WELCOME TO TERRORLAND

WELCOME TO TERRORLAND

MOHAMED ATTA & THE 9/11 COVER-UP IN FLORIDA

DANIEL HOPSICKER

THE MADCOW PRESS

Library of Congress Catalog Control Number 2003112217

Daniel Hopsicker, 1951-
    Welcome To TerrorLand — Mohamed Atta & The 9/11 Cover-up in Florida / by Daniel Hopsicker.
p. cm.
Includes index
ISBN 978-0-97529-067-5
 1. Terrorist Events—United States—September, 11, 2001- 2. United States - Politics and government—1989- 3. Political Corruption—United States—History-20th Century 3. Conspiracies—United States 4. Atta, Mohamed (1968-2001) I. Title.

First Edition

Published in the United States by The MadCow Press
Distributed to the trade by
MadCow Press
PO Box 577
WALTERVILLE, OR 97489

Printed on acid-free paper.
Manufactured in the United States of America

10 9 8 7 6 5 4 3 2 1

FOR RITA & NORMAN REILLY,
whose love & kindness form an enduring legacy...

WITH APPRECIATION

This book could not have been written without the support of friends and the kindness of strangers.

During a time when our country's "free press" has been mostly missing in action, being a "dissident journalist" is well nigh impossible without the encouragement and assistance of people who are determined that the truth not be silenced.

I want to thank first of all my family: my Mom and Norman, who believed in me when I couldn't buy a thrill in the major media (I still can't); and my sister Carol, brother David, and brother-in-law Bob, for assistance above and beyond the call of duty.

To my friend and colleague Kris Millegan, whose good humor and steady hand are a major reason this book exists, and to Ed Bishop, whose graphic design has made it pleasing on the eyes, I remain in your debt.

A huge and humble thank you to Lois Battuello, a brilliant and indefatigable researcher whose knowledge and assistance buoyed me up when I felt like sinking like a stone, and kept me going through the niggling harassments designed to stall my efforts.

To my good friend Dr. David Stern, whose Deep Politics website was an early inspiration to those of us who saw the promise of the Internet to keep the Truth alive in a world of media whitewash, I owe a debt of friendship and gratitude.

I salute the courage of the people of the aviation community in Venice and Southwest Florida, and of local law enforcement there as well, who testified to what they saw and heard. And I salute the fortitude of the eyewitnesses who raised their voices despite the warnings and intimidation of the FBI, and defied the most un-American official conspiracy of silence they attempted to enforce.

Your example has been an inspiration, and has re-affirmed what it means to be a citizen of a country sometimes called The Last Best Hope, which is that, quite simply...

Real Americans won't be silenced.

Contents

INTRODUCTION

Oo ne day while fumbling through my morning routine two years ago, I happened to glance at the Today Show while making coffee, and watched a Boeing 767 cross the sky, right over Katie Couric's shoulder in the monitor above the news desk, and explode into the South Tower of the World Trade Center.

It was the most surreal event ever seen on this planet. Minutes later, I was among the untold millions worldwide watching human beings hanging out of 100th story windows.

And then they began to jump.

Tiny human figures, barely visible, wavered through the smoke on the upper floors. They were specks against the gleaming superstructure as they fell, bathed in the light of a late summer morning in New York.

U.S. networks soon cut away—on the pretext that it was just too horrible to air—as the figures began dropping in groups of two's and three's from their perches and falling into the canyons below. But you only needed to see one body fall to feel a gut-wrenching anguish tear at your stomach.

Many, we learned later, jumped holding hands. And all I remember thinking was: "Those poor people."

Given the rate of falling bodies, something like 125 miles per hour, someone calculated that before they hit the pavement they had been falling for eight or nine seconds.

It must have seemed an eternity. Minutes earlier, some of them had been stirring "sweet and lo' and "non-dairy coffee whitener' into their mugs before heading to their desks.

And now this.

A fireman looked into the camera of the two French brothers shooting a documentary that morning (later aired on CBS) and asked, "How bad does it have to be before jumping out a 100th story window seems like the better alternative?"

If you fall from a great height you're dead before you hit the ground, I read somewhere, because your heart stops. Although I want to, somehow I find that hard to believe.

I have an unforgettable image of a man dangling out a window on an upper story, being shot from a camera a long distance away, so you couldn't see his face distinctly in the wavering haze. He was still dressed in summer clothes, wearing white pants.

He was soon to be dead. I was grateful not to see a close-up of his face that would show whether he already knew it. He was someone just like me, except I was sitting at home sipping coffee and he was getting ready to leap to his death.

Two years later the memory remains indelible. Later someone posted still shots on the Internet capturing an image of a man in white pants hurtling past the building on his way down.

It was him.

At some point soon thereafter I discovered in myself a burning desire to understand how this had come to pass.

Here's the purpose of this book:

Those who saw innocent people slaughtered owe an obligation to bring the perpetrators to justice.

Justice, vengeance, a duty to our dead—call it what you will, it demands adherence to a simple progression. Identify the people responsible, find them, and bring them to justice—*all* of them—even ones with non-Arab names, should any be found.

We owe it to them. It's a sacred duty which is somehow part of what being human *means*. If I were murdered in cold blood, I'd want someone to do it for *me*.

But there's a problem. Let me put it bluntly: Our government has not told us the truth about what happened. Nor do they appear to be committed to tracking down and punishing everyone responsible. Individuals in the U.S. Government possess an agenda that differs from this one, it has become painfully clear.

This discovery was almost as searing and painful as the black day itself. In the aftermath of the attack, we learned—and in short order—that *we the people* were to be kept in the dark about the most momentous event of the still-young 21st Century, just as we had for the last half of the 20th Century.

To date, the American people have still not been briefed about what happened that day, and why. We didn't hear the cockpit recordings. We didn't see pictures of the terrorists boarding the planes. We weren't told how they managed to get onboard.

We haven't been told why, afterwards, the FBI as if by magic knew the identity of the terrorists' ringleader almost immediately.

"We the people' weren't shown evidence that would prove the government's contentions beyond a reasonable doubt. When it came to answering questions about the attack, the message the government delivered to the people was: "You're not cleared for that information."

Never in this nation's history—at least never in living memory—has the flow of information from government to press and public been shut down so quickly and comprehensively. Washington, the place from which America's "official story' emanates, went into almost total information blackout. Some people found themselves reading Pravda.

Overnight, the Bush Administration laid down an across-the-board and centralized control of the public's right to know.

In the wake of the 9/11 attack officials in Washington promised explanations. They reneged. Secretary of State Powell promised a "white paper."

We're still waiting.

It was left to British Prime Minister Tony Blair to present the prosecution's case against Bin Laden, and he sketched out the Cliff Notes version of the evidence. Tony Blair said, "Al Qaeda is a terrorist organization with ties to a global network."

That made sense. The idea that Mohamed Atta and his henchmen needed help from an international organization while they were in the U.S. was easy to understand.

Logistical support is difficult to arrange from caves.

But what *kind* of global network? Blair didn't say. Blair's "global network" remained elusive, un-named, shadowy, and undefined.

Several weeks later the FBI denied that this *global network* existed, and proposed instead a "Lone Cadre Theory" which became the operative assumption in their investigation.

"The 19 hijackers who carried out the worst act of terror ever to occur on U.S. soil worked with little outside help as a single, integrated group," the Washington Post reported. "As more of the conspiracy becomes understood, government sources now say that the investigation so far suggests the 19 had 'no major help' in the United States.

"The FBI investigation into the plot is preliminary, and the conspiracy's precise nature probably will not be understood for years," the paper said.

If it is a conspiracy whose precise nature won't be understood for years, we wondered, how can the FBI already know the terrorists had received no outside help?

The FBI, of course, has spent several decades living down their "lone gunman" theory of the JFK assassination. Perhaps this is why their "lone cadre" theory has not been widely accepted. An Agency with a marked preference for lone (nut) gunmen was floating a lone cadre trial balloon.

Atta's cadre was a lone cadre. Acting alone, at least while in the U.S. There was no one else involved. No Higher Ups.

Tony Blair's global network statements had been rendered inoperative, without explanation, by the FBI.

Think nineteen *lone gunmen*. A squadron of Lee Harvey Oswald's. Think Watergate. Whitewater. Kennedy.

Think *cover-up*.

Through it all, no one in the major media—America's vaunted free press—looked askance. For anyone who has lived through this country's recent history, there was an unmistakable and familiar feeling in the air...

Another cover-up was descending like a blanket of fog.

Was it plausible that the 9/11 terrorist conspiracy, presumably launched by Al Qaeda, brought down the World Trade Center without outside assistance?

During those brief moments when the FBI *was,* presumably, looking for international networks which may have assisted the terrorists, were any organizations *protected* from scrutiny?

The September 11th attack is fast becoming one of the biggest mysteries in American history. Worse, even the pretense of respect for the "public's right to know" has now been discarded.

After the Kennedy Assassination, for example, the government at least felt obliged to appoint an independent investigation, and quickly. Forget for a moment that the Warren Commission was stacked with political hacks; at least the *forms* of representative democracy were respected.

Forty years ago, in the supposed "bad old days' of official secrecy, before we moved into the sunlight of our more "enlightened" times, the government at least told the American public where supposed assassin Oswald had been living at a secret base in Japan, in Russia, New Orleans, Mexico City, Dallas...

Now even that bit of *noblesse oblige* is a thing of the past, because they're lying to us about when Atta arrived in the U.S. and where he spent his time while he was here.

Worse, nineteen months after the attack the independent 9/11 investigation had still not gotten underway. Bush Administration spokesmen like Vice President Cheney fiercely lobbied Congress in an attempt to prevent any independent investigation at *all.*

The Bush Administration was successful—not in capturing bin Laden—but in thwarting the creation of an Independent Commission for over a *year.*

On the 9/11 investigation, the Bush Administration adopted the same strategy they scorned when Clinton used it during the Monica debacle:

"Deny. Deny. Deny."

Then, in a gesture that must have been designed to display his capacity for irony, Bush named Henry Kissinger to head the 9/11 commission.

In our post-modern global village filled with 24-hour news channels, we know far less about the life of Mohamed Atta than we did forty years ago about Lee Harvey Oswald.

Why is that?

One plausible explanation is that there has been a government-imposed media blackout. One of history's greatest crimes has gone without serious public examination or investigation.

Given the immensity of the tragedy, we find this reluctance to investigate more than inappropriate...

It's *suspicious*. What are they trying to hide?

Late in a 2-year long investigation in Venice, Florida into the training of the terrorist hijackers, our suspicions were confirmed by the Chairman of the Congressional Intelligence Committee which investigated 9/11, Senator Bob Graham.

"Frankly, there is a piece of information which is still classified which I consider to be the most important information that's come to the attention of the joint committee," Graham said on CBS's *Face the Nation*.

"I was surprised at the evidence that there were foreign governments involved in facilitating the activities of at least some of the terrorists in the United States.

"We hope that it will be declassified. I think it is an important part of our judgments as to where our greatest threats are and what steps we need to do to protect the American people here at home," Graham said.

His Republican co-chair, Senator Richard Shelby, indicated that the unease was bipartisan. "Time is not on our side," Shelby said. "You know, we were told that there would be cooperation in this investigation, and I question that. I think that most of the information that our staff has been able to get that is real meaningful has had to be extracted piece by piece.

"There is explosive information that has not been publicly released. I think there are some bombshells out there," said Shelby. "I know that."

Pressed for detail, Graham told reporters, "Most of that information is classified, I think overly-classified... It will become public at some point when it's turned over to the National Archives, but that's 20 or 30 years from now."

To remain a Republic, a representative democracy, Americans should hear the truth a lot sooner than that.

We should hear it *now.*

One reason for the widespread distrust of the official explanation of the 9/11 attack—there are dozens—is the truly shocking fact that the FBI never finished its 9/11 investigation.

Less than a month after putting a 4,000-man FBI task force on the case, President Bush *called off* the FBI's investigation into the 9/11 terrorist conspiracy, on the pretext that the manpower was needed to fight the anthrax threat, then in the headlines daily.

When the anthrax scare was over, however, the FBI did not go back to finish its 9/11 investigation. After announcing their massive presence on the case, we never heard from the FBI in any meaningful way again.

Nor was any report ever issued to the American people of their findings, even though Bush Administration spokesmen like Secretary of State Powell promised there would be.

There is one small ray of hope. After Dallas, it took twenty years before polls showed a majority of Americans no longer believed the official story of a lone gunman in the Kennedy Assassination.

But there is already a pervasive and widespread skepticism about the official explanation for the 9/11 attack. The skepticism is visible everywhere… except, strangely enough, in our national media.

Lily Tomlin said it best: "No matter how cynical I get," she said. "I just can't keep up."

"Time is not on our side," said Republican Sen. Shelby.

The same sentiment was put poignantly a few years back, at the launch of *George* magazine. Its founder, JFK Jr., was asked if he would use his new magazine to investigate his father's murder.

No, he said. Too much time had passed.

"Time," he said, "is the great enemy of the truth."

He was right.

The memory of 3,000 dead people commands us to do the best we can to find the truth about how it is they came to die on September 11, 2001. Today the clear task in front of us is to deconstruct the "official story" about the 9/11 attack in as close to "real time" as possible. In the absence of a free press, the job becomes more difficult.

Although there are a dozen burning questions about 9/11 worthy of book-length investigation, we chose to focus on just one. Mohamed Atta in Florida. Who. What. When. Where. Why.

We did it because we have not received an explanation we find satisfactory from our government. In fact, it appears as if they think we don't deserve one.

Nor have the supposed perpetrators been brought to justice.

"When people at Ground Zero cheered President Bush as he stood amid the still-smoldering ruins... they weren't cheering for 'regime change in Iraq,'" wrote Maureen Dowd in the *New York Times.*

"They wanted the head of Osama bin Laden."

We still haven't gotten it, as least as of this writing. We thought bringing Osama bin Laden to justice was our whole objective in Afghanistan. Apparently we were mistaken.

The actions of CIA and American military commanders in Afghanistan, as reported in the *New York Times,* do not reflect an emphasis on rigorous pursuit of Osama bin Laden, even when he was right there to be had.

In a Sept. 30, 2002 front page article ("10-month Afghan Mystery: Is Bin Laden Dead or Alive?") the *Times* reported that people who were on the ground in Afghanistan during the siege of Tora Bora believe U.S. commanders did not act with anything like the zeal you'd expect from people whose mission was hunting down America's Most Wanted Man.

American forces in Afghanistan, the *Times* reported, "have not been helped by the suspicion here at Tora Bora, where bin Laden was all but trapped, that indecisiveness on the part of American commanders, or perhaps reluctance to risk casualties, may have helped him (bin Laden) escape.

"If (bin Laden) fled to Pakistan," the article continues, "he did so over snow-choked mountain trails that were not blocked by American or other allied troops until after the bombing—an oversight that some of the allies point to as having squandered the best opportunity of the war to snare America's most wanted man.

"Within weeks high-ranking British officers were saying privately that American commanders had vetoed a proposal to guard the high-altitude trails, arguing that the risks of a fire fight, in deep snow, gusting winds and low-slung clouds, were too high," said the *Times.*

"Similar accounts abound among Afghan commanders who provided the troops stationed on the Tora Bora foothills—on the north side of the mountains, facing the Afghan city of Jalalabad," continued the *Times* story. "Those troops played a blocking role that left the Qaeda fugitives only one escape route, to the south, over the mountains to Pakistan."

One Afghan commander told of pleading with Special Forces officers to block the trails to Pakistan. "Their attitude was, 'we must kill the enemy, but we must remain absolutely safe,'" said warlord Hajji Zaher. "This is crazy."

We were incredulous. Low-slung *clouds?* The snow was too *deep?*

It seems inconceivable that America's Special Forces would have backed down or insisted on remaining absolutely safe in a fight to capture the leader of the forces that attacked America on 9/11 and took 3,000 innocent lives.

An order to "stand down," if one was given, must have come from *above.*

So incompetence in the failure to bring to justice the chief criminal in the 9/11 attack is *not* the worst possible scenario we will be forced to consider. The worst possible scenario supported by available facts would be that the failure of U.S. commanders to capture Osama bin Laden may have been *willful.*

Two years ago 3,000 of our number perished in gruesome and horrible ways. It seems clear that if we want to know the truth about that otherwise unremarkable September morning, we will to have to find it ourselves.

The only thing I can think of worse than having to watch people dropping out of windows 100 stories above Manhattan, is having to watch it and then having your own government lie to you about who did it and why.

I can't tell you I know *why* they're lying.

But in the coming pages I believe I can prove they are.

CHAPTER ONE

WELCOME TO VENICE

This is the story of Mohamed Atta, a black-hearted psychopath, in Florida, a pirate's paradise. If either had been different, September 11th might never have happened.

We started with two simple questions: Why Atta? Why Florida?

Except to point out his cold stare and unfriendly manner, little attention has been paid to the personality of Mohamed Atta, the man authorities quickly dubbed the "terrorist ringleader." "J-Lo and Ben" receive more in-depth coverage in a week than the man who engineered the murder of 3,000 people.

Based on the accounts of eyewitnesses to Atta's actions in Florida, we discovered that Atta exhibited behavior that can only be described as psychotic. In fact, far from deserving the heroic mantle placed on his shoulders by Arab radicals, self-respecting Islamic fundamentalists should be ashamed that he sprang from their number.

Mohamed Atta wasn't a hero. He was a psychopath.

Before illustrating why Atta richly deserves that label, we want to first take a look at the "Florida as pirate's paradise" part of our equation. What attractions were there in the Sunshine State that made it the Hamburg cadre's overwhelming choice for "home away from home"?

Something has been struggling to emerge into our national consciousness concerning the physical location of most of the terrorist conspiracy's activities in the U.S. Mohamed Atta and his inner circle were in *Florida* while pursuing their murderous designs. The plot was masterminded from Florida.

What to make of this choice? Although media attention kept pointing away from the state—to Phoenix, San Diego, and Minneapolis—14 of the 19 hijackers voted with their feet and hung their terrorist shingle out in a state which has been governed since 1999, it must be said, by the current President's brother.

With an entire continent seemingly at their disposal, the terrorists chose Florida to be their American beachhead, and then base.

Why did Mohamed Atta, a man described by many who met him as a really "natty dresser" lead his cadre from a bustling European metropolis with an internationally-famous red light district to a retirement community in a place where the only "action" involves senior citizens lining up for the early bird special?

It's an odd choice. It's not as if Florida reminded young Arab men from desert kingdoms of the trackless wastes back home. The state that made Don Johnson, Elian Gonzalez and pink flamingos famous is as far from being a desert kingdom as it gets.

There's the weather, for one. While a mecca for northerners during winter, Florida in early July, when the FBI says Atta arrived in Venice, is a steamy place. Even the natives head north until it cools off.

"Florida," wrote one early Spanish explorer, "is full of bogs and poisonous fruits, barren, and the very worst country that is warmed by the sun."

Some people will tell you not much has changed.

Yet 14 of the 19 hijackers based themselves in the Sunshine State. And since 15 of the 19 terrorist hijackers were Saudi, the story of the terrorist conspiracy is, perforce, a story about *Saudis in Florida.*

The conspiracy which took down the World Trade Center is a story about young Arab men practicing "touch and go's" at obscure Florida airports, like the one in Venice, and checking in and out of hotels in Florida destination resorts like Orlando.

In the weeks after Sept. 11 the nation began to ask questions of Florida. Television commentators spoke of a "Florida curse." In truth, strange news had been emanating from that steamy world for some time.

The connection between Florida and most of the hijackers in the deadly attacks had state leaders questioning whether the Sunshine State had become a haven for international terrorists, where the world's nefarious characters feel free to congregate in a modern-day Casablanca.

"First we couldn't count the votes. Now we're hosting terrorists," said one state lawmaker.

"My God, Florida is always involved in these things," said Oscar Westerfield, a retired FBI official who specialized in foreign counter-intelligence and is now a security consultant in Tampa. Florida Governor Jeb Bush disagreed. After the attack, Gov. Bush defended the flight schools as "victims of fanatics."

After moving to Venice, we received a missive from someone who minced no words in his explanation for the attractions of Florida to the terrorists:

"You reside in a druggie mobbed-up state that also houses a lot of foreign unfriendlies with ties to various international bad guys, is run by a Bush, and where people become alligator bait and get lost in the swamps quite frequently," wrote our friend. "Additionally, there seems to be a major overload of paramilitary types floating in."

If you think that sounds extreme, listen to what one of the state's own senators had to say. Florida long has been "a lair for spies and now terrorists," said U.S. Sen. Bob Graham, D-Fl., chairman of the Senate Intelligence Committee, in the Sept. 14, 2001 *Orlando Sentinel Tribune.*

Graham said, "Florida itself is a significant crossroads of international intrigue and clandestine collection."

What Graham is referring to is explained in a conversation between two lawyers outside the federal courthouse in Miami, one local and one from Washington.

"You know the most wonderful thing about Miami is its location," said the local lawyer.

"What do you mean?" the visitor asked.

"It's so close to the United States."

So while Mohamed Atta and Florida are a surrealistic pair, they also make a certain sense together. He always drove a Pontiac Grand Am, in a rainbow of colors. Atta was an Arab Don Johnson, starring in his own Miami Vice, and he looked and sounded, said eyewitness Brad Warrick of Pompano Beach, who rented several cars to Atta, "as if he'd been in this country for a long time."

Atta and his cadre of terrorists lived in Florida, drank in Florida, and stuffed $20 bills down stripper's g-strings in skin joints all up and down the state.

And they learned to fly in Florida, too, mostly in the tiny town of Venice. It made nary a ripple when news first surfaced, though only briefly, that three of the four terrorist pilots learned to fly in a retirement community on Florida's Gulf Coast.

Mohamed Atta and sidekick and bodyguard Marwan Al-Shehhi were the ones identified as having been flight students there. Then it was reported—in a strangely muted tone for what was big news— that others of the terrorists had been in Venice as well, including Siad Jarrah, said to have been at the controls of the plane that went down in western Pennsylvania.

Three of the four 9/11 pilots learned to fly at two flight schools at the tiny Venice Airport. A terrorist trifecta out at the Venice Airport. Venice, Florida is the biggest 9/11 crime scene that wasn't reduced to rubble. But it hasn't been treated that way. And no one has offered any reason why.

Both flight schools were owned by Dutch nationals. Both had been recently purchased, at about the same time. A year later terrorists began to arrive, in numbers greater than we have so far been told. All of this must be just a freak coincidence, according to the FBI.

We call it their "Magic Dutch Boy Theory."

How had the FBI known the exact identities of the hijackers less than 24 hours after the attack? If their files had been so readily in hand, why hadn't they apprehended them *before* they killed thousands? And when conscientious FBI agents did try to raise alarms about known Al Qaeda sympathizers at U.S. flight schools, why were they ignored?

The only answer ever given by the FBI to why the terrorists came to the U.S. to learn to fly was "because flight training is cheaper in the U.S."

But Atta and Marwan ended up paying more than double what flight training costs elsewhere, according to aviation experts. So price was apparently not the object. And besides, in Florida alone there are over 200 flight schools.

What inducements led them to the two in Venice?

Flight school owner Rudi Dekkers inadvertently released paperwork showing that Atta and sidekick Marwan Al-Shehhi paid $28,000 each for what the chief flight instructor at a nearby flight school, Tom Hamersley of Jones Aviation, explained to us was available at his school—as well as dozens of others—for a fraction of this price.

Were the inflated prices Atta and his minions paid some kind of *terrorist surcharge?*

As days and then weeks passed with no word as to why so many terrorists had been in Venice, we grew increasingly suspicious.

The ugly truth was that there had been no official explanation for why terrorists beat a path from the Baltic Sea to Florida's Gulf Coast.

Was it that no one knew? Or was it that they *did?*

Venice, Florida, is an unlikely center of intrigue. But the Venice Airport, set beside an unsuspecting population of golf-playing retirees, is another story, we discovered. It has a history as a free-booting port of call for an international cast of Lear jet-setting rogues, spies, villains and terrorists.

Most of the key terrorists had Venice connections. Hamburg cadre member Ramzi bin al-Shibh, a candidate for 20th hijacker, was on his way to Venice until he was denied a visa.

Ramzi's replacement as the so-called 20th hijacker, Zacarias Moussaoui, we discovered, had also been in Venice, with Arne Kruithof, one of the two Dutch national flight school owners.

Kruithof told a local aviation executive he'd been grilled for two days at the Sarasota Courthouse about his connections to Moussaoui, by an Assistant Attorney General from the Justice Department accompanied by top-level officials from the FBI, in town taking depositions from potential witnesses in Moussaoui's upcoming trial.

Even if it stopped right there, wouldn't it seem Venice would be fertile soil for investigative journalists looking for "behind the scenes" reports about the terrorist conspiracy's activities?

Yet when we rolled into town two months after the attack, we didn't find ourselves rubbing elbows with Mike Wallace or Bob Woodward at Clock's Restaurant downtown. And we weren't tripping over clusters of hard-drinking journalists at the bar at the Crow's Nest on the Gulf.

In fact, there *were* no investigative reporters nosing around in Venice. Speculation about why the terrorists found a tiny retirement community on Florida's Gulf Coast so congenial to their plans has not been voiced in the major media.

We find this more than passing strange.

But then, we knew quite a bit about Venice before we got there, since our parents have had a winter house there since retiring almost 25 years ago. The family gets together there almost yearly for a few days of quality "family time" in the balmy Gulf breezes. Because of this personal history we began to doubt the official explanation, or lack of same...

Venice is on Florida's sleepy Gulf Coast, sandwiched among the better-heeled resorts of Naples, Sanibel Island, Boca Grande—a Bush family favorite—and Sarasota, home to Katherine Harris.

Popular pastimes include shuffleboard, golf, and leafing through magazines in doctors' waiting rooms. Restaurant traffic peaks at 6 p.m. Crosswalks allow extra time to get across the street, and have that beep feature in case you can't see.

The town's claim to fame—till now—was that every year Venice hosts the "Shark's Tooth and Seafood Festival," said to be a unique event showcasing "the shark tooth capital of the world."

When it comes to shark teeth, all that can be said is that they don't get many people real excited. The gee-gaw shops lining Venice's main drag get tourists in with the shark's teeth, and move them on to something else. Those few who go wild for sharks' teeth suffer, we think, from a paucity of imagination, and have altogether too much time on their hands.

Venice's *real* distinction is that it has the second oldest population in the entire United States. The median age is 69. Local advertising skews towards wheelchairs, home health care, funeral directors, specialist physicians, and estate planning. Commercials for "The Clapper" play in heavy rotation.

So by billing itself as the shark tooth capital of the world, the city fathers may just be putting their best foot forward, because there's no cachet in being known as "the assisted living capital of the world."

Despite the elderly population, one thing felt familiar to Atta when he got to Venice, oddly enough. When he was a student at Technical

University in Hamburg studying—supposedly—urban architecture and planning, he hung out at a place called Sharky's Billiard Bar. After moving to Venice he hung out at a restaurant and bar just across from the Venice Airport, also called Sharky's.

Small world.

Although Dekkers testified he hadn't seen Atta in many months, Atta was seen at the Venice Sharky's just two weeks before 9/11 meeting with the flight school owner.

Stuck in the sweltering middle of nowhere, 30 miles of mangrove swamps from the nearest real town, a retirement community of overwhelmingly white people does not appear to have much to offer healthy 30-something men, even if they were terrorists.

And it doesn't seem like an ideal place to hide an operation comprising several dozen dark-skinned foreign nationals.

So, why *did* young men choose to spend their final year on the planet in a town where handicapped parking spaces at the supermarket fill up fast? Why would healthy young men gravitate toward a retirement community *anywhere?* 'Cuz it ain't Hamburg. There's no red light district, unless you count the traffic signal downtown.

One possible answer is that bivouacking in Venice was someone *else's* decision. But of course, if Mohamed Atta and his Hamburg cadre didn't just wander in Rudi Dekkers' flight school door, we have an entirely different story than our government has so far been telling.

When we rolled into Venice two months after 9/11 the town was quiet on the surface, but jittery underneath, a discovery made after being pulled over by the local Venice Police twice on our first day in town. In 25 years of visiting the parents we don't remember even seeing a cop.

The Venice Airport was under around the clock 24-7 surveillance. A police cruiser roved the perimeter. Although this stretched the resources of a small department, there seemed no reasonable explanation for it. Were local officials expecting the terrorists to make a vengeful return appearance? More likely, the terrorist would be sending a postcard saying "Thanks for the help! Wish you were here!"

It made no sense. Later on we learned that all three of the top city officials filed for concealed weapon's permits at about the same time. It still didn't make sense, but now it seemed more serious.

On each of the two occasions we were pulled over, we identified ourselves as a visiting journalist, and since neither stop resulted in a ticket, but just a friendly wave, we concluded they were some kind of local law enforcement custom. A "meet and greet."

On the second occasion, we asked the officer if it would be prudent to pay a courtesy call on the police chief. He allowed that it might. So we did, stopping at the new police headquarters to say hello. And we're glad we did, because the sergeant on duty proved congenial, which gave us a chance to ask a few questions about Rudi Dekkers, the owner of Huffman Aviation, who had been everywhere on television during the days after the attack.

It was a simple question, really. We wanted to know if Dekkers had any local "priors." But it made Sergeant Marty Treanor sigh. Then he started to say something, thought better of it, and sighed again.

He said he couldn't tell us if Dekkers had been in any trouble in Venice, because all of his files were gone.

"Gone?"

"The FBI took all our files, everything. They loaded the files right outside this window," said Treanor, indicating a parking lot outside the station, "into two Ryder trucks, then drove them right onto a C-130 military cargo plane at the Sarasota airport, which took off for Washington with Jeb Bush aboard."

We will come back to visit the question of the Governor of Florida's national security responsibilities. The important point was that *taking* files was a lot different than *copying* them. The FBI wasn't taking any chances.

In the immediate aftermath of 9/11, Venice City Manager George Hunt said to reporters, "It's really just coincidence that terrorists chose such a place (as Venice) to be their training ground for the unspeakable."

Was that true? Determining whether it was or not would be complicated by the fact that the FBI had dutifully confiscated anything that looked remotely like evidence.

What the FBI was doing with it is still anybody's guess.

Our suspicions that there was something wrong with the official story would grow steadily. But the first indication we had that they might be correct came in that first encounter with local law enforcement. The police spokesman seemed troubled that he lacked the ability to respond to questions about the possible criminal background of flight school owner Rudi Dekkers.

It sounded as if he would have *liked* to. He sounded none too happy about the fact that all police files pertinent to 9/11 were gone. At the time we wrote it off as just stepped-on toes, a little resentment by local law enforcement when they were brushed aside by federal agents.

But maybe it was something more.

After a week in Venice we realized in some horror that the terrorists had been flying right over our parents' house several miles east of the airport. There were lots of them flying at one time, too, apparently, in virtual squadrons, according to the local *Venice Gondolier*, in a story written while Atta was at the Venice Airport.

The City Council heard numerous complaints from residents, upset about student pilots taking off at the Venice Municipal Airport and flying low right over their homes, as each circled the Airport, and practiced landings, again and again, in a maneuver called a "touch and go."

One local resident, Walter Fife, a clearly indignant fellow, told the Council he had counted 90 student flights over his house in a two hour period. There were, he figured, about 15 planes flying overhead six times each.

Fifteen planes. A terrorist squadron. Bin Laden Air.

When Fife's wife Gerda contacted Huffman Aviation, reported the *Gondolier*, an employee there suggested the Fifes could move out if the noise bothered them.

The City Council took no action, not even to reprimand the Huffman employees for being rude to Walter Fife's wife Gerda, although we bet they wouldn't like it if somebody was talking trash to their mom.

Huffman Aviation had some juice in Venice.

Unraveling the connection between the terrorists and the unlikely place to which they flocked became our major endeavor. It would take more than a year before any answers became clear.

On the other hand, the answer to our *second* question—Why Atta?—came all at once after we had finally been successful in a months-long quest to track down Mohamed Atta's erstwhile American girlfriend, who wasn't eager to be found.

We learned from her what it was about Mohamed Atta that made him uniquely qualified to fly into a skyscraper without flinching.

Our search for the terrorist ringleader's girlfriend is fully covered later. For now, we'll just say that after a lengthy process of digging we found the young woman named Amanda Keller who local news accounts stated had lived for a short time with Mohamed Atta.

When she "hooked-up" with Atta, Amanda Keller was a willowy 20-year-old "lingerie model" and stripper with spiky pink hair. She worked nights for an escort service called Fantasies & Lingerie which catered to a mixed crowd of politicians, judges, high-rollers and socialites of both sexes, just down the street from Cheetah's, a strip club Atta was known to frequent in nearby Sarasota.

Amanda was Mohamed Atta's live-in girlfriend in Venice for more than two months. And while the full story of her experience awaits a later chapter, one supremely horrific experience should be brought up now, because it clearly shows Atta to have been someone capable of driving a Boeing 767 airliner into tons of steel and glass.

The two went out almost every night, during their brief time together, Amanda told us, to clubs like Area 51 and Margarita Maggie's in Sarasota. They were, as she described it, part of a whole scene. "When we went out we would meet pilots from Africa, Germany, and there were always lots of Arabs," she said.

But, the good times didn't last long, and after just two months, Amanda was ready to move on. But instead of clueing him in during a quiet dinner in a restaurant somewhere, she dumped him in a humiliatingly public fashion, in a night club where they were partying with a bunch of Atta's friends.

Amanda met a good-looking long-haired party animal who she noticed dancing bare-chested near her. We'll let her tell the story…

"We were at Margarita Maggie's in Sarasota near the Quay," she began. "Angelina, Olivia, Timothy, Juergen, Sabrina, Mohamed, Wolfgang… they were all there."

"And Mohamed, like a dumb-ass, was standing on top of a speaker dancing. The man could not dance to save his life, he was real stiff, just kind of shaking, doing that old 'Roxbury head bob' thing, you know? He embarrassed me instantly when we got there, and I pretended I didn't know him," Amanda said.

"I was dancing onstage, because onstage the guys can't come up and dance with the girls. I was up there with a whole bunch of other girls and Angelina. And this cute guy was dancing right below us, and the light was hitting him, and he had this long beautiful hair, and he looked at me, and I got real embarrassed."

The cute guy's name was Garret, we heard.

"I had seen Angelina hug him earlier in the night, and I said to her, 'You've got to introduce me to him.' Mohamed was just a few feet away watching, and I didn't give a damn," she said.

"And we finally started dancing and he handed me his shirt, and Mohamed got really pissed. He (Garret) wrapped his shirt around my legs and was dirty dancing with me, and he slid me down off the stage and began brushing his lips against mine, and kissed me," she said.

"Mohamed came over and tapped me on my shoulder, and I said, 'What the hell do you want?' And he said, 'What are you doing?'" she said, mocking Atta's apparently British-accented English.

"And I said, 'I'm dancing!' Garret walked over to get himself a beer, and Mohamed said, 'I'm leaving.'

"And I said, 'See ya.' And he said, 'When are you leaving?'

"And I said 'Whenever I feel like it!'

"He asked me about Garret, saying, 'Who's that?'

"And I said, 'I guess he's the new one.' And I stayed until the club closed."

That night Amanda went home with her new beau. Things were never the same between her and Atta again.

"The day I stopped liking him," she mused aloud, "was when I saw him for the first time out at the pool, wearing a lime-green Speedo. He had a flank-y ass."

A lime-green speedo, when we thought about it, was one of those perfect details that make sense instantly. It was the shock of recognition: that's exactly the kind of Euro-trash look someone like Atta would affect.

Mohamed Atta in a lime-green speedo at the pool, revealing a flank-y ass.

There's nothing exceptional in this story... so far. Another half-sad, half-comical "hook-up" gone wrong. But events now began to spin out of control. Although Atta's money paid the rent, the apartment lease was in her name, Amanda explained. One night soon after meeting Garret, the "hot new guy," she brought him back to the apartment. She told Atta he could deal with it. He could move out. Or he could check with the landlord.

The hot new guy was sleeping over. The hot new guy was in the "big bed." Atta was on the couch. After discussing what she should do with the apartment house manager, who corroborated her story, Amanda Keller unceremoniously dumped Atta's three suitcases and Gold's gym bag onto the parking lot underneath their second floor apartment, and called him a cab.

"He told me he'd get even with me," she says. "He said, 'You will be sorry for this!' "

One week later she found out what he had meant, upon returning from a long night at the escort service to the apartment that was now hers alone.

Amanda kept a pet dog, and several cats as well, one of whom had just had a litter, she informed us haltingly. There were six adorable kittens. But when she opened the door to her apartment, she didn't hear any kitten noises, which was strange...

And then she hit the overhead light. Voice cracking with emotion, she told us what she saw: there were dead kittens—no, *pieces* of dead kittens, kitten parts—strewn all over her living room.

We asked her to repeat what she was saying, mainly because we couldn't believe what we were hearing.

She walked through it again. "I came home from work, after breakfast with Page (a co-worker), and then went down to the beach to talk for a while, so it was about 9 a.m. when I walked into my apartment," she stated.

"She (the mother cat) had had a litter of six, and only one survived. The mother cat was dead, gutted on my kitchen table. And there were little baby cat parts all over the place.

"The only ones to survive were my little dog, that hid under the couch, and my Siamese, who sat on top of the fridge behind the cookie jar. There were dead kittens with their heads cut off, little body parts everywhere, I saw little baby legs and everything. It was awful. My friend, Page, had to clean it up. I couldn't do it."

In an apartment directly across the street from the Venice Airport, an American girl who had spurned Mohamed Atta was stepping around kitten parts. She moved out that same day and never returned.

Numerous descriptions of Atta have painted him as menacing, dark, glaring, sometimes just wooden. We heard speculation, from people who had been in his presence in Venice, that he looked as if he might have been brainwashed, not that anyone in town had ever seen any-one who had been brainwashed, but he looked the way they thought somebody in that condition *might* look.

But after listening to Amanda Keller's story, corroborated by emi-nently-credible witnesses in coming pages, we're confident we got the answer to one of our big questions about the 9/11 attack: why Mo-hamed Atta had been the one chosen to commit one of history's most unspeakable crimes.

It was because he *could*. He was capable of it. Not merely capable, but seemingly perfect for the job.

Mohamed Atta was a psychopath. A Kitten Killer.

We're in Jeffrey Dahmer territory here.

While the FBI's phony chronology of Mohamed Atta will be ex-plored later, it's worth noting that the events just described took place in Venice fully four months after the FBI says Atta left town.

The FBI has said nothing at all about his numerous appearances in Venice after finishing flight training at Huffman in December 2000.

We don't know why. Perhaps if they admitted Atta had been in Venice a lot more than they'd told us, they would have to answer questions about what he was doing while he was there that authorities would prefer not to see raised.

Questions that might open up what legendary Southern Senator William Fulbright once called "an endless can of worms." Fulbright was speaking about the Bay of Pigs invasion.

But he might just as well have been describing the 9/11 cover-up in Florida.

When we finally tracked her down, Amanda Keller displayed the reluctance to talk about her brush with history we soon discovered was common among people who had been contacted by the FBI after 9/11.

Reporters had camped out on her doorstep in the days after the attack in a vain attempt to get her to talk. She told them that au-thorities had told her not to say anything. And then she disappeared, going into seclusion in a place where she had every right to think she would never be found.

Until she told us her story, after we finally managed to show up on her doorstep, she had spoken just eleven words to reporters, which sum up "the way things were" in southwest Florida in the aftermath of the 9/11 attack.

"I can't really discuss anything," Amanda Keller told reporters.

"I'm afraid I'll get in trouble."

CHAPTER TWO

THE ATTEMPT TO ASSASSINATE GEORGE W. BUSH

Two hours before terrorist hijackers began crashing airliners into the Twin Towers of the World Trade Center, four Arab men in a white van pulled up to the guard gate of the hotel where George W. Bush was spending the night, the Colony Beach Resort Hotel on Longboat Key in Sarasota, Florida, and launched an attempt to assassinate the President of the United States.

The attempted assassination had very likely been coordinated by terrorist ringleader Mohamed Atta, just then passing through airport security 1000 miles away in Portland, Maine.

Several days before Bush's arrival in Sarasota, according to eyewitnesses, Atta had been meeting with co-conspirators at a Holiday Inn barely two miles down the beach from the hotel where Bush would be staying.

Two hours before the assassination attempt was launched, Secret Service agents guarding the President in Sarasota received a dramatic predawn warning of an imminent threat.

That two years later Americans have been told nothing about these events illustrates both how seriously U.S. officials took the attempt, and how far they have been willing to go to keep a tight rein on information. Whoever said "the first casualty of war is the truth," said a mouthful.

We discovered the assassination attempt while sifting through local news coverage in the aftermath of the attack, acting on a friend's cynical dictum that the only real news you get when something big happens is in the first 24 hours, before the cover-up is put in place.

We had been scrutinizing news accounts from the confusing early hours and days following the 9/11 attack. We were looking for big news stories that inexplicably and immediately died, without explanation or follow up.

It's called "suppressed news," and we hoped to discover a few nuggets. But we didn't just find nuggets. We found *boulders*.

Amazing things were happening in Sarasota during the pre-dawn hours before September 11th, events which we discovered had surfaced briefly in news reports before disappearing, never to be heard from again.

We did our job by piecing together two separate news reports from Sarasota—one a local television newscast, the other a town newspaper—that together lead to the inescapable conclusion that during the intrigue which was swirling in Sarasota before dawn that day, terrorists were looking to kill George W. Bush.

The first report stated that a pre-dawn warning of imminent attack had been delivered to President Bush's Secret Service detail in Sarasota, and aired on the Sarasota ABC affiliate's evening newscast.

"The warning of imminent danger was delivered in the middle of the night to Secret Service agents in Sarasota guarding the President," reported Monica Yadov of ABC's Sarasota affiliate, "and it came exactly four hours and thirty-eight minutes before Mohamed Atta flew an airliner into the World Trade Center."

The second story is a chilling eyewitness account of the attempted assassination in progress. It came from the Longboat Observer, which literally covers the waterfront in upscale Longboat Key, where Bush spent the night before the attack.

"At about 6 a.m. Sept. 11, Longboat Key Fire Marshall Carroll Mooneyhan was at the front desk of the Colony Beach & Tennis Resort as Bush prepared for his morning jog. From that vantage point, Mooneyhan overheard a strange exchange between a Colony receptionist and security guard," the paper reported.

"A van occupied by men of Middle Eastern descent had pulled up to the Colony stating they had a "poolside" interview with the president, Mooneyhan said."

Neither of the two reporters knew of the other's report. But both had covered different angles of the same story… a concerted attempt by four Arab men posing as journalists to gain access to President George W. Bush at 6 a.m. on the morning of September 11th, for the purpose of ending his life.

Here's how it went down:

Zainlabdeen Omer, a Middle Eastern native residing in Sarasota, contacted Sarasota police in the middle of the night to tell them a friend of his, who had made violent threats against President Bush in the past, had just shown up—and unexpectedly—in Sarasota, ABC's Yadov reported.

The man whom Omer warned authorities about was identified in the Sarasota police report of the incident only as "Ghandi."

Omer said Ghandi told him he was in town to get a friend out of jail… But Omer had heard Ghandi make violent remarks about Bush in the past, and since the President was in Sarasota at the same time, Omer feared his friend might be in Sarasota to kill the President.

The warning was initially given to the Sarasota police, who called in the Secret Service. Within hours Secret Service agents were searching an apartment in Sarasota.

Turns out, Omer was right. They arrested three men, all from the Sudan, and took them in for interrogation. The questioning lasted, according to one of the three, Fathel Rahman Omer, for ten hours.

"The police came and arrested me and three other people,"

Fathel Rahman explained in the ABC interview. Rahman said he couldn't help the Secret Service.

"So you know nothing about the President coming to Sarasota?" asked Yadov.

"I know nothing," he replied. "I know nothing about Osama bin Laden, nothing like that."

Moving quickly, the Secret Service next swooped down on a local beauty supply store, whose owner had been fingered by Omer as being a close associate of "Ghandi."

The owner of a liquor store next door watched as agents raided the place. "Very shortly after the World Trade Center attack, we noticed four or five agents swarm the building next door," explained Greg Breslich, owner of North Trail Liquors in Sarasota.

"We always thought there was something strange about that establishment. We saw a lot of people go in there, but never saw anyone come out carrying any beauty supplies."

Agents detained and questioned the owner of the beauty supply store, a Muslim named Hakim. Hakim, too, had disturbing information for the Secret Service about Ghandi, reported Yadov.

He told agents Ghandi was a member of the SPLA, or Sudanese People's Liberation Army, a Christian and animist guerrilla group fighting the fundamentalist Muslim government in Sudan.

Whoa! Sarasota, Florida, seems a little far afield for sub-Saharan freedom fighters. What could they have been doing there? Pricing retirement real estate?

Maybe they had been receiving covert training in the swamps, which is a southwest Florida tradition. Bay of Pigs invaders stormed the beaches here practicing for Cuba, a local Sheriff told us.

And why would operatives of a guerrilla organization fighting against a government of Islamic fundamentalists closely allied with Osama bin Laden want to assassinate, of all people, George W. Bush? It didn't make sense.

But once you admit the possibility that there exist sub-Saharan Christian animist guerrilla fighters in whitebread Sarasota, Florida, anything seems possible.

We were able to confirm much of ABC reporter Monica Yadov's account. The arrest of the Sudanese men made national wire service reports on the day after the attack. The Associated Press said the Secret Service interrogated four Sudanese men in Sarasota after getting a tip that the men intended to harm President Bush during his visit to the city.

But the men taken into custody had been released, and the incident found to be "unrelated" to the attacks, said the AP story. The Secret Service also dismissed the report, saying the warning was "coincidental" to Sept. 11.

The Special Agent in charge of the Presidential detail in Sarasota told reporter Yadov that the President was never in any danger, and the connection to the SPLA, and the warning that the Secret Service got before the terrorist attack, was all "just a coincidence."

For good measure the FBI weighed in, pooh-poohing the story to reporters asking about the significance of the warning. In the vague and wary way government spokespeople seem to have patented, FBI spokesman Sarah Oakes said, "Nationwide the FBI has received over 200,000 such tips, with more than 5,000 of the tips coming into the Tampa office alone."

The explanation would have to do. No one would have anything more to say. Another mystery averted by your friends in public service. When your credibility as an agency has already been shredded, as the FBI's has, there's not much left to lose. Their denial made no sense, but it served to stop further investigation into the predawn warning.

Stopped it on a dime.

Until reporter Yadov went looking for Hakim, the owner of the raided beauty supply store, and discovered that Hakim's beauty supply store wasn't there anymore. Hakim was missing, too. He left in something of a hurry after being released by the Secret Service, Yadov learned. Gone. No one knew where.

And Hakim wasn't the only witness to disappear in Sarasota. Zainelabdeen Omer was missing too. The man whose warning of imminent havoc had been right on the money was now unavailable for comment. He quit his job and left town, just ahead of reporter's questions.

Hakim and Omer joined the swelling ranks of 9/11 Missing Witnesses. We like to think of them as just all being on vacation together somewhere, maybe on an Island of Lost Witnesses.

Some of Omer's friends could still be found, however.

One told Yadov, "Omer got in a lot of trouble with the law. All I know is he can't leave town."

"So you think he's still somewhere around?" she asked.

On camera, Omer's friend shrugs and says, "Should be. If he's still alive."

It's a chilling moment. *If* Omer's still alive? Why wouldn't he be?

Where are the missing Sudanese men today?

The Secret Service doesn't know. Yadov checked with the INS. Was Omer being detained? The INS wouldn't say.

Their responses sounded a little cavalier, especially from people who take very seriously their job of protecting the President, unless by being part of a deliberate cover-up they thought they *were* protecting the President. But two years later?

But if it *was* a cover-up. How could you tell? One sure way, we figured, would be to look for signs of witness intimidation. If authorities were actively discouraging people with firsthand knowledge from talking, then you can be pretty sure that something's rotten in the state of Denmark. Or Florida.

Was there evidence of witness intimidation? Yes… The eyewitness to the incident at the front gate of Bush's hotel who came forward, Carroll Mooneyhan, was a Longboat Key Fire Marshal. He had been milling in the lobby of the Colony Beach Resort at 6 a.m. along with Secret Service agents waiting to accompany Bush on his morning run.

When reporter Shay Sullivan of the Longboat Observer interviewed him about what he'd seen, Mooneyhan probably didn't know enough to dummy up. He was local. He was honest. He was a fireman. So he talked.

And even though reporter Sullivan knew nothing about Yadov's corroborating report of an earlier predawn warning, the savvy reporter immediately suspected that Mooneyhan had witnessed a foiled assassination attempt.

Mooneyhan told the Observer that he had been waiting at the front desk in the lobby of the hotel when a white van arrived at the hotel's guard gate carrying four Middle Eastern men.

The men in the van identified themselves as a television news crew with an appointment with the President, claiming they had a "poolside" interview scheduled with Bush after his morning run. They even asked for a Secret Service agent by name, Mooneyhan said.

Secret Service agents at the guard station told the men to contact the President's public relations office in Washington D.C. to schedule an interview. They turned the four Arab men away, but they let them go. "In light of the attacks, Mooneyhan wonders if what he witnessed is related to the events of Sept. 11," reported the paper.

So did the FBI. Sort of.

"That's very strange," an unnamed agent with the Sarasota field office of the FBI said, when informed what happened. Sullivan wrote, "He said he would direct agents to look into the matter."

The FBI's blasé reaction wasn't enough to put Sullivan off the story, however. He noticed that the ploy used to attempt to gain access to Bush had been used, and *successfully*, just two days earlier by bin Laden operatives to murder the Taliban's biggest foe.

Two Arab men pretending to be journalists arrived to conduct an interview with charismatic Northern Alliance leader Shah Massoud on September 9th in Afghanistan. They used the ruse to gain an audience with the legendary guerrilla leader, who fought against the Soviet invaders in Afghanistan in the 1980s, and was now leading the resistance against Taliban rule.

Massoud Khalili, a Northern Alliance leader who was there, said, "Shah Massoud said, 'OK Let's film.'"

Then the "journalists" blew themselves up, killing Massoud. One of the two "journalists" detonated a bomb hidden inside their television camera, killing their intended target and themselves.

The blast almost claimed his life as well, said Khalili. "I was screaming and then again I saw the noise from the camera. Then I saw the hand of Commander pushing me back and I was unconscious. I'll never forget the face of my friend stained with blood," he told CNN.

The Northern Alliance immediately said it had evidence that Massoud's assassination was the work of bin Laden… but not *just* Osama bin Laden. Many, like Massoud's companion Khalili, thought bin Laden had outside help as well.

"One thing we believe is that it was a global network of Osama plus some others who killed Commander Massoud. I believe they also said it was a global network of Qaeda and others who brought this catastrophe in New York," Khalili said.

There's that "global network" again.

Based on eyewitness accounts, the Sarasota assassination attempt was probably coordinated by Mohamed Atta himself, reported the Observer: "If three eyewitnesses are correct, terrorist hijacker Mohamed Atta came to the Holiday Inn Hotel & Suites-Longboat Key Sept. 7th—the day the media announced President George W. Bush would be coming to the area Sept. 11 to speak at a Sarasota school. Atta may have been there to meet a second hijacker, Marwan Al-Shehhi."

A waiter at the Holiday Inn, Frank Boyal, said while he was there Atta didn't stray far from the bar, the paper reported. Atta and his companion had both ordered the hotel's $18.95 "Surf and Turf" buffet.

"They were just here," he said. "I remember the face."

When we visited the Holiday Inn Hotel, the bartender at the hotel pub, Darlene Sieverts, confirmed for us that Atta had most definitely been there. "Mohamed Atta sat right on that bar stool you're sitting on now, drinking rum and coke," she stated. "But I didn't have any real interaction with him. A bartender can tell when a customer doesn't want to talk, and he didn't.

"About fifteen minutes after he arrived he was joined by a second man, who indicated that he didn't speak English when I asked what he'd like to drink," she continued.

"The second man motioned for Atta to intercede, but instead of ordering something for him Atta asked for the bill. He left a $20 bill to cover a $4 tab."

Seiverts' recollections were echoed by other hotel employees, who remembered seeing Atta dining in the hotel restaurant with a second man.

In Sarasota, just a few days before the attack, Mark Bean, the hotel's assistant food and beverage director, identified the second man as Marwan Al-Shehhi.

One need only compare what we've just learned about the fateful morning of September 11th with what was reported to have happened to begin to understand how complete the 9/11 information embargo has been.

The AP story, for example, made no mention of a van filled with Middle Eastern men attempting to gain access to the President as Bush was leaving for his morning jog.

They also neglected to report the predawn warning of an imminent attack. Instead, media accounts of that morning at the Colony Beach Resort sound much like this one, from the *London Telegraph*: "Bush awoke in the magnificent surroundings of the Colony Beach Resort on Longboat Key… on the morning of his 234th day in office, with a light, warm breeze slipping in from the ocean. After breakfast, Bush led his Secret Service crew on a four-mile run around the nearby Serenoa golf links," reported the paper.

"On his return to the Colony, the President showered, changed into a lightweight, dark blue suit, and, still glowing from the morning's exertion, sat down for the first routine intelligence briefing of the day. It was 8 a.m."

We'll stop there, because it doesn't get any better. Although we learn that Mr. Bush was wearing a lightweight dark blue suit they spare us the detail that he had been a target for assassination.

In light of what happened in Sarasota that morning, the true beginning of what we know as the 9/11 Attack was probably Shah Massoud's assassination in Afghanistan on September 9th. Had the white van with four Arab men, the "TV crew," gotten close enough to Bush, his fate would have been the same as Massoud's.

That same morning, about 8. a.m., a Longboat Key resident standing on the Sarasota bay front waiting to watch the Presidential motorcade go by noticed something unusual for Sarasota… a dilapidated van.

Inside the van, he told police, were "two men of Middle Eastern descent screaming out the windows "Down with Bush" and raising their fists in the air."

What the shocked Sarasota resident probably witnessed was the frustration of men stopped tantalizingly short of eternal access to more virgins than you can shake a stick at.

When we finally reached him by phone, Carroll Mooneyhan, the fire captain who saw the launch of a quickly hushed-up assassination attempt on the life of George W. Bush, told us, "I was visited by the CIA and the Secret Service after 9/11. I have a career to think about. I have to be careful what I say."

And that was the last we heard from him.

CHAPTER THREE

NO SNIGGERING
ALLOWED

If people *with careers to think about* were being pressured into keeping silent about something as serious as an assassination attempt on the President, what *else* might authorities be covering up?

Try: "almost anything." And then delete "almost."

When we began interviewing eyewitnesses to Mohamed Atta's sojourn in Florida—what historians call primary sources—we were soon in the midst of a major "anomaly" in the official story. There was a problem in the FBI's timeline about when Atta first arrived in the U.S. to set up his terrorist HQ.

The FBI states Mohamed Atta landed in America on June 3, 2000.

We interviewed a good dozen credible eyewitnesses who could tell them they were wrong. Didn't they *know* that?

They did. The logic is inescapable… if *we* knew it, we had to figure that *they* knew it as well. After all, they had a massive 4,000-man investigation team. They could put 3,999 more investigators on the street than we could.

They interviewed the same people we did, and heard the same things we heard. So the FBI was not wrong on Atta's timeline by *accident.* They were not making what could be considered honest mistakes. They were *lying.*

Things were worse than we'd imagined. How much worse became clear when we began to compare the truth as we found it with the official story of Atta's activities and movements.

From a number of sources, including the *New York Times* and the *Washington Post*, we compiled the reported milestones in the FBI's chronology of Atta's time in the U.S. Let's start with the official story as recounted in *Time* magazine (Oct. 8, 01):

"On June 3, 2000, he (Atta) arrived in Newark, N.J., from Prague with a six-month tourist visa. Within a month, Atta and Al-Shehhi signed up for flight training at Huffman Aviation International in Venice, Fla."

That's simple enough. What the FBI says happened next was reported in the Sept. 23, 2001 *Ft. Lauderdale Sun-Sentinel*:

"South Florida became Atta's home for almost 14 months. Al-Shehhi traveled with him. They lived in Nokomis (next to Venice) a southwest Florida suburb, as they learned to fly small airplanes at Huffman Aviation from July to November 2000. That December, they apparently moved to southeast Florida as Atta shelled out about $1,500 for him and Al-Shehhi to gain six hours in a jet simulator at SimCenter in Opa-locka."

Okay, we think we've got the FBI's story, which goes like this: Atta arrives in the U.S. in early June, begins flight training at Huffman in Venice in July, then leaves Venice in December and moves gratefully on to the jazzier precincts of the Miami area.

It is a simple, straightforward timeline. Just for safety's sake, let's hear it one more time, in the sworn testimony of Huffman Aviation's Rudi Dekkers—the colorful and controversial Dutch national whose numerous post- 9/11 TV appearances made him a minor celebrity—before the House Judiciary Committee.

"On July 1st, 2000," Dekkers testified, reading from a prepared statement, "Mohamed Atta and Marwan Al-Shehhi arrived at Huffman Aviation in Venice, Florida to inquire about taking flying lessons."

"After a description was given about our flying school, they said they would let us know what they would decide about the flying lessons. On July 3rd, 2000, Atta and Al-Shehhi came back to Huffman Aviation to sign up for lessons" said Dekkers.

"On December 24th, 2000, Atta and Al-Shehhi rented a Warrior from Huffman Aviation for a flight... one to two days later Atta and Al-Shehhi returned to Huffman Aviation to make final payments on their outstanding bills. Because they were not taking any more flying lessons, they were asked to leave the facility due to their bad attitudes and not being liked by staff and clients alike. Huffman never heard about or from them again."

The official story, we can say with confidence, is that after getting their pilot licenses Mohamed Atta and Marwan Al-Shehhi left Venice forever by Christmas of the year 2000.

In the remaining eight months and 11 days before the attack, the FBI's chronology leans heavily, though not exclusively, on Miami-area locations:

Atta is living in an apartment in Hollywood, and then another in Coral Springs. He abandons a stalled private plane on a runway in Miami, purchases global-positioning devices in Fort Lauderdale, trains on a sophisticated full-motion simulator in Opa-Locka. He rents single-engine planes in Belle Glade, at the Palm Beach County Airport, and in Gwinnett County, Georgia.

He consults a pharmacist in Delray Beach, hangs out at Shuckum's Raw Bar in Hollywood, gets a traffic ticket in Broward County, and has frequent meetings in Paterson, New Jersey.

He flies commercial from Fort Lauderdale to Boston. From Boston to New York, to Prague, back to Newark, from Newark to Fort Lauderdale, then to Madrid from Miami, to Las Vegas and back.

While far from comprehensive, this run-down clearly illustrates the official story about Atta, which is that after December of 2000, he is *never* in Venice. When the FBI speaks of him, the word "Venice" does not pass their lips.

Two weeks after the attack the FBI released photographs and brief bios of the hijackers along with a "request for the public's assistance in obtaining more information about these individuals."

Their bio on Atta omits any reference to Venice: "Mohamed Atta. Possible Egyptian national. Date of birth used: Sept. 1, 1968. Possible residences in Hollywood, Fla.; Coral Springs, Fla.; and Hamburg, Germany. Believed to be a pilot."

This is beyond strange. The six months Atta was in Venice comprises roughly half of the time he was in the U.S., according to the FBI's own calculations. Yet there's no mention of Venice in his official FBI bio.

If you saw Atta in a supermarket in Ft. Lauderdale the FBI would like to hear from you, since they list Atta living in Hollywood and Coral Springs residences.

But if you were calling the FBI with a hot tip on seeing Atta huddled in conference with somebody in Venice, apparently they already knew all they needed to know about that, thanks.

The FBI's attempt at misdirection is obvious. This is a big clue that whatever they're covering up about Venice is big enough for them to doctor Atta's entire story to hide it.

All the FBI would have to do to learn that their chronology—the basic tool of investigators—was off by *miles* would have been to talk to some witnesses in Venice, as we did, or even just read the local newspapers. Because the local newspapers of record in Venice and environs had simply done their job, and reported what credible eyewitnesses told them about their encounters with the terrorists.

They didn't know they were in areas deemed "sensitive." They were like the fire chief on Longboat Key who'd blurted out what he'd seen because he wasn't "clued-in" enough to keep his mouth shut. They were local, thank god.

By interviewing dozens of eyewitnesses—often before the FBI got to them—these newspapers performed an invaluable public service. They reported the eyewitness testimony of people who had first-hand knowledge about Mohamed Atta and his terrorist cadre.

For that, future historians will be grateful, even as we are.

Worse for the FBI, these witnesses stories corroborate each other in ways that definitely give them the ring of truth. Unwittingly, local people saw things that gave them possession of what's been called "inconvenient knowledge."

What is inconvenient knowledge? Here's a quick example: if you had been in Dealey Plaza when Kennedy was shot, and happened to notice Lee Harvey Oswald standing right beside you on the curb chomping on a chili dog while the motorcade went by, you would have seen something tremendously inconvenient. Even if you didn't want it, you would have inconvenient knowledge.

Just *seeing* something, though, only constitutes "possession." What they treat far more seriously is seeing something and then talking, to, say, a reporter. This is "possession with intent to distribute," a more serious crime. Under certain circumstances, it can occasionally prove physically harmful.

But consider this: if your inconvenient knowledge contains information hot enough to affect the destiny of the Western World, you could be in trouble even if you *don't* talk. Because how do "they" know you won't someday snigger inappropriately at the mention of Lee Harvey Oswald, and drop a hint. Something like, "That Oswald boy sure does love his chili dog!"

At a bare minimum you would find it necessary to refrain at all costs from ever mentioning the name "Oswald" in a sentence containing the words "chili dog."

But inconvenient knowledge is nothing to make jokes about. Just ask those already in our story who unwittingly came into possession of some. Life can change real fast, as Zainlabeen Omer, and his buddy Hakim, wherever they are, undoubtedly understand.

Things can happen.

When Mohamed Atta and his sidekick Marwan came to Venice, they first lived with a Huffman Aviation employee named Charlie Voss. They'd needed someplace to stay when they got into town, Voss told reporters.

Later, flight school owner Rudi Dekkers testified to Congress that he gave the terrorist duo Charlie's number, an act of "kindness" for which Charlie apparently still holds a grudge.

Voss gave a stilted statement to reporters on his doorstep on the day after the attack, which sounds like something a Justice Dept. attorney wrote down for him and made him repeat until he had it memorized.

"FBI agents informed me there were two individuals that might have crossed our paths who were students at Huffman Aviation, my employer, and the FBI told me they were involved in yesterday's tragedy," Voss said.

The "two individuals" who "might have crossed Charlie's path," Atta and Marwan, lived with the Vosses for just a week, and quickly wore out their welcome. They were asked to move when the Vosses grew tired of remarks they were making which Charlie's wife Drucilla characterized as "arrogant" and "sarcastic."

"The ringleader, Atta, he creeped me out," Drucilla told reporters. "I made them leave."

Atta and Al-Shehhi then signed a 6-month lease with Steve Kona, a member of the Venice Fire Department, renting a small two-bedroom house on Laurel Drive in Nokomis just north of Venice, where they lived from July through December, 2000.

Since the attack, the house has become something of a tourist attraction. To avoid any identification with the hijackers who once lived there, the current occupants have an American flag flying outside all day. Every day.

In an interview six months after the attack, landlord Kona told us, "I just maintained the grass over there in the summer; they actually dealt with the rental agency for the rent each month, but I would see them occasionally when I was over there mowing."

Like many who knew them, Kona spoke of liking the bear-like Marwan, often described as being friendly and accessible…

"Actually, Atta kept kind of secluded. His cousin, I talked to him a couple of times. He was friendly, but Mohamed Atta, no, I never spoke with him the six months he was there."

Kona was clear about the time period during which Atta and Marwan had rented from him: the same July through December time period when they are said to have been at Huffman Aviation.

"They rented it just for that six months, about the same amount of time they were here for their pilot's training. And then they left," Kona said.

According to the FBI, that's just about the whole Venice story. A week with the Vosses, then six months in a pink two-bedroom house in Nokomis. Over and out. On to Miami, right?

Not so fast.

Charlie Voss and Steve Kona were *not* Mohamed Atta's only two landlords in Venice. The terrorists had a *third* landlord there as well. And when this individual stepped forward alarm bells must have gone off all over FBI Headquarters in Washington.

Start with this account in the *Venice Gondolier* three days after the attack, headlined: "FLIGHT SCHOOL MAY HAVE CHARGED SUSPECTED TERRORISTS EXTRA RENT."

The gist of the account was that Huffman Aviation had rented an apartment for $550 a month, and then turned around and sublet it to students at an outrageously high markup.

It was hard to muster indignation over the terrorists being victims of rent-gouging. But the story also contained information which mat-ter-of-factly destroys pretty much the entire edifice of the FBI's of-ficial story.

"Two men suspected of terrorizing the heart of America this week resided in a Venice apartment earlier this year," said the paper.

"While attending flight school at Huffman Aviation in Venice, Mo-hamed Atta, 33, and Marwan Al-Shehhi, 23, lived with four other Middle Eastern students near Venice Airport at Sandpiper Apart-ments. The six Middle Eastern men shared a two-bedroom, two-bathroom apartment in unit 26, said Charles Grapentine, manager of the apartments."

Atta had a third landlord in Venice. That same day the *Charlotte Sun-Herald* reported essentially the same thing.

This was one landlord too many for the FBI's official story.

And it had the same basic effect on the FBI that reports of a "second gunman" had 40 years earlier. But alas for the official story, and the FBI, there was a list of witnesses—an inconveniently long one—who knew first-hand that the terrorist ringleader had lived at the Sand-piper Apartments.

For one, there's Amanda herself, after we'd located her. "I found the Sandpiper," she told us, "met Charlie, thought he was really nice. Mohamed used a check to pay for it. The name on the check was Mo-hamed Arajaki, the name he said was his. The FBI told me they found bank accounts of his all over under numerous different names."

Then there was the couple that managed the Sandpiper Apartments. Charley Grapentine and his wife Paula never had any doubt who their tenant had been. When she saw it on TV, Paula immediately recognized Atta, said the *Gondolier.*

"Paula Grapentine immediately recognized the face of a suspected ter-rorist who may have trained for the World Trade Center attacks at Huff-man Aviation in Venice. He was her next-door neighbor. They lived at the Sandpiper Apartments, unit 26, in Venice until earlier this year."

Even the postman confirmed the identification, as did the tenants next door to Atta and Amanda's apartment. None doubted that the terrorist ringleader had been in their midst. As it turns out, Mohamed and Amanda had been anything but an inconspicuous duo.

Atta lived at the Sandpiper "earlier this year," reported the *Gon-dolier*, meaning of course earlier than the Sept. 14, 2001 date of the story. Maybe you see the problem.

At the time these eyewitnesses say Atta was at the Sandpiper, the FBI says he was no longer in Venice. The Grapentines, and the other Sandpiper Apartment eye-witnesses, were about to discover the consequences of possessing "inconvenient knowledge."

Although at least two other newspapers covered the story, reporter Earle Kimel made it his own in the *Sarasota Herald-Tribune,* owned by the *New York Times.* In the aftermath of 9/11, Kimel had understandably focused on the local angle. The terrorists in Venice was a huge story for a sleepy little town. If it hadn't been so heartbreakingly-tragic, it might have felt like Christmas to reporters there.

As Venice was discovered to be increasingly important to the story of the terrorist conspiracy, the headlines over the paper's reports changed to reflect it, going from: "FBI LINKS THIRD TERRORIST TO VENICE;" to "FOURTH TERRORIST SUSPECT MAY HAVE TIES TO VENICE;" to: "FIFTH PILOT TRAINEE VANISHES."

In his initial account of Atta's third Venice landlords, Kimel recapped what the FBI had released about Atta's stay in Venice. And right away he noticed a huge discrepancy between local eyewitnesses and the official account:

"Voss and his wife, Dru, asked the pair to leave after less than a week. The two men lived in a Nokomis rental home from July 2000 to January 2001, according to the home's owner. Huffman flight instructors have said they believe Atta left the area shortly after receiving his pilot's certification.

"However, Atta may have been in Venice as recently as April. Charles Grapentine, the manager of Sandpiper Apartments on Airport Avenue in Venice, said he remembers seeing Atta at the complex for about three weeks in April. He said Atta was living in the apartment of Amanda Keller."

When we finally found Amanda Keller, one of the first things she said was how distressed she had been when she learned that her former landlord had talked to the press. "When I saw Charlie talking in the newspaper I knew they were going to jump all over him. I thought, 'Charlie, no. Can't you just wait?'"

Kimel's story was where we first learned that terrorist ringleader Atta had had an American girlfriend while in Venice. Somewhere out there was a girl named Amanda Keller, who undoubtedly had one whale of a story to tell.

News accounts of Atta's stay at the Sandpiper don't just stray from the FBI's account. They flatly contradicted it.

After just weeks in Southwest Florida, we had the chilling feeling that someone—or something—big was being hidden down in the mangrove swamps of Southwest Florida...

Something in Venice.

When we showed up at the Sandpiper Apartments, over six months after the attack, we learned we were in luck.

The shock had begun to wear off, and the FBI agents had stopped coming around. After climbing the stairs to unit 26, Atta and Amanda's second floor apartment, we knocked on their next-door neighbor's door.

Stephanie Frederickson was home. She invited us in.

And she talked.

CHAPTER FOUR

THE "THIRD LANDLORD"

40 years ago, the worst nightmare for the Warren Commission was that someone would walk through the door with proof for the "second gunman" theory. A second gunman was to be avoided at all costs, because what if someone had seen a "third gunman"? This was something they were going to nip right in the bud.

News of Atta's "third landlord" in Venice was treated in the exact same way. A third landlord brought unwanted attention to the role of the Venice Airport in the terrorist conspiracy, and there was an enormous can of worms there, waiting to be opened.

The Venice Airport is a string of non-descript buildings and hangars running for several blocks down one side of Airport Avenue just before it dead-ends at Casperson Beach on the Gulf of Mexico.

Across the street is the Sandpiper Apartments, a drab two-story stucco building, next door to the equally-colorless Lemon Bay Apartments, also maintained by the same management.

When we arrived at the Sandpiper we made a beeline up the stairs to unit 26, Atta and Amanda's unit. It certainly looked normal. Nothing to indicate that a mass murderer had walked through that door, or walked down those steps.

When we stopped at the apartment next door, Stephanie Frederickson, a pleasant-looking 50-year-old housewife, answered, smiled as we told her why we'd come, and invited us inside.

Stephanie Frederickson is nobody's idea of a "conspiracy theorist." She cares during the day for the baby of a friend needing help. She had not sought publicity, nor had she spoken to the press. And a good thing too. From what she told us, she clearly believes she would have been in trouble if she had.

We were soon sharing iced tea while she told us what had happened at the complex after the attack. The only interruption came when the baby she was caring for, a sparkling-eyed little girl, woke up from her nap.

In the first few days after the attack, all of the local newspapers in the Venice area—the *Sarasota Herald Tribune, Charlotte Sun,* and *Venice Gondolier*—reported that Mohamed Atta had lived at the Sandpiper Apartments.

The Sandpiper, Stephanie explained, had been home to a transient tenant population which included an ever-changing roster of foreign pilot trainees learning to fly at the twin flight schools across the street, Huffman Aviation and the Florida Flight Training Center. Many of the tenants who were flight school students were Arab, along with sizable Dutch and German contingents.

All had come to learn to fly, supposedly, in the single engine trainers speckling the tarmac across the street. We say "supposedly" because we will soon hear that Mohamed Atta *already* possessed pilot's licenses—from a half dozen nations—when he arrived in the U.S., ostensibly to learn to fly. So just "what all" Atta was doing while he was a flight student was not yet clear.

Atta's stay at the Sandpiper was a small part of local news coverage. No particular emphasis was placed on it. The local papers were full of stories about unsuspecting townspeople who discovered, to their shock and disbelief, that "their paths had crossed" with the terrorists.

Several accounts quoted landlord Charles Grapentine saying Atta had been living in his apartment building, with Amanda Keller in April, in apartment 26 on the second floor. Atta was also said to have been close to a group of six Middle Eastern men who had been renting a downstairs apartment.

One of the men in the downstairs apartment had been positively identified as Atta's "sidekick" Marwan Al-Shehhi, who was in fact his bodyguard. So the public record—*the public record in Venice,* anyway—was clear.

Somehow though the news of Atta at the Sandpiper wasn't included with those of the other two Venice landlords: Steve Kona, owner of the house the terrorist duo rented for six months, and Charlie Voss, the Huffman employee, with whom they lived for a week.

Why was that? If reports of Atta living at the Sandpiper were any less credible than the others, local newspapers wouldn't have carried them. They weren't lacking for stories about terrorist sightings. Atta had been seen all over town. He dressed "in khakis and polo shirts." He seemed "fairly quiet and aloof."

"The only thing I can tell you about him is he drank Bud Light," said a waitress at the Charlotte County Airport.

Becky Cover worked in the deli of Publix supermarket a mile from the airport. "I was on the phone with my mother-in-law when they started showing pictures of three different guys on TV. Atta was one of them. And immediately I recognized the faces and I told my husband then, "My God, those are the three guys. They were just in the store a week ago.... They got subs."

Becky says the terrorist pilots were in Venice just one *week* before the attack. They got subs. This is, of course, inconvenient knowledge, and would not be music to the FBI's ears.

Like a number of other witnesses, Becky mentioned the terrorist ringleader's malevolent presence. She said that Atta "didn't speak, just stood and glowered."

"I didn't like the way he just stared at you," she told us. "It would have been different if they would have talked to you like you were a normal person, like 'hi, how are you today.' But he just stood back and just glared at you with his dark eyes."

Few people we spoke with who had met Atta were surprised it had been him piloting a plane in the attack. No one said what you usually hear, which is, "Oh no. Not him. It *couldn't* be."

No national newspaper picked up the reports of Atta living at the Sandpiper. One paper, the *New York Times,* even sent a reporter who made persistent attempts to spike it, winning him the enmity of Sandpiper residents, including Stephanie Frederickson, who knew different.

During our afternoon at the Sandpiper with Stephanie Frederickson and Charley and Paula Grapentine, we learned that even before the

Sept. 11th attack, Mohamed Atta had stuck out in a way that made him hard to forget.

"He was very unfriendly," said Paula Grapentine. "He wouldn't talk to women."

Atta stopped by the Grapentines' apartment one time to discuss something regarding the complex, Paula stated.

"He came to talk about something and said, 'I don't talk to women and you're supposed to look down when you talk to me,'" Grapentine recalled.

"He treated women like they were under him."

We heard the same complaint from neighbor Stephanie Frederickson, who confirmed the Grapentines' account. Atta and Amanda lived next-door for several months, she explained, and he was no picnic as a neighbor.

What she really wanted to talk about, though, was how she, and other building residents like the Grapentines, had been harassed and intimidated by agents of the FBI, in an effort to keep them from talking to reporters.

"The question they (the FBI) asked was always the same," said Frederickson. "You aren't saying anything to anybody, are you?

"At first, right after the attack, they told me I must have been mistaken in my identification. Or they would insinuate that I was lying. Finally they stopped trying to get me to change my story, and just stopped by once a week to make sure I hadn't been talking to anyone. Who was I going to tell?"

She shrugs. "Most everyone around here already knew."

Frederickson said a *New York Times* reporter to whom she spoke accused her of making it up. He urged her to stop talking about it.

What makes this strange is that the reporter need only have read his own local newspaper to learn the story of Atta's American girlfriend had been confirmed by a number of witnesses.

A competent and intelligent grown woman, Stephanie Frederickson knows what she saw. She resented the FBI agents' heavy-handed and repeated assertions to the contrary. And she wanted us to know about it.

Real Americans won't be silenced.

"Amanda moved in next door first, saying she had come from Orange Park (near Jacksonville)," Frederickson began. "Then one day in the middle of March she brought home Atta. She had only been here for a short time before he showed up, just a couple of weeks.

"She told us she met him at the bar at the 44th Aero, across the street at the airport, which was remodeling at the time and not really re-opened yet, but the bar was still doing business.

"Amanda said to me, 'I'd like you to meet my friend Mohamed Atta. He's from France.' I looked at her to see if she was joking, but I guess she wasn't," stated Frederickson.

"Later when I saw her alone I asked her if she realized that Mohamed Atta wasn't really a French name, and that he was definitely *not* French. She looked at me like I was nuts. I didn't know if she *really* believed he was French, but it was clear to me that he wasn't."

When she arrived at the Sandpiper Apartments with Mohamed Atta in tow, Amanda Keller was a good-looking, sexy twenty-year-old with pink hair living a fast life. She is still remembered fondly by some in Venice.

But when we first heard she thought Atta was French, however, we concluded that she was perhaps not the sharpest knife in the drawer. This may have been a little hasty; after we met her we discovered that Atta spoke fluent French.

Atta and Amanda's brief relationship was troubled, Frederickson said. While Atta's cheesy taste for infidel flesh is well-known, when it came to his *own* girlfriend he apparently balked at sharing glimpses of it with others.

This created difficulties, since his girlfriend was a "lingerie model," and it became something of an issue for the couple.

"That's when she started dressing really slutty, and dyeing her hair pink," Frederickson said. "She wasn't going to let herself be controlled by him."

The more we heard about Mohamed Atta, the more his image as an Islamic fundamentalist began to crumble. An Islamic fundamentalist who shacks up with women with pink hair fits no definition of "Islamic fundamentalist" we've come across.

Pink hair doesn't seem Wahabbi.

But perhaps Atta wasn't who we've been told us he was... Considering the bombshell Stephanie Frederickson casually dropped into our conversation, between burpings of the baby. We already knew that Atta was a Kitten Killer.

Now we learned he beat his girlfriend too.

"There were a couple of times he beat her up that I know about," Frederickson said, "mostly over the slutty way she dressed to go to meet her escort service clients. Her hair was always done up in a half dozen funky colors and she always dressed… well, you know, like a hooker," said Stephanie.

"Fantasies & Lace would send a car and driver to get Amanda," she said. "And I would hear the driver and Atta arguing out on the balcony. Atta didn't want her to leave.

"The third time it happened—the third time he beat her up—she put him out," states Frederickson. "She threw his two suitcases, and a blue Gold's gym bag which he always carried around with him over the balcony railing onto the driveway in front of the apartments, and called a cab to come get him."

Frederickson was glad to see him go.

"He was a really nasty guy," she says. "He had no patience, and seemed mad at the world. One day, I remember, it was raining out, and I left my apartment at the same time he came out of his. He didn't have a car that day, for some reason, so I offered him a ride.

"He got furious, and shouted at me, 'You do not speak to me unless I speak to you first!'

"I said get over yourself, Bub," she said. "You're in America now.

"Atta said, 'American women are all bitches.' I told him the least he could do was thank me for offering him a ride."

Apartment manager Charlie Grapentine, a grizzled former marine in his early 60s, remembers when Amanda performed her informal eviction. Later we learn from Amanda that she sought his counsel first, on what to do about the unworkable arrangement.

Amanda's name was on the lease.

Grapentine told her to kick him out.

"Atta always carried a fanny pack around his waist," Grapentine said. "I remember Amanda once telling him that she needed some new clothes, and he reached in and peeled off a few hundreds from a thick roll of cash he had stuffed inside the fanny pack."

The FBI did not receive apartment manager Grapentine's recollections any more warmly than they had those of Stephanie Frederickson.

In fact, says Grapentine, the FBI was positively frosty, especially on the subject of talking to reporters.

"They called me a liar, and told me to keep my mouth shut," states the ex-marine grimly. "Nobody likes to hear that: that they didn't see something they know they saw."

Frederickson and Grapentine, both still angry, felt their personal integrity had been attacked. The FBI, more concerned with squelching the story, apparently didn't mind stepping on a few toes in the process.

What did they think the attraction was between Atta and Amanda?

"Atta and his crew were always flush with lots and lots of money," Stephanie replied promptly.

"Those guys were all really party animals."

Although the six Arab men at the Sandpiper may have had money to burn, their living accommodations didn't reflect it.

"I lived next door to Amanda and Atta on the second floor, but then moved downstairs to my father's apartment to help him, because he had had surgery and couldn't climb stairs any longer," says Frederickson.

She remembered some of the crew of Middle Eastern men who took over her old apartment... like "Sid," a nice gentlemen with a red car. Sid was Siad Jarrah, she later learned. And the big guy named "Mahmouti" was probably Marwan Al-Shehhi. He lived in Nokomis, where he had a cousin, Sara, a pharmacist.

"Atta's pals took my old apartment. One time I stuck my head in, and there were at least eight of them living in a small two-bedroom place, with sleeping bags spread out everywhere."

The student pilots living at the Sandpiper and hanging out with Mohamed Atta hadn't all been Arab, she said. "Pierre" came looking for a bride. "Patrick" came from Holland.

The one subject we were getting nowhere with was Amanda's current whereabouts. She had gone to ground. No one knew where. We checked bars we learned she had been known to frequent, and former employers. We learned nothing.

Amanda Keller was another witness who had disappeared.

We tried to track down the man she left the Sarasota nightclub with the night she broke up with Atta, Garret Metts.

"Garret was a dark-haired guy, a good-looking little shit," remembered Stephanie.

Unfortunately, Garret was now dead. Killed in a car accident. His brother, who remembered Amanda, gave us the names of several of her girlfriends, and we began looking for *them*.

The reason for our urgency was that it was clear after interviewing Charlie Grapentine and Stephanie Frederickson the FBI had been extremely anxious to suppress news of Amanda Keller and Mohamed Atta's dalliance.

There must have been a reason.

One of the things which puzzled us was why Amanda hadn't sold her story to a tabloid. A girl who makes her living as a "lingerie model" could probably use the money. Certainly the tabloids would go nuts to get her story.

"Terrorist's Girlfriend Bares All!" would sell a lot of papers in the check-out line. Why hadn't she? Was something preventing her? Or someone?

We found a clue on the 1-year anniversary of the attack, filed by the Associated Press. The headline said it all:" One year later, 19 hijackers still a tangle of mystery and contradiction."

We thought, is that on purpose?

While Atta had been living at the Sandpiper Apartments, apartment, manager Paula Grapentine told reporters, he had "a lot of visitors."

The building's owner, Vicky Keyser, told authorities that the students smoked a strange tobacco which smelled like marijuana. This will be by no means the last reference to drugs we will come across in connection with the terrorist conspiracy.

It was clear the FBI didn't want the public to know that Mohamed Atta returned—or maybe even *remained*—in the Venice area after receiving his multi-engine commercial pilot's license on December 21, 2000.

Maybe it *would* open up that "endless can of worms" Sen. Fulbright talked about. This notion received some support when we discovered another local news account about Mohamed Atta and Amanda Keller, one we'd missed, because it didn't come from Venice, but from North Port, the next town southeast of Venice…

According to witnesses there, interviewed in the *Charlotte Sun-Herald*, Atta and Amanda engaged in a very un-Islamic three-day drug-and-booze-fueled party in Key West.

At the time of the party weekend, late February, 2001, Atta was living in a rented house in North Port that he and six other Middle Eastern men rented in early January and left in early March, after being evicted.

Far from leaving Venice, Florida forever in December, Mohamed Atta had still been in the immediate vicinity, in North Port, in January and February 2001, and then in Venice with Amanda during March and April.

What had he been *doing* there? And why was the FBI lying?

CHAPTER FIVE

"ENAMORED OF MOHAMED"

Mohamed Atta's three-day binge in Key West made the news—the local news, at least—in the immediate aftermath of the 9/11 attack, before disappearing without a trace, down the rabbit hole, never to be heard again.

This is, once again, extremely strange. It wasn't that it's not newsworthy. In the land of *Entertainment Tonight*, the sheer salaciousness of the tale should have guaranteed that every national reporter younger than Sam Donaldson would be beating it down to the Keys on the double.

But they weren't.

Back in the early days after the tragedy—when authorities couldn't use the name "Mohamed Atta" without the appellation "Islamic fundamentalist" in front of it—the story of Atta in Key West might have made a big difference.

In little things. Like notions of who had attacked us, and why.

The idea that the 9/11 attack stemmed directly from fanatic Islamic fundamentalism might have been "rendered inoperative" if Atta's hijinks in the Keys had surfaced, for the very good reason that Islamic fundamentalists don't do coke in hotel rooms in Key West.

The story of Atta's trip to Key West broke in the *Charlotte Sun-Herald*, where reporter Elaine Allen-Emrich's account offered revealing insights into the nature and workings of the terrorist conspiracy's operations in the U.S.

"Hunt for terrorists reaches North Port," read the headline in the paper, which covers Venice, North Port, and Port Charlotte. "As authorities continue to dig through the rubble in Tuesday's terrorist attacks, agents were digging through North Port to find one of the many missing pieces to the puzzle of who declared war on the United States and why."

FBI agents were combing the town of North Port two days after the attack, said the paper, looking for North Port landlords Tony and Vonnie LaConca, who had rented their Agress Avenue home to "someone whom authorities think may be connected with Tuesday's attacks. Agents questioned the couple for two hours concerning a man they knew only as 'Mohamed.'"

This is not strictly true. The LaConcas knew the man's full name, or at least the full name he gave them. It was on the check he used to pay for his rent. Unless you're Elvis or Madonna, banks make you use your whole name on your checks.

It wasn't true, but it was definitely *useful.* We have already seen that when the FBI doesn't want the public to know an individual's true identity, they give him one name. "Ghandi." "Hakim." Now "Mohamed."

It's a crock.

Mohamed "was associated with a local woman believed to be Amanda Keller, a local restaurant manager," the *Sun* reported.

LaConca told the FBI that Keller had "dishwater-blond hair, was big-boned and freckled, and seemed to be very enamored of Mohamed."

The FBI was looking for Keller for additional questioning, said the paper, "but she might be missing."

"While talking to Keller and Mohamed, the couple learned he had a pilot's license to charter small planes of four to six people and was going to school at Huffman Aviation in Venice to train for a commercial pilot's license," said the *Sun.*

Sounds like Mohamed Atta. The paper felt on safe ground mentioning it. "Huffman was the school that enrolled Mohamed Atta and Marwan Al-Shehhi, both identified as suspects in the hijacked jet assaults on the World Trade Center and the Pentagon."

The LaConcas told agents the man was about 25, 5 feet 10 inches, 160 pounds, had "dark, perfect" skin, and was clean cut and very polite. "He was a very handsome guy," Vonnie LaConca told reporters. "He had beautiful, unblemished skin."

Mohamed Atta's black heart did not always manage to conceal his good looks, apparently. He also looks younger than thirty-three, even in the mug shot picture we've all seen a million times.

"Mohamed was associated with a local woman believed to be Amanda Keller, a local restaurant manager, LaConca said. The FBI is looking for Keller for additional questioning, but she might be missing.

"Keller, who allegedly met Mohamed while working at Papa John's Pizza in Venice, told the couple she would translate because Mohamed spoke limited English," the story continued.

"She said he was French/Canadian. She told the LaConcas that he was not a U.S. citizen. A Papa John's employee confirmed that Keller was a manager there, but has not been to work for some time."

This is further confirmation of Amanda Keller's relationship with Mohamed Atta, and also confirmation of Stephanie Frederickson's account that Amanda thought Atta was French.

Keller was a restaurant manager when she met Atta, she will tell us later. Before she switched to a more lucrative line of work, she managed the local Papa John's. And it is there she first met Atta, which is why—two days after the attack—the FBI was looking for Amanda Keller...

"In an effort to locate Keller, agents accompanied Tony LaConca to the North Port Police Department to pick up a Feb. 25 police report in which Keller had called police about harassing cell phone calls.

"According to the police report, after Keller called police about the calls, a computer check was conducted and showed an outstanding warrant from Marion County on a worthless check charge," the story said.

"Mohamed bailed her out of South County Jail," Vonnie LaConca said. "We told agents this because we thought they (FBI) might be able to get his last name from the reports."

Mohamed had used a check to bail her out of jail, Amanda will tell us. She knew him as Mohamed Arajaki, which was also the name on the check. "The FBI told me they found bank accounts of his all over in numerous different names," Keller stated.

"This is a written paper trail," would be the FBI's thinking on the matter. "It will be made to go away." Barring extraordinary circumstances, we predict that neither check will ever see the light of day.

The only request Atta made to the couple, reported the paper, was that they provide him a desk in which he could do his aviation homework.

"He didn't even care if the house had a bed, all he wanted was a desk," said Tony LaConca.

Here is where our story begins to get up close and personal.

Let's go *backstage, for the behind the scenes* look at Mohamed Atta's wild life that would have been aired already, if not for wartime censorship.

Although he was in this country for—at least—the 14 months the FBI says and probably much longer, we haven't heard any personal accounts from Americans who knew Atta.

Read on, for reasons why not!

Reporter Allen-Emrich's account said Mohamed Atta and his American girlfriend Amanda Keller had partied for three days straight in a very un-Islamic drug-and-booze-fueled binge in Key West.

The LaConcas told her they learned this from a then-employee of Vonnie LaConca's cleaning company. "After meeting Mohamed and Keller on Feb. 21, the former employee joined the couple on an adventure to Key West the following day," said the paper.

"They were gone for three days," said Tony LaConca. "They didn't sleep—it was a continuous party."

LaConca said Mohamed footed the entire bill for the weekend, including buying Keller and the unnamed employee new clothes, alcohol, drugs and hotel stay.

However, the couple said, Mohamed did not have a job.

"The two girls were introduced to two men from Germany that they said were Mohamed's friends," Tony LaConca continued. "I thought it was strange, because Mohamed didn't appear to be French-Canadian or German."

Atta was meeting "two men from Germany" in Key West, who we will later learn flew in solely to meet him. This is the first hint we have gotten that all of Mohamed Atta's associates don't face East five times every day.

Who were these Germans? Part of Tony Blair's "global network"? The story says nothing more about them. We will learn later who the men are from Amanda herself.

The LaConcas told the paper that the FBI tried to locate and interview Vonnie's employee who'd gone on the jaunt. She goes nameless in the story. Nameless witnesses must be even more dangerous to the official story than one-named ones.

Whatever her true identity—and this is *really* interesting—she was, according to the *Sun-Herald*, "uncooperative to the agent."

Maybe it was because she had *kept in touch* with Mohamed…

"However, Vonnie learned the former employee made telephone contact with Mohamed last week," the paper said.

This *is* big news. A deliberately-unnamed woman had received a phone call from Mohamed Atta less than a week before the attack.

Were any confidences exchanged? We wanted to ask. Unfortunately, she's gone. No one knows where.

Maybe the Island of Lost Witnesses.

We're also dying to know more about Mohamed Atta's two German friends in Key West. *Sun-Herald* reporter Elaine Allen-Emrich apparently felt the same way…

"The FBI in Tampa would neither confirm nor deny that any agents were interviewing people in the North Port area," she reported. Asked for more information about Atta's wild weekend, an FBI spokesperson identified only as "Pam" said, "We recommend that you check in with CNN for current information. Any press statements can be found on televised stations like CNN."

The discovery that an American girl was romantically involved ("very enamored of Mohamed") with the terrorist ringleader makes Amanda Keller an extremely important witness to the terrorist conspiracy's activities. We went looking for Amanda.

We didn't feel like checking in with CNN.

CHAPTER SIX

LOOKING FOR AMANDA

Our first stop in the search for Amanda was at the *Sarasota Her-ald-Tribune's* local Venice bureau, where reporter Earle Kimel helped break the story of Atta's American squeeze.

We asked him if he had any clue about what had happened to her. Was she just a reluctant witness? Or had she been frightened into silence? Kimel knew a bit about recalcitrant witnesses; he'd found some strippers who had danced for Atta in a Sarasota strip joint, for example, but then encountered resistance from the strip joint's management when he wanted to ask them a few questions.

Their response was to throw him out of the club.

"A dancer at the Cheetah Lounge in Sarasota also reported seeing one of the alleged terrorists (Atta) at the strip club," Kimel reported. "Several other Cheetah employees, shown pictures of the men who trained in Venice, said they looked somewhat familiar... A club man-ager escorted a *Herald-Tribune* reporter out of the club shortly after-ward, saying the Cheetah had no comment."

Maybe the manager didn't want publicity. But probably he didn't want his girls to talk because he'd been *clued-in* on the need for se-crecy. Whether the strippers had knowledge about Atta was fast be-coming rhetorical.

Kimel said he had no idea where Amanda Keller was currently. He thought she'd left town, wished us luck in finding her, and with a weak smile let us know that if we *did* find her, he had a few questions he'd like answered, too.

Our next stop was Fantasies & Lingerie, where Amanda had worked as a private dancer. Like Cheetah's, it's just down the street from the Sarasota Airport.

It turned out to be a locked-down facility in a run-down strip mall. No windows. One door. Locked.

The only access was though an intercom.

The manager told us to go away. He had no employees named Amanda. No, he would not come out.

Next.

Kimel's second story about Atta and Amanda included a brief phone interview he'd done with her. She was speaking to him from her mother's house in the northern Florida town of Lady Lake, said the article.

"In a telephone interview late Friday, Keller said she met Atta through a friend and let him stay in the apartment with her and her then-boyfriend, Garret Metts, because she felt sorry for him. She said authorities told her not to say anything at all about Atta," reported Kimel.

Garret Metts is, or was, the "hot guy" Amanda met in a Sarasota nightclub while with Atta.

Kimel's account contained the eleven words, she said before lapsing into silence. "I can't really discuss anything," she told him. "I'm afraid I'll get in trouble."

Amanda's mother had met Atta, too. "Keller's mother, Susan Payne of Lady Lake, remembered Atta," Kimel reported.

"I didn't like him; he just seemed strange," she said.

We eventually lost count of the number of eyewitnesses who told reporters Atta "creeped them out."

Atta dressed in a casual yuppie fashion, said Amanda's mother.

Her daughter told her he mostly kept to himself. Amanda had taken him in because he said he had nowhere to stay, she said.

"Stray dogs, stray cats, stray people, she was always taught to help anybody out when they needed help," Payne said.

A real humanitarian, we're sure, concerned with children and every living thing. But since she'd also been, if only briefly, the girlfriend of a man with the blood of 3,000 innocent human beings on his hands, somebody should have been asserting the people's right to know here.

But it's strange. Nobody did.

We went looking for Garret Metts, the "studly" boyfriend for whom Amanda dumped Atta, only to discover he had been killed the previous summer in a car accident.

We visited his last known address, a modest two bedroom ranch house in South Venice. There we met Garret's younger brother, who remembered Amanda well…. When your older brother's dating a stripper with pink-to-orange-to-dyed-blond hair, he let us understand, you tend to pay attention.

Amanda and Atta even lived briefly, he said, with Garret's family.

We checked the neighbors, and discovered several who knew all about Amanda Keller and Mohamed Atta.

In fact, one neighbor said that the lady across the street still had Atta's dog. From her description, we recognized that she must be talking about the little dog who survived Atta's kitten-killing spree by hiding under a couch.

Garret's brother passed on the names of some of Amanda's girlfriends: Olivia. Angelina. Page. They used to hang out together at a bar called Crawdad's on the Intracoastal Canal, which wends through Venice.

We were puzzled when we couldn't find Crawdad's listed in the phone book. Then we learned it had closed a year ago, and the owners had moved on to open a new place called The Big Easy.

On the chance that the clientele of Crawdad's had followed the owners to their new place, we stopped by. And although it was only late afternoon the bar was busy already, filled with a mix of prosperous-looking older men sipping whiskey, catered to by an attractive young wait staff, busy killing the hour between five and six. One young waitress, we noticed, had something shiny sticking out of her tongue… A diamond stud.

We thought: These could be Amanda's people.

We struck up a conversation at the bar, and several beers later had made contact with a blond woman in her twenties named Laurie, who had known Amanda.

The only problem was, she didn't want to talk about her. She gave as her reason for protecting her friend: "Who wants to be known as a terrorist's girlfriend?"

It made a certain sense. Still, privacy concerns in matters pertaining to 9/11 seem clearly outweighed the search for the killers of 3,000 people.

So we drove up to Lady Lake, a smallish town tucked into the hill country of northern Florida. We thought we'd try to get in touch with Amanda's mother, Susan Payne. But the house had been abandoned. There was broken glass all over the driveway. Susan Payne had died months ago, a neighbor told us. Another daughter, Tammy, had moved away.

On a sweltering hot August day that seemed to come right out of the movie *Body Heat* we visited Amanda's former residences in the Venice area. We found another house where she had lived, this one on Manasota Key, near North Port. But it too was vacant. Then, in Port Charlotte, just to the south of North Port, we pulled up to another of Amanda's former residences and got lucky…

A man was mowing the lawn in front of the house. He knew Amanda, sure. His stepson had lived with Amanda two years ago, he said. He appeared not to have much use for either. He and his wife, the stepson's mother, were raising the stepson's two children. The stepson was something of an "unfit parent."

He couldn't tell us where the stepson was, but he knew he was no longer with Amanda. The stepson's living arrangements were currently fluid.

We regrouped. It was time to review what we had already learned. We reread news accounts, and in the process discovered another story about Amanda and Atta, that had come out a week after the initial flurry of reports.

We were amazed at what it contained… The *Sarasota Herald-Tribune* was reversing itself, though not through a retraction.

Amanda Keller had *not* lived with Mohamed Atta, the paper now reported, but with *another* Mohamed.

A Mohamed who had somehow previously escaped mention.

The headline offered a clue to the contortions somebody was going through to offer this news to the world. The paper, as we've seen, was counting the ever-increasing number of terrorists said to have passed through Venice in its headlines...

They were up to five: "FIFTH PILOT TRAINEE VANISHES. 'Mohammed' slept on her couch, a Venice woman says."

"Investigators have identified a fifth man of Middle Eastern descent who trained to fly in Venice, but they don't know if he was involved in the Sept. 11 attacks because they can't find him. He told the people he lived with in Venice earlier this year that he was moving to Paris," the paper reported.

"The man, known as "Mohammed," stayed at Amanda Keller's unit in the Sandpiper Apartment complex on Airport Avenue in April. Authorities would not release the man's full name, and Keller would not divulge it, citing instructions from the Florida Department of Law Enforcement."

There had been a *fifth* terrorist pilot in Venice, authorities were now asserting. By itself that is not too surprising; there may have been dozens.

His name was Mohammed, with an extra "m" in the middle.

Strangely, enough, the similarities between him and the terrorist ringleader didn't end with their similar names. The two Mohameds shared a *lot* of characteristics...

Like Atta—who, as we've seen, told Amanda he was French—this new Mohamed also had a French Connection, of sorts... He said he was moving to Paris.

Also like Atta, this "other Mohamed" had an "icky"personality.

"He would leer," Tammy Payne, Keller's sister, told reporters. "God was he creepy."

This other Mohammed's chief—and apparently only—salient characteristic seemed to be that he was *not* the Mohamed whose last name was Atta.

"Investigators recently asked Keller about the man because his name appeared on a list of flight students at Venice area flight schools," said the story. "They aren't sure whether he was among the 19 men who hijacked the jets that crashed into the Pentagon, the World Trade Center towers and in rural Pennsylvania. But his training in Venice and his disappearance have attracted their attention because of four other men who authorities say trained in Venice to prepare for the attacks."

So, there was a second terrorist named Mohamed in Venice. But authorities wouldn't release his full name. Amanda Keller told reporters she wouldn't either. This second Mohamed had vanished without a trace. But despite their vagueness on his identity, whereabouts, chronology, and participation in the 9/11 attack, authorities knew one thing about him to an absolute dead certainty:

He wasn't the terrorist ringleader.

It hadn't been Mohamed Atta waking up to pink hairs on his pillow in the morning… It was this *other* "Mohammed."

Even for a cover story, this one seemed a little thin. For an outright lie, it looked pretty bald. But—and here's the point—it didn't *have* to be fully thought out. It was for local consumption. It put to bed rumors about Mohamed Atta's American girlfriend. The local paper didn't question further.

It was the way things were in Florida after the 9/11 attack.

There *had* been some initial confusion, authorities admitted. But Amanda Keller herself was now available to clear it up.

"Keller said comments attributed to her in the *Herald-Tribune* on Saturday, saying that Atta lived in her apartment, were wrong. She said that it was this unidentified fifth man, also named Mohamed, that stayed in her home.

"In an interview at her mother's house, Keller wouldn't talk about the man who stayed on her couch. But she did say the attention she's received from police and the media has been unwelcome."

As a lingerie model, Amanda was probably quite capable of dealing with unwanted attention.

What to make of this Fifth Pilot Theory? We found the whole story strange.

Was it plausible that someone—actually, a half-dozen people—had mistaken the man with the 1,000-yard stare whose picture had been seen everywhere around the world… for someone *else?*

We thought a big clue was that the *New York Times*-owned *Sarasota Herald-Tribune* had pulled Earle Kimel, who'd discovered the connection, off the story.

Were there any other crucial 9/11 witnesses who had conspicuously changed their stories? As a matter of fact, there were. In fact, there were several striking examples right in—where else?—Florida.

Shuckum's is a dive bar in Ft. Lauderdale with the requisite nautical theme, complete with life-size shark mounted on an ocean-colored wall. Mohamed Atta and two of his henchmen were drinking heavily there six nights before the attack, reported *Time, Newsweek* and wire service stories reprinted worldwide.

The networks all had correspondents *go live* from Shuckum's.

FBI Agents had shown up at Shuckums just 12 hours after the attack. They showed employees—especially manager Tony Amos and bartender Patricia Idrissi—photos of two men.

Bartender Idrissi says FBI agents told her "they were on the plane and passed away."

"We were able to recognize both gentlemen," Amos told reporters. He identified a man in a photo bearing the name Mohamed underneath, who, along with two other men, had each consumed at least several drinks.

The guy, Mohamed, was drunk, Amos said.

The two and another man "got wasted" in his place, he said, downing "chicken wings and cranberry juice, Stolichnaya and orange juice, and Captain Morgan's spiced rum and Coke."

"Atta drank Stoli vodka for three straight hours," remembered bartender Idrissi. "The guy, Mohamed, was drunk. They were wasted."

Idrissi said the men told her they wanted to eat but didn't like what was on the menu, so she sent them to a Chinese restaurant a few doors down. "They were very rude," she said.

They didn't want to pay the bill. When asked if they could afford the $48 bar tab, Atta's face had darkened. He pulled out a thick roll. "'You think I can't pay? I'm a pilot for American Airlines. I can pay my fucking bill.'

"Atta and two of his buddies seem to have gone out for a farewell bender at a seafood bar called Shuckums," *Newsweek* reported.

"Atta drank five Stoli-and-fruit-juices, while one of the others drank rum and Coke. For once, Atta and his friends became agitated, shouting curse words in Arabic, reportedly including a particularly blasphemous one that roughly translates as 'F—k God.'"

Time magazine put it this way: "It was at Shuckums, on Sept. 8, that Mohamed Atta and Marwan Al-Shehhi did some pre-mass murder tippling. Atta drank vodka and orange juice, while Al-Shehhi preferred rum and cokes, five drinks apiece."

One eyewitness interviewed at Shuckum's described Atta as having something more than just an eerie presence.

"He was just kind of strange, because he was just staring," the woman told Brian Ross on NBC. "And every time I'd walk in and out, he had the same look on his face, so God knows what was going through his mind. Now I guess we know what was going through his mind. He had a very intense-looking face, very intense-looking eyes."

Along with other reports of heavy drinking which were surfacing, the report was at odds with the portrait—the official story—that was beginning to emerge of the terrorist ringleader, raising questions about whether Atta was *really* a fanatic and puritanical Islamic fundamentalist? Wahhabi desert dweller—or just a guy who knows the importance of Stoli's authentic Russian heritage when you're letting the night unfold. Were they sure he was Islamic Fundamentalist?

Maybe Atta was Islamic Stolichnaya.

Then a witness's conspicuous retraction came to the rescue of the official story. Night manager Amos changed his story. Mohamed Atta drank nothing stronger than cranberry juice that evening at Shuckum's Bar, Tony Amos now said.

He was sitting quietly by himself. It had been Atta's companion Marwan and a third man that did all the drinking.

Case closed.

Everyone by this time had seen the brooding mug shot of Mohamed Atta, complete with unnerving icy stare. Is it *at all* plausible that Atta could be mistaken for someone else? For the teddy bear, Marwan?

We wanted to ask Tony Amos. But when we stopped at Shuckum's we discovered that neither he nor bartender Idrissi were there any longer. No one knew where they'd gone. The current bartender, before she realized she said too much, indicated their leave-taking had been somehow 9/11 related.

Amos and Idrissi had purchased tickets to the Island of Lost Witnesses. Hopefully round trip.

A week later, when the *Los Angeles Times* mentioned the night at Shuckum's in a story on the terrorists' final days the reports of heavy drinking were gone. The story didn't even mention it:

"That same night (Sept. 7) down the coast in Florida, Atta and Al-Shehhi went to Shuckums sports bar in Hollywood along with a still unidentified third man. The owner, Tony Amos, says Atta sat quietly by himself and drank cranberry juice and played a video game, while Al-Shehhi and the other customer tossed back mixed drinks and argued."

Why did the restaurant manager change his story? We read carefully through the detailed early accounts of the incident, and were left—as we suspect you are—with a startling conclusion.

The manager's retraction was *coerced*, because the two employees' initial remembrances of the encounter were just too full of vivid details. Amos says they had chicken wings and Stoli, Capt. Morgan's Spiced Rum and Coke. He said Mohamed was drunk, his voice was slurred. Bartender Idrissi recalls how many drinks (5) each downed, and said Atta paid her with a $100 bill from a thick wad, but left only a $3 tip.

Bartenders remember things like that.

Stories of the terrorist ringleader's two-fisted drinking habits—we will be hearing more—lead inevitably to doubts about an official narrative which insisted that the villains who attacked defenseless civilians and broke the hearts of Americans were cave-dwelling religious fanatics who had been cast out of their own society.

Well, what if they weren't?

After all, it's not as if the Shuckum's story was the only drinking incident: there were many. The *London Sunday Mail*, to cite just one example, reported Atta and Al-Shehhi spent a thousand dollars in 45 minutes on Krug and Perrier-Jouet champagne at a Palm Beach bar called 251 Sunrise.

Marwan was with a short blonde, said the paper, while Atta was with a six foot tall busty brunette in her late twenties. This has the ring of truth. Sidekicks don't get to pick first. The *Mail* reported both of the women were known locally as "regular companions of high-rollers."

Are there Islamic fundamentalist high-rollers?

If the truth can be so easily manipulated as the incident at Shuckum's seems to show, then "inconvenient knowledge" about the hijackers might contain information that would force a reappraisal of just who, in fact, our enemy *was*.

What remained were sanitized reports, like the Sept. 22 *Washington Post*:

"The Friday night before the attacks, Atta and two other men—one of them another suspected hijacker, Marwan Al-Shehhi—spent 3

1/2 hours at a sports bar in Hollywood, Fla., called Shuckums. Atta played video games, a pursuit out of line with fundamentalist beliefs. But the manager on duty that night has said that he doesn't recall seeing Atta drink alcohol."

Were we witnessing evidence of a federal *clean-up crew* in action? Were they *scrubbing down* Florida and sanitizing the public record of inconvenient knowledge?

We knew one thing. We still wanted to find Amanda Keller.

Because the "Fifth Pilot" was the "Unknown Terrorist." His entire existence, for the record, consisted of his stay with Amanda. There were no follow-up stories about him.

No "Fifth Pilot Identified" headlines.

Even his name remained a mystery. He was Mohammed No Last Name. He went totally unmentioned in later in-depth news accounts about the Hamburg cadre's key members.

He was The Man Who Was Not There.

After serving the purpose of disabusing the public of the notion that Mohamed Atta had lived with Amanda Keller in March and April of 2001, he retired from earthly existence, was immediately forgotten, and has never been mentioned again by the press or by authorities.

Except for Amanda Keller saying so in her retraction, there was absolutely no evidence that he had ever existed at all. And yet this transparent ruse was somehow strangely successful in keeping the press from going after the story.

The part that really hurts is not so much that they take us for fools and get away with it…. It's that they might be right.

We made a new rule of thumb: "When the FBI identifies someone with only one name, don't believe anything they say."

And we continued to search for Amanda Keller, and finally got the break we'd been hoping for. On our third or fourth phone call to the police chief of Lady Lake seeking information on Amanda and her family, he turned us over to "Debbie," the department's detective in charge of juvenile and child welfare cases.

Debbie already knew quite a bit about Amanda. She had known her and her family, as well. Police had been called out to their place regularly. They had been involved in a lot of "domestics."

Despite being only 21, Amanda Keller had two children, Debbie stated. She was divorced from the children's father. He had had her "Baker-acted," which meant she was declared a threat to herself, and not a fit parent. There had been a court fight, the result of which was that Steve Keller, the father, won custody of the two toddlers.

Amanda had had drinking and drug problems. For that matter, so had her husband. Amanda's mother, Susan Payne died three months after September 11, sometime in December. After attending her funeral, Amanda "abducted her two children from the parent with lawful custodial care and fled the state," Debbie stated.

She took her children to a maternal aunt's house in a large Midwestern state, and turned herself in to state authorities there. Custodial arrangements were now being worked out jointly by the two states.

Amanda was working to put her life together, Debbie told us. She was sober. She was in a stable living environment. Amanda's aunt was involved. She and her husband had been two immature kids with babies, she said.

"Amanda had absolutely no parenting skills at the time, and she was from a family where there were no parenting skills."

The situation was being monitored, Debbie stated. Would we like the aunt's phone number?

We made an unsuccessful attempt to sound nonchalant.

Yes, please, we replied. That would be nice.

CHAPTER SEVEN

MOHAMMED ATTA'S
SECRET WORLD

If the media had just treated Mohamed Atta like they do any other celebrity, like O. J. writ large… If *Entertainment Tonight* had just taken viewers for a sneak peek backstage into the private life of one of history's greatest villains… If Mohamed Atta had only gotten the media spotlight accorded J-Lo's latest boyfriend… 9/11 might not remain such a near-total mystery.

The reason they didn't is simple. They couldn't. They weren't allowed to. But if they *could*… If they could, reporters would still be camped out on Amanda Keller's doorstep, the way one *New York Times* reporter was, until the FBI ordered him to go home.

We finally found Amanda. Overall, she was not a happy camper…

About press harassment, she said, "A *New York Times* reporter named Chris—young, tall, kind of heavy, dark hair and a dark goatee—came to my house. And he was mad because I wouldn't talk to him. But I was still reeling from Garret dying, and this dude would NOT leave me alone. I stood outside arguing with him forever, and he was trying to trip me up, get me to say something, and I said, I don't know what the hell you're trying to do," she said.

"And I called the FBI agent that had been calling me—right while this reporter guy was standing there—and said, this guy won't leave me alone. The FBI agent said let me talk to him, so I handed him the phone. And I don't know what was said, but after that he left me alone."

Amanda Keller may have had "scorching-hot" details of life with a terrorist ringleader...

But the FBI had other ideas.

When we met Amanda Keller, she didn't look at all like what we'd been expecting. While she and Atta lived together she was moving in pretty fast company, so we'd been expecting—maybe not a pink-haired stripper—but still, someone who chewed gum and had a really *really* short attention span.

Instead, the now 22-year-old Amanda Keller looks just like what she is today: a young mom, raising three small children and living with a man with a day job.

She was dressed in a pullover sweater and jeans, with natural light brown hair framing an attractive face. She even wore glasses, which made her blue eyes look a little watery.

In short, it was hard to visualize how she could ever have been wild enough to attract the jaded Atta's attention. Compared to what we'd heard about her, she looked positively matronly.

Only later, after she pulled out photographs taken two years ago, posing with the boyfriend for whom she'd left Atta without a backward glance, did we begin to understand what Atta must have seen in her... a 20-year-old hottie.

She didn't look like that now. It was a composed young woman who came to our hotel to meet us. She even brought her sister.

Amanda Keller said she's suffered the same bullying harassment from the FBI that the other intimidated witnesses at the Sandpiper Apartments were forced to endure. Even *after* she left Venice, she said, FBI agents called her every other day for several months after the attack, just as they had with Stephanie Frederickson.

"There was a police car constantly watching the house," she said. "When we burned some leaves in a burn barrel, a police officer came over and told us we weren't allowed to burn anything because we were on some FBI list, and they were afraid we might be burning documents or something."

Pretty serious surveillance for a girl who lived with some *other* Mohamed... Was this why she recanted her original statement?

"Because of the intimidation by the FBI," she replied. "They told me not to talk to anybody, to keep my mouth shut. The newspaper quote was accurate: 'I can't say anything because I'm afraid I'll get in trouble.'"

The FBI nearly convinced her that she didn't know whom she'd been living with for two months, Amanda said. It was easier just to go along with what she was being told.

"When I saw Charlie (Grapentine) talking in the newspaper I knew they were going to jump all over him. I thought, 'Charlie, no! Can't you just wait?'"

We were hearing *way* too many stories from eyewitnesses of FBI intimidation and harassment for it to be blamed on a few over-zealous agents, or a couple of "bad apples."

Something weird was going on in Southwest Florida... Something—dare we say it?

Something un-American.

Whoever Mohamed Atta ultimately turns out to have been, meeting Amanda brought us a huge step closer to the truth. Still, as we began to listen to her tell her story, we were mentally assessing the believability of what she was saying, until we had arrived at our conclusion.

We think a reader should be able to do the same. So we'll let her tell her story in her own words, as much as we can, just as she told it to us, in a three-and-a-half hour interview we filmed with her at a secret location. The only condition she set on our interview was that we not reveal where she is living today.

We agreed.

We began by asking her how she came to be in Venice in the first place. Frankly, we had wondered if she had been some kind of *perk* of Atta's "job."

But the story she told was virtually identical with what we had heard from the Lady Lake detective, featuring youthful immaturity compounded by casual drug use, along with big dollops of domestic violence. Meeting Atta was an accident.

Amanda was just 19 when she moved to Venice, but she already had two children. Her recently-divorced husband had "pulled a fast one on her," she said, and was granted custody of the kids.

In the aftermath, she felt bereft, devastated...

Pink hair was on the horizon.

She moved to Venice with her boyfriend-of-the-moment, who was from nearby Port Charlotte. "Robert liked to move around a lot," she explained.

He also liked to beat her. While looking for a way out, she worked an assortment of jobs. At one of them, in early February, 2001, she met Mohamed Atta.

"I worked as a manager at Taco Bell and McDonalds in Port Charlotte, then got hired at Papa John's in Venice," she said. "I'd worked there for 2-3 weeks before I met Mohamed."

Atta came in with people whose names she learned later: Peter, Stephan and Juergen, none of which sound Arab, oddly enough.

Her account of meeting Atta jibes with the Sept. 14, 2001 *Charlotte Sun* report: "Keller, who allegedly met Mohamed while working at Papa John's Pizza in Venice… A Papa John's employee confirmed that Keller was a manager there, but has not been to work for some time."

Her emotional state at the time could be described as fragile.

"I was at an ultimate low, living with a guy I wasn't happy with, abusive, and missing my two kids. I wanted to figure a way out without getting hurt," she explained.

"Mohamed comes in, I'm standing there covered in dough, baseball cap, hair pulled into a pony tail, looking my ultimate worst.

"Mohamed asked one of my employees to have me come over and wait on him, and so I did… I said, 'Can I help you?'

"Mohamed said, 'Do you know how pretty you are?' And I just looked at him kind of funny and said, 'Are you going to order a pizza or what?'

"So Mohamed said, 'How would you like to go out for dinner?' I declined, and went and made them their pizza. I can remember their pizza cause it was weird; it was like every single thing you can put on a pizza, all at one time. It was disgusting.

"After that they came back every day," she continued. "Sometimes a couple of times a day. And they ordered the same nasty pizza over and over again."

Many of Mohamed Atta's close associates while he was in Florida weren't Arab, apparently. They were German.

"Peter and Stephan were from Austria, Juergen was German, they had nice (German) accents, yah, yah…. Peter asked me if I had any girlfriends he could introduce me to, and at that time I didn't because Robert didn't allow me to have any friends.

"And Mohamed would tell me how pretty I was, and he compared me to a flower that was still closed up, and a bud that hadn't yet bloomed. He told me I had a natural beauty about me."

This sounds like flowery Islamic rhetoric, or maybe the words of a practiced seducer. Spies learn that sort of thing, we've heard.

"I had a cell phone," Amanda continued, "Mohamed asked for my phone number, he'd come in every day for two and a half weeks, and I gave it to him. Then he called me one day and said he'd just gotten evicted from this house he lived in with seven other guys in North Port, which I saw later when I helped him move out."

This was a major clue... If Mohamed Atta was not in Miami in February of 2001, where the FBI says he was, but on the Gulf coast, in North Port, just south of Venice, then something was well, truly rotten in the state of Denmark...

"He (Atta) asked me if I knew of another apartment he could rent," she continued. "He said he didn't care if it even had a bed as long as it had a desk. He told the lady there that too."

This matches a detail in the *Charlotte Sun*: "The only request Atta made to the couple, the LaConcas said, was that they provide him a desk in which he could do his aviation homework. 'He didn't even care if the house had a bed, all he wanted was a desk,' said Tony LaConca."

Atta and Amanda's doughy courtship proceeded apace, until one day she came to be with Atta when he rented from the LaConcas.

"I helped him move from a house in North Port, and he asked me to talk to the landlady, because he didn't like American women, and she (Vonnie) happened to be the one renting the apartment," Amanda said.

"'How can you like *me* if you don't like American women?' I asked him. 'I'm as American as it gets!'"

Mohamed replied that he didn't "translate" well with American women.

"So I talked to the landlady for him," Amanda said. "He was curt and rude with her, so she told him when it was time to pay the rent just to stick it (the check) in the freezer, so she wouldn't have to deal with him."

At right about this time she decided to leave Robert, she says. Just days later, after her and Atta's three-day party in Key West, she agreed to get a place with Atta. She remembers the date, probably from repeating the story over and over to the FBI.

"So on February 25, 2001 we went to Key West for 3 days…. It was me, Mohamed, Peter, Stephan and Linda. Linda knew the owner (of the newly-rented house) and told me she was a stripper."

Linda, who the *Sun-Herald* reported got a phone call from Atta during the week before the attack, is the woman later characterized as unhelpful with the FBI.

That was when we realized that Amanda Keller didn't have to be a rocket scientist to help unearth information about the terrorist conspiracy. And the first case in point is that the terrorist ringleader was about to party for three days with people whose names do not appear to be Arab.

Based on her descriptions we will later be able to positively identify at least five of Atta's close German associates during the time he was in Florida. They were *not* fellow student pilots, but individuals with whom he appeared to have long-standing relationships, said Amanda, and with whom he attended "meetings."

Our thoughts were racing as we listened to Amanda tell the story of their Key West excursion…

"I had a beat-up '81 Ford Granada, and he (Atta) asked me to meet him," Amanda began. "He was driving a rented white Grand Am. The place he lived in, in North Port, wasn't too far from where I was living.

"We went to Key West, and he took this long, out-of-the-way route. He was really familiar with Florida. He knew a back way to Ft. Lauderdale on the way back. He drove to Daytona Beach and Naples and Ft. Myers all the time. He always rented cars out of Tampa. A red Pontiac, a green Pontiac and a white one, all Grand Ams.

"I slept most of the way, he and Linda stayed awake."

Mohamed Atta cruised towards Key West accompanied by two girls who knew how to party. Amanda remembers thinking Atta may have even met Linda before…

"Linda instantly latched onto him, at Vonnie and Tony's, when we went to move his stuff into Vonnie's place," she explained.

"She had black hair, mid-twenties, said she was a stripper in Sarasota. Her and Mohamed acted like they knew each other. On the car ride down they acted like they were old friends. She sat in the front seat, I was in the back to stretch out because I knew I was going to end up falling asleep."

She dismisses whatever suspicions she had with a wave.

"Linda was kind of easy, sort of, just open for business. She was really clingy with me too, though. It was kind of uncomfortable."

Before reaching Key West, they rendezvoused with Atta's German friends.

"We met with Peter and Stephan, at one of the first islands before you get to Key West, Largo. They had already been on their way down. Then we stopped at a Bell's outlet on Largo, and we went crazy and bought a bunch of clothes."

The original Sept. 14, 2001 *Charlotte Sun* article confirms, in a backhand way, Amanda's account of a shopping spree:

"While he was writing the checks, the couple noticed Mohamed had brand new clothing, all still with tags on them from a local mall, the couple remembered."

Peter and Stephan were the two German men that Atta's North Port landlord said the girls met on the trip. "The two girls were introduced to two men from Germany that they said were Mohamed's friends, Tony LaConca told the *Sun.*

"'I thought it was strange, because Mohamed didn't appear to be French-Canadian or German.'"

When the group checked into a hotel in Key West, there was also something odd about the room assignments. "We rented 3 different rooms in Key West," Amanda said.

"In one room nobody slept. It was where they put their flight bags. Then they locked the room down. Peter and Stephan slept in one room. And me, Mohamed and Linda slept in the same room."

She adds immediately, "But nothing happened, no threesomes, cause I'm not a lesbian."

Amanda may have been a "private dancer," but she wasn't terribly worldly otherwise. She was from a small town in North Florida, and hadn't traveled much. The free-wheeling Key West made quite an impression on her.

"It was my first time ever in Key West and I was shocked—there were naked people everywhere! We walked out on this pier and there was this naked guy right in front of me, and I freaked.

"Mohamed said this was normal for where he was from, France, where there were nude beaches everywhere. But I looked down and I was mortified."

So Amanda *did* think Atta was French. In her defense, when we hear more about Atta's claimed French connections later, there are details which make her belief seem slightly-less hopelessly naïve.

Another big surprise: their trip to Key West mixed business with pleasure. Atta and his German pals had a dinner meeting which Amanda said she wasn't allowed to attend.

"We went to Sloppy Joe's, went to Rick's Rooftop Bar, and took a boat ride to see the dolphins, me and Linda did, while Peter, Stephan and Mohamed went to the Hard Rock to meet some people for dinner. They just said they had to meet with some people at Hard Rock. They didn't tell me who it was."

Who was Mohamed Atta meeting in Key West? All Amanda knows is that they flew in just to meet Atta...

"Somebody had flown in to meet with them in a single-engine plane—to come speak to them. When they came back, they met up with us on the dock, and everybody was somber-looking and kind of quiet."

Amanda's description of their demeanor when they returned from the meeting makes it hard not to conclude that it had involved discussion of actions that would leave thousands dead.

"Later we were walking through some shops, a chapel by the sea, looking at some necklaces and Mohamed turned to me and out of the blue said, 'Why don't we get married?'

"And I said, 'What the hell are you talking about? I just met you!'

"And he said, 'Well this way I can have my visa and I can stay here.' Peter and Stephan started laughing, and told him, 'You're not in the right country.' And Mohamed got really mad at me.

"And I said, 'How the hell can you get mad at me for not wanting to marry you? I just met you, plus I just got out of a bad marriage.'

"Pointing at Peter and Stephan, Linda said, 'I'm getting ready to marry one of you two.'

"So we went by Diva's, and it was the first time I ever saw a drag queen, and I was standing there talking to them. They had their pictures taken with a drag queen. Peter, Mohamed and Stephan were all standing next to the drag queen, who stuffed his hand down all their pants in the pictures, and Peter and Stephan both laughed it off, but Mohamed got really angry," said Amanda.

The truth is always stranger than fiction. Somewhere there are photographs of terrorist ringleader Mohamed Atta being groped by a drag queen in Key West. This is startling, and not a little surreal.

But given numerous accounts of Atta's proclivities, which included frequent visits to strip clubs, it's not at all unbelievable.

"He (Atta) was mad because I was standing there talking to the drag queens," she continued. "So he stopped at this store, a Cuban cigar shop, and they bought big fat cigars and began smoking one which smelled really *really* bad."

Perhaps Atta was used to being fawned over. He had, after all, a full-time bodyguard (Marwan), acolytes, and minions. But in Key West he was forced to play second fiddle to his young blonde companion, who was clearly the center of attention. Getting a big fat Cuban cigar must have been small compensation.

"And we walked past Sloppy Joe's and the bartender—I was wearing a purple top that tied around my neck in three places and came down my back in a v-shape, and a khaki skirt, and chunky shoes—and the bartender called me into the bar, saying, 'Hey Blondie! Come in here! Shots are on me!'"

Blond babes get treated different. Stop the presses. Atta would have to learn to cope. "He (the bartender) lined purple hooters down the bar, and there was a drag queen and Linda and me drinking shots with him. And Mohamed got really mad at this, and told me I shouldn't be drinking in public. And I said, 'I don't know who the hell you are, you're not my father!'"

There was, already, trouble in paradise.

"This was where it first started. I was telling him, 'You're not going to run me.' But I was also trying to be nice about it, because I was looking at him (Atta) as a way to get out of my relationship with Robert," explained Amanda.

"After that we went to Rick's Rooftop bar, and I didn't see the sign cause someone was standing in front of it, but it said "clothing optional," and Linda and I went first and we got up there and there were just naked people standing everywhere! The one that sticks out in my mind was a woman who must have been 80 years old, dancing in nothing but a tattooed thong."

An 80-year-old woman wearing nothing but a tattooed thong is exactly what an Islamic fundamentalist would expect to find in America. If Atta minded this display of Western decadence, he kept it to himself.

Then, again, he'd probably seen it before.... Amanda says she was surprised to see how well Atta and his chums knew their way around Key West.

"We went back to the hotel, and I couldn't find my way, but the guys knew exactly where they were going, and I said, 'How did you guys remember?' And nobody answered me."

Again the next day Atta had a business appointment. But this time Amanda got to ride along.

"Next morning we went to the Key West Airport, and they pulled over at a beach nearby, and there were flight students from the airport, and Peter, Stephan and Mohamed talking with the flight students, and they introduced me, and I remember one guy said he was from Africa. They were all talking in a language I couldn't understand," she said.

An aviation executive in Venice who'd recently flown into the Key West Airport filled us in on its colorful history.

"For a long time down in Key West, the Sheriff's Department was under orders to keep all the dope sniffing dogs out of the airport," he said.

"At one time the Sheriff would even send patrol cars to escort the dope going up the road to Miami. At least they aren't doing that any more.

"But after the World Trade Center attack, it was only 4 hours before the FBI showed up at Big Pine Key. There were a bunch of Arabs on Little Pine Key," this executive said.

"They were gone three hours before the FBI got there."

Amanda said something which may be important about the curious hotel room that Atta rented but nobody slept in, vacant except for the men's flight bags.

"They were drinking the whole time we were there," she said. "And they were doing drugs, but not in front of me. They would go into the locked down room where no one slept, saying they needed to look at their manuals, and when they came back you could tell their jaws were locked, and they started chewing gum like there was no tomorrow.

"They didn't do drugs in front of me until after I had met everyone back at the apartment in Venice, at the Sentinel Apartments," Amanda stated. "Once I had met everyone there they felt comfortable with me and pulled out the coke."

Atta was a juiced-up Islamic fundamentalist.

Atta was coke-head Wahhabi.

We've never heard of anything like that.

CHAPTER EIGHT

MOHAMED ATTA, CYBER-TERRORIST

After their non-stop three day Key West bash, the revelers headed back to North Port in Atta's rented white Grand-Am.

Having decided to move in with Mohamed, Amanda now faced the difficult hurdle of retrieving her clothes and other possessions from the apartment she shared with soon-to-be-ex-boyfriend Robert. As she suspected, Robert turned out to not be a very good sport.

"Mohamed asked me to get an apartment when we got back from Key West," she explained. "He asked if I would find an apartment and split rent with him. He was an option for me to run and never look back, so I said OK."

What happened next culminates in a twist of fate so cruel and ironic—or cruelly-ironic—that it should be in the dictionary.

After listening to North Port landlord Tony LaConca describe what he knew about Atta, FBI agents wanted to know more about Amanda.

So LaConca took them to see the local police. From the Sept. 14, 2001 *Charlotte Sun*: "In an effort to locate Keller, the agent accompanied Tony LaConca to the North Port Police Department to pick up a Feb. 25 police report in which Keller had called police about harassing cell phone calls," the Sun reported.

The *harassing phones calls* were from boyfriend Robert, who was threatening her with physical violence if she left him, she explained.

"The night we came back from Key West I got arrested right in front of Vonnie and Tony's apartment. Mohamed bailed me out of jail. It was $150 bucks.

"What happened was Mohamed drove me to pick up my stuff," she recalled. "And Robert came out and hit me. I had told him I was leaving him before leaving for Key West, and he said he would 'fucking kill me.' He started wailing on me, and I was bloody. I had cuts on my arms and everything," she said. "And Mohamed did nothing, just sat there in the car. He was a big pussy."

It was strange to hear this young American woman coolly describe a man responsible for 3,000 deaths as *a big pussy*.

But maybe he was. We'll soon hear more tales portraying him in a less than manly light. Back in North Port, what happened next isn't the cruelly-ironic thing yet. But it *is* ironic:

"So I called the police in front of Vonnie and Tony's apartment." Amanda told us. "And the police came out and arrested *me!*"

"According to the police report, after Keller called police about the calls, a computer check was conducted and showed an outstanding warrant from Marion County on a worthless check charge," the *Charlotte Sun* reported.

"The police ran my name, and a check I'd written at an animal shelter had bounced, so they arrested me," Amanda explained.

So instead of her ex-boyfriend being arrested for assault, it was Amanda who got popped and had to "go downtown."

"Mohamed bailed her out of South County Jail," Vonnie LaConca had told reporters. "We told agents this because we thought they (FBI) might be able to get his last name from the reports."

That must have been what the FBI wanted: the bail document which Atta had to sign to get Amanda released. They were erasing any paper trail.

Her bounced check was for a small amount, to the Humane Society in Bradenton, for charges incurred when she went there to adopt a cat, she stated.

Amanda said the checking account Atta used to bail her out was in the name of "Mohamed Arajaki."

Now here's the cruelly-ironic part:

Mohamed Atta bailed Amanda Keller out of jail for bouncing a check which she wrote to the Humane Society to adopt a cat…. Two months later Atta dismembered that same cat and left it gutted on her kitchen table during his rampage through her apartment.

Atta rented the LaConca's place in North Port for a week, just the time it took Amanda to find the apartment at the Sandpiper across the street from the Venice Airport.

At this point in telling us her story, she made a chance comment which turned the direction of our investigation southward from Venice to North Port and neighboring Charlotte County.

Amanda had helped Atta move to the LaConca's rental house from the house where Atta and six other men were being evicted, both in North Port, she said. But something about where Atta had been living didn't add up.

"The house was huge inside," Amanda said. "It was immense and beautiful, nicely and very expensively furnished. Their landlady was kicking them out, Atta said, because she wanted the house back. She was getting $300 a week from seven different people."

Seven guys paying $300 apiece is $2,100 per week, which may not be much in LA or New York, but is virtually unheard of in an area which caters, as we've seen, to seniors.

Why was the rent so high? Another *terrorist surcharge*?

Atta told Amanda, when they "hooked up" at the end of February, that he had lived in the "immense and beautiful" North Port home for just two months.

So we now know that Mohamed Atta didn't move to Miami when he left Huffman Aviation in December of 2000. He shuffled down the block to nearby North Port, still on Florida's Gulf Coast, and still near Venice.

If he had rushed off to a place filled with tall European models, like South Beach, it might make sense.

But he didn't.

His appetite for infidel pleasures was certainly a healthy one. It took him from the Cheetah Club to the Pink Pony to Harry's Bar in New York. So why was he still hanging around Venice? What was he doing?

Here's the answer: Mohamed Atta was going to flight school at the Charlotte County Airport, just a short drive from the "immense and beautiful" North Port home he was renting.

And once again we have a local official to thank for knowing about it. "Sheriff: suspected terrorist may have lived in Charlotte County" was the headline of the Sept. 21 story.

"Sheriff Clement told the *Charlotte Sun-Herald* that Atta had lived in the area and attended a flight school at Charlotte County Airport," the paper reported.

Clement told reporter Christy Arnold that the Sheriff's Office had forwarded several tips to the FBI about Atta, who used an alias in Charlotte County, but he would not discuss specifics.

"Gathered intelligence and a recently obtained e-mail containing a photo of a dead child may link suspected terrorist Mohamed Atta to Charlotte County and Punta Gorda," said Sheriff William E. Clement.

"It gives me a bit of chill knowing they were here. Atta may have, at one time, resided in the Punta Gorda area and may have attended flying lessons at Charlotte County Airport.

"It looks like some of these terrorists were here and then went to Venice," Clement told reporters.

Whoa… How could Atta have been in Charlotte County *before* moving to Venice, supposedly his first residence in the U.S.?

Local reporters understood the significance of the revelation. They asked the FBI to confirm or dispel reports about terrorist sightings in Charlotte County. The FBI's non-response was, as usual, non-instructive: "The FBI has information but the FBI cannot disclose the information because the investigation is pending," said Sara Oakes, the FBI's Tampa spokeswoman. "I can confirm to you that the FBI has followed thousands of leads and interviewed people across the country."

We've heard them give this same speech several times already. When the FBI starts quoting statistics about how massive their investigation is, they're almost always hiding something.

When we interviewed Sheriff William Clement of Charlotte County, the source of the initial reports of Mohamed Atta having lived in Charlotte County, he was no more happy to see us than Longboat Fire Captain Mooneyhan had been.

Apparently there had been some serious thought given, locally, to the proposition that instead of talking about Mohamed Atta having lived in his jurisdiction, the Sheriff should have kept his mouth shut. Although Clement is a big man, as southern Sheriffs tend to be, he appeared somewhat chastened by the experience.

But real Americans won't be silenced. And so he matter-of-factly confirmed to us that Atta had been in Punta Gorda in the Spring. The reports had it right: terrorist ringleader Mohamed Atta had been living under an alias "in rural Charlotte County, just south of Venice on Florida's Gulf Coast."

That's a geographical description of North Port.

The Sheriff said that right after the attack he began receiving phone calls from local business owners in Punta Gorda—Charlotte County's only town—who recognized Atta from his photograph in the newspaper. Soon he had learned enough to tell reporters that Atta had been in flight training at the Charlotte County Airport.

The owners of the flight schools at the Charlotte County Airport denied it, including David Byers, owner of Professional Aviation, where Atta was suspected of attending. The school had served an international clientele, including dozens of Tunisians, before suddenly going bankrupt at the end of February, 2001, the exact same time Amanda said Atta moved back to Venice with her, right across from the Venice Airport.

"He may have had friends here," Byers said. "Perhaps he was visiting, but he was not at our school as a student."

Byers was whistling in the dark. A little more than 48 hours after the attack, the school received a visit from the FBI.

"FBI agents seized records from a financially troubled flight school at the Charlotte County Airport, Professional Aviation, that recruited students from Tunisia and went out of business in the spring of 2001, after tipsters said they saw Atta there late last year or early this year," the *Sun* reported.

Brian Ross of NBC News knew something was going on in Charlotte County: "And yet more evidence of the overseas money trail has been found at a flying school in Punta Gorda," he reported. "The owner says FBI agents seized records relating to at least 12 foreign students whose tuition was paid with foreign wire transfers.

"They were very interested in the German transfers, and they were very interested in the Middle Eastern transfers," Byers told him.

Byers' pupils soon became a focus of intense scrutiny from the FBI. At least eight of them were questioned at least several times each.

But what of the strange report of a "recently obtained e-mail containing a photo of a dead child?" What had that been about?

The e-mails, at least five, written and sent by Mohamed Atta, first came to light after being reported to authorities by Jim Kantor of Eastern Avionics at the Charlotte County Airport, we learned.

Kantor had corresponded by e-mail with Atta, who purchased some pilot gear from the firm. Another employee told local reporters they received e-mails from Atta containing Arabic writing with references to Allah.

Kantor turned the e-mails in to the police.

"The sheriff said he thought the e-mail was a political article written in both Arabic and English. He said it showed a photo of a dead child killed in a riot in the Middle East. He would not elaborate," the *Sun-Herald* reported.

The Sheriff told reporters that the names on the e-mail list of some 40 individuals would be the focus of intense scrutiny from the FBI. He was careful to point out to us that, for the record, his local law enforcement agency's investigation had ended when they turned over the e-mails to the FBI.

Later we came into possession of Atta's e-mail correspondence from a source close to the case, and immediately discovered that the names on Atta's e-mail list *should* receive intense scrutiny…

The e-mail addresses of several of the names on Atta's "terrorist e-list" appear to have been, or still are, employees of U.S. defense contractors.

One name on Atta's e-mail list, for example, apparently works at a Canadian company called Virtual Prototypes. The firm's website says the company helped prototype the avionics instruments in the F-15 jet fighter, the F-22 Raptor, the B-2 bomber and the Apache Longbow.

Another address on the list, paradisehasaprice@hotmail.com, may be that of a female suicide bomber in Chechnya.

The correspondence contains information of a relatively mundane socio-political nature. In one, he bemoans the passing of a Muslim figure and asks for prayers. Another of Atta's e-mails reads today like a non-negotiable demand from Paradise…

"I demand the decision-makers in the American University in Cairo withdraw their threats of dismissing a Muslim female student who refused to take off the Niqab… and adhere to their claimed 'non-discrimination policy' printed in their catalogue," Atta wrote.

A "Niqab" is a face veil, according to Islamic sources, and a "Niqaa-bi" is "a sister who covers her face and hands when in public or in the presence of any man outside her immediate family."

After verifying the authenticity of the Atta e-mails with local officials, we shared them with a reporter from a local news channel who had helped break the story of their existence. Amy Ochier's subsequent report led the local news that night on NBC's Charlotte County affiliate.

What was it about Charlotte County, and the Charlotte County Airport, that attracted the terrorists? When we asked one well-placed local official, the answer was a shock. The Charlotte County Airport and surrounding area were teeming with international activities of a distinctly "spooky" kind, he said

We get an inkling of how *much* strange activity goes on at the Charlotte County Airport when the Sheriff told us, a little sheepishly, that 23 helicopters have been stolen there in the last several years… Stolen from the *Sheriff's* Department. Later, wags at the airport told us that the helicopters hadn't really been stolen…

They'd just been "released on their own recognizance."

CHAPTER NINE

THE SECRET HISTORY: ATTA IN FLIGHT SCHOOL

The story of Mohamed Atta's stay in the U.S. has not yet begun to be told, but remains shrouded, deliberately hidden, part of this country's secret history, that history, in other words, in which lone gunmen play no role.

Nowhere is this more visible than in the official story about Mohamed Atta at American flight schools which is an exceedingly simple one: he went to Huffman Aviation for six months. Period.

Following that experience, the FBI says his only additional training was in flight simulators, where he supposedly got the "feel" of piloting an airliner.

But the real history of Atta as a student pilot at U.S. flight schools is an altogether more elaborate tale than that. For example, Atta's first flight school in the U.S. has never been named. It's identity remains a mystery.

We're not sure why, but it does. After that he attended Huffman Aviation in Venice. Jones Aviation in Sarasota was next. Then Huffman Aviation again.

After leaving Huffman for the second time, Atta and Marwan trained during January and February of 2001 at Professional Aviation at the Charlotte County Airport.

When that school went suddenly and mysteriously bankrupt at the end of February 2001, Atta and Marwan returned to Huffman Aviation... for the *third* time.

We discovered where Atta went after leaving Venice (and Huffman) at the end of December, 2000 when we learned of a post-9/11 investigation into suspected espionage by students at Professional Aviation which left a paper trail subsequently uncovered by reporters.

That's the big picture. Here's the big question: Was Atta *actually* undergoing flight training at all of the flight schools he attended?

Whether Atta was actually a student pilot during all of the time he spent at the just-mentioned flight schools is still unanswered.

But the reason for its importance is because there is *another* plausible explanation for how Atta spent his time in flight school. Instead of pilot training, Atta's status as "foreign flight student" may have merely been a "legend," or "cover story," that allowed him to move freely around the United States while engaged in activities not limited to coordinating and readying the 9/11 attack.

Whatever he was up to while attending U.S. flight schools, learning to fly could not have been his only—or maybe even chief—motivation, because Mohamed Atta was already a licensed pilot when he arrived in the U.S., Amanda Keller told us. An *experienced* licensed pilot.

One day while Atta was rummaging through his flight bag—the same bag important enough to warrant its own room in Key West—Amanda got a look inside.

"The thing the FBI was most interested in was his pilot bag," she told us. "They asked about it a lot. He kept it locked, and they wanted to know whether I had ever seen anything in it.

"I told them, 'Yes, one day he opened it briefly, and there were a lot of papers in it, and there was a blue log book in a different language.' Mohamed was fluent in almost any language you can think of," she continued. "He had a kind of Daytimer in there, too. And a folder with all these different ID's in it. And that's when I saw one—because it fell out—a little blue and white thing the size of a driver's license. It had his picture on it, and it looked like a mug shot, or a prison shot. And it didn't look like him, and I asked him, 'Who is *this?*'

"And he said, 'That's me.' He told me it had been taken back when he was in some kind of militia-type deal, like a military-type deal, he said. He compared it to our military only they teach you different tactics. He didn't elaborate.

"He didn't say where it was from, either" she said. "But the writing looked like a cross between Hebrew and Arabic... those little frilly lines. He told me he spoke Hebrew. I said bullshit. So he started speaking it, and I guess he did."

We longed for a fuller explanation of the "militia-type deal" to which Mohamed Atta belonged, and wished he had dropped the ID in front of an eyewitness who might have recognized the issuing organization.

Still, this is crucial information. What Amanda said next shed even more light: "He told me that he went to different countries and studied. He had pilot's licenses from several different countries. But all the pictures looked different. All the names were different. He had a license to fly from just about every country he had been to. He went to pilot's school in all these countries.

"He said no matter where he decided to live, he could always fly," she said, "because he said it was his path, he had always wanted to be a pilot.

"I asked him, and he told me his last name was spelled different in different languages, but he always kept the first name Mohamed. There was one (pilot's license) from France, one from Germany.... He also had one in the Homeland, he called it," she said.

"Homeland" is a word we've all grown used to since 9/11. But it was strange to hear that Atta used it too.

What Mohamed Atta told Amanda Keller about himself was what a spy tells a civilian: a *cover story*, a legend. He probably had a number of them... "He said his father was a commercial jet pilot from France," said Amanda.

"His mom was from the Homeland. He said they ran from there, moved to France, and that he went to Lebanese private schools.

"I didn't know what to think," she said. "I don't know what countries connect to what other countries. If you were to show me a globe, I could pick out the U.S. and Canada, but not much more. I never paid any attention."

That Amanda believed his story wasn't too surprising. Most of us accept other people at more or less face value. Amanda wasn't trained to spot spies, and she clearly wasn't a geography major.

And there's another thing worth mentioning.... Keller wasn't all *that* interested in Mohamed Atta while she knew him, she told us candidly. He was a very brief way station on her own personal journey, her time with him had been a matter of convenience. If he hadn't become instantly infamous after the 9/11 attack, Amanda told us, she would probably have never thought about him again.

The official story of Mohamed Atta's progression through American flight schools in the run-up to the Sept. 11th attack begins when he and Marwan Al-Shehhi arrived at the squat beige hangar of the Airman School in Oklahoma early in July of 2000, and asked to take a look around.

Although Venice would receive most of the media spotlight, two days after the attack a school official in Oklahoma confirmed that Atta and Al-Shehhi had first visited their school, the Airman Flight School, staying overnight at the school's dormitory in the nearby Sooner Inn, before deciding to train at another facility.

The school's admissions director told reporters she gave them her standard half-hour tour: the six flight simulators, the classrooms, the airfield. The two men then thanked her and left: "They did a school visit in July of 2000 but went elsewhere for whatever reason."

After this brief mention of the terrorists visit, media interest in the Oklahoma flight school quickly waned. This is strange because—just like Huffman Aviation—the Airman Flight School in Norman, Okla. was something of a magnet for associates of Osama bin Laden.

The most famous of the terrorists who have been identified as having trained there is Zacarias Moussaoui, the French national and so-called "20th hijacker" accused of conspiracy in the Sept. 11 terror attacks, who spent three months there during 2001. Yet the Oklahoma school's involvement with Al Qaeda terrorists begins much earlier than that…

At the trial of four men charged with the 1998 bombing of the American embassies in Kenya and Tanzania, prosecutors introduced evidence that an Orlando, Florida cabdriver named Ihab Ali, bin Laden's personal pilot, trained at Airman Flight School in the early 90s. Ali was indicted for refusing to answer questions about his ties to the bin Laden organization, including his "pilot training in Oklahoma," according to court papers.

There is something strange about the FBI's relationship with Airman Flight School. It provides a striking example of what looks like willful failure—despite specific warnings—to detect the terror threat before it happened.

Since the FBI was aware that a number of suspected terrorists had attended the Oklahoma facility, a reasonable assumption would be that agents must have taken extra-special interest in the school, and especially its Arab students.

Nothing could be further from the truth.

"Two agents were sent to Moussaoui's Airman Flight School in Oklahoma to investigate," said a Sept. 25, 2002 story in the *New York Daily News*, "including one who had been sent to the same school two years earlier, to check on someone identified as Osama Bin Laden's personal pilot. The agent said he had forgotten about the connection."

Two weeks before the 9/11 attack, an FBI agent arrived at Airman Flight School to investigate Moussaoui. The same agent had been to the school two years earlier on a case involving Osama bin Laden's personal pilot, but claims to have forgotten when visiting the school the second time.

Does this pass the *smell* test? If your answer is: "No, it does not," join the growing ranks of those who doubt the government's explanations for the 9/11 disaster.

It is arguably the biggest "dropped ball" in American investigative history. Even the top Republican on the Senate Intelligence Committee felt the stirring of something otherworldly going on.

Calling for hearings to look into whether U.S. intelligence missed warnings that could have prevented the attacks, Republican of Alabama Sen. Richard Shelby told reporters, "You go back and see what was the evidence… that maybe we missed.

"Maybe they didn't miss it. Maybe they didn't go after it."

This is shocking stuff. Shelby appears to be suggesting deliberate malfeasance.

During the emotional chaos in the aftermath of the attack, no one noticed that the Airman Flight Schools director gave a description of the so-called "20th hijacker" which used the same verbiage Huffman Aviation's Rudi Dekkers used when speaking to reporters about Mohamed Atta.

"He was pretty bad in the plane. He was just difficult to teach," she told reporters. "Every conversation with him was difficult. He was demanding and arrogant—not a nice guy."

Both Dekkers and his Oklahoma counterpart stressed that their terrorist students had a bad attitude. Their message seemed to be "terrorists are not nice people."

No one questioned why these two particular flight schools had done such land office business with Osama bin Laden's henchmen.

Whatever their reservations about Oklahoma, Florida would offer an inviting welcome and prove to be a congenial place for terrorists to learn to fly, and Atta and Al-Shehhi signed up for flight training at Huffman Aviation in Venice in early July.

But between their visit in Oklahoma and when they showed up in Venice three weeks later is a span of time that is a real mystery.

That's because the flight school Mohamed Atta and Marwan Al-Shehhi first attended in the U.S. has not been named.

It is unknown. It is a mystery flight school.

The name of the first school Atta attended would seem to be one of the first facts uncovered in the 9/11 investigation. But it hasn't been.

Although the FBI said Huffman Aviation was the first flight school Atta attended, the owner of Huffman Aviation, Rudi Dekkers, denied it. He disclaimed responsibility for the terrorists having been allowed into the U.S., passing any blame onto the flight school the terrorists first attended. It was *this* school, Dekkers said, which held responsibility for Atta's INS paperwork and visas, not his.

On the morning after the disaster anchor Jane Clayson of the *CBS Morning News* asked Dekkers, "How was it that they (Atta and Marwan) could gain access and admittance to your school?"

"Well, they didn't came [*sic*] through our paperwork," Dekkers replied. "Like if they were calling from Europe and we know two months ahead and we know they are showing up. As I say, they came from another flight school out of Florida. Probably that flight school did all the INS paperwork with them in their country."

Another flight school out of Florida...? He was equally vague later that day on ABC's *Good Morning America*, except he had changed the location of the unnamed first school. Correspondent Jim Mora asked Dekkers: "Now, how did they get to you? Did they apply to the school? Did they just show up?"

"No, they just walked up into the front door," Dekkers replied.

"Apparently they were flying at another school—I've heard Tampa; I can't confirm that."

This is a really obscure flight school. It has no name. It's located somewhere in Florida near Tampa. Strangely, Dekkers' reference to

Atta's first flight school—attended *before* he came to Huffman Aviation—went completely un-remarked upon in the national media.

Dekkers didn't just mention the mystery flight school once or twice. He did it numerous times. "The two men were clearly from the Middle East," he was quoted as saying in the Sept. 13 *New York Times.* "They complained that they had begun instruction elsewhere but didn't like the school."

Did the *New York Times* ask Dekkers where "elsewhere" had been? They did not. The *Washington Post* reported a similar story on Sept. 19, quoting Dekkers saying Atta and Al-Shehhi showed up complaining about the experience at "another school."

"Another school elsewhere."

Did the *Post* ask for the name of this flight school located elsewhere? They did not. Or if they did, they're not letting us in on it. The *Washington Post*, like the *New York Times*, forgot to ask.

Making this omission seem even more sinister is the *Post's* own headline: "Hijack Suspects Tried Many Flight Schools" promising, at a bare minimum, a story containing a list of the flight schools "tried."

When two of the largest and most respected newspapers in America are both guilty of an omission this glaring, what other conclusion is there than that a massive cover-up is in progress?

Even in his sworn testimony before the House Judiciary Committee on March 19, 2002, Dekkers is vague about the earlier flight school attended by Atta and Al-Shehhi. This time he places it "up North."

"They had stated they were unhappy with a flying school they attended up North," Dekkers told the Committee. None of the members of Congress in attendance asked about this first school.

It's as if the Warren Commission had said Lee Harvey Oswald lived some place before moving to Dallas… and left it at that.

What remains unclear is how Atta and Al-Shehhi qualified for flight instruction in the first place. As foreigners, while studying at Huffman Aviation the men would have been required to obtain student visas.

Dekkers said the school helps students obtain the visas. "We send them the paperwork and they go to their embassies."

Richard Nyren, a British classmate of Atta and Marwan, told a reporter that it's not easy to get a student visa, even with the help of the school. He said he had to provide bank statements to show he had money to cover his lessons and living expenses and a house mortgage to prove he would return to the United Kingdom. His student visa was rejected the first time he applied because he hadn't submitted enough information, he said.

Yet Mohamed Atta and Marwan Al-Shehhi, who Dekkers identified as being from Afghanistan, waltzed right in.

Imagine that.

From July through December they were at Huffman Aviation, with a brief three-week stint at nearby Jones Aviation in Sarasota. Then in December the terrorist duo moved 40 miles south to Professional Aviation at the Charlotte County Airport, where they underwent flight training the FBI has chosen not to tell us about.

Atta's sojourn in Charlotte County is not in the official story, which is *really* strange, because it is the FBI itself which is the source of this knowledge, in a memo from the Bureau to the INS introduced in court during the deportation hearing of a Tunisian student suspected of espionage. (If they had known we would be paying attention, they would have probably used a military tribunal.)

Professional Aviation at the Charlotte County Airport catered to a student body consisting mainly of foreign nationals from the small Mediterranean country of Tunisia, considered a moderate Arab state.

There were so many Tunisians at the school that it made the news well before the 9/11 attack.

"From the steady hand on the throttle to the aviator sunglasses, Mariem Ezzahi looked every bit like the experienced pilot she hopes to be back in her native country of Tunisia," reported the *Charlotte Sun-Herald*, in a feature story. "Mariem's goal is to become a commercial pilot like her late father, who flew jets for Tunis Air, the country's national airline."

Alas, Mariem would get stiffed by the owners of the school. So would dozens of other Tunisian students left stranded by the bankrupting of a flight school there.

Local news was filled with accounts of the scandal at the Charlotte Airport. Some foreign students had lost their life savings. Amid a flurry of media attention, students picketed the company's offices and staged a sit-in. Television news crews from Charlotte County and Fort Myers broadcast their plight.

The students claimed that they had paid more than $170,000 for flight training and received virtually nothing.

"With the promise of quicker, cheaper training, Florida flight schools recruited students from the Arab nation," reported the *Charlotte Sun-Herald* in March 2001. "But what a group of young Tunisians ended up with was an education in far more than flying. Many of them lost tens of thousands of dollars each when the school they paid to attend, Professional Aviation in Punta Gorda, closed.

"Many of the students had given its owner, David Byers, thousands of dollars in advance to cover training and housing costs," the paper reported. "Now their money was gone."

Students protested for days outside Professional Aviation's offices, holding signs with messages reading, "Where is our money, what about our future?"

The story of Zouhiaer Sdiri, a Tunisian student, was typical, said the paper. He left his wife and job in Tunisia to acquire his pilot's license in Charlotte County in the hope of someday flying commercially. But he received little instruction for the amount of money he paid.

"I have built so many dreams on this endeavor," Sdiri said. "I have only had 3-1/2 hours of flight time and a headset to show for the $7,000 I paid."

"He (Byers) thinks because I am not from this country, I don't know the law," former student Fares Smaoui told reporters. "But I know what fraud means."

"I paid $17,000," said another Tunisian student. "They stole it from me. I lost my future."

The story of stranded and bilked Arab student pilots received extensive local coverage. But in the days after the 9/11 attack when national reporters asked questions about reports of numerous foreigners training at the Charlotte County Airport, an airport official there had the presence of mind to cover it up.

"I don't think either (school) had international students," said airport director Cindy Anderson.

If the stakes are high enough, and the press docile enough, you can get away with almost anything in 21st century America. Cindy Anderson did.

While Mohamed Atta and his band of terrorists were making themselves at home in Florida, some of their American "hosts" were preying on the flood of Arab flight students turning up in large numbers, joining the ranks of German and Dutch flight trainees.

When Professional Aviation went bankrupt, a number of Arab student pilots there, including many of the dozens of Tunisian students who had paid as much as $25,000 up-front for flight training, moved up the road to begin attending flight school in Venice. Mohamed Atta was one of them. It marked the third occasion he and Marwan returned to Venice.

The FBI says they were only there once.

So Amanda Keller's testimony that Atta was living for two months in North Port, close to the Charlotte County Airport, before moving into the Sandpiper Apartments across from the Venice Airport in early March with her, dovetails perfectly with these accounts of Arab students moving up to Venice in March 2001 after Professional Aviation ceased operations.

In the flush of full disclosure Sheriff Clement had told reporters that Atta had been in flight training at the Charlotte County Airport. Though news accounts noted the flight schools denied he had been there, the connection had been made.

Atta and Al-Shehhi, the *Sun-Herald* reported, "often flew to the Charlotte County Airport where Professional Aviation was located, and authorities have linked some of the e-mail sent by the two hijackers to a Professional Aviation computer."

In an attempt to pin the blame for the bankruptcy on the students' shoulders, a mechanic at the defunct school told reporters that one student was involved in an incident at a local dance club that Amanda told us she and Atta had frequented together.

"One of the students damaged a school car in the parking lot of Area 51," the mechanic said.

News accounts also contained what is likely a direct reference to Atta's eviction from the "immense well-furnished house" which Amanda said he was living in when she met him.

"Students also claimed they have received an eviction notice at one of the homes where they reside in Deep Creek," reported the *Sun-Herald*.

Three of the Tunisian students who had attended Professional Aviation were taken into custody during the week after the attack.

One of them was 21 year-old Maryem Bedoui. Bedoui had been one of the Tunisians who moved to Venice when Professional Aviation went under. There she studied at Dutch national Arne Kruithof's Florida Flight Training Center, a block from Huffman Aviation.

During a deportation hearing in Bradenton, Florida, three months after the attack, Bedoui told the Judge that she was friends with one of Atta's roommates, but she denied knowing Atta, and denied as well any involvement or knowledge of the 9/11 plot.

However, the FBI noted in a letter to the immigration judge about the case that Bedoui attended flight schools in Punta Gorda and Venice, Florida, at the same time that hijackers Atta and Marwan Al-Shehhi trained at a nearby flight school, inadvertently revealing information indicating they have knowingly fabricated their own chronology of Atta's time in the U.S.

Presenting evidence for why Bedoui should be deported, the FBI's letter stated Bedoui had attended Florida Flight Training Center in Venice *at the same time* that Atta and Al-Shehhi were just blocks away at another school.

But Maryem Bedoui didn't enter the U.S. until 2001. And according to the FBI's chronology Atta and Al-Shehhi were at Huffman only from July to December 2000.

So according to the FBI's own reckoning Atta was in Venice months after they say he left for good. The *Sun-Herald* reporter noted the contradiction, and went to federal authorities seeking answers to give their readers.

"FBI spokeswoman Sara Oakes declined to comment Friday about the discrepancy," reported the paper.

Why had the FBI shown their hand? Probably because they didn't think anyone would catch the slip. And they must have been a little anxious about Bedoui, who, during a solo flight two weeks before the attack, made an unauthorized nighttime landing at a Lockheed Martin airstrip near Orlando. The site is the headquarters for Lockheed Martin's Missiles and Fire Control Division, which develops advanced combat, missile, rocket and space systems, all of which are deemed somewhat sensitive to national security.

Bedoui told the judge she had run out of fuel and landed rather than risk crashing.

"I was out of fuel," Bedoui said. "If I don't land, I crash."

Since the facility was closed, Bedoui said she spent the night there in her plane.

An immigration judge ordered her to return to Tunisia.

"In ordinary times," the judge told Bedoui, "that may not be a big thing. But these are not ordinary times."

Federal authorities never made public any details of the arrests of the three Tunisians. The matter was cloaked in such secrecy that two federal agencies were fighting over who was in charge.

Each pointed the finger at the other. FBI spokeswoman Sara Oakes in Tampa said the FBI had only assisted the INS in making the arrests.

"They were not arrested on FBI violations," Oates said.

But in Miami, regional INS spokesman Rodney Germain told reporters, "We are assisting the FBI. Because of the sensitivity of the investigation and the importance of the information, we can not release any information."

In the end, the big losers were the flight students, who were out large sums of money. Some of the students filed a criminal complaint against the company with the Charlotte County Sheriff's office, after trying to question Professional Aviation's owner, David Byers, about flight time and a refund of their money.

"We were supposed to meet with David this morning at 8 a.m., but he did not show up. He told us not to worry, that he wasn't going out of business," Youssef Abdelkrim told reporters.

Byers did not return phone calls or requests to answer the door at his Port Charlotte home. Maybe that was because the situation involving the Tunisian students was not the *only* problem Byers faced...

"David is past due on the rent at the Charlotte County Airport for January, February, March and April so we are in litigation on that matter," said Fred Watts, Charlotte County Airport executive director.

Was this just a case of a hard-working small businessman who couldn't make it work? Not to the local paper, it wasn't. They smelled fraud.

"The records imply that Byers simply did not pay his bills or taxes. Among other creditors are phone companies such as Sprint, MCI Worldcom and Qwest Communications, utilities such as Florida Power & Light, Charlotte County Utilities and the Charlotte Harbor Water Association, and cable company Comcast, Florida's Department of Revenue and Department of Labor, as well as the Internal Revenue Service."

"Among the rest of the 116 people and businesses who have claims against Professional are services such as gas companies, exterminators, air conditioner repairmen, body shops and aviation companies such as national giant Raytheon and Punta Gorda's Mod Works."

David Byers, owner of Professional Aviation, slipped out the back door with a lot of foreign students' money. In a later chapter we will see an Orlando flight school do the exact same thing. Although on the surface the two flight schools are not in any way related, we believe both will be shown to have been covertly associated with each other... and to Huffman Aviation in Venice as well.

There are strong similarities between Professional Aviation in Charlotte County and Huffman Aviation in Venice, each supposedly a free-standing business in competition with the other.

Professional Aviation had been going bankrupt at exactly the same time that Huffman Aviation's Rudi Dekkers was generating embarrassing coverage in the local press for his inability to pay his rent at the Venice Airport.

Numerous witnesses at the Charlotte County Airport had confirmed reports that Mohamed Atta was there during a time when the FBI says he was somewhere else.

What was going on? Why didn't the FBI just quietly change their chronology to accommodate the facts? Why were they ignoring an elephant in the living room? What were they trying to hide?

We discovered that they weren't trying to hide an elephant. That would be silly.

They were trying to hide an Ark.

CHAPTER TEN

23 MISSING HELICOPTERS

What the FBI is trying to hide, through the simple expedient of lying about Mohamed Atta's U.S. chronology, ironically sits in plain sight today at Charlotte County Airport.

It's the first thing Mohamed Atta and Marwan Al-Shehhi saw every time they drove into the Airport, after exiting Interstate 75 onto the county road running alongside.

It's an Ark. A Flying Ark.

Tied down at one corner of the Charlotte County Airport is a vintage DC-3, garishly painted to look like an airborne Noah's Ark. Hippos, giraffes and elephants adorn the silver sides of the plane, climbing towards the cockpit. The colorful oddity, the most conspicuous plane at a small rural airport, has been parked there since being seized by law enforcement two years ago.

It belonged to Frank Moss, a notorious 80s-era drug smuggler who briefly achieved a certain notoriety during the Iran-Contra Hearings, after it was revealed that Oliver North knew that Contra supply planes from Moss's Hondu Carib airline were also being used for drug runs into the U.S.

North was, no doubt, shocked. But despite the unfortunate publicity, Frank Moss has apparently soldiered on, and the airborne Ark isn't even the first plane of his seized there.

That honor belongs to a DC-4 which the U.S. Customs Service was chasing off the west coast of Florida in the mid-'80s, while it was busily dumping what authorities drily noted "appeared to be a load of drugs."

When it landed at Charlotte County Airport on March 16, 1987, it was seized by the DEA. An address book found aboard contained the Virginia telephone number of Robert Owen, Oliver North's courier. In a memo to North, Owens said that Moss's "DC-6 which is being used for runs [to supply the Contras] out of New Orleans is probably used for drug runs into the US."

Moss had been under investigation for narcotics offenses since 1979, it turned out, by no less than *ten* different law enforcement agencies. But America is the land of the second chance, and thus Moss was one of the first pilots chosen to fly Contra supply missions. He was there at the inception of the "Contra cocaine" business run with the tacit approval of shadowy government figures like then-CIA Director Bill Casey.

Moss also regularly dropped duffel bags—military issue, *natch*— filled with Contra cocaine onto the Louisiana "farm" of Barry Seal, the biggest drug smuggler in American history, according to the U.S. Government. Besides being big in the drug business, Seal was a life-long CIA operative, something which quickly became "inconvenient knowledge" during Iran-Contra and, later, the Clinton Scandals, where the *Wall Street Journal* called him the "ghost haunting White-water."

Both Charlotte County Airport, and Venice 40 miles to the north were unlikely hotbeds of covert activity, and it is no doubt just another "freak coincidence" that Barry Seal's Iran-Contra buddies have their fingerprints all over operations at two tiny airports frequented by the terrorists. Still, Atta *had* hung out in both places…

What was up with that?

Late one afternoon we met with two County law enforcement officials in the area. They told us that the somnolent west coast of Florida has been teeming with activity of a turbulently spook-ish kind for as long as some in local law enforcement can recall.

"You know, of course, that there is at least a 40-year history of covert training in this area," the older official stated. "They used Useppa Island just off-shore to train for the Bay of Pigs."

Actually, we hadn't known.

"The only city in Charlotte County, Punta Gorda, was pretty much founded by a group of 'former' CIA agents," said the second official, a little wearily, we thought. "They built Punta Gorda Isles, a big upscale development on Charlotte Bay."

How much strange activity went on at the Charlotte County Airport where Atta and Marwan trained and spent time?

Well, for starters the airport is currently home, the officials told us, to major intrigue involving the disappearance of at least 23 helicopters... *from the County Sheriff's Department.*

The helicopters had been procured through a General Services Administration Military Surplus program, and then spirited out of the country, to exotic and faraway destinations where the Charlotte County Sheriff has no apparent law enforcement jurisdiction.

"Right now the Charlotte County Sheriff's Office has a flyable helicopter in Chile," the current Sheriff told us mournfully. "But we can't get it back. We've had absolutely no cooperation from the Feds."

The program under which the Charlotte County Sheriff's Department procured their helicopters is the same one that resulted in felony convictions of "former" CIA agents in Arizona in the Forest Service C-130 scandal in the mid-90s. There a C-130 military cargo plane loaned to the U.S. Forest Service to fight wildfires in the West also went "missing...

When it was discovered, on a runway at the Mexico City Airport, there was a billion dollars worth of cocaine aboard.

So it's not as if local law enforcement doesn't have a pretty good idea of who's been swiping helicopters in Charlotte County, we were informed. But knowing it and being able to do anything about it are apparently two different things.

The helicopters were "misplaced" over a period of three years, said the Sheriff, beginning in 1996. The thieves had pretty ecumenical tastes...

"We've lost all kinds: Hueys, Bell Jet Rangers, Hughes 500 helicopters. When we discovered it we took it immediately to the State's Attorney. They locked up the local force captain. But the FAA has never prosecuted anybody, and they show zero interest in helping us get our copters back."

"You wouldn't think Charlotte County would need 23 helicopters," laughed Coy Jacob, an aviation business owner at the Venice Airport. "They'd be bumping into each other in the air."

"Charlotte County has always had kind of a shadow," he explained. "There's a fellow who rebuilds helicopters who has always been in quasi-problems with the FAA with his helicopter parts. Jamie Hill."

Jamie Hill had been a target of the Charlotte County Sheriff investigation, we'd learned. "He's got seven helicopters sitting on his property today that don't belong to him," one local law enforcement source stated. "He's got millions of dollars of aircraft parts with the numbers filed out."

Jamie Hill's partner in the company strongly suspected of having been a conduit for the disappearance of 23 helicopters from the County Sheriff's Air Wing turns out to be another notorious covert operative with a significant presence at the Charlotte County Airport. Dietrich Reinhardt's name, which could have been lifted straight out of transcripts of the Iran-Contra Hearings, had also been linked with Barry Seal's infamous Mena, Arkansas cocaine smuggling.

We discovered that one of Reinhardt's companies active at the Charlotte County Airport, Caribe Air, had been doing business with Rudi Dekkers' Huffman Aviation.

Caribe Air was an especially notorious CIA proprietary whose past included "blemishes" like having all its aircraft seized at Mena, Arkansas after government prosecutors accused the company of using its planes to transport cocaine worth billions of dollars into the U.S.

It was beginning to feel like Old Home Week in Charlotte County. Reinhardt—apparently not content with the distinction of being business partners with a man suspected of making helicopters disappear—was linked to the man who trained both pilots who crashed airliners into the Twin Towers of the World Trade Center.

Dekkers had had a "maintenance contract" with Reinhardt's company. This is no doubt just another freak coincidence.

Why would Dietrich Reinhardt know Rudi Dekkers? What would they have to talk about? Maybe Dekkers' "maintenance contract" involved vacuuming out the planes.

You wouldn't want to trust that kind of job to just *anybody*.

Reinhardt had also operated the now-defunct St. Lucia Airways, referred to as a CIA proprietary company in a Senate intelligence committee report. Reports in the *Washington Post* linked St. Lucia planes to the delivery of Hawk and TOW missiles to Tehran, Iran in

1985 and 1986 as part the covert arms-for-hostages deal between the United States and Iran.

But busy guys like Dietrich are hard to get on the phone. The *Post* reported, "Attempts to reach Reinhardt by telephone in Frankfurt, Germany, were unsuccessful. His telephone had been disconnected."

Was Dietrich Reinhardt German?

Reinhardt's St. Lucia flew a C-130 military cargo plane often seen delivering arms to a remote airstrip in Zaire in 1986. The *New York Times* reported the weapons were on their way to Angolan rebels. But Reinhardt denied any involvement in arms shipments to Angola, saying the cargo was relief goods for Zaire.

Zaire is one of the African countries said to have been involved in blood diamonds, supposedly a bin Laden organization specialty.

Is it just coincidence that the Florida airports where Mohamed Atta spent the most time are both linked to American covert operations? We remembered a question we'd asked in a conversation we'd had just a week after the attack with a gentleman who was "sort of retired" after spending 35 years working for something "very much like" the CIA.

Nine days after the attack, we told him, we'd read reports saying that 15 of the 19 hijackers in the far-flung network of terrorist pilots and thugs got their money from the same source.

We were incredulous at this news, and asked, "How could the Agency not have known about 15 foreign pilots all paid from one source?"

He answered carefully, speaking to us kindly, the way you would to a child not terribly bright.

"I would assume that they *did* know," he told us. "It would be almost-impossible for them *not* to."

Of course. They must have. They must have looked "the other way," just as somebody—the previous Sheriff—had to have been looking the other way while *somebody* slipped away with 23 helicopters. He had to have known what has happening. Helicopters make noise taking off.

We had begun to discover that local law enforcement officials in South West Florida weren't stupid, or unobservant. But there was a limit to their powers, especially when faced with federal operations.

When we interviewed the former Venice Chief of Police, for example, he seemed a little embarrassed, even apologetic, about what he had been forced to allow at the airport in his town. He asked that we not judge city officials too harshly. They had little or no control over what went on at the Airport, which was a federal jurisdiction.

"The Venice Airport is the kind of place where it's not unusual to see a military Blackhawk helicopter touch down at three in the morning and then take off again 30 seconds later," said the Chief, shrugging. "Or the airport can be quiet and deserted one minute, and the next have 5,000 paratroopers landing. That's just the way it is here."

What we discovered at Atta's home port in January and February of 2001, the Charlotte County Airport, was shocking, and where our investigation was headed was beginning to become plain.

One of the most disturbing moments of our time in South West Florida came when we sat down with two local law enforcement officials who could be considered fairly typical Southern Sheriffs, both of whom ventured the opinion that—based on what they had witnessed of a 40-year long history of CIA-connected covert operations in their area—they believed that the CIA was somehow involved in, if not responsible for, the World Trade Center attacks.

We expect talk like that from wild-eyed "conspiracy theorists," but not law enforcement officials, who say they've spent their careers watching questionable activities with which they could not interfere.

Meanwhile, back at the ranch, the FBI has been as silent as Mullah Omar about the milieu which Atta and his Hamburg cadre slipped into as smoothly as a harem girl into pajamas. And it wasn't just these two SW Florida locations, we soon hear; instead, the entire stretch of coastline from Naples in the south to Sarasota in the north on close examination looks like some kind of international pirate's domain, filled with men flying the jolly roger.

We were alarmed at how many of the people in Florida's "cowboy flyboy" world that the terrorist ringleader moved in had also been shadow players in a spook-filled world, whose lives and careers seemed to be bound up in an awful lot of America's recent secret history.

Were they bound up with Mohamed Atta's as well?

CHAPTER ELEVEN

"SAUDI PRINCE" MOHAMED ATTA?

To pierce the veil of the official story about the terrorist conspiracy and arrive at something better resembling the truth required a little understanding about what it is that spies *do*. They do a lot of things, but one of the things they do, before going out to do those things they do, is to create for themselves a "legend," a cover story. A lie that holds together long enough to let them slip away.

Saying spies create legends is just a polite way of saying that they lie. Habitually, regularly, reflexively and for a living. It is a craft. They are professionals. They do it well.

This creates a bit of a problem for us civilians. No one likes to think of themselves as someone who can be successfully lied to. A sucker. But we all can, and we all have been. So it's important that we admit the possibility that when it comes to Mohamed Atta, as the Firesign Theater put it memorably, "Everything you know is wrong."

The government's explanation of Atta as a "fanatic Islamic fundamentalist" was, as we've seen, fraying at the edges. So just for a moment we're going to assume that we've been successfully lied to about Atta, and put aside everything we've been told. We're going to pretend Mohamed Atta wasn't the wild-eyed religious zealot we've been told he is, and see if that clears up any of the many "anomalies" about the official explanation of who he was.

What if, instead of a xenophobic Islamic fundamentalist, Mohamed Atta had been a Prince. A Saudi Prince. If that idea makes you feel you've slipped down the rabbit hole, don't worry.

You've got company.

Before we'd finished tracking down people who we discovered had been close to the terrorist ringleader in the U.S., we'd been continuously amazed at the sheer rich pageantry of corruption, criminal activity and deviant behavior they exhibited...

Busy with everything from smuggling aircraft into the U.S. over the Arctic to sabotaging planes and helicopters to crash. We met ex-KGB Colonels in Miami working for the Russian Mob; heard about a Saudi Prince and his entourage at loose ends at an Air Force base near Pensacola while a helicopter that President Roosevelt gave his father, King Faisal, was repaired; we learned of wineries in South Africa owned by members of the family of the Prime Minister of the Bahamas, and million dollar "loans" to televangelist Jerry Falwell that he'd forgotten to repay. Bugged phones, double agents, a mysterious Pakistani with State Department connections flying daily to Havana, and an ex-CIA pilot who used to fly U-2s over Russia...

Atta's U.S. associates were responsible for or involved in: a Lear jet seized in Orlando by Uzi-toting DEA agents with 43 lbs., of heroin onboard with it's pilot talking unconcernedly on his cell phone while agents leveled their guns; suspected skulduggery in the Mormon Temple in Orlando; a gold mine in the Caribbean; high technology smuggling out of southwest Florida; missionary flights to Havana carrying—not the word of God—but bag-fulls of gold Rolexes for sympathetic Cuban officials who already had Bibles; the interesting part-time job of the chief pilot for Venezuela's Air Force One; robot planes at the Venice Airport; and a "really tall blond woman whose parents were KGB."

For somebody looking to go unrecognized, Atta knew a lot of people. Far from being the secretive ringleader of a "lone cadre" which slipped through Europe and America unnoticed, Atta moved in some pretty interesting circles.

Compared to some of the bizarre lives we will soon be witnessing, the idea of Atta as a Saudi Prince doesn't seem too over the top. There is even evidence that he may have been using it as one of his cover stories, or legends.

Atta's flight instructor at Huffman Aviation told another student pilot, Dr. Anne Greaves, an English osteopath, that Mohamed Atta had connections with the Saudi Royal Family, and that Atta's status as a member of the Saudi elite warranted him having a full-time body-guard (Marwan) with him at all times in the U.S.

The revelation was buried in the news right after 9/11. It resurfaced later in an Australian Broadcasting Corporation's investigative pro-gram, *4 Corners*, a Down Under *60 Minutes.*

Anne Greaves lifelong passion for aviation led her into pursuing her dream of learning to fly at Huffman Aviation. She was there at the same time as Mohamed Atta and Marwan Al-Shehhi were there.

"When I checked with my instructor on one occasion about their (strange) habits," she told *4 Corners,* "I was informed that the men we now know as Mohamed Atta and Al-Shehhi actually had royal connections with a Saudi House and that Al-Shehhi was his body-guard."

Australian TV correspondent Liz Jackson attempted to pin down de-tails: "This story about Mohamed Atta being royalty and Al-Shehhi be-ing his bodyguard, was that something just that Huffman's told you? I mean do you think that was something that they even believed or…"

"It was my impression that it was generally believed," Greaves said. "Because it was my instructor who told me this at the time so I had the impression that that was generally believed, yes."

"That Mohamed Atta was royalty?"

"That he had some connection of the Royal House of Saudi, yes."

"And Al-Shehhi was his bodyguard?"

"That is what I was given to understand. So in a way it made sense to me that there were always two because I never saw Al-Shehhi take the controls of the aircraft. It was always Mohamed Atta but never-theless Al-Shehhi always accompanied him on his flying lessons."

This is amazing testimony from an eye-witness with no visible ax to grind. If a student pilot at the school had had a bodyguard flying with him at all times during flight training, this detail could not have been missed by the school's owner.

The show's host asked Rudi Dekkers, "Now there have been stories that he presented himself as an Arab prince, is that correct?"

"Well, no," Dekkers replied. "If he was a prince, yes or no, I can't state that because we never heard them talking about that, we never heard anything, we have heard that one of my students who was here in the same time that Atta and Al-Shehhi was here, and I think it was Miss Greaves, that she stated in the London newspaper that he was a prince, that their clothing was expensive and that Al-Shehhi was his guard."

"Nothing of that we have seen here in the five months they were here," continued Dekkers. "They were absolutely low profile, they clothed themselves like we all do. They were just there in jeans, sneakers, regular American."

Jeans, sneakers. Regular American.

It sounded nice. But it wasn't true. Numerous witnesses said otherwise, like Bob Gaff, a Huffman flight instructor, who told reporters in interviews the day after the attack what a sharp dresser Atta was.

"You see how we're all dressed?" asked Gaff, who was clad in a T-shirt and jeans. "This guy used to show up in leather shoes, shined shoes, dress slacks, silk shirts, all the time."

But neither said, "Jeans, sneakers. Regular American."

Brad Warrick, who rented three cars to Atta during the last six weeks before the attack, told us, "Mohamed dressed to the nines. You know, nice. Nice pants and shirt. Just business like. Nice clothes, business like. He carried a briefcase."

"Jeans, sneakers. Regular American." It doesn't even sound like Dekkers is talking about the same guy.

A restaurant owner in Nokomis who had a memorable encounter with Atta and his terrorist compatriots, described in a later chapter, was asked how Atta had been dressed when he came into her restaurant.

"They were dressed in Florida type shirts, the silk, you know, with the pattern, that kind of thing, lots of jewelry. *Lots* of jewelry. I thought they were Mafia," said Rene Adorna of the Pelican Alley.

All of these descriptions are a long way from "jeans, sneakers, regular American." It's a small point, but telling. Did Dekkers lie in an improvised on-camera attempt to discredit Anne Greaves' account? It raises a red flag about his veracity during his innumerable television appearances in the wake of the disaster.

Another comment by flight student Greaves seems clearly prescient in light of what we would soon discover.

"I just thought it very strange that two Arabs had selected an airfield or a flying establishment that was really very quietly situated," she said.

"I remember thinking at the time I found this very strange, because normally royalty learn at military establishments for security reasons alone."

Atta *had* learned at U.S. military facilities, we discovered. As many as seven of the hijackers were in this country at the invitation of the U.S. Government. Keeping this knowledge secret has been an objective of the cover-up currently in progress.

On the Saturday following the Tuesday attack, the *Los Angeles Times* broke the story in a long article on their front page..

"A defense official said two of the hijackers were former Saudi fighter pilots," reported the paper, "who had studied in exchange programs at the Defense Language School at Lackland Air Force Base in Texas and the Air War College at Maxwell Air Force Base in Alabama."

The story went wide the next day, Sunday, Sept 15th. *Newsweek*, the *Washington Post* and the *Miami Herald* all reported as many as seven of the terrorist hijackers in the Sept. 11th attacks received training at secure U.S. military installations.

"Two of 19 suspects named by the FBI, Saeed Alghamdi and Ahmed Alghamdi, have the same names as men listed at a housing facility for foreign military trainees at Pensacola. Two others, Hamza Alghamdi and Ahmed Alnami, have names similar to individuals listed in public records as using the same address inside the base," the *Washington Post* reported.

"In addition, a man named Saeed Alghamdi graduated from the Defense Language Institute at Lackland Air Force Base in San Antonio, while men with the same names as two other hijackers, Mohamed Atta and Abdulaziz Alomari, appear as graduates of the U.S. International Officers School at Maxwell Air Force Base, AL, and the Aerospace Medical School at Brooks Air Force Base in San Antonio, respectively," the *Post* said.

According to the *Post*, seven of the suspected hijackers had been in the U.S. receiving military training. *Newsweek* said U.S. military officials gave the FBI information suggesting that five of the alleged hijackers received training in the 1990s at secure U.S. military installations. Three of them listed their address on driver licenses and car registrations as an address on the base of the Pensacola Naval Air Station which houses foreign-military flight trainees.

"Pentagon spokesman, Col. Ken McClellan, said a man named Mohamed Atta had once attended the International Officer's School at Maxwell Air Force Base in Montgomery, Ala," reported *USA Today*.

Mohamed Atta attended International Officers School at Maxwell Air Force Base in Alabama. An Islamic fundamentalist learning snappy salutes in the Officer's Club?

This is a huge chunk of inconvenient knowledge. There were going to be a lot of questions. Someone was going to have to answer… for a *lot*.

"But Atta is a fairly common surname in the Middle East," the *Post* quoted Laila Alquatami of the Arab-American Anti-Discrimination Committee as saying, and the suspected hijacker's first name is "probably the No. 1 name that is given to babies, in honor of the prophet Mohamed."

The *Boston Globe* reported the Pentagon's denial: "Some of the FBI suspects had names similar to those used by foreign alumni of U.S. military courses," said the Air Force in a statement. 'Discrepancies in their biographical data… indicate we are probably not talking about the same people.'"

How easy was it to tell the Pentagon was lying? Think about it. It is neither plausible nor logical that the reports were false because of seven separate cases of mistaken identity. One or two, maybe. But seven? No way.

Still, after this vague and perfunctory Pentagon denial, the story had an exceedingly short half-life. The Pentagon denied it. The media dropped it. It went away. There was no follow-up.

Had the *Washington Post*, the *LA Times, Newsweek,* the *Miami Herald* all been wrong?

None of the papers offered a retraction.

How could a story as major as this—that many of the terrorists, including ringleader Mohammed Atta, had been in the U.S. to receive training at U.S. military facilities—have gotten *lost?*

It wasn't lost, we discovered. And it wasn't wrong, either…

It was *suppressed.*

The first thing we noticed in the Pentagon denial was that "probably not talking about the same people" doesn't strike quite the right tone of specificity one might expect of an investigation into people responsible for vaporizing 3,000 human beings.

It's not just vague. Given the circumstances, it's almost criminally-vague.

When the Pentagon unveiled their big new bunker-busting bomb in Afghanistan, they didn't describe it as being a "kinda big" bomb, did they? No, they called it a "satellite-guided, two ton bunker-busting bomb known as the EGBU-27."

Yet now Air Force spokesmen were persuading *Newsweek*, the *Washington Post* and the Knight Ridder newspapers to drop an immensely important revelation on the basis of statements like "name matches *may not necessarily* mean the students were the hi-jackers."

What if Nixon's press secretary Ron Ziegler had been able to wave Woodward and Bernstein off as the Watergate scandal came to light, by saying the burglars "probably didn't have" White House ties?

The only answer we could see was that the initial press reports, while true, were also inconvenient, and were deliberately suppressed. Could America's vaunted free press be involved in an ongoing cover-up of something of this magnitude? We tried to find out. But we were stonewalled every step of the way.

We weren't the only ones being stonewalled. When *Newsweek* reported that three of the hijackers received training at the Pensacola Naval Station in Florida, home state Senator Bill Nelson fired off a fax to his friend, Attorney General John Ashcroft, demanding to know if it were true.

The Senator has still not received a reply, we heard from his spokesman, when we called his office eleven months later.

"In the wake of those reports, we asked about the Pensacola Naval Air Station but we never got a definitive answer from the Justice Department," stated the Senator's press spokesman.

"So we asked the FBI for an answer 'if and when' they could provide us one. Their response to date has been that they are trying to sort through something complicated and difficult."

"Speaking for Senator Nelson," concluded the spokesman, "we still do not know if three of the terrorists trained at one time in Pensacola or not."

From the spokesman's somewhat wry tone, we understood that he didn't expect Attorney Gen. Ashcroft to respond to Senator Nelson's request until hell freezes over and Ashcroft skated down from Heaven to test the ice.

If a home state Senator couldn't get a response, there was little chance we could. Still, we called the Pentagon and spoke to a Major in the Air Force's Public Affairs Office who had been involved, she said, in crafting and disseminating the original Pentagon denial to the press.

She was the Public Information Officer who read the Air Force denial to the media, so she was familiar with the question, she told us, and she offered to help us achieve clarity.

"Biographically, they're not the same people," she explained patiently, using the same language contained in the Air Force's press release. "Some of the ages are twenty years off."

"Some of the ages?" Could she be, perhaps, just a *little* more precise?

Negative.

Let's make this real simple, we said. We were only asking about *one* of the seven purported terrorists reported to have received military training in the U.S.

Mohamed Atta.

Was she saying that the age of the "Mohamed Atta" who had attended the Air Force's International Officer's School at Maxwell Air Force Base was different than that of "terrorist ringleader Mohamed Atta?"

Not exactly, she admitted. She could not confirm that—*in this specific instance*—they had different ages. What she could do was once again deny that the International Officer's School attendee named Mohamed Atta had been the Mohamed Atta who piloted a passenger plane into the World Trade Center.

However, she could offer no specifics for her assertion, and repeatedly declined requests for biographical details about the Mohamed Atta who *had* trained at Maxwell Air Force Base. None of this kept her from shamelessly soldiering on.

"Mohamed is a very common name," she said.

It was indeed, we told her, making one final effort. We said we would be happy to help the Pentagon's investigative effort, especially since they were busy with other concerns. We offered to take it upon ourselves to track down the Mohamed Atta who had attended the Air Force's International Officer's School to confirm, once and for all, that he was not the Mohamed Atta said to have flown a jetliner into the side of a skyscraper in Manhattan.

All she had to do was tell us where the Mohamed Atta who *had* attended International Officer's School at Maxwell AFB was *from*.

We would take it from there. Solve the mystery at no cost.

"I don't think you're going to get that information," the spokeswoman stated flatly.

Still, we pressed her again, and probably to the point of rudeness, to provide a few lonely specifics, and we were rewarded when she finally said, in exasperation: "I do not have the authority to tell you who (which terrorists) attended which schools."

It was hard to read this as anything other than a back-handed confirmation. When she said that she didn't have the authority, the clear implication was that someone else *does...* Somewhere in the Defense Dept. a list exists with the names of Sept. 11 terrorists who received training at U.S. military facilities.

She just didn't have the authority to release it. End of story.

One obvious reason for this cover-up would be sparing the Pentagon the embarrassment of having to admit that some of the terrorists—including ringleader Atta himself—had only been in the U.S. to begin with to receive U.S. military training. But this may not be the most important consideration, which is why we've placed the story of "Atta as Saudi Prince" alongside reports that the terrorists received military training at secure U.S. bases.

Anyone receiving training in U.S. military programs, we learned, would *not* fit the portrait of a fanatical Islamic fundamentalist that's been painted of Mohamed Atta.

Gaining admittance to the International Officer's School at Maxwell AFB in Montgomery would have required Atta to be extremely well-connected with a friendly Arab government.

We learned just how well-connected and well-placed foreign nationals who attend International Officer's School are after finding the resume of Colonel and Staff Pilot Mohammed Ahmed Hamel Al Qubaisi, an International Officer's School graduate from the United Arab Emirates, posted on the Internet.

Currently, his resume stated, he was a Defense Military Naval & Air Attaché at the United Arab Emirates embassy in Washington, after serving stints in his country's Embassy & Security Division as Chief of Intelligence, and in the UAE's Security Division/Air Force Intelligence & Security Directorate as Security Officer.

It's safe to say that Mr. Al Qubaisi is pretty dialed-in in the UAE, and the furthermost thing from a terrorist. He's a member of the Arab elite. It even looks like he's a spook.

So was Mohamed Atta.

And because he was, we're in a whole different ballgame than the one they've been announcing from high overhead in the Pentagon booth.

We heard from someone who works on Maxwell Air Force Base in Montgomery, the former wife of a CIA pilot. "I have a girlfriend who recognized Mohamed Atta. She met him at a party at the Officer's Club," she told us.

"The reason she swears it was him here is because she didn't just meet him and say hello. After she met him she went around and introduced him to the people that were with her. So she knows it was him."

Saudis were a highly visible presence at Maxwell Air Force Base, she said. "There were a lot of them living in an upscale complex in Montgomery. They had to get all of them out of here."

"They were all gone the day after the attack."

CHAPTER TWELVE

THE SAUDI COVER

Within minutes after Mohamed Atta's name was identified as the main suspect in the 9/11 attack, reporters began digging through newspaper archives for anything that might have been printed about him in the past.

What turned up was reflected in a question on the morning after the attack that Jane Clayson of the *CBS Early Show* asked of Rudi Dekkers, the Huffman Aviation co-owner then in the midst of his whirlwind round of media appearances...

"Let me ask you this," Clayson began. "One of these men is widely considered to be responsible for a bus bombing in—in Israel. How was it that they could gain access—admittance to your school?"

Authorities immediately denied that the Mohamed Atta who masterminded the demolition of the World Trade Center was the same Mohamed Atta who, fifteen years earlier, had blown up an Israeli bus. There were two separate Arab terrorists named Mohamed Atta, they said, one who bombed a bus in 1986, and a second who flew a commercial airliner into the World Trade Center Towers.

We found a May 21, 1987 story from Damascus on the Chinese Xinhua Overseas News Service with a headline reading "SYRIA ACCUSES U.S. OF DETERIORATING BILATERAL RELA-TIONS."

"Abu Nidal, head of the Fatah revolutionary committee of the Palestine Liberation Organization threatened to sabotage American interests all over the world if Washington decided to hand over Mohamed Atta, a Palestinian arrested in New York, to the Israeli authorities on trial for murdering a bus driver in Israel."

The context was a recently announced U.S. decision not to send back its ambassador to Damascus unless Syria's Hafez Assad took steps first to prove that his government was no longer supporting terrorism. "American accusations of Syrian support for terrorism were baseless," declared the Xinhua report.

La plus ca change.

"Future terrorist ringleader" Atta was eighteen at the time of the bus bombing—an age when youthful idealism is often perverted into violence—but a quick search through newspaper indexes revealed that "bus bomber Mohamed Atta," also known as "Mahmoud Atta," was indeed much older, thirty-three in '86. He'd be fifty-ish today.

"Mahmoud Mahmoud Atta, 33, charged in the firebombing of a crowded bus on Israel's occupied West Bank on April 12, 1986, that killed one civilian and injured three others, was held Thursday without bail until the policy issues can be addressed," UPI reported on May 8, 1987.

That seemed to settle the question: Bus bomber Atta is a much older man than the terrorist hijacker.

Smoke. No fire. It happens.

By pursuing the story we'd gained a little incidental knowledge: "Mahmoud" is another was of saying "Mohamed," the same way men named "John" are sometimes called "Jack."

Interestingly, "bus bomber Atta" felt there was some confusion as to his identity: "Atta, also known as Mahmoud El Abed Ahmad, claims he is not the person authorities were looking for," UPI reported.

So at a minimum we have two Arab radicals with the same admittedly not-uncommon name. Probably just coincidence... unless the name "Mohamed Atta" was used by numbers of Arab terrorists.

Bus bomber Atta's globe-trotting ways were also eerily similar to terrorist hijacker Atta's peripatetic movements. Newspaper accounts said the bus bomber fled from Israel to Athens, and then on to Venezuela, where he was arrested. When he arrived at JFK Airport, after flying from Caracas "accompanied" by FBI agents, the U.S. Prosecutor in the case said Atta's passport showed "numerous trips around the globe."

Terrorist pilot Atta got around a lot too. Prague, Madrid, Miami, Manhattan. Maybe being a spy hasn't changed that much.

But there's something big and important to understanding 9/11 here. Because there had been a "bus bomber Mohamed Atta," the *name* "Mohamed Atta" was on a special CIA-FBI federal watch list, which should have red-flagged the terrorist ringleader to authorities on numerous occasions.

In fact, an NBC report the day after the attack attributed the FBI's quick zeroing in on Atta to the simple fact that they already knew who he was. They'd seen his name before, linked, said NBC's Kerry Sanders, to the bus bombing in Israel.

"Agents were in Hollywood, Florida serving search warrants inside an apartment complex," Sanders reported. "They left with several boxes of evidence. The attention was really focusing on one person, Mohamed Atta, 33 years old, somebody who they know, because they've seen his name before, linked to a bombing of a bus in Israel in 1986."

"Atta, 33, who was born in the United Arab Emirates, was listed as a suspect in a bus bombing in Israel in 1986. That landed him on a CIA-FBI-Immigration & Naturalization Service watch list," reported NBC's Sanders.

Here's the Big Question. If the *name* "Mohamed Atta" was on a federal watch list of people tied to terrorist activity because of "bus-bomber Atta," why didn't this fact get "hijacker Atta's" ass caught *before* the attack?

Were they *that* incompetent? NBC anchor Brian Williams—he of the oft-remarked unnatural tan—gave voice to it first, the night after the attack. "There will be many people asking tonight," he said, right over the public airwaves, "just what it is we are getting for all those tens of billions of dollars being spent on intelligence."

Could that be it? Simple incompetence? Why didn't they catch Atta if he was running in and out of the country with a notorious name? They had ample opportunity. For example, the terrorist ringleader had had police on his tail late on the night of April 26 in Broward County, Florida. Red and blue flashing lights and a police siren beckoned him to pull over. Atta pulled his red Grand Am to the curb, and was arrested during the traffic stop for not having a driving license, but he easily bailed out and drove away.

Street cops aren't looking for international terrorists during routine traffic stops. Not before 9/11, they weren't, anyway.

But what explains the fact that Atta was able to fly from Miami to Madrid and back, with no hassles... *despite* the fact that he had over-stayed his visa.

"At least one of the Boston hijackers, Mohamed Atta, was able to enter the United States despite having been implicated in a 1986 bus bombing in Israel, according to federal sources," the *Boston Globe* reported three days after the attack.

Officials said Atta's name was on a federal watch list. Yet the INS readmitted him with no problem upon his return to the U.S.

Simple incompetence? Or something more sinister...

"In interviews with the *Globe* yesterday, flight instructors in Florida said that it was common for 'students with Saudi affiliations' to enter the United States with only cursory background checks, and some-times none."

Ah-ha. Gotcha. Students with "Saudi affiliations." This was new, or new to us: students with Saudi affiliations were accorded special treatment in Florida, said flight instructors there, that allowed them to enter and leave the U.S. more easily.

Saudis were getting special treatment in Florida from our govern-ment. That much seemed clear, even though we weren't sure we had a working definition yet of what "special treatment" meant. And it wasn't just Saudis who got special treatment, reported the *Globe,* but students with *Saudi affiliations* as well.

Saudis had a lot of juice in Florida.

Chuck Clapper, owner of an air charter company in Lantana, Flor-ida, told the *Globe* that several Florida flying schools had contracts with Saudi Arabian Airlines that enabled them to bypass much of the red tape involved in obtaining visas for their students.

Saudi Arabia had authority to "pass through" anyone they wanted. They didn't even need to be Saudi. They just needed "Saudi affiliations."

"The Saudi cover may have enabled one of the dead hijackers, Mo-hamed Atta, to deflect attention from the fact that he was wanted in Is-rael in connection with a bus bombing in 1986," the paper reported.

"The Saudi Cover." It sounded like the title of a Robert Ludlum nov-el. Because he had "Saudi cover" Atta got special treatment in Florida. Atta's passing himself off as a Saudi Prince made more sense.

Indeed, the benefit of having "Saudi Cover" goes back some time. The former head of the American visa bureau in Jeddah from 1987 to 1989, Michael Springman, told *BBC News Night:* "In Saudi Arabia I was repeatedly ordered by high-level State Department officials to issue visas to unqualified applicants."

"People who had no ties either to Saudi Arabia or to their own country. I complained there. I complained here in Washington… to the Inspector General and to Diplomatic Security, and I was ignored. What I was doing was giving visas to terrorists—recruited by the CIA and Osama bin Laden—to come back to the United States for training to be used in the war in Afghanistan against the then-Soviets."

"Forced to give visas to terrorists" sounds like a good headline. Too bad we'll never see it. It pretty much capsulated American diplomat Springman's story. Was it a method still in use to bring Saudi-affiliated individuals into the U.S. when Atta arrived?

When Atta arrived a dozen years later, were "special people" still getting in and out of the U.S. this way?

In passing, it should be noted that the "Atta was a bus bomber" story was also twisted and used in some pretty sophisticated disinformation, when a broadly-based e-mail campaign started fingering "tar baby" Bill Clinton for being responsible for releasing Mohamed Atta from jail.

The Oslo agreement between the Palestinians and Israel had required release of so-called "political prisoners," explained the disinfo. However, the Israelis would not release any with "blood on their hands."

That's where that dastardly Clinton comes in. As American President he supposedly "insisted" that *all* prisoners be released, even those *with* "blood on their hands." Some people thought it sounded like our Bill. At any rate Atta was freed, and came back to thank the U.S. by flying an airplane into Tower One of the World Trade Center.

There was not a shred of truth to the story. But it obviously took someone some little time and effort to first package the lie so cleverly, and then disseminate it widely, during a confusing and uncertain moment in our national life when news accounts actually said that U.S. intelligence agencies were recruiting psychics to help predict future attacks. (The FBI and CIA refused to comment, except to confirm investigators had been told to "think outside the box.")

The national mood was dicey. Enough to warrant the *Washington Post* to gushingly report that the FBI, "after decades of pursuing gangsters and drug kingpins to great acclaim, was rushing to remake itself as the nation's primary line of defense against terrorism."

"Great acclaim" was a little rich. "Decades of great acclaim" is rich enough to give the flack who wrote it gout. The only *acclaim* for the FBI we'd heard came from those who want to see it abolished for a long and sordid history distinguished by scandal, incompetence, and worse.

Sometimes much worse. Remember? "Atta, 33, an Egyptian, was on the FBI's master list of suspected Arab terrorists, specifically as a possible operative of bin Laden," reported the Sept. 13, 2001 *London Daily Telegraph.*

"Federal authorities have known for at least three years that two associates of bin Laden had trained in the United States as airline pilots," reported the *Boston Globe,* citing an FBI memo dated May 18, 1998.

The *Globe* doesn't say why the FBI did nothing about it. Neither does the memo, we'll wager. Not since the days of J. Edgar Hoover and Efram Zimbalist Jr. have the American people believed much in this particular Federal institution. Congress has rumbled with murmurs that it is beyond reform and should be abolished.

All of which makes it all the more puzzling when the FBI turned up so Johnny-on-the-spot at Huffman on the day of the attack. After spending decades not being able to find their ass in the dark with both hands, the beleaguered FBI shows up at Huffman Aviation in Venice less than eighteen hours after the attack. It usually takes them that long to have lunch.

This is one of the most remarkable facts about 9/11—remarkable in the sense that it should receive close scrutiny. It looks like the FBI already knew who he was, as well as where he was, or would have been, if he hadn't vaporized himself and thousands of others. They had *known* who Atta was.

Here's a newsflash: The FBI got to Venice a lot sooner than has been reported. Instead of piling out of cars during the middle of the night 18 hours after the attack, they had Huffman Aviation employees in Venice under surveillance just a few hours later. A former Huffman Aviation manager told of a car filled with FBI agents pulling up and parking right outside his house during the middle of the afternoon on the day of the attack.

"They (the FBI) were outside my house four hours after the attack," this still-shaken aviation professional stated. Like many eyewitnesses we spoke with, this longtime aviation executive spoke of being intimidated and harassed by FBI agents. They didn't strong-arm him to make him think harder and cough up some useful leads, but to ensure he kept his mouth shut.

We've heard about this already from other people, too, haven't we? It's becoming a refrain. Hide the children honey, here comes the guy in Florsheim shoes bouncing a sap off his thigh again.

"My phones have been bugged, they still are," the former Huffman executive said. "I thought these guys (Atta & Co.) were double agents. Why is that so incriminating?"

"Double agents."

He'd said it. We had wondered as much ourselves. He said no more, except to indicate that he has lived in some fear for his life since the 9/11 attack, which is why he'd be very obliged if we didn't use his name.

"I gleaned early on that the operation I was working for had government protection," the Huffman exec stated. "They (the terrorists) were *let* into this country. How did the FBI get here so soon? Ask yourself: How'd they got here so soon?"

"Let" into this country? By *whom?* To do what?

Later we learned of a conversation this former Huffman executive—who was at the school the whole time Atta was—had with another aviation executive at the Venice Airport, who had asked him: Why'd he quit working for Rudi?

His response was a little frightening. "I had to leave and get out" said the former Huffman exec. "I wish I didn't know as much as I know. I told them they had nothing to fear from me. I had a contract to get paid and expected them to pay me."

Asked why he stopped cooperating with our Venice investigation—he stopped talking to us after just a few conversations—he said, "I've got a family to worry about."

The aviation executive he was talking to operates a maintenance facility right next door to Huffman. So he was naturally curious. What was going on at Huffman that made it so difficult to talk about now?

"You don't want to know," replied Dekker former manager. "I've got a family, you've got a family. My wife doesn't want to know any of this stuff and if you're smart, you'll do the same."

Whoa, now! We haven't heard any voices like *that* on Larry King Live! At the time of this conversation we'd been poking around in Venice for a year. It wasn't long enough to have figured things out much, but it was apparently long enough to have warranted mention at the Airport.

"He made it crystal clear that Hopsicker knows far more than he thought he knew," the second aviation exec told us. "He said, 'I know more about Wally (Hilliard) than I want to know. But I can't talk to Hopsicker any more. I can't do that to my family.'"

Maybe this is why, or partly: "FBI Knew Terrorists Were Using Flight Schools," headlined the *Washington Post* on Sept. 23, 2001. "The FBI has been aware that four or five groups linked to Osama bin Laden have operated in the United States, and known for years that suspected terrorists with ties to Osama bin Laden were receiving flight training at schools in the United States," the paper reported.

"Federal authorities have been aware for years that suspected terrorists with ties to Osama bin Laden were receiving flight training at schools in the United States and abroad, according to interviews and court testimony."

"A senior government official acknowledged to the *Post* that law enforcement officials were aware that fewer than a dozen people with links to bin Laden had attended U.S. flight schools," the paper said. "However, the official said there was no information to indicate the flight students had been planning suicide hijacking attacks."

Here's a more important question: if the FBI knew that a dozen Al Qaeda terrorists were attending U.S. flight schools, why didn't they do anything about it?

The Saudi Cover? The explanation was growing increasingly plausible. Saudis had been running loose in Florida, we will soon hear, privileged and protected. Some make it sound as if somebody sold the Sunshine State to the Saudis.

From Amanda Keller, we learned that even if Atta wasn't a Saudi Prince, he had a big Saudi connection. They were having an argument about religion one day, she said. Provoked by a comment that

Islamic customs like stoning were barbaric, Atta extolled some of the virtues of Islamic life as he saw it.

"Mohamed said, 'You American people are so stupid. You think you're so great and powerful, but you wouldn't even know if something was happening.'

"I said, 'Please. You people are over there killing each other for no damn good reason,'" Amanda told us. "'What makes you think you're so fucking great? What are you fighting over? It's just ignorant.'

"And he got mad at me, because I told him ignorance wasn't bliss. I said, 'You treat your women like shit.' And he said that's how women were meant to be treated. And I'm like, 'Oh really?'"

Even as she talked we thought: We would have paid to watch this scene play out.

"He would make fun of how we believe in God," she stated. "He said 'What do you people do for your god? You don't do anything for him.'

"And I just looked at him. He was talking to me about how American women are free to choose abortions if they want, like that was immoral, and I said, 'You guys stone people to death if they get pregnant and they're not married.' I said, you want to talk about barbaric? *That's* barbaric. Stoning somebody to death, what does that accomplish? You guys are so damn crooked that you would stab your brother in the back and not think anything about it.'

"He said, 'You don't know what you're talking about,'" she continued. Atta told her there were many rich people who funded what he did.

"He said that there was someone in Florida—some rich Arab—who had a lot of money. He said, 'Are you aware that when we come over here, your people pay to have us set up businesses?'

"Eventually, he told me, his people were going to try to take over this country. He said, 'I've been in this country many times before. I can come in and go out of America and no one ever knows.'"

This is a side of Atta we haven't seen before. Arrogant, but with a reason. He's not an infidel. He's styling. He's got Saudi Cover.

Atta wasn't the only one in Venice with Saudi Cover.

He had "friends" at Huffman who were covered too. Saudi links to the owners of Huffman Aviation began to be uncovered shortly after the attack, in a story in the *Tampa Tribune* about bin Laden family members in the U.S. flying out of the country while all other aviation except military traffic had been grounded.

"The twin-engine Lear jet streaked into the afternoon sky, leaving Tampa behind but revealing a glimpse of international intrigue in the aftermath of terrorist attacks on America," the paper reported. "The federal government says the flight never took place. But the two armed bodyguards hired to chaperon their clients out of the state recall the 100-minute trip Sept. 13 quite vividly."

The paper's headline was "Phantom Flight from Florida," maybe because the federal government says the flight never took place. It carried a Saudi Arabian prince, the son of that nation's defense minister, as well as the son of a Saudi army commander, from Tampa to Lexington, Kentucky, where other Saudi princes had been purchasing racehorses in Bluegrass Country. From there, they flew a private 747 out of the country.

A spokesman for the Federal Aviation Administration's regional office in Atlanta told reporters, "It's not in our logs… it didn't occur."

No one in the government would acknowledge to the *Tampa Tribune* what had happened. The White House referred questions on the trip to the State Department, which denied involvement, the paper reported, and the National Security Council, which did not return messages.

But two armed bodyguards hired to get their clients out of the state remembered the trip vividly: Dan Grossi, a retired Tampa cop who had worked in internal affairs and homicide, and Manuel Perez, a retired FBI agent involved in counter-terrorism. The men also provide security for the National Football League at Raymond James Stadium.

"They said it was happening," Grossi told the *Trib*." This was out of a Tom Clancy movie."

Grossi said he was told that clearance for the flight came from the White House after the Prince's family pulled a favor from former President Bush.

Grossi and Perez recalled the strange feeling of flying in the near-empty sky, knowing of the ban on private flights. "My first reaction to the pilot was, 'We're not going to get shot down are we?'" Perez said.

The enforcement of the empty skies directive was so stringent that even after the United Network for Organ Sharing sought and gained

FAA clearance to use charter aircraft on September 12 for critical deliveries of organs for transplant, one of its flights carrying a human heart was still forced to land in Bellingham, Washington.

But apparently the Saudis all got home okay, so that's some relief.

The *Tampa Tribune* report offered tantalizing glimpses of privilege accorded Saudi nationals denied to American citizens.

We figured the evacuation of the Saudis to have been accomplished through the CIA, and tried to track down the owner of the Lear in question. Since the plane took off from a private hanger at Raytheon Airport Services in Tampa, we contacted them first.

Raytheon is a major defense-intelligence industry player which spent the past decade expanding, purchasing notorious E-Systems and then merging with Hughes Electronics' defense operations (Hughes Aircraft).

When we asked who had owned the Lear that took off from their facility that morning, we learned that Catch-22 is still alive and well. Raytheon said we would have to ask the owner of the plane to tell Raytheon they could tell us who owned the plane.

"I checked our policy on disclosing owner/customer information and we decline to do so unless that owner requests that we release the information," a Raytheon spokesman told us with a faint smirk.

Since we didn't know who the owner was, how could we first ask them for permission to release their names?

Later a knowledgeable aviation source told us that the Lear jet in question had come from a Naples, Florida charter service.

"Wally Hilliard owns the only charter Lear service in southwest Florida," said the source. "If a Lear was flying that day, it would have been his."

Hilliard of course is the financier who purchased Huffman Aviation for Rudi Dekkers, and it had been the terrorist's American beach-head. So not only had Hilliard financed the operation which trained Mohamed Atta and assorted other members of his terrorist cadre to fly, but he apparently also owned a Lear jet used to extricate Saudis from the Raytheon facility in Tampa.

Tampa, of course, is also home to the Pentagon's Central Command (CentCom). It was the place from which the war in Afghanistan was run.

"Everyone's got deals with the Saudis," protested a retired Special Forces Commander at McDill AFB pressed back into service for the Afghan war, when we brought the Lear flight up to him.

"Why point a finger at this one incident?"

The FBI pointedly stated—early on—that they knew about terrorists rotating through flight schools like Rudi Dekkers' in Venice, Florida. But they always left hanging the question of why they did nothing about it. Why so reticent?

Was there a covert operation being run by another branch of the government that was using the Venice flight schools as a "portal" into a military training network that didn't check ID's real hard?

Was that why the FBI left the operation alone?

A longtime Florida observer told us bluntly that what we were dealing with was "market forces." It was the climate of intrigue created by the commodities that were being traded on Florida's overactive black market that created conditions which allowed Arabs from desert kingdoms to wander around the state as easily as if they'd been listening to Tom Petty albums all their lives.

What commodities? What black market? What had been going on that we were missing down in Venice, Florida?

As they say in TV-Land, "Let's take a closer look."

CHAPTER THIRTEEN

"EVIL IN OUR OWN BACKYARD"

On the morning of September 12, 2001, a small unexceptional town tucked into an out of the way corner on the off the beaten path Gulf Coast of Florida awoke to find itself the center of the world's attention.

Reporters arrived in waves at the tiny Venice Airport after the identity of the terrorist pilots from the World Trade Center attack and their relationship with the local flight school became known.

NBC's Kerry Sanders' report was typical: "Thirty-three-year-old Mohamed Atta, on the flight manifest of one of the suicide flights, one of those who the FBI suspects took the controls of the hijacked jet. Where did he learn to fly? Venice, Florida."

Venice, Florida where answers to some of the most important questions about what had happened were sketched-in, at least in pencil, combining to form what would rapidly become the government's official explanation for the attack.

We want to revisit a few of the key moments of that "morning after" which helped shape our perceptions. But instead of the dumbfounded shock through which we initially watched what happened that day, this time we're fortified with some hard-won knowledge.

We've all had time now to deal with the shock. The plain fact was that, like most people, we had never seen anything so horrific as what we saw September 11th. Our critical faculties had been swept away by it. There were too many poignant details filling our hearts which none will ever forget. Nor should we.

Like the chilling phone call from a flight attendant aboard American Airlines Flight 11 detailing the frantic struggle on the doomed plane as hijackers slit a passenger's throat and stormed the cockpit. Madeline Amy Sweeney's last words to her ground manager in Boston were to tell try to tell him where the hijacked plane seemed to be headed: "I see water and buildings. Oh my God! Oh my God!"

Or the stark terror faced by hundreds of men and women stranded a thousand feet in the air above a raging inferno burning on the floors below them: They had two choices, die in the fire or jump into the void and plummet for nine seconds before hitting concrete.

There was no Door Number Three.

The scenes of chaos and terror in New York were coming to us live. Those people leaping out hand-in-hand. That woman's dress billowing as she fell. A bare-chested man tumbling end over end.

Awful things were happening—live—that human beings should never have to witness, much less endure. We felt it deep. Chaos had been loosed upon the world. Upon *our* world.

Bodies littered the plaza, but we didn't see any of that until later on. Arriving at the scene, the chief of police and the Mayor saw a pair of feet in their shoes laying unattached to a body. The head of a middle-aged man went rolling down the street. A woman was sliced in half by a large sheet of glass falling out of the Towers.

Then came the stories, like Jeremy Glick's, who called his wife to tell her to lead a full life, that were almost ineffably sad.

The wisest words we heard came from New York Mayor Rudolph Giuliani, asked in a news conference to estimate how many lives had been lost.

It was too early to know, he told reporters. He said, "The number of casualties will be more than most of us can bear."

He was right.

It was in this state of shock and mourning that most of us first heard and let uncritically wash over us explanations for who had committed this unspeakable crime.

But now, with the passage of time, we can take a more clear-headed look at some of what was happening in the immediate aftermath of the attack.

The FBI first went to Huffman Aviation at 2:30 Wednesday morning. Sue DeSantis, the office manager, let them into the darkened flight school. They returned at 11 a.m., seized files, and carted away at least eight boxes of records.

On television, Rudi Dekkers was everywhere being interviewed. What the designated hitter is to baseball, Dekkers was to sound bites about the terrorists who had been living among us.

Dekkers was the designated "interview-EE."

At Huffman Aviation the parking lot quickly filled with satellite news trucks from all the major networks. Reporters from all the major newspapers and news magazines were hanging out in the lobby. Some were watching the story unfold on the TV in the reception area; others were standing outside smoking and trying to chat up employees.

Everyone was there to talk to Rudi Dekkers. He was on the *Today Show*, ABC's *Good Morning America*, the CBS *Early Show*, the Dan Rather CBS *Evening News*, *Larry King Live*, CNN *LIVE* with Greta Van Sustern, Peter Jennings on *ABC World News Tonight*. He even entered Bill O'Reilly's *No Spin Zone*.

Rudi was doing a lot of fast talking, a talent which local newspapers had already noted he possessed. Waiting for interviews, reporters exchanged ironic side-bar items so bizarre you knew they were true. One of Flight 11 hijackers left a Koran in a strip club in Daytona Beach. The coffee shop at Huffman Aviation gave its entrees aviation-related names. The bacon cheeseburger was known as the "Emergency Descent."

While Al Gore and George W. Bush had been fiercely contesting an election all over the state in the biggest news story of the previous year, Mohamed Atta and Marwan Al-Shehhi had been buzzing up and down the coast of that same state in Cessnas.

Who knew?

Standing under the glare of TV lights on the apron of the Venice Airport the day after the attack, Rudi Dekkers told us what he knew. Or at least he seemed to... in retrospect, as we'll see, it looks as if he may have been making up big chunks of it up as he went along.

Over and over, Dekkers denied any responsibility for the terrorists being in our midst. "They came in through the front door," he told reporters. He said they claimed to be Afghans who had entered this country from Germany.

"They were normal students and worked very hard. They lived nearby and bicycled here every day," said Dekkers.

At 46, Rudi Dekkers was a round, middle-aged, unprepossessing and slightly florid man who nonetheless spoke and answered questions with what one reporter noted was a "clipped Dutch accent and a tone that suggests he's used to barking out orders."

If a global network had assisted the development of the terrorist conspiracy which led to the operation, Rudi Dekkers would be the first place to look. Both before and after the attack, an unexplained element of intrigue was swirling around him.

Yet Dekkers seemed free with advice, both to law enforcement and Congress, about preventing future attacks. He had saved the day, he said, when those slackers at the FBI were about to leave his flight school without all of the pertinent records.

"It was yesterday, 2:30 a.m. they called my managers here in Venice and wanted the C-2 files," he explained on CBS. " I came in at 7:00 in the morning, they were still there, I talked briefly with them. They told me they were ready to go. I told them that we had more customers, clients from the Middle East and I thought it was a good idea to gave them all my files. So I gave them a couple of hundred files from the last years."

Good save, dude.

One of his staffers set up a press conference in what looked like a classroom. Some rolled their eyes at the idea that this man was holding a news conference, wrote one reporter who was there. There was talk that Dekkers was a media hound. As it turns out, the talk was correct.

"I asked him why he was doing so many interviews," his office manager Sue DeSantis told us months later. "Rudi said because it was the best free advertising we would ever get."

Mr. Dekkers was, apparently, not one to waste time on remorse when there was a buck to be made.

The beefy Dekkers was at times a little difficult to understand. He spoke defensively through a thick European accent, but his defensiveness was easier to understand than his accent. Who wouldn't be defensive in such an intense media spotlight over such a numbingly horrific event?

Yet, and this is important, despite all his "face time," his testimony was surprisingly devoid of revelations or insights. We didn't learn much, except that he didn't like Atta.

"If you see the picture in the newspaper, you see the face, tell me what you think," he said. "I just didn't like the face. I have no explanation."

He did, however, sort of like the chubby one. "The other guy," said Dekkers, referring to Al-Shehhi, "was the teddy bear. He was friendly. I have found out, in my life, that chubby guys are always a little bit more friendly."

The day after witnessing 3,000 vaporized bodies, Rudi Dekkers holding forth on Larry King on his theory about the jolly nature of chubby guys seemed more than just a little beside the point.

But, they let him get away with it.

Dekkers insisted to all who would listen that, where the terrorists were concerned, he was filled with an unspeakably murderous rage:

"This morning at 7:00 I heard what happened, and the first thing I questioned myself was, if I would have known, I would kill them with my own bare hands. If I have a Muslim coming in right now I think I'm going to be a human being and tell them get the hell out of my property here."

In another interview he said, "We feel awful that we had these awful men, no, these monsters, in this school. If I saw them now, I would want to murder them, kill them, like every other American at this moment."

His reassurances may have had a purpose. Tensions were running high.

About 3 p.m., officers from the Sarasota County Sheriff's Office and the Venice Police Department arrived at Huffman Aviation, saying they were looking for a suspicious blue Toyota that reportedly was on the premises.

"I hope they're not going to plant a bomb here, if they're really here," said an employee behind the desk who did not want to give his name.

Several minutes later, the law enforcement officials left the building, saying there was no danger. The vehicle had belonged to a Brazilian news crew.

"A couple of people called and said, 'How could you do this'?" explained Greg Woods, a flight instructor at Huffman. "Emotions are very high."

Earlier that day, the *Venice Gondolier* ran a huge black headline across the top of the paper: "Evil in Our Back Yard." Underneath was a picture of Rudi Dekkers facing a phalanx of TV cameras, speaking into a forest of microphones.

The irony of the juxtaposition did not go unnoticed.

"At first everyone just thought it was kind of funny," said a family member of a Huffman employee, "because it made Dekkers look like he was the 'evil' in our backyard, which the newspaper probably didn't mean.

"And then it hit me that he'd started his flight school not long before those two terrorists moved into town. And it gave me the chills."

Less than 24 hours after the Sept. 11 attack, Rudi Dekkers, whose school will eventually be shown to have trained a veritable squadron of terrorist pilots, seemed impervious to suspicion.

What suspicion? He was schmoozing with the King himself on *Larry King Live*.

"Were they of a nationality other than American?" King asked.

"No, they were—my people took copies of their passports when they came in, because they need to show a ID And, apparently, they were—one of them was an Afghanistan. I don't know what the other one was," replied Dekkers.

"I don't see the files myself because I have my managers taking care of that. I have spoken with one of them on several occasions. And Mr. Atta, I spoke to him one time five minutes."

Larry King showed why he is famous for never preparing for an interview, asking Dekkers, "That's Mohammed Atta, right?"

"Mohamed Atta, that's correct."

Hard-hitting American journalism is the envy of the Free World.

Larry King's sign-off with Dekkers was love and kisses:

"Rudi, thank you," King murmurs. "I know how tough this must be for you."

Tough for the rest of us maybe. Not tough for Dekkers. CBS's Jane Clayson on the CBS Morning News asked him: "And I know it is difficult, because you in some sense feel a little bit of responsibility, don't you?"

"No, we don't feel responsible for what happened at all," Dekkers replied. "No. Not nothing."

He was just running a business. There was a mercantilist approach to much of what he said.

"I don't need anything from you, just a check to start flying."

He likened flying lessons to shopping for groceries.

"We're just a business."

The stream of Middle Eastern men who walked up to his counter, thrust out cash money—ten thousand dollars at a time—what did we expect him to do? Not take it?

It had not registered on him as a source for concern. All he did was take their money, and then teach them to fly.

But he didn't teach them to fly *into* anything.

Most took his point. But for Dekkers' school, at a tiny airport located on a former military installation, the connection to terrorists Mohamed Atta and Marwan Al-Shehhi prompted troublesome questions about his operations.

Dekkers said his school was typical of what existed in Florida and the rest of the United States. For years, he said, flight schools have been advertising on the lucrative foreign market. More than two-thirds of Huffman's students were from overseas. He owned another flight school further south in Naples, FL that also catered to foreigners. In a wire service report three days after the WTC disaster, Dekkers was quoted saying, "I can tell you that there's definitely some flaws in the system."

Later we would realize it had been one of his few truthful statements.

"The day that all this occurred, we felt very, very sad like all the other Americans," he said, on the *CBS Morning News*.

Expressions of sympathy are clearly in order. But Dekkers isn't American, he's Dutch.

His flight school offered instruction in light single-engine aircraft, he said. But not in commercial jetliners. He insisted the terrorist pilots couldn't have learned to hit skyscrapers with 757's merely from enrolling in his school.

He had followed the law. He repeatedly stated the terrorist pilots—Atta and Marwan—were people who basically walked in off the street into his school at the Venice Airport.

Dan Rather, the only newsman in Dealey Plaza during the Kennedy Assassination, didn't see anything then and not much has changed. Rather asked Dekkers, "Is this unusual for someone to come from Afghanistan or, for that matter, anyplace overseas, show up at the door and say, 'OK, I'll pay you the $10,000. Train me to fly.' Is that unusual?"

"If—if we call that 2 or 3 percent of the business is that way and it's unusual, yes," Dekkers replied. "But there are numerous students who are not happy with the flight school where they are and they just are already in the United States and they go to another flight school where they're happy. They told us they were flying in—in another area where they were not happy and they wanted to change flight schools."

There had been *another flight school.*

Federal investigators returned to Venice Municipal Airport late the day after the attack and combed through records at the Florida Flight Training Center, owned by Arne Kruithof.

Like Dekkers', Kruithof was a Dutch national. His doors were closed while federal investigators, who declined to say what they were looking for, worked inside.

A sign on the door read: "Due to a national emergency, we will be closed until further notice."

Kruithof said he couldn't talk about the federal investigation that had shined a spotlight on the small airport and the two Dutch-owned flight schools. "All our records were sacrificed yesterday (Wednesday) as part of that investigation. I can't release any information about what was taken."

In all, 27 terrorists were trained to fly, the *LA Times* reported. Among the four hundred foreign nationals who rotated through Dekkers' two flight schools—the second down the road in Naples—an as yet undisclosed number had been terrorists. While the number remained undisclosed in the months ahead it was nonetheless slowly growing.

There was no speculation in the media, however, about why young men with a pronounced weakness for lingerie models and strippers had chosen a sleepy enclave filled with widows with blue hair, so far from the pleasures of infidel flesh.

Take this pop quiz. Multiple choice. You've only got a year to live. Would you go move to Leisure World? Or head to Vegas?

While Dekkers insisted the terrorist pilots had only the most fleeting of associations with his flight school, and hotly denied being anything other than a victimized businessman, questions remained. There were over 200 flight schools, just in Florida alone.

Yet somehow the hijackers leaned towards one or the other of the two schools in Venice. The twin Venice flight schools were the terrorist's American beachhead. Rudi Dekkers' Huffman Aviation was the terrorist's Omaha Beach. What had made these two schools so popular with the terrorist cadre?

No one asked.

The only investigation being conducted pointed a finger directly at an obscure outfit most had never even heard of called Al Qaeda. The Base.

While the FBI was, presumably, actively looking for any international networks that might have assisted the terrorists, were any likely suspects overlooked? Maybe even *protected* from scrutiny? Maybe the FBI should have taken a peek closer to home.

Because it did not seem like the FBI was looking too deeply or too hard. We interviewed numerous material eyewitnesses with important information who were never contacted by the FBI, which supposedly fielded 400 agents in Florida until the anthrax attack changed their focus.

"The FBI came down almost immediately after September 11," said Huffman office manager Sue DeSantis, the employee who let the FBI into the school at 2.30 in the morning. She later told us. "It just totally amazed me that they took everything Rudi said as the truth."

Could the FBI be, somehow, *institutionally* incurious? Or maybe they didn't need to investigate Rudi Dekkers because they already knew who he was.

Danielle Clarke was the office manager at Ambassador Aviation in Naples. "The first thing I noticed on Sept. 11 when I walked into Ambassador was they had all these TV's on, one big one in reception, and another in the student room, and they had never been on before," she told us.

Clarke said she noticed something strange about the way the FBI agent who was there talked to Rudi. "I could hear them in the other office. The FBI agent was coaching Rudi on what to tell the reporters outside."

For some reason, a lack of enthusiasm permeated the FBI's investigation of Rudi Dekkers, the man who ran the FBO (fixed base operation) at the tiny airport as well as the flight school.

Forty years ago, the Bureau displayed a similar lack of enthusiasm in investigating another man who ran an FBO, CIA agent David Ferrie in New Orleans.

A researcher called to say that Dekkers sounded phony to her when she'd seen him on TV.

"The single biggest weak link in the current case is Rudi Dekkers of Huffman Aviation in Venice Florida, just minutes away from where the President was when the attack occurred," she wrote. "He's the guy that trained the pilots. Look at his corporate records, they're on file—on the Net even. Look at his links to companies that claim they're leasing 757's and 767's from an airline that doesn't own any. Look at how many businesses he's involved with. Look at who flies in and out of the airport where he operates. Find out why he hasn't filed his required annual reports with the Florida Secretary of State's office listing his officers."

We found it bizarre that no one in the media questioned Dekkers publicly about what role he may have played, or what he may have done to facilitate what happened on September 11.

If the FBI was buying his explanations, however, it wasn't on account of his sterling reputation.

Two weeks before the World Trade Center attack, Nicole Antini, an employee of Dekkers, filed suit to enforce settlement of a sexual harassment suit against him. "I tolerated Rudi's advances because I needed to keep my job," said the former Dekkers' employee in court documents.

"As long as I have worked at Huffman Aviation, I have been subjected to sexual harassment by Rudi Dekkers," she stated.

Court documents revealed that this wasn't just garden variety sexual harassment. No inadvertent touch or misunderstood word. The employee was eighteen. Her employer, Rudi Dekkers, had apparently gotten a thrill from sticking broom handles up the back of her dress when she wasn't looking. Several months later, he would be invited to testify before the Congress of the United States of America on preventing future terrorist attacks.

We still find this odd.

Amanda Keller knew Rudi Dekkers. "I saw Rudi Dekkers. He's a total pervert. A nasty, nasty man," she told us.

"He said to me one time, 'What would it take for me to have a piece of you?'"

"I looked at him and said, 'You're lucky I don't hit you,' and his secretary applauded me. He told her to sit down and shut up."

So Dekkers wasn't being shielded from serious scrutiny because he sang loud in church. What, then? Why was Rudi Dekkers protected? And by whom? Flight school owners don't have juice like that.

Where did he get his stroke?

Rudi Dekkers was covered, we discovered, by the same umbrella his flight student Mohamed Atta huddled under. Rudi was a grateful beneficiary of "Saudi Cover."

While Dekkers had been minimizing his involvement with the terrorists in front of reporters in Venice the day after the attack, across the state in Vero Beach, CNN reported, FBI agents were searching houses occupied by Saudi pilots they found suspicious who said they were on a 15-month pilot's course at Huffman Aviation.

News accounts reported the same thing. One said, "Some of the kamikaze pilots had pilot licenses that indicated they were sponsored or employed by Saudi Arabian Airlines, which is owned by the Saudi government."

Not a single reporter pressed Dekkers on his Saudi connections, He got a pass.

The story of his cozy Saudi relations doesn't end there. It goes right to the bin Laden family itself.

By three weeks after the attack, people were standing clear of Rudi Dekkers on the tarmac at the Venice Airport. Former associates pled ignorance. Key employees declined comment, saying they were "no longer with the company."

Late at night in Venice, when it got really quiet, you could almost hear the mournful sound of people whistling past the graveyard. Some seemed already to be constructing a defense. Venice Airport Manager Larry Heath told reporters the city's relations with Huffman hadn't been the same since Dekkers took over, as if he weren't one of the city officials responsible for approving his presence at the Airport.

Airport Manager Heath allowed that the revelations about Venice's connection to the terrorist attacks were "absolutely amazing."

He said, "I hope it doesn't give us a black eye."

CHAPTER FOURTEEN

THE VENICE
"MAGIC DUTCH BOYS"

One of the most puzzling questions about 9/11 has to do with the competency and skill displayed by the terrorist pilots. What's curious is that Atta and Marwan's flight school instructors in Florida said they were poor students and poor pilots. The impression created was that the duo were zealots, brand-new commercial pilots on a misbegotten mission.

Despite this testimony, numerous observers cite the pilots at the controls of the hijacked jets for a cool efficiency which provoked a grudging respect for their *professional* talents.

Was Atta a better pilot then they let on?

"Their capacity to operate the aircraft was substantial," said Attorney General Ashcroft. "It's very clear that these orchestrated, coordinated assaults on our country were well-conducted, and conducted in a technically proficient way."

An ex-military pilot told us: "They swooped down on the World Trade Center like a pair of fighter jets. The terrorists were flying bulky 200-ton Boeing 767 jetliners so smoothly they obviously had considerable flying skills."

"The hits on all three 9/11 buildings were damned difficult, and not at all the 'stuff' of new commercial pilots," he continued. "It's possible they were former fighter pilots, cycled through Florida flight schools used as a 'cutout.'"

Investigating the large-scale training of possible terrorist pilots would become a crucial law enforcement concern. An FBI list of more than 220 people wanted for questioning as possible associates of the hijackers contained at least 32 pilots, five student pilots and 12 aircraft mechanics. Dozens of those sought for questioning were trained as pilots.

Remember: "Your 'legend' is your cover story, the lie that holds together long enough to let you slip away." Mohamed Atta's "Islamic extremist" legend had begun falling apart in South Florida's bars and strip joints, just as Lee Harvey Oswald's "communist" legend did when news of his presence at anti-Castro paramilitary camps in Louisiana came out.

Let's take a look at the legend of Rudi Dekkers as "flight school owner," to see if it, too, is beginning to fray around the edges.

For his part, Dekkers professed no concern over his role in the tragedy. Summing up his sentiments about it, he said, "At the beginning, it was bad. We had some death threats. Now, basically, all we hear is good news. People come up and say, 'Aren't you the guy who owns Huffman Aviation?' And they shake hands with me."

Just as the "Magic Bullet Theory"—one bullet passing through multiple bodies, intact and unharmed—was the only way the Warren Commission could sell its lone gunman story, the FBI's version of what happened in Venice relies on similarly-twisted logic.

It's called the "Magic Dutch Boy Theory," and it's required to explain how all those terrorist pilots could have been at two separate Dutch-owned flight schools and have it all just be another freak coincidence.

Dekkers, who is, of course, Dutch, had purchased Huffman in the year before the terrorists began to arrive. While everyone else was pondering the Internet bust, Atta and Marwan spent their days in small Cessnas, building time.

The terrorist duo practicing touch and go's in the humid September air on Florida's Gulf coast were joined by a third terrorist, Siad Al-Jarrah, who moved in next door to Huffman at Kruithof's Florida Flight Training Center.

Like Dekkers' school, this second Venice flight school had also recently changed ownership. The new owner was—of all things—another Dutch national. Arne Kruithof was from Rotterdam in the Netherlands.

Other members of the Hamburg cadre came too. Bald-headed Zacarias Moussaoui was in Venice, and Ramzi bin al-Shib paid money to attend as well as others we will hear of later.

Dutch national Kruithof's purchase of the second of the two Venice flight schools while countryman Dekkers purchased the other has led to the two being dubbed the "Magic Dutch Boys."

But they've got more than a nickname. They've got a whole theory named after them. The notion that it is just coincidence that almost all of the key members of Atta's Hamburg cadre came to Florida to learn to fly at two separate recently-purchased Dutch-owned flight schools at the tiny Venice Airport is called the "Magic Dutch Boy Theory."

Someday, perhaps, it will be taught in college, in the history of the 21st Century. The chief tenet of the "Magic Dutch Boy Theory" is: "Two foreign nationals purchasing flight schools at the same airport at about the same time which are soon hubcap-deep in Arab terrorist pilot-wannabees is just a magical, or freak, coincidence."

It is the official position of the chief investigative agency of the United States Government, the FBI.

Others disagree.

"Two Dutch boys buying adjacent flight schools which shortly thereafter get 'overrun' by terrorists is one damn Dutch boy too many," growled one nationally-known law enforcement figure.

"It's untidy."

"It seemed kind of odd when Dekkers bought his flight school here," said Coy Jacobs, owner of Mooney Aviation, "because the only other flight school in town is owned by Arne Kruithof, and he's Dutch too and the odds of that are pretty slim."

Bob Mudge is the genial editor of the local *Venice Gondolier.* He told us: "I've heard a lot of rumors that I haven't been able to substantiate about connections between them and other businesses here and entities and agencies outside the area. It's certainly something you have to say is a very interesting coincidence."

If the appearance of two Dutch nationals purchasing flight schools months apart isn't just a freak coincidence belonging in *Ripley's Believe it Or Not,* then the FBI is covering up something in Venice.

Were Rudi Dekkers and Arne Kruithof acting as "cut-outs" in an effort to provide that ever-popular "plausible deniability"? Was Huffman funneling their trainees into further training?

Could the CIA have been running a covert operation in Venice? Training pilots for Osama bin Laden, in an effort to penetrate his organization that somehow had gone horribly wrong?

Someday they'll be adding a "Magic Dutch Boy Wing" next to the "Magic Bullet Wing" of the Secret History Museum.

We came across a business profile written about Rudi Dekkers months before the 9/11 attack. The two flight schools at Venice Municipal Airport catered almost exclusively to international students, said the Sarasota Herald.

Rudi Dekkers had trained some 800 foreign students at his school during the past two years. Dekkers told reporters he had 200 students at this facility at any given time, and estimated 80 percent were foreign.

Venice residents said Florida Flight Training also had numerous international students.

Dekkers, 44 at the time of the attack, was born in Holland, and began flying in 1981, in between working as a computer salesman and real estate broker.

In 1985, he earned his European commercial pilot's license and left Holland for the warm beaches and pretty blue waters of the Florida Gulf Coast, where he settled with his wife Astrid in Naples, and "quickly fell in love with the States."

"Dekkers does have some financial support from sources other than customers," reported the paper, citing a retired Naples insurance magnate as one big backer. Dekkers also owned Ambassador Airways in Naples, the story said. He had been operating charter flight services for nine years.

That "financial support from sources other than customers" the article references is Wallace J. Hilliard, a 70 year-old "retired" insurance executive originally from Green Bay, Wisconsin. Even before the tragedy of September 11th, both men's dealings had lifted eyebrows at the Venice Airport.

Though they got a free ride from the national media, that was not the case with people at the airport, where, among their aviation peers, a cloud of suspicion hung over their operations.

Arne Kruithof was expected to testify at the trial of the so-called 20th hijacker, Zacarias Moussaoui, we learned; where he would also presumably be grilled about his relationship with Rudi Dekkers, as well as his partner Pascal Schreier, a German national living in Munich.

Their joint company, Aviation Aspirations, provided both financial assistance and also what the company called a "Mentor Programme." About their "mentoring programme," their literature said, "The help is both financial and practical. We now provide one-to-one practical assistance from experienced Professional Pilots (our Mentors) whom we have established throughout the world."

The company's motto was "Better training because we care."

We wondered what they meant by "special mentoring." Was a "mentor" the same as a "handler"? Was Aviation Aspirations a front for recruiting intelligence assets in the guise of training people to fly?

Dekkers and Kruithof insisted they had never met each other until they separately decided running a flight school in Venice seemed a good idea. The truth, however, would turn out to be an altogether different proposition.

"I knew Rudi Dekkers," said Tom Hammersley, former chief flight instructor at Kruithof's school. "My former employer, Arne Kruithof, and Rudi Dekkers, they are both Dutch. They go back a long time."

So Dekkers was lying. When people lie, it's usually for a reason.

Another odd link between Dekkers and Kruithof was a German named Pascal Schreier, who had recruited students for them in, among other places, Hamburg, where Atta's Hamburg cadre was based.

Probably just a freak coincidence.

"I know Pascal Schreier, too," Hammersley told us, when we asked about him. "I worked with him as part of Florida Flight Training Center. He's a German boy, and he did a lot of recruiting of students over in Europe, sending them over to Arne."

Although the two Venice Dutch Boys ran what were supposedly competing flight schools, strangely, Pascal Schreier appears to have been in business with both of them. He was an officer of a company called Florida Sunrise Aviation at the Venice Airport. Dekkers was an officer in a company at the same airport called Sunrise Aviation.

Another freak coincidence?

Rudi Dekkers said Atta and his sidekick just showed up at his facility one day. He had, instead, been actively marketing his flight school in Germany at *the exact time* Mohamed Atta and his terrorist cell left Hamburg and moved to Florida.

Dekkers began an aggressive European marketing campaign right after purchasing Huffman, said a story headlined "New owners of Huffman Aviation have global presence," in the *Venice Gondolier.*

Dekkers talked to the paper about his plans for the newly-purchased company. "The world is my working place," he boasted.

"I won't forget Venice, but I'm going to market throughout the world, Germany, France, Belgium. That's our goal, to get people to come in here from all over the world."

His plans were apparently successful. They soon changed the make-up of his two flight schools. Foreign nationals came to account for over 80 per cent of the student pilots enrolled with him.

His two schools were training four hundred foreign nationals a year, said the paper.

After Atta moved from Germany to train with Dekkers' flight school in Venice, at least four other members of the same terrorist cell moved there to train as pilots as well, according to German prosecutors.

We met a wizened old pilot who's flown in the area for over 15 years. Two years ago, said Danny Schultz, he'd noticed a change in the type of pilot trainees. "Many times I went to lunch with these folks, and some of them could hardly speak English, from various countries in the Middle East. There was a recent influx of these types of trainees. Before, you'd never seen much Middle Eastern traffic. Then one day, all of a sudden they're marching across the tarmac."

What if Mohamed hadn't gone to the mountain, but, instead, the mountain—in the guise of the portly Dekkers—had come to Mohamed?

If Atta was in contact with Dekkers' recruiters while still in Hamburg, instead of just showing up in Venice, that could explain statements by officials early on that the key to unraveling the plot might not lie in the United States, but in Germany.

Rudi Dekkers, as we've seen, had "Saudi Cover." But it went well beyond a contract with Saudi Arabian Airlines. The French newspaper *Le Monde* reported that Osama bin Laden's Geneva, Switzerland-based brother Yeslam had also been sending student pilots to Venice for training.

Yeslam bin Laden is one of three half brothers of Osama bin laden who head the Saudi Bin Laden Group, the parent company of the family's far-flung business ventures, which include construction, tele-communications and finance. He has been called a key figure in the family's business empire.

Swiss police questioned Yeslam because one of his companies, Av-con Air Charter, had offered flight training to clients at the Venice flight school attended by some of the hijackers. As a result of what Le Monde called "a still unexplained coincidence," the pilots of Yeslam bin Laden's company trained at Huffman Aviation in Florida, the paper stated.

"I didn't chose that flight school," Yeslam protested. "I don't have contact with my half-brother since over 20 years ago."

Swiss magazine *L'Hebdo* reported that Swiss federal inspectors were seeking information on the activities of several bin Laden family companies, including Geneva-based Saudi Investment Company, a financial clearinghouse for the family's international investments, and Avcon Business Jets SA, which owned a fleet of private jets which it leased to clients.

In a rare public statement, the head of the bin Laden family business explained that he had only invested in aviation "because I am passionately fond of flying."

But, he said, he was also passionately fond of "tennis, skiing and the cinema." Yeslam said that Avcon "rents planes, provides services to clients, but didn't participate in the instruction of pilots."

Yet Mohamed Atta and his sidekick bodyguard Marwan had told the chief flight instructor at one of their schools that their future plans were with the nationally-owned Saudi airline.

"I asked them (Atta and Marwan) specifically about what their goals were, and they said they wanted to learn to fly so that they could go fly for 'Saudia.' For people coming from that part of the world, 'Saudia' would be the premier airline of the Middle East," stated Tom Hamer-sley, the terrorists duo's chief flight instructor at Jones Aviation.

Then we learned that, incredibly, four additional 9/11 terrorist sus-pects at Dekkers schools had fled the U.S. in haste just days before the attack. Three of the fleeing students were Saudi nationals. All four had been training at one of Dekkers' two flight schools. Aviation observers at the airport shook their heads. It heightened the sense of intrigue which swirled around the controversial Dekkers.

News of the additional terror suspects schools broke in accounts of FBI raids on a house in the Miami area.

FBI agents spent two days in South Florida searching an unoccupied Palm Beach County home which had been hastily abandoned by a Saudi family just two days before the attacks on the World Trade Center and Pentagon.

Saudi Mohammed Almasri and his family had first moved into the home in question in July 2000, the FBI said. His son was a student at Huffman Aviation at the same time hijackers Mohamed Atta and Marwan Al-Shehhi studied there.

The other three new terror suspects had been training at the Dekkers-owned Ambassador Aviation, in Naples, 100 miles south of Venice.

One of the three fled the U.S. in haste just days before the attack. The sad story of 22 year-old Marwan Mohammed Shemina provides a glimpse into the intrigue going on at Dekkers' schools.

Shemina, who told school officials his father worked for the United Nations in Rome, abruptly ceased training and disappeared under mysterious circumstances days before the 9/11 attack, stated Danielle Clarke, a former flight training executive at the school.

School officials spoke with the FBI about Shemina's sudden departure, she said, as well as the departures of two other Saudi student pilots just before the attack: Kamran Hussain, traveling on a UK passport, and Ahmad Badri, who had a Swedish passport.

Unlike most student pilots, who are enthused to learn to fly, Marwan Shemisa was an extremely reluctant 19 year-old student pilot, said Danielle.

He holed up in his hotel room and wouldn't emerge to begin flight lessons until after his mother had been dispatched from Rome to buck up her son.

"Marwan didn't want to be here," Clarke said, "He arrived two weeks late, took two lessons, and then took sick and stayed in his hotel room for 10 days. When his father called the school, I asked him if we should ship him back."

"'Absolutely not,' he said. 'He's over there to achieve something and he's not coming back.'"

Shortly thereafter his mother arrived, a Libyan woman wearing traditional Arab clothing who lived in Rome, and Marwan began taking flight training again, but without any enthusiasm, said Clarke.

"He didn't look at all happy. He appeared very depressed, and only brightened up when talking about playing football (soccer) in the streets of Rome. So one day I asked him, 'What is it with you?' I said, 'You don't know how lucky you are to have your parents paying for flight training!'"

"I want to be a football player," he told her.

She asked him if he would like her to relay his desires to his parents. "No. They want me to be a pilot," he replied, "You don't understand, I don't have any say in the matter."

Then, the week before the attack, and just two days shy of completing his courses and getting his multi-engine license, Marwan Shemina's father—who had previously been insistent his son stay and take lessons—abruptly commanded him to leave.

"It's ridiculous, like dropping out of college a few days before the end of your last semester," she explained.

Danielle implored the father to let his son finish his courses. "Couldn't you extend his stay by just two days so he can finish his multi-rating license?" she asked.

His reply: "Absolutely not."

On the unhappy youth's final day at the school, Danielle asked if he was looking forward to going back to Italy.

Even today, Marwan Shemisa's reply is chilling. He had had another change of plans he told Danielle. He was headed for what authorities later called the assembly point for most of the hijackers.

"I'm not going back to Italy," Marwan said. "I'm going to Boston."

"What? Why are you going to Boston?" she asked.

"Because I have to," he said. "You don't understand, I don't have a choice."

Several days after his sudden departure the hotel he'd been staying at called the school, asking what they should do with his clothes and several very large trunks, all of which he'd left behind, as if in haste.

Marwan Shemina disappeared on September 6, 2001, taking a flight to Boston. It is not known for sure if he was on board any of the hijacked planes. The school has not heard from him.

But he was telling the truth about one thing: His father did work at the U.N.

"Eighty per cent of his tuition was being paid for by the United Nations, which was where he said his father worked," said Danielle. "I took it to be a perk of his father's job at the U.N."

There was something *else* strange, too... The FBI had been more interested in the two Saudi students that disappeared. They had not appeared concerned with Shemisa.

"But when they returned the school's records to us, there was only one file missing: Marwan Shemisa's," said Danielle Clarke. "That file never reappeared, although we are supposed to have it by law."

We were able to get a brief interview with the financier whose money purchased both of Dekkers' flight schools, 70 year-old Wallace Hilliard, of Naples, FL. One of the things we asked him to explain was the large number of Arab students in his flight schools "marching across the tarmac."

Hilliard angrily denied reports of the number of Arab students with a terrorist bent who had flocked—so far inexplicably—to his and Dekkers' flight schools. He said, "I'm sorry, what you are saying is grossly untrue. I believe that there were two Arab students, not 22, only two. There were two, period. Two total."

In point of fact, news of the four additional terror suspects brought the current total of 9/11 cadre terrorists known to have been enrolled at flight schools owned by the "Magic Dutch Boys" to *eight*.

Rudi Dekkers' figure alone stood at five.

We also asked Hilliard about his associations with persons of clearly dubious repute, Dekkers among them.

"I've done some stupid things," Hilliard replied. "I have done some very stupid things with airplanes, and it has cost me lots of money."

One of the "stupid things" Hilliard is referring to was the seizure of a Lear jet he owned, on the tarmac of Orlando Executive airport in early July of 2000. DEA agents brandishing automatic weapons surrounded the plane before discovering 43 pounds of heroin onboard.

That deal had cost somebody lots of money. We hoped it wasn't Hilliard.

CHAPTER FIFTEEN

CHALK & CHEESE

The world would have little need to take note of Wally Hilliard and Rudi Dekkers were it not for the fact that their purchase of Huffman Aviation, for an undisclosed sum in June of 1999, set in motion a chain of events that ended in tragedy.

It was their business decision which sixteen months later resulted in people hanging at dizzying heights out of windows high above New York.

Atta's Hamburg cadre, and the Arab terrorist bombers of the early 1990s—several of whom also attended flight schools in the U.S.—clustered in a handful of flight schools. The terrorists didn't have complete and unfettered access to any U.S. flight school they pleased. They were funneled through only a few *special* schools: the Magic Dutch Boys, Airman in Oklahoma, and a couple in Arizona and California. The so-called 20th hijacker, Zacharias Moussaoui, who also has links at the Venice Airport, spent three months at Airman and everything was cool. When he showed up at a flight school in Minnesota not in this "special category," flight instructors at the school called in the FBI the *very next day.*

Wally Hilliard and Rudi Dekkers weren't even in the flight school business, we slowly discovered. These were not two guys forming a partnership to make a profit selling goods or services.

The Dekkers-Hilliard partnership lost money from the first day it began. There was no hint it mattered to either man.

It is widely known—and confirmed by Hilliard himself in filings at the Sarasota Courthouse—that the Naples financier lost between five and seven million dollars in his aviation partnerships with Dekkers.

But that was clearly all right with him, because when they bought Huffman Aviation, they were *already* losing sizable amounts of money every month at the *first* flight school they'd purchased, in Naples.

"When they bought Huffman, they were already losing $40,000 a month on the Naples school," said Stuart Burchill, a former Hilliard accountant. "It was ridiculous. No one could understand why they'd want to double the pain."

Their decision, to their own accountant, made no *business* sense. Whatever Dekkers and Hilliard were doing together during the two years and six months between the purchase of Huffman and the 9/11 attack, had nothing to do with prospering in business.

Nor were Dekkers and Hilliard diehard aviation enthusiasts using the flight schools as playthings, or a hobby. Dekkers was far too busy with a variety of illegal ventures to have been any sort of connoisseur of flight.

And while the 70 year-old Wally Hilliard *is* a pilot, he has an unfortunate "tic" that would seem to indicate that he could find a more suitable hobby than flying… He suffers from a narcoleptic condition which causes him to fall asleep at irregular intervals—while at the controls of airplanes he is flying, for example.

So whatever their motivation for turning up at the Venice Airport as new owners of Huffman Aviation, they weren't just two entrepreneurs looking to share in the glorious promise of free enterprise.

The fact is, Rudi Dekkers never made a dime teaching people to fly airplanes, and the "legend" of Rudi Dekkers as "flight school owner" is a sham.

This is important information in any real understanding of what happened on 9/11, because the controversial Dekkers is not just a run-of-the-mill con-man and quick-fading historical footnote. Dekkers was at the critical nexus of the terrorist conspiracy.

When Atta and Marwan made their fateful journey to America, when they arrived in Venice it was Rudi Dekkers assigning bunks on this side of the Big Pond.

Records from his flight school were deemed sensitive enough to have merited being escorted back to Washington by Florida Governor Jeb Bush aboard a C-130 cargo plane which left Sarasota less than 24 hours after the September 11 attack.

So, if Hilliard and Dekkers weren't in the flight training business, what business *were* they in? What kind of business were they transacting while terrorists practiced touch and go's on the runways at the Venice Airport?

And why would someone go through the motions of *pretending* to be in a business they really weren't in?

The answer is simple, straightforward, and, we think, ultimately inescapable: Rudi Dekkers and Wally Hilliard used owning the two flight schools as *cover* for their other activities.

The first person we asked about Dekkers when we first arrived in Florida was a man who had just recently been pressed back into service, out of nearby McDill Air Force Base in Tampa, because his experience in the early '80s running "Northern Alliance guys" in Afghanistan was deemed useful. He had also been a "troubleshooter" during the Presidency of Ronald Reagan. What he told us was chilling.

"Rudi's greedy, and when you're greedy you can be *used* for something," he muttered darkly. He would offer nothing further.

Charlie Voss put it into perspective, in an interview on his front doorstep six months after the attack. Voss was the former Huffman Aviation bookkeeper who provided a place for Atta and Marwan to stay when they got to Venice. His house had been surrounded by reporters the day after the attack.

Now things were quieter, and Charlie had some surprising things to say. Clearly, he'd been mulling over the same things we had.

"When something doesn't make obvious business sense," he said, "sometimes it's because things are being done for another reason that doesn't have a lot to do with dollars and cents."

When we asked for a comment on his former boss Dekkers, he said, "His business did not add up."

The "business" begin with an article in the June 15, 1999 *Sarasota Herald-Tribune* announcing the take-over of Huffman Aviation:

"Venice Municipal Airport's flight school and charter and aircraft maintenance services have swapped hands among Naples owners, who own a similar operation called Ambassador Airways at Naples Airport," said the paper.

"They bought the Venice business from Stanley Huffman of Naples, who founded the company 25 years ago."

There were some odd "anomalies" in the circumstances surrounding the purchase of Huffman Aviation that occasioned comment out at the Venice Airport. When Hilliard and Dekkers arrived brandishing a big roll and proceeding in short order to purchase the flight school, they paid such an inflated price for the business that it appeared to local aviation observers that money was no object.

There was talk. Rumors flew.

"They made the deal overnight," explained Coy Jacobs, who owns Mooney Aviation, a sales and maintenance facility right next door to Huffman Aviation.

"They just blew into town. They did no due diligence to the best of my knowledge. That's a cardinal *no-no*. I mean, you don't just come in and buy a business like that overnight."

He painted a picture of conditions at the time of the sale.

"Huffman was not for sale three days ago," said Jacob, "and then Rudi shows up with Wally, who owns some Lear Jets. They were here a day or two… met with Stan Huffman, he named a number, they said yes and wrote him a check, and then they notified the City of Venice of what they had done… *after* the fact.

"And that's a criteria," explained Jacob. "You *cannot* transfer properties at this airport, and most federally funded airports, without the governing authority's approval.

"It (the sale) was a shock to everybody at the airport. In fact, the City Council, the City Attorney and I think even for that matter the manager of the airport weren't even aware of it until well after the fact."

If the city of Venice didn't approve the purchase the two were stuck owning a business they couldn't run. They were taking a big financial gamble. What made the two men so confident that local officials would bless the transaction? What had made them sure of getting government approval?

When the sale was announced, Venice City Manager George Hunt told the *Gondolier* he had not been officially notified of the purchase. "We wish Stan (Huffman) well, and we would welcome Ambassador Airways. They have a fine reputation in Naples."

These are the first words out of Hunt's mouth about Rudi Dekkers, and they're wrong. The only reputation Rudi Dekkers enjoyed in Naples was as a deadbeat and occasional scumbag. Rudi wasn't an unknown quantity there at all. He had a tarnished history, which the Venice City Manager could have learned by picking up the phone and asking a few questions, as we did.

Time after time, we discovered that government entities had inexplicably smiled on the fortunes of Dekkers and Hilliard's aviation partnership, until it began to seem as if they had a "rich uncle" in government somewhere.

The FAA, for example, protected Dekkers on a number of occasions. An aviation mechanic who worked for him told of criminal acts Dekkers committed which the mechanic had been forced by law to report to the FAA. Especially eighteen thousand feet in the air, where safety is an important consideration...

At least it's supposed to be.

"Rudi Dekkers did an import of an airplane," the mechanic explained. "We found dents on the front of a wing and replaced sheet metal, and then we found ribs that were crushed. This renders an airplane un-airworthy. And yet he still sold the plane.

"I turned Rudi Dekkers into the FAA. They didn't do a damn thing."

Another aviation mechanic who worked for Dekkers over a period of years, Dave Montgomery, laughed when we asked him if this story could be true. Montgomery said when he found something wrong with an airplane Dekkers bought, Dekkers had fired him. Adding insult to injury, Dekkers then bounced his last payroll check.

John Villada, who managed Wally Hilliard's huge jet fleet, confirmed Montgomery's story. "Dave Montgomery worked for Rudi for three years as his Chief Mechanic till he found something wrong with an airplane Rudi bought. Rudi fired him, and then bounced his last payroll check."

Rudi Dekkers reputation at the Naples Airport got so bad, we learned, that he couldn't even buy gas there... for *cash*.

"When he bought Huffman Aviation for big bucks he couldn't even pay his rent at the Naples Airport," said a Naples aviation executive "His reputation as a deadbeat was so bad that the local Fixed Base Operator refused to sell him aviation fuel, even for cash."

Dekkers' reputation in Naples preceded him to Venice, except with government officials like Venice City Manager Hunt. Aviation business owner Coy Jacob said people there knew he had been basically run out of the Naples Airport.

"All we knew was that he was operating a flight school, an unsuccessful flight school in Naples. He had some run-ins with the FAA, I think he had lost his license, or had been reprimanded," said Jacob.

A Naples aviation observer, Rob Tillman, confirmed Dekkers record of illegality there. "They got busted by the FAA, crashed some airplanes, violated air space enough to get grounded, chartered airplanes with no license... you name it."

And then there's the problem of Dekkers' "extensive business aviation experience" cited by newspapers.

Dekkers didn't have any.

"I've always had some suspicions about the way he breezed into town out of nowhere," said someone close to the scene at Huffman. "Just too many odd little things. He has, for example, absolutely *no* aviation background as far as anyone can tell."

"Breezed into town out of nowhere" and "no aviation background" were not comments that square with portrayals of Dekkers in news accounts about the purchase of the flight school, which stressed his broad aviation experience.

"Ambassador Airways owners Rudi Dekkers, 42, Naples, president, and Wally Hilliard, 67, also from Naples, are both experienced pilots. Their Ambassador Airways owns several jet aircraft including Lear jets," read one local news account.

Owning a fleet of Lear jets may bestow a certain *je ne sais quoi,* but that hardly erases a colorful history of unscrupulous and illegal business practices. Dekkers crossed the line with aviation professionals we spoke to...

He put lives at risk to make a buck.

"He would take in people's planes to rent out while they were idle," one aviation mechanic who worked for him stated.

"Then he would come to me and want me to put switches on the Hobbes meter. It's like disconnecting an odometer on a car. It's a direct FAA violation and an extremely dangerous practice, because you can no longer tell when the plane is due for service," the mechanic explained.

"But he wanted to do it because it let him rent out planes without having to pay the plane's owner their cut."

Huffman was the only full-service fixed base operator, or FBO, at the Venice airport. An FBO sells gas, provides mechanical services and otherwise caters to private aviation, and is usually a center of activity at the airport. In other words, something of a civic resource.

"When Wally found Rudi Dekkers, Dekkers had already been thrown out of Naples as a con artist," said Naples aviation observer Rob Tillman. "Plus he had tax problems. He didn't pay tax on shit. And this is the guy to whom Wally sold Florida Air."

"Who approved Dekkers buying the FBO in Venice?" asked an irate aviation insider at the Venice Airport. "He'd been thrown out of Naples... how come they let him buy the 'diamond' of Venice?"

Rudi Dekkers literally arrived with a bang at the newly-purchased Huffman Aviation's headquarters, according to Charlie Voss. "On his first day running the company, he took a girl into his office and noisily copulated with her on his desk, just to let everyone know that he was the new rooster in town. Everybody could hear them. It was disgusting."

We found a number of people willing to talk about Dekkers on the record.

We heard from numerous sources that Rudi Dekkers had been the object of a serious multi-agency federal investigation during the mid-90s. Apparently authorities found a number of fruitful investigative leads to pursue...

"Rudi owned a computer business doing illegal activities at the Naples Airport," explained Tillman. "When Wally and Rudi were romancing, Rudi was smuggling aircraft back into the U.S. over the Arctic."

International Computer Products was the name of Dekkers' computer firm, active during the 1990s, we learned.

Naples aviation executive John Vellada confirmed the accounts. "There was a warrant for Rudi's arrest for smuggling computer chips," he told us. "Both the DEA and U.S. Customs were interested in him back in '93 and '94."

"Everything he ever did, from A to Z, was illegal."

A major source of conjecture around the airports in both Naples and Venice was what were the two partners doing together. They were considered an Odd Couple—universally, so far as we can tell—by observers at both airports.

Danielle Clarke was a French pilot who moved to Florida after spending twenty years as a flight instructor in Britain. She became Dekkers' and Hilliard's flight manager at Ambassador Aviation.

"It was an unholy alliance, unless there was a reason for that alliance to be," she told us. "They were just so incongruous. It was like watching the Pope and Saddam Hussein together."

"One of the big topics of conversation around the Naples Airport was *what do you think about the Wally situation?*"

"We were *all* trying to figure out Wally's relationship with Rudi. They were like 'chalk and cheese.' Nobody ever understood how they came together, but they were always together," said Clarke.

Amanda Keller used an American equivalent of "chalk and cheese" when she described seeing the corpulent Dekkers and the slight Hilliard together at Huffman.

"It was funny to see the chubby guy and the little guy walking together. They were like Abbott and Costello or something."

Rudi Dekkers had an erratic sense of cash management that often led to speculation among aviation observers. He went from dead broke to flashing a Big Roll in the blink of an eye.

"Rudi would write a lot of bad checks, disappear for a while, and come back with lots of cash," an airport observer recalled.

"Huffman Aviation was a little jewel when he bought it, and it had a really good reputation," another aviation executive told us. "He took a profitable business and ran it right into the ground. So he's got a business that's losing money hand over fist, and yet he was awash in cash. It just doesn't add up right."

"I can recall times when Dekkers owed money to everyone at the (Naples) airport," said a business owner there. "And then he would leave town for three weeks or so in the Lear, and come back flush."

Rudi Dekkers' financial profile changed overnight, said Coy Jacob in Venice. "Just about a year before he bought Huffman, he asked me for a ride from Venice to Naples, an airplane ride, which is maybe a 20 minute flight. I said yeah, sure, I'll take you down there with one of my pilots if you buy the gas," Jacob related.

"He didn't even have the money to buy gas for an airplane to go down and back, and yet a year later he shows up and plops a million seven, a million eight or two million dollars on the table as if it were paper money."

People who work in general aviation in Venice and Naples have a seemingly unlimited supply of stories portraying Dekkers as a shady character.

"I spent 5 years working at an avionics shop in Naples," one aviation mechanic told us. "There were a lot of things about the guy that just did not add up. He's claimed to me, for instance, that he's a New York cop. He's even got a plaque on his wall, with words to that effect.

"A New York *cop*? You tell me: How does a Dutch con artist get a plaque claiming he's an officer with the New York Police Department?"

His question has been ringing in our ears for a long time. It was also, perhaps just coincidentally, the second reference to the NYPD we'd heard recently in South West Florida. The first had been when Amanda Keller recommended someone who could confirm a story about Mohamed Atta harassing her at work.

"The bouncer at Fantasies & Lingerie was a big bald guy named Nick, a retired NY City detective," she said. "You could talk to him."

But, Rudi Dekkers was not the *only* Dutch national flight school owner at the Venice Airport with curious and unexplained associations. The second "Magic Dutch Boy" could be equally mysterious, according to Coy Jacob.

"Arne Kruithof sat across from my desk one day and told me he had trained at a U.S. military installation in southeast Missouri," said Jacob.

"I'm from Missouri, and there aren't any military bases there training foreign nationals that I know of. But the thing I kept wondering was," 'What's a Dutch national doing training at a secure U.S. military facility?'"

Dekkers had a specific objective in mind when he came to Venice, witnesses said. He wanted to operate in complete *privacy…*

"I know that he (Dekkers) wanted to buy out everybody on the block, so to speak, and he wanted to have a monopoly on the airport," chief flight instructor Hammersley told us. "That was one of his goals. Then, I just saw it as a short Dutch man with a French complex, called a Napoleon complex."

Dekkers and Hilliard exhibited a peculiar secretiveness, unusual in small town businessmen.

"I flew down to Naples one day, and the deputy in charge of airport security said something funny," Coy Jacob told us.

"He said, 'Wally and Rudi never talk inside a building, they go out to an airplane and talk inside the plane.'"

And as the Rudi Dekkers we heard about came from people aware of his penchant for sexually harassing young female employees, some as young as eighteen, it removed any doubts about his character for us.

"I personally witnessed him sneak up behind this kid that worked for him and stick something that looked like a broom handle up the back of her skirt," stated one eyewitness angrily. "And Dekkers is a fat slob of a middle-aged guy. It was sick.

"Even though he's married he was always after the young girls who worked for him to take little 'rides' with him in his helicopter, always for a half an hour or so at a time."

Dekkers settled one lawsuit brought by Nicole Antini, an 18 year-old girl who used to work for him, the *Gondolier* reported. Records were sealed, and the settlement enjoined the girl to keep silent, which she did.

But when the beefy Dutch national tried to renege on the settlement's terms, the young girl's attorney filed a motion to enforce the settlement agreement, and the sealed complaint became public information for the first time.

It included contemporaneous notes taken by Nicole and painted a vivid portrait of life at Huffman Aviation during the time Atta and Marwan were there.

"As long as I worked at Huffman Aviation I have been subjected to sexual harassment by Rudi Dekkers," the girl told the court.

"Can I bite into you?" Dekkers asked her on one occasion, stated her notes. Told that he was "sick," Dekkers replied, "I know, I just can't help it. Look at you: your hair, your face, your ass… you're a hot girl!"

On another occasion the middle-aged Dutch national asked his young female employee, barely out of high school, if he could "buy her."

"Buy me what?" she responds.

"You know, just *buy* you. It should be like in the olden days. I should be able to just buy you," Dekkers replied.

In the same conversation, Dekkers wondered aloud what the reaction would be if someone walked into his office while he was tucking his shirt back into his pants.

"Wouldn't that be funny if somebody walked in now as I'm putting my shirt away? They would think I was fucking you!"

Once Dekkers asked her, "Did you see that Russian girl I had in here? I couldn't hire her, because she's Russian. But I did tell her I had a job for her."

"In the pilot shop?" the young employee asked.

"No, I told her she could give me a blow job," Dekkers replied.

Dekkers, the girl wrote, told her, "You're beautiful when you're mad."

To which she replied, "You have no right touching my pants."

The young woman's allegations were confirmed by numerous other women who had close contact with him, including Amanda Keller, Mohamed Atta's former live-in girlfriend, who knew Dekkers from waiting in the flight school lounge for Atta to land.

"Rudi Dekkers… He's a total pervert," she said. "A really nasty, nasty man."

"He said to me one time, 'What would it take for me to have a piece of you?' I told him I didn't know what he was talking about. He said, 'Oh come on you know what I mean,'" Keller told us.

"He's lucky she (Nicole) was the only one with enough nerve to sue him," said a woman close to a Huffman executive. "He sexually harassed nearly every girl there, including the young 18 year-olds working in the restaurant."

Almost everyone at the small Venice Airport was aware of numerous allegations of sexual harassment against him. "Yeah, I heard that," Coy Jacob said. "That was the rumor around the airport."

"The airport is a small community. It's like a microcosm of society, most airports are. People—women leave, and I've heard that there have been problems down there."

His former office manager in Venice, Sue DeAngelis, wouldn't be specific with her complaints about sexual harassment from her boss.

She said she was thinking of suing him herself. But she did say, a little grimly, "I put up with a lot of stuff from him. It was ugly. My experience with Rudi was unbelievable."

One of Mohamed Atta's flight instructors at Huffman, Greg Woods, wrote to us about how hellish an experience it had been awaiting "the biweekly arrival of a depraved cuckoo bird in his private helicopter, screaming insults at various employees, sexually harassing the purposely chosen young and unsuspecting office workers and leaving everyone dazed and unbelieving at the upheaval of their routines."

The man whose glib tale about the terrorist hijackers walking in his front door was the foundation for the FBI's story about them in this country is a liar, a cheat and a thief, yet the FBI expected the American people to believe him, because without Rudi Dekkers' testimony the official story was back at Square One.

Maybe that's why although he was interviewed by every "news-hour journalist" in America, there was nary a hardball question from the lot of them.

Local newsmen observed that, through it all, Dekkers had been acting as unconcerned as a diplomat with a parking ticket.

"He acted like he had some kind of diplomatic immunity," *Gondolier* Editor Bob Mudge said, shaking his head at the memory.

Maybe Dekkers did.

Former bookkeeper Charlie Voss told of hearing him talk with his bankers in ways ordinary people wouldn't, for example. "I've heard banks call him up 'cuz he's bouncing checks in his accounts, and heard him say to them, 'I haven't got time to keep track of that.'"

The character—or lack of same—of Rudi Dekkers matters for only one reason. If Dekkers is lying about being an innocent and victimized business owner, then Mohamed Atta didn't *just happen* to stumble into his Venice, Florida flight school, and, in Dekkers we would be looking at the "Southeast Regional Manager" for the global network said to have assisted the hijackers.

With what we've already learned about Rudi Dekkers, we didn't expect that his track record for telling the truth would be all that great... And we were right. He was the opposite of a "straight-shooter," said people who know him well.

"I've certainly had occasions when Mr. Dekkers had told me something that turned out not to be true," said *Venice Gondolier* Editor Bob Mudge with a smile.

"It's common knowledge around the airport," said Coy Jacob. "In fact the phrase you hear a lot of times is: 'You can't believe what he says.' He doesn't have a lot of credibility."

Former employee Charlie Voss was "not even a short-time friend of Rudi's," he told us. "I don't have too much to say about him. But if his lips are moving, he's lying. And if he's not lying, his lips ain't moving."

From the day of the attack until now there has been an unspoken question hanging in the air at the Venice Airport, said a flight instructor who knew both Dutch national flight school owners well. "To what extent he would go to succeed?" asked Tom Hammersley.

He shrugged. "I don't know his character well enough to comment on it. I think in a lot of ways he's very ambitious."

Over the placid golf courses and shuffleboard courts dotting the Florida Gulf Coast during the year before the attack, the clock was ticking. But on the ground the only sound was the noise made by Dekkers himself. Well before the 9/11 attack he was being characterized in the local *Venice Gondolier* as a fast talking con-man of dubious repute. A headline from the day after the attack read: "Huffman Aviation no stranger to headlines."

"Huffman Aviation Inc., has had problems in the last few months with the city of Venice, Sarasota County and the state of Florida, but the school keeps flying," the paper reported.

Huffman Aviation wasn't paying its rent out at the airport. Dekkers was a deadbeat.

"I don't think I knew anything at all about Rudi, even his taking over of Huffman, until April or maybe early May of last year when he missed a rent payment—right after I found out he was behind on several months rent," said Bob Mudge, editor of the *Venice Gondolier*.

"The only fixed based operator at the Venice Municipal Airport was I think at that time three months behind in his rent and had gotten a demand letter being threatened with eviction."

Dekkers was receiving a rolling drumbeat of bad press. "Huffman Rent Is Late Again," ran the paper's May 12, 2001 headline.

"When Huffman Aviation paid three months of overdue rent, company president Rudi Dekkers said the rent wouldn't be late again.

'No, we won't have this any more,' he said during an interview," the paper reported.

Coverage got even less flattering as time went by: "City Threatens Lessee With Eviction, Again," was the embarrassing headline on June 9, 2001, just three months before the terrorist attack.

Not threatened with eviction. Threatened with eviction *again*.

"Huffman Aviation, Inc., is again on notice from the city to catch up on its rent payments or face eviction from the airport," said the paper.

Nothing about Dekkers' rent status had changed by mid-summer. The continuing saga made Huffman Aviation a regular item in local coverage.

"Huffman Rent Late Again," headlined the *Gondolier* in late July. "For the sixth straight month, Huffman Aviation, Inc., has failed to pay its rent to the city on time," read the account.

When, less than a month before the September 11th tragedy, Rudi Dekkers finally paid Huffman Aviation's rent, even that was considered newsworthy.

"Huffman pays rent," the paper headlined.

It must have been good for a chuckle. But back when the *Gondolier* was highlighting Rudi Dekkers' shortfalls, it wasn't of interest, except locally. No one thought to question Dekkers about how he came to be suddenly flush with cash. He wasn't notorious, yet.

But when we first learned the "news"—months after 9/11—that he had finally managed to pay Huffman Aviation's rent on time, our blood went cold. Because where did he come up with the money?

If something changed in Rudi Dekkers financial condition just three weeks before the attack, we wanted to see him hauled in for questioning.

Another question was why Dekkers, whose "clients" were forking over more than double the going rate for flight training, had always been late paying his rent.

Even after collecting a terrorist surcharge, Dekkers came up short. We weren't the only ones who wondered. Bill Warner, a private investigator in Sarasota probing so-far unpublished connections there to the terrorist conspiracy, said he couldn't believe what he was seeing.

"General aviation has been in serious downturn since the attack. At the Venice Airport, it's been—understandably—even worse... Remember the stories about how Rudi Dekkers had so much trouble coming up with his rent at the airport?" he asked.

"Rudi Dekkers isn't having trouble paying his rent anymore," he said, a little in awe of the implications of what he was saying.

Less than a month before the September 11th attack, things changed for the better for "flight school owner" Dekkers.

Rudi finally got caught up on his rent. Imagine that.

In the aftermath of the attack, while general aviation suffered, every aviation concern at the Venice Airport was late at least once with their monthly rent.

Every business but *one*...

Before the attack Rudi Dekkers' Huffman Aviation became a standing joke in Venice, Florida because he couldn't pay the rent on time. But after the attack?

Even with the disastrous affect 9/11 had on general aviation, with every aviation concern at the airport missing payments, one business paid on time each and every month, like clockwork.

Huffman Aviation.

CHAPTER SIXTEEN

"RUDI THE CROOK"

Since terror flight school owner Rudi Dekkers was not in any regular sense a businessman, we began to entertain slightly-darker scenarios for what he was doing and how he *just happened* to be in such close proximity to Mohamed Atta's terrorist cadre.

Dekkers repeatedly evinced lack of interest in running the business side of Huffman Aviation, the Venice FBO, the bread and butter of the operation, and this fact was noted by the Venice aviation community.

"People with helicopters at FBOs are generally looking to defray their expenses by renting out things like helicopters. That's what they're in business for," explained Danny Schultz, who's been flying for fifteen years in the skies over Southwest Florida. He said he's still puzzled at the lack of interest shown by Dekkers in his nominal business.

"I needed to rent a helicopter for a property appraisal a while back," he continued, citing an example. "I called his (Dekkers) office several days in advance, because he was the local chopper supplier, he's got the FBO in Venice. And they told me he would call me back. It was a sizable usage of the chopper, which would be very financially rewarding. But he never got back to me. He didn't even give me the courtesy of a reply."

"All I can say is that, at the time, I thought it was *odd*," stated Schultz, shaking his head. "And this was long before Rudi became famous after 9/11."

Whatever Rudi Dekkers was about, it wasn't making a buck in general aviation. Longtime local pilot Schultz described abrupt changes in the aviation *scene* once Dekkers took over at Huffman…

"We have a designated flight examiner at our small airport, he was one of the few in this area," explained Schultz. "He stayed busy most of the time with foreign students, giving them their FAA check-rides. I often went to lunch with him, and these folks would come too, and some of them could hardly speak English. They were from places like Libya, various countries in the Middle East."

It hadn't always been that way in Southwest Florida.

"This was a recent influx of this type of trainee," said Schultz.

And that's why understanding the true identity of the Dutch national who in 1999 purchased Huffman Aviation is so important: Rudi Dekkers was responsible for the flood of Arab student pilots that began "marching across the tarmac."

Mohamed Atta and his Hamburg cadre were part of that "flood."

So, who *is* Rudi Dekkers?

We interviewed a number of people who worked with or for Dekkers in the last few years, they were unanimous in the opinion that Dekkers is a highly dubious character.

Danielle Clarke has observed Dekkers close-up at the Naples Airport since the early 1990s. Born in Lyons, France, she was passionate about flying since girlhood. She moved to Naples, Florida a decade ago, after a long marriage to an English flight instructor, during which they taught flying in Britain. When he died, she told us, it was time for a change of scene.

And Florida had a reputation as a sunny place.

"Rudi was a wheeler-dealer back to 1990 in Naples," she recalled. "First time I saw him I said to myself, *'There's* a crook! Never get associated with him. He'll be bankrupt before the end of the year.' Then, after I'd seen him for a while, I'd say to myself, 'There goes Rudi the Crook.'"

Danielle was a shrewd judge of human nature, apparently, because Rudi *is* a crook. He's wanted in his native country. We learned from a law enforcement source in Venice that after Dutch authorities recognized him during his many appearances on CNN, he was re-indicted on financial charges in the Netherlands. The cop credited *Larry King*

Live with performing a function usually reserved for *America's Most Wanted.*

Even in the U.S., ordinarily such a friendly and forgiving place for him, Dekkers' legal troubles were mounting. By the end of 2002 he had also been indicted on a charge of criminal fraud by the state of Florida. When we called Dekkers for comment on his indictment, he professed to be unaware of any pending charges.

"My lawyer in the Netherlands has said nothing to me about any indictment," he said. "I can't imagine that I could have done anything wrong."

The Florida State's Attorney was telling a different story. "Dekkers owes $3 million to the government of the Netherlands, from the mid-1990s, we discovered," stated Florida State's Attorney Jonathan Greene, leading the prosecution of Dekkers in Sarasota.

Dekkers owed $3 million in the Netherlands as the result of pledging assets he didn't own to secure loans he had no intention of repaying, the same crime for which he'd just been charged in Florida.

After a judge in Sarasota signed a warrant for Dekkers' arrest, the local *Gondolier* called him for a comment.

Dekkers said, "Wow, I'm surprised."

Florida State's Attorney Greene sounded faintly amused at the intrigue swirling around Dekkers.

"I knew nothing about Rudi Dekkers, except the particulars of this one charge, but I've learned more," he said, figuratively rolling his eyes. "I've gotten at least 15 to 20 calls, for example, just to *congratulate* me for charging him."

"There was also a Federal investigation alleging illegal exportation of technology against him a while back, " Greene told us. "They're working on some Federal stuff on him now."

This confirmed a big piece of the "Rudi Dekkers puzzle." We'd been hearing, from numerous sources, that Dekkers had been the subject of a multi-agency federal investigation in the mid-90s. An investigation in which several federal agencies pool resources must have indicated some strong federal interest in Rudi Dekkers' activities.

John Vellada, the tanned and smiling son of an expatriate Cuban family who came to America in the early '60s, knew Dekkers when he was exciting all that federal attention. He was also, until recently, the jet manager for Wally Hilliard's fleet of planes.

"There was a warrant for Rudi's arrest for smuggling computer chips. Both the DEA and U.S. Customs were interested in him back in '93 and '94," he said.

"What I heard was that he was buying the chips, taking boxes and putting a certain amount of chips in, and then hiding the rest underneath to evade customs.

"He has a warrant in Holland for smuggling-in chips," Vellada said. "He's not allowed back in Holland. He got busted for smuggling chips and money fraud. I remember when DEA, Customs, everyone was after him over here."

To have aroused the interest of the Drug Enforcement Administration, Dekkers must have been involved with smuggling something besides computer chips…

"Why was the DEA interested in Rudi? Nobody ever knew. That was everyone's big question," Villada replied. "All I know is the DEA was here, US Customs, Holland officials… That's when I learned he had had to flee Holland."

We had confirmation from Florida State's Attorney Jonathan Greene that it was true. Dekkers had been under suspicion of illegal exportation of high technology, Greene had said. So a man wanted in his home country, and also the target of a multi-agency federal investigation, was invited to testify in front of the Congress of the United States of America, where he was free with tips on preventing future terrorist attacks.

How was this possible?

Even more importantly, after the 9/11 attack Rudi Dekkers had been seemingly instantly relieved of suspicion. No journalist inquired about whether he had been engaging in illegal activity at the same time the terrorist conspiracy was making use of his facilities.

We called the Netherlands Embassy, Washington, D.C. Was it true Dekkers was a wanted man in Holland?

"We don't give this information out to journalists," explained Embassy spokesman Harry DeWitt, who nonetheless said "you can make what you will of the fact that I am referring you to the Ministry of Justice for an explanation. I've been told to say nothing."

The man at Huffman Aviation standing in front of the TV cameras, Rudi Dekkers, was a linchpin in the official story. His testimony had shaped the initial accounts of the hijackers.

Why had Dekkers become the annoited *interviewee*? Didn't the U.S. *know* Dekkers was a crook before he went on television? There is only one answer, we think. Rudi Dekkers was one of their own, or he belonged to them, at least. He said what they wanted him to say… because he *had* to.

He was a criminal. He had been caught by federal authorities back in the mid-90s. But he had never been charged. Why not?

The answer is simple, and yet stunning: Rudi Dekkers had "rolled," and become a government "confidential informant." He was, in criminal parlance, "working off a beef."

In the dozens of sound bites he fed to the world's media about Atta and Marwan in the days after the attack, he lied, and lied effectively… for the people for whom he worked. They even coached him on what to say.

This explains how two Dutch nationals, Kruithof and Dekkers, could each buy flight training schools at the off-the-beaten-track Venice Airport, and not face questioning about it later when three of their students are found to be piloting planes used as guided missiles on a September morning.

There were people taken into Federal custody whose connections with the terrorists were far less suspicious than theirs.

Plus, both men were foreign nationals presumed to be flight risks as a matter of law.

Yet neither was being held.

While dozens of journalists milled aimlessly at Huffman Aviation in the frenzied days after the attack, only one noted that Dekkers' story kept changing. Reporter Rochelle Renford expressed her suspicions about Dekkers on Sept. 29, 2001, in the *Sarasota Weekly Planet.* "Would it be reasonable to expect Dekkers to give the same information to every news outlet?" she asked.

"Perhaps. But that was not the case. When Dekkers first appeared before the press on the day after the attack, this is what he said, He didn't know the suspects. He wasn't the one who took their money so he was unsure how they had paid for their training. He didn't see their passports so he wasn't sure where they were from. He denied having had many interactions with them at all."

"On Wednesday, he told some reporters, including me, that his interaction with the two suspects came from a couple of brief conversations when he passed them in the halls," Renford wrote. "His employees had dealt with their enrollment."

"But by Sunday's reports, Dekkers was serving up anecdotes about the two men, telling one reporter, 'He sat right there last year when he came to talk to me about taking lessons here.'"

According to Renford, on the day after the attack a reporter from the *New York Times* asked Dekkers about reports that the two men (Atta and Al-Shehhi) were from Germany.

"Didn't it strike you as odd that they were from Germany? They didn't look German, did they?"

"Don't tell me what people tell you," Dekkers barked in response. "I have never heard that they're from Germany. I have never heard that they speak German." Renford wrote.

"Dekkers gave a different answer on *Larry King Live*. Now he *did* know where they were from... Dekkers now recalled that Atta told him he had come from Germany. But when Dekkers, a Dutch native, began speaking to Atta in German, the Middle Eastern man just got up and walked out of his office. Dekkers said he found it odd.

"Whereas on Wednesday he'd blasted a reporter for asking about a German connection," wrote Renford, "on Thursday he told me an anecdote about one of the suspects saying he was German.

"Dekkers wasn't just remembering new details," she concluded. "He was learning how to tell a story."

Because national reporters apparently had no clue about his shady local reputation, and his inability for six months straight to pay his rent on time, no one questioned how Dekkers had come to be so flush with cash just three weeks before the attack.

But it did strike some people as strange, like Bill Warner, a private investigator in Sarasota who made it his business to delve into Rudi Dekkers' financial affairs to explain his sudden pre-9/11 change in liquidity.

"Rudi Dekkers somehow came up with $10,000 in late October (2001)," he told us, "to finally pay off the woman's (Nicole Antini) sexual harassment suit. He also came up with $ 56,000 in early November to pay off another law suit with FH1100 Manufacturing Corp.

"But he had filed a UCC with M&I Bank Northeast for all inventory of Huffman Aviation way back in March of 2000. So he appears to have had no source of additional financing for this $65,000 cash outlay in late October and early November 2001.

"There are enough judgments in his name and his companies name to paper his office walls," said Warner. "How do you obtain that much cash under such severe conditions?"

If somebody had been "protecting" Rudi Dekkers from financial harm, all that changed with "the INS thing" six months after 9/11, said airport insider Max Burge.

"Rudi got indicted because he embarrassed the President of the United States with the INS bullshit."

The "INS bullshit" refers to Rudi Dekkers' return to the national stage exactly six months to the day after the attack. He'd gotten a second 15 minutes of fame and made headlines again when he called in reporters to reveal a government bungle when he received in the mail, on the six month anniversary of the attack, INS approval of visas for Mohamed Atta and Marwan Al-Shehhi.

It had been a very bad day for the INS. In addition to provoking "outrage" on Capital Hill, the hapless INS's bungling was said to have made even President George W. Bush "pretty hot."

The CIA and FBI *had* been taking all the post-9/11 heat.

But suddenly the tide of public opinion turned against the lowly INS, and a finger of blame began to be pointed towards what was no doubt a swell bunch of guys forced to spend their time standing around in the hot sun at border crossings doing their best to look the other way. It didn't seem fair.

Dekkers displayed the INS letter to reporters. He said the arrival of the yellow INS forms had come as a shock.

"We thought we had put this behind us," he said. "And it had to happen right on the six-month anniversary."

"Poor Rudi" caught the public relations break of the new century. The cameras were rolling again, and he was back in the limelight— jetting to Washington, D.C., this time to advise the INS on how they might improve their system.

Even *The New York Times* raised an eyebrow. "The error seemed particularly difficult to explain, because Mr. Atta and Mr. Al-Shehhi were among the most infamous of the 19 hijackers," said the *Times*.

It was a triumphant performance for Dekkers, who said he viewed the INS mistake as long-sought vindication. He told reporters, "When they hit the buildings they were approved to be here. I could not show (until now) that we applied for the right paperwork. "Therefore I am happy that I can do that now."

A reporters asked, "So you feel vindicated?"

"Yes," Dekkers replied. "I don't expect when I get in on Monday morning to get two permits for Atta and Al-Shehhi. I thought they were behind me already and my life goes on."

When we saw him speak these words on camera, we thought: Not so fast, pal.

He was clearly enjoying the moment, however, and dispensed some advice to the American government. "The flight schools didn't do anything wrong. The government needs to look at itself and look at procedures and see what they can change so this will not happen again."

Dekkers, at that point, seemed to need some kind of turnaround in his fortunes to alleviate all the bad publicity he had been getting locally. A *Gondolier* editorial even suggested, for the first time, that it might be time for Dekkers to go. "If he won't be more helpful, the city should re-examine whether it wants Dekkers' business to remain at the airport," said the editorial.

When we originally asked people in Venice how they had felt on learning the news that the terrorist pilots had trained right in their town, a woman in the deli of Publix market echoed widespread community sentiment when she told us, "They wanted to go burn down the airport."

So, slipping quietly out of town would have seemed the outcome the Dutch national would be desperately seeking. But Dekkers called attention to himself just when he should have been laying low. And now the President of the Unites States himself was pissed. Certainly no one enjoys being left hanging, twisting slowly, slowly, in the wind.

We remembered that budding screenwriters are taught that sometimes the best thing that could possibly happen to your character turns out to be the worst thing. Because that's the way life is.

Rudi's second moment in the headlines would come back to haunt him. Aviation consultant Max Burge told us, "He hasn't been protected for at least a month."

It was a measure of revenge for Burge. Rudi and Max had crossed swords in an aviation deal. Dekkers had looked at him, Max said, and sneered: "You're not a player."

Now Max Burge was returning the favor. He said, proudly, "I made sure that the indictment developed. I made sure Wally had the right attorney."

The first time we met him, Max Burge had identified himself as a business consultant for the American government. He was a square-jawed, no-nonsense, former Marine and riverboat pilot from Mississippi, in Venice to broker the sale of Huffman Aviation to new owners. It appeared he might be playing an unofficial role at the Venice Airport; a position that might, in hindsight, have been filled a little sooner.

Max had had business at the Venice Airport with some of the "players" involved, he told us, so after 9/11 he had checked "with some people" to ascertain if any of his business associates at the Airport had any culpability in the attack.

"I was told that Rudi doesn't check out clear," he said. "When I asked about Dekkers, I was told, 'He's bigger than national. He's transnational.' And I was warned to stay away from him."

Something had now changed, apparently, because Burge was talking about Dekkers.

"In the drive to indict Rudi," he told us, smiling, "virtually every branch of the U.S. government lent a helping hand. Everybody offered to help in any way they could. The INS was especially helpful."

"I hear Rudi owes $5.5 million to Wally," he tossed out casually. "I hear Rudi's helicopter has a stolen government engine in it."

"His indictment opens up Pandora's Box," Burge concluded. "If he runs, you'll have it. It's also about getting a hold of him. And it opens up a big can of worms."

We couldn't believe it. There it was. The can of worms we'd been waiting for.

Burge made a prediction. "If he doesn't flee, he'll be arrested in the next couple of weeks."

He was.

When Rudi Dekkers tried to use the INS snafu to his public relations advantage, even as he was claiming to feel "vindicated," new details were being released that showed he was nothing of the kind.

Dekkers shared the now-famous INS form with the Associated Press, which noted that, on the visa application, Atta's name is mis-spelled "Mohomed." It was an understandable mistake, since the Huffman

Aviation assistant who filled them out, 18 year-old Nicole Antini, was just then being sexually harassed by a middle-aged Dutch boor.

We saw something else important: the AP said that the INS documents indicated the academic term cost each of the two terrorist pilots $27,300. This was now the third, and highest, figure that had come out, since somehow the exact amount Dekkers charged the terrorists was one of those things that never gets pinned down.

Dekkers had changed his story twice. And now it was revealed that Atta and Al-Shehhi had paid nearly $30k each, almost $60,000 between them.

Dekkers had been quoted in numerous places saying that between his two schools he had been training 500 foreign nationals a year. And 500x $30,000 is a fairly significant 7-figure number. So how come, out at the Venice Airport, Dekkers had been unable to pay his rent?

It was clear that Rudi Dekkers was more than an innocent business owner victimized by wily terrorists. There was a darker reality lurking behind his widely-promoted public persona.

For example, we learned to our amazement that at the same time Dekkers had been unable to pay Huffman Aviation's rent for six months in a row, he had been launching an *airline*.

We weren't the only ones taken aback at this development. There had been amazement at the Venice Airport as well…

"When we heard that Hilliard and Dekkers were starting an airline by early 2001, everybody at the airport's jaw dropped," Coy Jacob told us. "When someone walked in my office and told me Dekkers was starting an airline, I told him 'Sure, and I'm building a shuttle launch facility here at the Venice Airport.' That's how ridiculous it was."

Yet, we found a glowing paean to Dekkers' business acumen in a *Sarasota Herald Tribune* article on Rudi's new airline, called Florida Air, or FLAIR.

"Run by an ambitious, optimistic and fast-talking Dutch citizen named Rudi Dekkers, the airline, using 11-seat Cessna Grand Caravans it borrowed from Alaska Air subsidiary Harbor Air, opened for business Feb. 15. By March, it added Jacksonville to its route list, and if the airline catches on with Florida travelers it might expand to other cities, including Pensacola, Atlanta and Savannah, GA"

And right about then was when we learned that Dekkers' partner in his new airline was in business with the Mob.

CHAPTER SEVENTEEN

SECRETARY'S DAY

In the history of crime in America the golden age of bank robbery was supposedly the 1930s, a decade that spawned the legends of John Dillinger, Bonnie & Clyde, and Willie Sutton, famous for robbing banks because "that was where the money was."

But perhaps the real Gilded Age of Crime will someday be recognized as having been our own... After all, more cash just disappeared at Enron than has ever been stolen in all the bank robberies in America put together. And Enron is just one example, and may just be the tip of the iceberg...

In the Spring of 2001—while Mohamed Atta was at his school—Rudi Dekkers did something so incredible that we spent over a year examining it in befuddled amazement. At the same time he was receiving the most painful kind of humiliating coverage in the local press ("Huffman Rent Is Late, Again"), Rudi Dekkers and Wally Hilliard blithely launched an airline.

They called it Florida Air, or FLAIR.

We were not surprised to discover no one in the local aviation community thought the move made any business sense. All agreed that FLAIR was a doomed venture from day one. Once again, the question was why were they doing it. If both had not had business with Mohamed Atta, it might not have mattered.

But they had.

They chose, as partner, a man named Rick Boehlke, who owned an air carrier called Harbor Air, in Gig Harbor, Washington. Boehlke was also, just then, a participant in Portland, OR., in the $340 million looting of pension funds of mostly Mob-led unions, like the Laborers Union.

We wondered: who had the temerity to steal pension money from Mob-led unions? Then we learned newspapers were calling the *looting* "Mob-led", too.

What were the odds that Rudi Dekkers and Wally Hilliard would go looking for a business partner and come up with a guy with Mob ties who's helping pull off a spectacular $300 million heist?

Was this just wretched bad luck, on top of the misfortune they'd already experienced because their flight school had become a magnet for terrorists?

Wally and Rudi must have been two really star-crossed dudes… Because if they weren't, then something sinister was going on.

Florida Air, the new airline, used Rick Boehlke's Harbor Air's license to fly. Boehlke also ended up supplying the new airline with both planes and pilots. What Dekkers and Hilliard were bringing to the party was an open question. Meanwhile, Mohamed Atta was still at Huffman Aviation, doing no one knows quite what.

Was it outside the realm of possibility that all three men—Dekkers, Boehlke, and Hilliard—worked for the same company?

A company, or network, specializing in "niches" like looting pension funds and training terrorists to fly?

Or… was this just another freak coincidence? What are the odds, that the men who helped terrorist ringleader Mohamed Atta establish his American beachhead would be in business with a partner who robs banks… from the *inside?*

However it played out, our understanding of what the terrorist conspiracy was doing in Florida would be shaped by what it was Rudi Dekkers and Wally Hilliard were discovered to have been doing—and with whom—while Mohamed Atta practiced touch and go's at their facilities in Venice and Naples.

Florida Air launched with great fanfare in the Spring of 2001. Dekkers and Hilliard had started another aviation business that did not make business sense.

During its brief two-month existence, Mohamed Atta may well have flown for the airline as a co-pilot. No one will admit it, but there were terrorists inside the cockpit of an American airline plane during the year 2001 who didn't need box-cutters to get there.

We discovered that the chance to fly as a commercial pilot with Florida Air, after taking flight training at "sister company" Huffman Aviation, had been a big part of Rudi Dekkers European sales pitch, and was played up in the company's advertising.

"I kept ads from flying magazines from 2000," said Bill Bersch, a former manager at Huffman. "'Come to Huffman to train, and then fly with our Florida Air airline.'"

"The flight school was advertised as a feed into Florida Air as future employer of Huffman's flight school students. Florida Air put the ads in everywhere, but when it came down to it they couldn't offer flying jobs, because there wasn't an airline for very long."

While this would seem to be a pretty serious crime, there had been no FAA investigation, which isn't surprising. During the course of his "aviation career" in Florida, Rudi Dekkers received so many free passes from the FAA that they should enshrine it with an exhibit at the Air & Space Museum.

When Dekkers and Hilliard's short-lived airline became germane to the 9/11 investigation, Rick Boehlke and Rudi Dekkers competed to see who could heap the most scorn on the other, attempting to divert attention from themselves. As someone once said, there's no honor among thieves.

Boehlke accused Dekkers of not having any experience running a commuter airline and training facility. "He (Dekkers) was an oxymoron the day I met him," Boehlke told Portland, Oregon KABC reporter Eric Mason. "I can't believe anyone handed him millions of dollars to run a business he had no experience in."

Boehlke also charged that Dekkers suggested his Huffman Aviation students hone their skills by acting as co-pilots on FLAIR's commuter routes in Florida, urging him to allow student ride-alongs on scheduled airline flights.

"That's illegal," said Boehlke. He left no doubt as to where he came down on the proposition. He said he had rejected the idea at the time.

Looking back, Boehlke said he was alarmed that Dekkers' desperate attempt to save his failing airline could have had dire consequences.

"Having a student without enough hours or that type rating as a co-pilot is not legal," an FAA spokesman said about Dekkers' scheme.

Boehlke demonstrated an eye for a good headline.

"There could have been terrorists on a ride-along!" he told reporter Eric Mason. He said a *chill* runs through him when he thinks about it.

"I was amazed knowing how close we'd been to that training environment. It would have given them legal access to cockpits and other secure areas in airports across the country," he exclaimed.

As we learned more about Rick Boehlke's checkered past, his claim to be "amazed" would begin to sound like the French Inspector in Casablanca who tells Bogie he's shocked—*shocked*—to find gambling going on at Rick's… while at the same time pocketing his winnings.

Reporter Mason had been interested in Boehlke for obvious reasons. "The financing that had gone between Mr. Boehlke and Florida Air, which was a sister operation to the flight training center which trained Mohamed Atta, was murky."

"Murky" is not a word you want to see applied to people who trained Mohamed Atta to fly.

We needed to take a closer look at Rick Boehlke, at Florida Air, and at Rudi Dekkers and Wally Hilliard's motivations for starting it. How many businessmen behind on their rent for six months *in a row* have the gall, or chutzpah, to at the same time start a new airline? Was it not enough for Rudi and Wally that they were already losing money hand-over-fist in their flight school venture, that they decided they might as well be losing millions in an airline as well?

Bill Bersch, a longtime aviation professional with experience as senior pilot for a regional air carrier, rues the day he hired on to help launch Florida Air. When he checked-in to start work at the airline's Venice headquarters, he was surprised at what he found.

"I functioned as the director of operations," Bersch said, "which meant my job was to decide which flights to cancel every day. I used to look at Wally and Rudi and wonder whatever made them think they could start an airline."

Flying the friendly skies for fun and profit played no apparent part of Dekkers and Hilliard's motivation that he could discern, Bersch said. It had all left him feeling baffled.

"I mean, I was on the executive team and here they were, trying to start an airline, and from August 2000 to the present we had all of four business meetings."

Bersch's professional frustration showed. "Wouldn't you think you would have at least weekly meetings if you were trying to start an airline? And then when you *could* get a meeting scheduled, somebody would tell you that it had been canceled, because Wally was in Havana."

Why "Wally was in Havana" would become a focus of our investigation, but at that time we hadn't any idea what it meant. Bersch passed on another big clue a moment later, while speaking of how poorly the company was managed.

"It was just ridiculous," he said. "For the better part of a year, we were paying eight pilots to do nothing."

"Paying eight pilots to do nothing" must have raised suspicions , we figured, around the Venice Airport. It had.

Coy Jacob said suspicions about Dekkers and Hilliard had been widespread, since well before Mohamed Atta came to town. Since 9/11 it had only grown more intense.

"When people operate suspiciously at airports around here, people start investigating," he told us. "I mean law enforcement hovers around most airports in the Southeast United States. They hover around airports around here, obviously. And they were told to stay away from that operation."

Told to stay away from that operation?

We had already discovered that, whatever else he was, Rudi Dekkers wasn't a businessman or flight school owner in any conventional sense, illustrated by the fact that at the same time he was launching a commuter airline he was thought of as a deadbeat in Venice and Naples. So he wasn't a "flight school owner."

Now we heard he hadn't been an "airline owner" either.

"The whole thing was strange as hell to me," said Bersch. "Here we had a business to run, but only a couple of times over the years did we even have staff meetings. The business didn't make any sense."

The airline made no more sense than the flight school.

What, then, had been its purpose? Had it served as *cover* for other activities?

"When something doesn't make business sense," former Huffman bookkeeper Voss said, "sometimes it's because it *does* make sense… just in some other way."

"FLAIR started out of here (Venice) which was a Dekkers-Hilliard thing which, again, just never made sense," Coy Jacob stated. "That airline startup thing was… the chances of that working were slim and none. It was a joke around here."

But after 9/11, this particular joke was no longer funny.

Bill Bersch's bad experience with Florida Air began as soon as he was hired. "Rudi hired me, August 2000, and shortly after, in October or November 2000, I met Wally," he said.

"We flew a Lear up to North Carolina to see people at Corporate Express, where Wally was looking to use other peoples' Certificates. They were always trying to run an angle around the regulations. The Department of Transportation doesn't like it when they find someone doing what Rudi and Wally were doing.

"They nearly crashed the Lear in a hard landing," continued Bersch. "Earlier I had told Dale (Kraus) that the tires were bald. Now we were landing in North Carolina in a rainstorm, the tires were bald, there were crosswinds, the plane spun 90 degrees, and from a passenger window I found myself looking straight down the runway."

Welcome aboard Florida Air.

Florida Air's first CEO, Bersch told us was Ian Alexander, whose business performance was somewhat hampered by the fact he was drunk most of the time.

"He used to live in Atlanta, came to work for FLAIR, and has since fled to Canada," said Bersch. "Wally and Rudi both directed him; Wally would tell Ian to do one thing, Rudi would tell him the opposite, or to do something else. I heard Rudi tell Ian to 'fudge numbers, shift them around.' Rudi would do this, Ian said, whenever Rudi had to show the numbers to an investor," said Bersch.

We wanted to know why Ian "fled to Canada."

"It was rumored Ian tried to take $90,000 using a company credit card," said Bersch. "FLAIR was like a money spigot. Ian never accepted responsibility and was drunk all the time, even in the morning… Is this any way to run a business?"

The long-suffering financier behind all these inexplicable money-losing aviation ventures, Wally Hilliard, was in the midst of taking yet another financial bath.

"The airline lost $800,000 in two months," said Stuart Burchill, Hilliard's former accountant. "All together, the airline ended up costing Wally almost $8 million."

Bersch's puzzling tale was typical of experiences we heard from a number of former employees of how Dekkers and Hilliard ran their new airline. "We were going to use Sarasota as a hub, fly state people up to Tallahassee, fly to Jacksonville with military people," he explained.

"Then they had to get Rudi out of the picture because he wasn't an American citizen. And so Rudi told them to name Doug Helterbrand to run it, who until two years ago was just a mechanic for Huffman Aviation who worked on Rudi's helicopter. What Doug really wanted to do was to be an airline pilot, but Doug has never worked for an airline in his life," continued Bersch.

"Yet in the business plan next to his name, it says he has 18 years of airline experience. And six months later, when they updated the business plan, it now said he had *twenty* years of airline experience. And when they introduced the management of the airline, Doug was listed as Director of Safety, an important job for a carrier."

"But Doug was just a Navy mechanic."

Florida Air's history was nasty, brutish, and short. Danielle Clarke, who has been around general aviation much of her life, says she had no idea what the two were doing.

"I like to think I'm pretty smart," she told us. "But Rudi and Wally would discuss Florida Air in front of me and I would never understand what was going on.

"They were losing absolutely horrendous amounts of money and I often wondered why Wally bothered to work."

Although Rudi Dekkers was listed as the airline's CEO, he wasn't even supposed to be an officer, we learned. Once again, his Dutch Uncle, "Uncle Sugar," was protecting him.

"Rudi is not a U.S. national, I don't believe he's a U.S. citizen," explained Coy Jacob. "And historically the FAA is pretty picky about who they allow to even own U.S. registered airplanes. Non-US citizens cannot register an *airplane* in the United States, let alone own an airline."

"Rudi was involved in the start-up of FLAIR, I think it was called, which was Florida Airline, simply," recalled *Gondolier* Editor Bob Mudge. "And I know he had a lot of problems with that. I think he was briefly in service, but FLAIR's period of service was real brief."

Mudge shook his head in mock disbelief.

"I've heard a lot of things about why that airline went into trouble, there were a lot of financial problems and I've heard problems with people not getting paid, and I had discussions with Dekkers about that at some point and he was blaming it on… I forget who."

Illegality was not just rampant at the airline; it was *de riguer.*

"Rudi and Wally were running a whole bunch of companies as if they were just one entity," Bill Bersch explained. "They had Florida Air, Dekkers Aviation Group, Florida Air Holdings, LLC, and even Florida Air Holdings, Inc. But since they intermingled funds all the time, I just thought of them as one company. They all had the same personnel and the same management, and they were all the same company."

So commingling funds was the preferred way of doing business for Wally Hilliard. We'd thought it was illegal. This became more important when we learned that Hilliard was involved with another flight school bankruptcy, in Orlando, where hundreds of students at Discover Air were ripped off when Hilliard's partner, the schools owner, skipped town.

"Nobody will ever know the extent to which these guys engaged in underhanded business deals," said Bersch. "They didn't pay state taxes, they didn't pay employee taxes."

No matter how many aviation observers we spoke with about Rudi and Wally, they were uniformly incredulous at the pair's actions. Longtime airline professional Bill Bersch, while ruminating out loud one day, may have put a finger on it.

"Rudi's name was popping up everywhere in DOT (Dept. of Transportation) or FAA records," said Bersch. "He was trying an angle with Air Tahoma, an Ohio and San Diego-based operation—it would shift locations as business arose. Rudi's name was associated with it. I have never seen a business run like that in my life. It was like they were only pretending to run a business."

His words rang in our ears.

"They were only pretending to run a business."

"Just a guess, but FLAIR probably lost $7 million," he continued. "There were other investors, this wasn't all Wally's money, but still... You have to wonder why Wally kept giving Rudi money. It didn't make any business sense."

Rick Boehlke, their new partner in FLAIR, was also in the business of general aviation. And he owned Harbor Air, called the "Navy's airline" because it serviced the big Whidbey Naval Air Station in Oak Harbor, Washington. Boehlke was as controversial in his hometown of Gig Harbor, Washington, we learned, as Rudi Dekkers was in Venice. How had Rick Boehlke "got in for a piece" of the massive looting of workers pension funds in Portland?

Hardest hit ($60 million) by the theft were secretaries and laborers from the Laborers Union, called the biggest Mob-run union in America. To make up for the money stolen from their pension funds, analysts said, some of the unfortunate secretaries would have to spend an extra decade working.

Happy Secretary's Day.

The looters not only got away clean, they even managed to keep it from making big headlines. If someone broke into Citibank over Labor Day and made off with $300 million, we're pretty sure it would lead the *Evening News*.

This appeared to be a classic inside job. Just as in the half-trillion lost in the Savings and Loan Scandal, almost no one was going to jail, and no one was offering to give any of the money back. The local Portland newspapers just claimed to be sort of puzzled by it all.

We asked ourselves: How much clout does *that* take?

Dekkers' partner, Richard Boehlke, was one very fortunate man. He got $26 million in pension funds to build a high-rise condominium which he had only budgeted at $12 million. So Boehlke pocketed $14 million before he even broke ground.

We wondered: Where do you go to apply for that kind of work?

Boehlke participated in what the Securities & Exchange Commission called, "the biggest fraud by an investment manager in U.S. history." This would be newsworthy all by itself. But he did it while simultaneously being involved in still-more funny business with Wally Hilliard and Rudi Dekkers, who were at that same time "in business" with Mohamed Atta.

This could be construed as one major fraud too many for coincidence.

It reminded us of what our Southern lawman friend said when we told him about two Dutch nationals owning terror flight schools in Venice. It was one damn Dutch boy too many.

Two words you hope you never hear applied to your retirement plan are "Ponzi" and "scheme." Clearly, Jeff Grayson, the pension manager who helped Richard Boehlke and numerous others get rich for free, had experienced more than just one or two weak moments.

To give away $340 million dollars, you'd almost have to experience weak moments from dawn till dusk.

For *years...*

Yet that's just what thousands of union members and their beneficiaries from Portland and elsewhere began hearing had happened to their pension and 401[k] retirement plans invested by Capital Consultants LLC, the Portland investment management firm headed by Jeff Grayson.

"There was a 'consultant' problem with Capital Consultants," someone close to the case said delicately. "The people he loaned money to were fast-talking sleazebags."

"Ex-money manager charged with fraud" read the October 6th 2002 headline of the Associated Press coverage of the looting.

"A federal grand jury indicted Jeffrey Grayson whose firm 'collapsed' losing hundreds of millions of pension investments. Grayson was charged with mail fraud, conspiracy, money laundering, witness tampering and paying a former union chief union trust funds in a scheme that cost Grayson's clients over $355 million in failed and fraudulent investments," said the account.

Moreover, the disgraced firm, Capital Consultants, had been instrumental in giving Richard Boehlke his business start. According to Boehlke they had underwritten Crossings International, his development company founded in 1984. With Grayson's backing, Boehlke got into the assisted living business, a hot market catering to America's growing population of senior citizens, and made a killing.

By 1995 Crossings International owned or operated 15 health care facilities on the West Coast, and was valued at more than $100 million. The money allowed Boehlke to indulge in his passion: flying. In 1987, the avid pilot started Crossings Aviation, a series of aeronautic-related businesses at the small Gig Harbor airport.

Amazingly, while supplying both the planes and the pilots for the new Florida Air, Boehlke's Harbor Air, like Florida Air, had also been going bankrupt. So were two other of Boehlke's companies, Crossings Aviation, and Crossings Development, the Portland entity which Boehlke used to build his condominium project.

Counting the number of bankruptcies associated with Rudi Dekkers and Wally Hilliard, we realized, would require both hands, and our toes would be on-deck.

One last Boehlke note: his condo project was called "Legends Condominiums." Remember what your legend is?

Probably another freak coincidence. Or maybe somebody's sick joke.

Somebody said the "M" word. We almost wished they hadn't.

"Boehlke would do anything for money, he was so desperate," an aviation executive in Gig Harbor Washington who had witnessed Boehlke's descent told us.

"I'm surprised he hasn't skipped the country by now, what with all the trouble he's gotten himself into farting around with those Mafia boys down in Portland."

Word of the "M" word's use somehow got back to Boehlke...

"I've known Jeff Grayson (Capital Consultants' former CEO) for 12 years," Boehlke huffed.

"I have never known him to have any shady or, you know, some have asked me about... Mafia affiliations."

When reporter Eric Mason first met him, Richard Boehlke told him he was someone else. Spies do that sort of thing, don't they? Lie about who they are?

"It's interesting, in the first conversation that I had with him he denied being Richard Boehlke," Mason told us. "I asked him, from the description I'd gotten, I said, 'Mr. Boehlke, can I get an interview with you?'

"And he said, 'Mr. Boehlke isn't here.'

"When I saw him again later, I said, 'Mr. Boehlke, I think you really need to speak to me. I've got some important questions for you.' He finally said okay, come on upstairs."

Rick Boehlke sounded like Rudi Dekkers in a Pendleton shirt.

"Boehlke owed retirement homes, pulled shenanigans, and got sued a lot," said Mike Picket, who owns an aviation business at the same small airport as Boehlke's bankrupt Crossings Aviation.

"He owned Crossings retirement homes. He got in trouble about something to do with a woman who passed away. He would do a lot for money."

Boehlke and Dekkers seemed too similar for it to be just a coincidence... For example, Boehlke's aviation company was evicted from its terminal at Sea-Tac International for failure to pay back rent. And Boehlke's aviation-related businesses didn't make business sense, either. "Richard Boehlke's former employees always wondered what the aviation business was really doing," reporter Mason told us.

"From the beginning they felt that the finances flowed from the real estate holdings and the retirement home into this aviation company, and that there was really no way this aviation company was really making money. So the question about what this aviation company was really all about still remains to be seen."

We have seen quite a bit of wondering about "*what this aviation company is all about.*" About Dekkers and Hilliard as well. Then, too, Boehlke also was said to have often and inexplicably received blessings from the US government.

Did Boehlke have a "Dutch Uncle," too?

Mike Pickett, of PAVCO Flight Center, owns one of the oldest aviation firms at the airport where Boehlke went bankrupt, and was very familiar with Boehlke's operation.

"The city gave this guy all sorts of favors," he told us.

Just like Rudi Dekkers.

We wondered why.

Boehlke's Harbor Air had invested $8 million in new planes to accommodate more passengers in 1999, for example, and company officials said 2000 was a profitable year. But the firm's debts had already mounted to the point where management just cashed out and split.

A Harbor Air employee could only speculate as to why the airline was going under. "Mismanagement of funds," said the employee. "(Passenger) loads have picked up tremendously. We have five or six flights in and out a day."

Mismanagement of funds.

Only pretending to run a business.

Was Rick Boehlke an innocent businessman having a horrible string of bad luck? Or had he been feathering a bank account in the Caymans? Like Rudi Dekkers, all his companies were losers… even his "flagship" assisted living company.

"Even Boehlke's Alterra Health Care went sideways," said an aviation observer in Tacoma. "The stock went from $38 three years ago to 22 cents."

The *cover* story we heard was: Boehlke lost $40 million in the stock market. We thought: yeah, right. Boehlke lived in the San Juan Islands. Like Rudi, he owned a helicopter. He would use it, sources told us, to blow the leaves out of the yard of his house in Gig Harbor, on the Puget Sound. Boehlke had an expensive yacht. So did Rudi Dekkers…

"Rudi has a $500,000 boat in Naples supposedly bought with Florida Air stock which is worthless, several planes, a helicopter grounded by the FAA for illegal parts and maintenance, a million dollar home, fancy cars, and lots of other toys," one scandalized Naples, Florida resident told us indignantly.

"Somehow he has all of these things and yet every one of his businesses is a loser. He took cash from Huffman to pay the girl in the law suit. He intermingles funds between all of his businesses. He reportedly screwed Dale Krauss, former owner of an FBO at Venice airport which Rudi bought, out of 100K. He may even be in this country illegally."

It appeared that, for both of these men, crime had somehow been made to pay.

One difference was that Rick Boehlke was gay. We thought, at least we won't hear any stories about broom handle parties on his boat.

Then we learned he held orgies on his seaplane.

"For the 53 year-old Boehlke, the sun-drenched parties aboard his personal Grumman Albatross with friends in the San Juan Islands were supposedly over," reported the local paper in the San Juan Islands.

"His huge flying boat sits for sale at the Tacoma Narrows Airport in Gig Harbor, along with other assets from his bankrupt aviation company. Observers in Washington noted that he was not, however, running noticeably short of cash."

An aviation source in Tacoma told us, cryptically, "Money was being provided by the Mafia to smaller operators willing to do what needs to be done."

Speaking of the Mafia, the Mob, the Syndicate, and/or organized crime: Another grateful beneficiary of the money they were giving away in Portland from the retirement pension funds of the little people was a Boca Raton lawyer whose complex web of international connections was legendary.

Rick Boehlke's friend Jeff Grayson had made a $6 million investment with Title Loans of America, a Georgia company that lends to individuals with low credit ratings at extremely high interest rates. The loans are secured by the titles to the borrowers' cars.

Some call it legalized loan sharking, which is pretty accurate, because Georgia Title is owned by Alvin Malnik, the man labeled in print as "Meyer Lansky's heir" so often he should put it on his business cards.

The New Jersey Casino Control Commission found Malnik to be a "person of unsuitable character" to have any role in the industry. Malnik was so intimately associated with organized crime figures that they denied licenses to two businessmen who had done deals with him. But it wasn't Malnik's gangster ties that made our jaw drop…

It was his connection with the Saudi Royal Family.

Alvin Malnik, who admits only to being a Jewish lawyer from Miami, has extremely close ties—*family* ties actually—to a leading prince of the Saudi royal family, King Fahd's brother, Prince Turki Al-Faisal.

Malnik's son, Mark, converted to Islam, changed his name to Shareef, and married the daughter of Sheik Al-Fazzi, whose other daughter is married to Prince Turki.

"The Saudi Prince not only blessed the marriage, but regularly works with the US organized crime associates," read one account.

"The Saudi King would frequently send his private 747 to Florida to pick up Malnik and his associates, so they could conduct business on the plane away from prying eyes."

In Miami, Malnik owns the Forge, a restaurant law enforcement sources call the biggest mob hangout south of New Jersey, attracting what one account called "men with big cigars and women with tiny resumes."

We wondered if Mohamed Atta ever smoked cigars there. As we have already seen, he and Marwan had been hanging out in the Miami area with women known to "consort regularly with high rollers."

An Islamic fundamentalist high roller sounds like a contradiction in terms.

We have been looking for evidence of a global network which authorities, early on, said must have been aiding the terrorists while they were in this country.

Boehlke, because of his proximity to terrorist flight school owner Dekkers and his concurrent participation in what the Securities & Exchange Commission has called "the biggest fraud by an investment manager in U.S. history," seemed to offer some clues.

Might the same "international network" responsible for stealing $340 million have been simultaneously training a terrorist air corps in Southwest Florida?

Reporter Eric Mason was thinking about it too.

"Boehlke received financing from Capital Consultants," he said, recapping. "And the financial officers of Capital Consultants, have been indicted on a number of charges, including fraud. Some labeled it a Ponzi scheme, and I think the prosecutors have made the case that there was a major fraud being perpetrated."

"And you have to ask yourself: where did all this money go? How much money can you lose and not have anything to show for it?"

Perhaps Rudi Dekkers, Wally Hilliard, and Rick Boehlke worked for s single unnamed airline, devoted exclusively to a very large client, a client—after the pension fund scam—more than $300 million dollars richer.

Call it "Global Network Air."

Lurking just beneath the surface of American life, it seemed, was massive corruption on an unheard of scale, presided over by modern-day Untouchables, members of an organization—*a global network*—operating well outside the law.

And getting away with it.

Tracking this enterprise, we sometimes felt as if we were watching the spotlight on a bathysphere playing across the dark shape of a giant octopus in the inky depths of the ocean, 20,000 leagues beneath the sea. It was fascinating, but also a little scary.

Of course, as with an iceberg, the real action's always down below the waterline... Seafarers say the truly dangerous part of an iceberg is the unseen part.

And that's the part where the crimes of 9/11 reside...

When President George W. Bush said all evidence pointed to bin Laden and his Al-Qaeda organization as being responsible for the attacks, he equated the Islamic group to the Mafia. He said, "Al-Qaeda is to terror what the Mafia is to crime."

Said Naples jet manager John Villada, about Rudi Dekkers: "Everything that guy ever did, from *a to z*, was illegal."

CHAPTER EIGHTEEN

A BASTARD NAZI,
A FLAMING GAY MAN &
JACKSON STEPHENS

An investigation into the terrorist conspiracy's movements and activities led to an inquiry into the backgrounds of the people with whom Atta did business. So far we'd focused almost exclusively on Rudi Dekkers, the man who assigned the bunks when they arrived in Venice.

As we've seen Dekkers, a Dutch national, was a fugitive from justice in his native Holland. After fleeing to Florida, he became the subject of a multi-agency federal law enforcement task force during the mid-90s, which investigated him for smuggling restricted high technology out of the U.S.

Unless smuggling high technology was just a crazy idea Rudi dreamed up one day—unlikely—Dekkers probably had so-far unrecognized ties to international organized crime.

And he ran a flight school in Venice, FL with the distinction of having trained—for sums far in excess of normal—both of the pilots crashing airplanes into the World Trade Center. At a time when Rudi Dekkers couldn't buy gas for cash at the Naples Airport, he had fronted for the purchase of Huffman Aviation in Venice.

By early 2001, it was now his rent at the Venice Airport that Rudi couldn't pay. Then, while Mohamed Atta was still in residence in Venice, Rudi launched an airline.

His airline partner was active at that moment in concert with the Mob in the massive looting of union pension funds controlled by an investment firm in Portland, Capital Consultants.

Somehow no one mentioned any of these connections to Larry King, or Dan Rather, or Bill O'Reilly, or Jane Clayson, or Greta Van Sustern, before they put Rudi Dekkers on the air, where he was instrumental in creating the "official story" of Atta's time in Florida.

None of these fine journalists, working for esteemed major media organizations, had seen fit to do the tiniest bit of due diligence on a man who had been the terrorist ringleader's first major contact in America, contact which continued, as we'll soon see, until less than two weeks before the attack, although Dekkers testified it ended in December of the previous year.

We'd slipped down a rabbit hole. And we were mortally offended, on behalf of the entire American nation, at a government that was manifestly lying to us about important matters concerning 3,000 deaths.

We were examining the possibility that both men belong to a shadowy "global network" which aided the terrorists while they were in this country, so Dekkers and Hilliard's connection with Rick Boehlke was of immediate interest.

Boehlke was going bankrupt at the exact same time as Professional Aviation in Charlotte County, while Atta was there, taking innocent people's dreams along with their money.

Some of them later wrote about it.

"The office is a ghost town and my phone calls are not being returned," wrote one disgusted student, in a discussion among bilked students over how to get their money back. Unfortunately these people got my block time money and ran away."

"Crossings Aviation took my money also and ran, does anyone know of a class action suit being filed? If so, please contact me," wrote another.

Rick Boehlke was bilking his flight students in Oak Harbor, Washington at the same time David Byers was slipping away with *his* student's money in Charlotte County, Florida, at the same time Rudi Dekkers couldn't, or wouldn't pay his rent at the Venice Airport.

The three supposedly unrelated flight schools were all on the ropes during the Spring of 2001. Boehlke's Crossings Aviation and David Byer's Professional Aviation at the Charlotte County Airport went under; Huffman Aviation wasn't bankrupt but they couldn't pay the rent. Maybe they couldn't let Huffman go bankrupt because the school was still training terrorists to fly, and would be, right up until days before the attack.

Like the other two schools, Boehlke's flight training school, Crossings Aviation, received a visit from the FBI, we learned. Investigators were looking into the background of a Federal Aviation Administration electrical engineer who took flight classes with Boehlke in 2000, reported local papers. Moulay Lalaoi denied any wrongdoing, but said he'd also been interviewed by the Secret Service.

Are these similarities just *coincidence*? If not, we've located the "global network" British Prime Minister Blair spoke about.

But, what was the *name* of the enterprise we had stumbled on?

Who had Rudi Dekkers and co. been working *for*? We didn't know anyone you could just walk up to and ask.

We maybe got a clue from Mike Pickett, the aviation executive who had watched Rick Boehlke with the same amazement with which aviation professionals in Florida watched Dekkers.

"When Boehlke came in he was just a restaurateur at the Gig Harbor airport," he said. "Then he became the General Manager for a German named Folker, a German industrialist buying up all the land in that area."

More Germans.

Jessica Daley, an attractive airline professional in her late twenties, worked for Rick Boehlke at Harbor Air and later transferred and worked for Rudi Dekkers at Florida Air. While Harbor Air was going under, Boehlke told Jessica to fly down to Florida and see Rudi.

"When I walked into his (Rudi's) office he was yelling and screaming at people," she recalled. "He said, 'People call me a bastard Nazi because I'm loud and I'm German. And I'm very demanding.'"

Dekkers told her he was German, not Dutch, Jessica said.

"When I flew down to Florida from Portland during the first week of March, 2001, Rudi didn't even want me to go back," she told us.

"He said, 'sit down.' He said, 'I want you to work for me. Make it feasible. What would it take to get you here?'"

Despite having reservations, she was immediately and enthusiastically hired by Dekkers to work Florida Air's station in Tallahassee.

"He offered me $2,000 to stay, and said he'd have people move my things down from Portland. He was in such a hurry for me to come work for him that he burst into a pilot's meeting and had someone fly me round-trip up to Tampa to change my ticket."

Jessica soon was sorry she'd come. Conditions were chaotic. Employees began comparing notes...

"All we knew was that Rick and Rudi had worked out some kind of sleaze deal," said Jessica. "Rudi had written a check for $500,000, and Rick was keeping it, no matter what. They were screwing each other so bad it was almost comical.

"Rudi came in with a lot of money, but he didn't know the first thing about running an airline. And Rick was a pilot, and he knew nothing about it either. At that time he owned the Oak Harbor, WA. Airport FBO. It was weird.

"What I could never understand was Rick was in so much debt it wasn't funny, yet he still flew up to Sun Valley, Idaho in the Albatross almost every weekend," she said. "He didn't seem to care."

Boehlke was never shy about exhibiting his ostentatious lifestyle, said Jessica. "You have to understand: Rick is a flaming gay man who, even though he was in desperate financial trouble, was having all the upholstery torn out of one of his planes because he didn't like the color."

Both Dekkers and Boehlke were devotees of the high life. What the kids call "living large."

"It was the need for cash that brought Florida Air and Harbor Air together, and it was the lack of it that caused both to flounder in the months that led up to the terrorist attacks," reported the *Tacoma News-Tribune,* in a story on twin failed airlines.

"But former employees of Harbor Air said Boehlke mismanaged the company long before the deal with Florida Air. Keith Chvatal of Gig Harbor said Boehlke 'promised Dekkers the farm but had already slaughtered the cows and shut the doors on the barn.' He and one other former employee, who spoke privately, said extravagant parties and spending preceded financial troubles at Harbor Air," said the paper.

"Chvatal said he's owed $400 by Harbor Air. He also wants his former boss to be made accountable for the losses. 'It's time (for Boehlke) to tell everyone where all of the money went.'"

If people like Boehlke ever tell people where "all the money went," we've missed it.

"The business had been there for thirty years and he had run it into the ground in less than three," said Jessica. "I remember taking a foreclosure notice on the FBO that came in the mail over to him one day. And when I handed it to him, all he was concerned about was whether the wine cellar on his yacht was stocked for his next weekend excursion."

"Rick owned a huge hangar at the Gig Harbor, WA. Airport where he would keep his *toys*," she continued. "We called the hangar 'The Toy Box.' He had two yachts in the hangar, the Grumman Albatross seaplane that he used a lot, a 'little' Lear jet, and a couple of 'tail-drag-gers.'"

"Tail-draggers," she explained, were old-style antique airplanes. Boehlke collected them.

"Things began disappearing from the toy box one by one," said Jessica. "First a Cessna, then the Lear. Things kept getting worse. Everything Rick touches that has to do with money ends up disappearing."

This we were able to verify for ourselves. Boehlke became wealthy when, in 1996, he sold his retirement home business to Alterra and cashed out. Then the rest of his businesses went under. And then Alterra tanked, too, someone that followed the stock told us.

"Even Boehlke's Alterra Health Care went sideways. The stock went down three years ago from $38 to 22 cents."

Somebody lost $37.78 a share. We're sure it wasn't Boehlke.

"Finally, just as they were about to be repo-ed, they sent the rest of the planes down to Florida," said Jessica. "And then Rudi found out that Rick had let the insurance on the planes lapse. They were flying uninsured.

"When Florida Air folded several months later, I'd seen a lot of things I didn't like," she told us, "and I wasn't going to do anything illegal for them. Doug Hildebrandt (the then-President) called me and wanted me to get a U-Haul and go out to the Tallahassee Airport, after it closed, and get out all of the company computers and security badges and stuff. But I didn't want to be involved.

"They sent out some guy in a Suburban. When he tried to snag the airport security badges I got suspicious, and had one of my employees go tell the airport manager what was going on. The airline was out of business, so why would he need the airport security badges?

"The airport manager came over in a hurry with security. He said 'Oh, no! This airline owes the city a lot of money.' And the guy in the Suburban just took off."

Florida Air's attitude towards airline safety was as brazenly-casual as the ad hoc raid on the shut-down Tallahassee airline counter would indicate. In retrospect, some of this is more than appalling.

It's chilling, to borrow Rick Boehlke's phrase, to consider that Mohamed Atta continued to be active at the Venice Airport and was around the operation.

Jessica was getting her first tour of Venice, she said, when they passed a room where a security training class was underway for a roomful of Florida Air pilots. The class is required before airline personnel are issued the security badges they must have to pass through airport security, she explained.

"The guy teaching the class didn't have the 'SIDA badge' that said he was qualified to teach the course. And he wasn't. I had a SIDA badge from Seattle, so I ended up teaching and certifying the class for the course," she said. "What I remember about the 30 or so pilots was that so many of them were foreign."

"That was very unusual. I'd never seen that many foreign pilots in the same room. There was several French guys, a Russian guy, several Brits. It's incredibly difficult for a French pilot to get a work visa to fly for the airlines in the U.S. When I asked about it what they told me was that 'restrictions were looser in Florida.'"

Two years later, Jessica Daley is still paying for her stint with Rick Boehlke and Rudi Dekkers. "Just a few months back I heard from a hospital I'd gone to after a horseback riding accident in 1999," she said.

"They wanted me to pay the insurance portion of my bill. That's when I found out that they had been taking money out of my paycheck for medical coverage, but then not buying the coverage. Isn't that amazing?"

What did it mean that Rick Boehlke operated his aviation business with as little regard for employees and the law as Rudi Dekkers did? Boehlke's Harbor Air's sudden halt to operations left customers without connecting flights, employees without paychecks and creditors without payment. Dozens of lawsuits and liens were filed.

Dekkers had an interesting and fairly extreme managerial style, said John Villada, a jet manager in Naples. "He got in a minor dispute with a mechanic over something, and Rudi was interested in going out and burning this guy's house down. He was serious. I couldn't believe it."

Like Boehlke, Dekkers thought nothing of stiffing someone leaving his employ by stopping payment on their payroll check. His Florida Air ran aground when pilots refused to fly because they hadn't been paid.

"A Harbor Air pilot, who had gone to Florida for the airline, said the company not only issued him bad checks for his pay, but also failed to pay him the living expenses it had promised," reported the *Tacoma News Tribune* on May 26, 2001.

Seeking comment from Boehlke, the paper came up with an unintentionally funny line which perfectly describes the attitudes of men who routinely get away, for whatever reason, with breaking the law: "A house sitter at the Gig Harbor home of Harbor Air President Rick Boehlke said Boehlke was in Europe."

"Rudi acted like he had diplomatic immunity," the managing editor of the *Venice Gondolier* had told us.

Perhaps he did, because, in another freak coincidence, some impressively well-connected people are involved from both sides of the political aisle.

Capital Consultants, later taken over by Mobsters, had been founded by Charles J. "Butch" Swindells, an Oregon financier and philanthropist who helped raise hundreds of thousands of dollars to elect President George W. Bush. In April 2001 Swindells was said by the Portland Oregonian to be waiting "in line to become the next U.S. Ambassador to New Zealand."

He wouldn't have to work an extra decade before retiring.

And the Laborers Union, whose pension fund money was still supporting Rick Boehlke in the style to which he had become accustomed, long after his businesses went bust, was led by Arthur Coia, a man who curried and got Bill Clinton's attention, and was often invited to official White House events and personal dinners with the Clintons.

Coia and his union were longtime big players in the chase for campaign money. The union's various political committees contributed more than $ 2.6 million in regulated and unregulated, so-called "soft money" donations in the 1996 election cycle.

When Coia was indicted under the RICO (Racketeer Influenced and Corrupt Organizations) Act, he told his compatriots: "I talked to Bill Clinton... don't worry."

And indeed, the complaint had been quashed. Coia was only tripped up by the same ostentatious style which made John Gotti so eminently expendable.

"Arthur Coia's love of Ferraris, including one that cost more than $1 million, proved his undoing," reported the Jan., 28, 2001 *New York Times.* "Until recently the president of the national laborers' union, representing workers at the bottom of the construction pecking order, Coia has agreed to plead guilty to fraud charges for failing to pay about $100,000 in taxes on the purchase of not just one Ferrari, but three."

In a spasm of truthfulness, the *Times* said, "There could be any number of other questions it might be interesting to ask of a Ferrari-collecting union official, but not in this country."

The chief and, indeed, only accomplishment of Boehlke and Dekkers unsuccessful airline was that it provided a rationale for the presence on the tarmac of the Venice Airport of a half dozen British Aerospace Jetstreams poised within easy reach of Caribbean hot spots.

Well, the airline *did* have one other accomplishment: it was publicly endorsed by than then-Florida Secretary of State Katherine Harris.

"As one of Florida's top politicians, Katherine Harris doesn't have much time to do a lot of personal traveling," reported the April 16, 2001 *Florida Times-Union* in Jacksonville.

"But twice in the past month or so, the secretary of state—who received national attention for her role in the November presidential election—has taken the 75-minute plane ride from her current home in Tallahassee to her old stomping grounds in Sarasota. Her choice of airline? Florida Air, a start-up commuter airline based here, grasping to be an air-taxi for the entire state."

"'She has taken the airline twice,' Harris spokesman Ben McKay said. 'She appreciates the convenience that Florida Air offers.'"

When we discovered this, it seemed innocuous. But then we thought: does Katherine Harris seem the kind of gal who goes around endorsing businesses run by guys who can't pay their rent?

"Sometimes when things don't make business sense," ex-Florida Air exec Bill Bersch told us, "it's because they do make sense... just in some other way."

Even in newspaper profiles of Dekkers' new airline in its hopeful pre-launch phase, aviation executives said they found it to be a highly dubious enterprise.

"Other start-up commuter airlines have run into problems in the past trying to serve Florida, including Air South and Air Florida," the paper reported.

"Quite a few airlines have tried to make money serving an intra-Florida market,' said Bill Pettit, head of marketing at Jacksonville International Airport, 'but they have all found it to be very difficult.'"

How did Rick Boehlke and Rudi Dekkers know each other? Who brought them together? Dekkers claimed he met Boehlke through a mutual friend in Ohio.

He's lying.

Portland reporter Eric Mason explained. "Richard Boehlke started in business creating freestanding retirement homes, and he at one point had the largest company, the largest holding of these freestanding retirement homes in the country."

"One of the retirement homes that belongs to the company that Richard Boehlke once held was just a stone's throw from the airport where Mohamed Atta was trained. You have to ask yourself, there's a lot of coincidences here. Are they just coincidences, or is there something more to it?"

The official story provides an answer. They are just coincidences. Or they are "freak" coincidences.

But, just a few hundred feet down the block from Huffman Aviation in Venice, Boehlke's company, Alterra, built a gleaming new assisted living facility during the 1990s. Surely there couldn't be any connection between the assisted living industry and covert operations? Could there?

There could. We needed to look no further than a round-up of the usual suspects. A block away from the Venice Airport, on the opposite side of the street from Boehlke's assisted living home facility, is a large and stately colonial building which looks eerily like the plush digs of the law firm in the Tom Cruise movie *The Firm*.

The elegant building certainly seems out of place alongside the weed-strewn airport perimeter. It was built, we learned, to house the national headquarters of nursing home giant Beverley Enterprises, which was owned at the time they built it by a name almost synonymous with American covert operations.

Gleaming like a movie set in Florida's sunshine, the opulent three-story red brick building is a monument to the rivers of money which have flowed through the financial empire of Jackson Stephens, whose name has been linked with every major American scandal of the past generation: from BCCI to Contra cocaine through Mena, Arkansas.

Today the stately building still houses Stephen's former law firm, local political powerhouse Boone Boone & Boone, a firm which worked so closely with client Stephens that at least one of his executives was permanently housed there. Some credit the Boone law firm with running the town of Venice still.

"I don't think you could safely say that they (Boone & Boone) run everything in town," one local journalist told us. "But you could safely say they run *almost* everything. They exert a strong influence here, including out at the airport."

In an ironic twist worthy of the spy fiction of John LeCarre, the very thing that made Venice seem to us such an unlikely destination resort for Arab terrorists—its elderly population—attracted the home office of a nursing home company controlled by a man whose name is synonymous with American covert operations during the past several decades.

The name of Jackson Stephens, though rarely the man himself, made appearances in all the most whispered-about scandals and cover-ups in America. He was named in the BCCI criminal bank scandal, figured somehow in the story of the death of Vince Foster, was linked to the stolen Promis software scandal of the Justice Dept., as well as the 1996 campaign finance scandal involving allegations of Red Chinese money.

Most notably, Jackson Stephens was a figure in the huge scandal—involving gun-running and cocaine smuggling at Mena, Arkansas during the 1980's—that was behind both the Iran-Contra and Whitewater Scandals

Were Stephens to be implicated in another intelligence-related scandal, it would be, for him, something like three or four in a row.

Stephens' colorful curriculum vitae also included having been the college roommate of President Jimmy Carter at the US Naval Academy. Interestingly enough, the U.S. intelligence agency to which Jackson Stephen's name has been persistently linked, the National Security Agency, was accused by furious government intelligence officials with destroying data pertinent to the Sept. 11 probe, meaning that possible leads stemming from the Sept. 11 attack weren't being followed because of the NSA action, reported the *Boston Globe*.

The founder of Stephens' law firm in Venice, Dan Boone, we discovered, was no slouch in the college roommate department. Back when both were Florida Gators his roommate had been former Florida Governor Lawton Chiles.

Bringing things full circle, Lawton Chiles, although a Democrat, had given Republican Katherine Harris her start in politics, naming her to the Board of the Ringling Art Museum in Sarasota.

Small world.

Stephens was the chief domestic campaign contributor to both George Bush Senior and Bill Clinton, in, of course, different campaigns.

"At first glance it might seem curious that former President George Bush would attend an event honoring Jackson T. Stephens, the biggest Democratic power broker in Bill Clinton's home state," read a typical report in the Arkansas press. "But Mr. Stephens, a self-made billionaire investment banker and philanthropist, is financing a cause that transcends politics: golf."

When not occupied with enough philanthropic activities, Mr. Stephens found time to later be fingered as the "Old Man," as Barry Seal called him, behind the Mena, Arkansas cocaine smuggling scandal which dogged Bill Clinton throughout his time in office.

The Venice Airport also surfaced briefly in the news at this time. During questioning of Oliver North during the Iran-Contra hearings, a man with an aviation business at the Venice Airport named Joe Duncan was alleged to have run guns to the Contras from the Venice Airport.

What are the odds you'd stroll down the quiet streets of your retired parent's retirement community, which just happened to have trained a bunch of terrorists, and stumble onto a gated palace stuck out in the boondocks, looking like Emerald City?

"I think it is a crying shame that Dan Boone and his crowd can raise obscene sums of money to control the election and make it impos-

sible for a candidate without great resource to run for city council,"
read an angry letter to the editor in the November 7th *Venice Gondolier.* "We might as well cancel future elections."

Jackson Stephens had been an influential presence for several decades in the tiny town of Venice, the Hamburg cadre's portal into the
U.S.

Chances are, he still *was.*

CHAPTER NINETEEN

A LEAR TOO FAR

As far as intelligence or drugs, I am more willing to think this is drugs-related—but I am only looking at this different now…. Before, when I worked with FLAIR, I was threatened not to talk to anyone about FLAIR or about people there. But now I don't have a job and they owe me $8,000.

Less than three weeks after Mohamed Atta and Marwan Al-Shehhi began flying lessons on July 6, 2000, a Learjet belonging to the true owner of Huffman Aviation, financier Wallace J. Hilliard, 70, of Naples, FL., was seized by Federal Agents at the Orlando Executive Airport after they discovered 43 lbs., of heroin onboard.

In the drug trade, 43 lbs., of heroin is known as "heavy weight."

We first learned of the heroin seizure during an interview with John Villada, an aviation executive in Naples who was intimately associated with Dekkers' and Hilliard's various aviation businesses. He managed the firm's dozen or so jets, he told us, and he, too, had been shocked and amazed at the casual and arrogant way the two men dealt with various federal officials and agencies, like the FAA.

Dekkers forged Villada's signature on a repair order, he told us, stating required repair work on the helicopter had been completed. When he discovered it, Villada said, he was legally compelled to report the violation to the FAA.

"When Rudi was reported to the FAA for violations, an FAA guy came out and sat us down and said, 'I suggest you back out of this.' I couldn't believe it. I called the FAA to report a violation and was warned to leave him alone."

Villada dropped a bombshell. "After Wally's plane was impounded with the heroin and his pilots had machine guns stuck in their faces, the DEA came to visit our maintenance facility and Wally shouted out to me—right in front of the DEA guy—'Make sure all the heroin and cocaine gets hidden!'"

"That was in August of 2000. When I found out later that the DEA wouldn't let him have his plane back, I knew why."

Hilliard's mock warning to hide the drugs, explained Villada, had been Wally's way of telling the DEA how little he thought of them. The DEA hadn't forgotten. Villada seemed surprised we hadn't heard of the bust of Wally's plane. Not for the first time we realized how puny our investigative resources were before the immensity of the story of Atta and his cadre in Florida, itself just a part—though a crucial part—of the true story of 9/11 that has not yet been told or written.

We had soon confirmed Villada's assertion: Hilliard's Learjet had been involved in a major bust in Orlando. Authorities called it the biggest seizure of heroin ever found in central Florida. Had Hilliard been an unwitting victim? Like Rudi, an innocent business owner victimized by a world he never made?

Financier Hilliard ran money-losing flight schools. Now we discovered he leased jets to drug smugglers too. *Major* drug smugglers. A story in the August 2, 2000 *Orlando Sentinel* called the bust "the largest find of its kind in the southeastern United States in recent years."

We had thus far been preoccupied with Wally's less camera-shy partner Rudi Dekkers. The "front man." When we asked ourselves what it is front men do, we realized the answer was: deflect attention. It was time to turn our attention to the other half of the "Wally-Rudi" equation.

Because while Dekkers busied himself training young Arab men to fly, his partner Wally Hilliard had been running a charter service providing jets used to carry heroin, not a line of work you'd expect a "retired Midwestern insurance executive" to take up as a hobby on retirement in Florida.

The city where the heroin bust occurred, Orlando, will figure more heavily in our story. Mohamed Atta used Orlando as a transportation hub.

Bob Simpson, a Yellow Cab driver in Venice, took Atta by cab from Venice to Orlando several times. The FBI asked him about ferrying the terrorist ringleader, Simpson told us. They'd identified him from the number of his cab, caught by a surveillance cameras at the Orlando Airport.

Orlando's growing importance as a major trans-shipment point for heroin prompted Congress to officially designate Central Florida a High Intensity Drug Trafficking Area. Heroin overdoses, we learned, killed more people in Orlando each year than anywhere else in Florida.

The investigation which resulted in the seizure of Hilliard's Learjet began after a Colombian national, Nassar Darwich, was arrested in Orlando with 1.3 kilos of heroin in the soles of shoes he was carrying, the *Orlando Sentinel* reported.

Busted, Darwich promptly "rolled" on his bosses and cut a deal.

As a result, DEA agents were waiting two weeks later when the Learjet landed at the airport on July 25. They swarmed the plane, according to eyewitnesses, brandishing machine guns.

The flight originated in Venezuela and then made a stop in Fort Lauderdale before landing in Orlando, with New York as its final destination, the paper reported. Passengers Edgar Valles and Neyra Rivas, both of Caracas, Venezuela, were arrested. Most of the heroin was found hidden in the soles of tennis shoes stashed in their luggage. Eventually five people in Orlando were convicted in connection with the seizure, including the two Venezuelans.

"The pilot was not arrested, according to a DEA spokesman, because of a lack of evidence," said the *Sentinel.*

More on this sad fact in a moment. The DEA had a sad fact of their own…

"It confirms the sad fact that a massive amount of heroin is coming through Central Florida," U.S. Drug Enforcement Administration special agent Brent Eaton told the paper. "It's very disturbing to the DEA that more and more high quality heroin is coming from Colombia and at a cheaper price."

The DEA had been "very disturbed" enough to look more closely at Wally Hilliard's jet charter operation. The result was their firm opposition to returning the Lear to Hilliard, even though no one from Hilliard's company, Plane 1 Leasing, had been charged with any crime.

"DEA would not return it, they auctioned it off, they told Wally they had 'reasons,'" said an aviation source in Naples. "It was the first seizure in history from a so-called 'innocent person' where they took and kept the plane."

It appeared there was strong evidence pointing to the conclusion that—at the very least—Hilliard's company knew what was going on. Affidavits later filed by the machine-gun toting DEA agents who surrounded the Learjet indicated Hilliard's company's involvement went much deeper than anyone was willing to acknowledge publicly.

"It was just blatant," said a manager who worked there at the time. "That same plane flew that same run thirty or forty times, ferrying the same people. And they always paid *cash* for the rental! The red flags could not have been raised any higher."

We confirmed that Hilliard's Learjet made frequent round-trips to South America with an official at Executive Jet Service, the facility which serviced it at Orlando Executive Airport. He said the plane made weekly down-and-back runs to Venezuela. It was what's called a "milk run."

Three weeks after the Lear was impounded by the DEA, Hilliard asked for it back. In a motion filed in the U.S. District Court in Orlando, he argued that he was an "innocent owner" unwittingly duped by a known individual.

"Plane 1 and its officers shareholders and directors were not aware of the identity of the passengers utilizing the Lear 35A on this trip other than Mr. Valles," stated Hilliard's motion. The company had been "unaware that the individuals chartering the plane were engaging in criminal conduct." Company executives were also "not aware of any facts from which they should have been aware that individuals leasing the plane were engaging in criminal conduct."

A few facts about Lear jets: it's the most popular of private jets, the ultimate accessory for celebrities, and dates back to the late 1950s, when they were designed by American entrepreneur and inventor William Lear. The first Lear took off in October 1963. Today, Learjet is owned by Bombardier, and the planes are built in Kansas. They range in price from five to twelve million dollars new. The plane which golfer Payne Stewart was aboard when it crashed was a Lear 35A... And Wally Hilliard wanted *his* Learjet back.

The U.S. Attorney's office opposed the plane's return. Their motion said, "because the property was used or acquired as a result of a violation of the Controlled Substances Act."

The Justice Department, through the U.S. Attorney's Office in Orlando, declined to prosecute the pilot of the plane, even though affidavits filed by the plane-side DEA agent in charge revealed the pilot of the plane, Diego Levine-Texar, who worked directly for Hilliard, the Lear's owner, had guilty knowledge and should have been charged.

Even while machine-gun toting DEA agents swarmed the plane, the affidavit stated, "The pilot of the aircraft, DIEGO LEVINE-TEXAR, frantically attempted to make a telephone call using a cellular phone. LEVINE-TEXAR ignored agents and police officers who repeatedly ordered him to drop the telephone.

"Agents had to physically remove the telephone from LEVINE-TEXAR'S hands," the affidavit continued. "Based on my experience I know that narcotics traffickers maintain frequent contact with one another while transporting narcotics and currency, I believe LEVINE-TEXAR attempted to contact other accomplices as to the presence of agents and other law enforcement officials."

Picture the scene at Orlando Executive Airport. DEA agents are storming the plane brandishing sub-machine guns, but the pilot won't get off his cell phone. Agents have to "physically remove the phone from his hands."

Pretty ballsy. Or pretty blasé. We wondered: Who is Diego Levine? We discovered that knowledge about Diego Levine was considered, at least in some quarters, highly sensitive. But eventually, from aviation sources in southwest Florida, some information surfaced...

Like Dekkers and Wally, Diego Levine had a "hall pass" from the FAA, which might explain his casual attitude while being busted.

"One time in Miami, Diego got busted because he had no pilot's license," related a Naples aviation insider. "He was a terrific pilot, but he just hadn't ever bothered to get his license. He *should* have been in trouble. But he said, 'the FAA lost my file,' and—as a *courtesy!*—the FAA administered a 4-hour test on the spot and let him go on his way."

Diego had some juice.

What we heard about Diego: He flies a huge Gulfstream jet that looks like the interior of a Ritz Carlton Hotel.... His father owns a big furniture manufacturing plant in Venezuela.... Diego was trying to buy a Cheyenne (airplane) for the Venezuelan Air Force.... Diego's day job was chief pilot for Venezuela's Air Force One.

When he wasn't arrested flying Hilliard's Learjet, was it just dumb luck?

That's too absurd. No, what we are looking at is protected drug trafficking. CIA-approved. Probably dressed up as a "controlled delivery."

No wonder information about him was considered "sensitive." Whoever he was, Diego Levine was no amateur free-lancer. Diego's calls to the FAA got promptly returned. Diego is "home team."

Space does not allow an adequate discussion of the concept that the narcotics which are distributed in the US—with the same precision and re-shelving as any other commodity—are imported through the good offices of this nation's "clandestine services." There are a shelf-full of books (one is ours) which explain this connection, and how it is that the world's largest consumer market for one of the world's largest industries can remain hidden from federal law enforcement authorities. (It can't.)

Here's why:

The DEA affidavit confirmed the frequency of Hilliard's Lear's trips to South America. It said pilot Levine "stated he had known (Venezuelan) VALLES-DIAZ for approximately nine months. He has flown VALLES-DIAZ to New York and Fort Lauderdale approximately 30 times during that time."

"LEVINE-TEXAR said that he and his company were paid a total of $600,000 for those trips, and that he was going to be paid $80,000 for the current trip after arriving in Orlando," the affidavit continued.

Thirty flights in nine months—a weekly "milk run" down and back to Venezuela—would have ignited grave suspicions at any legitimate charter jet company, said aviation observers. But the discovery that Hilliard's operation was paid in *cash* for each of the 30 flights removes any question about the enterprise's legitimacy, in the unanimous opinion of aviation observers in southwest Florida.

It *wasn't*.

Wally Hilliard was involved in two ways, Florida records showed, as the principal of Plane 1 Leasing, which owned the Lear jet involved, and as a partner in American Jet Charters LLC, the charter company that leased the Lear from Plane 1 Leasing. Hilliard was a partner and co-owner, along with Diego Levine and a man named Mark Shubin.

"They obviously weren't even bothering to hide what they were doing," noted one observer. Yet despite being caught red-handed Wally Hilliard claimed in court filings to have been an "innocent owner."

On November 3, 2000, Federal Judge James Glazebrook denied Hilliard's motion. Yet there are no public documents explaining why.

"Wally took a big hit on that one," stated someone at the Naples Airport. "The DEA was *not* going to let him have that plane back."

"The DEA was planning on adding it to their Border Patrol fleet," confirmed a spokesman for the Lear jet's current owner, East Coast Jets of Allentown, PA. They bought the plane, he told us, after an insurance company, which insured it against seizure for the lender, successfully wrenched it back from the DEA after Hilliard had been removed from the picture.

Then we made an amazing discovery. Wally Hilliard got his Learjet from the same people who supplied the Learjet—two decades earlier—flown by famous drug smuggler and CIA agent Barry Seal.

Federal records showed Hilliard got his Learjet from World Jet, Inc., owned by the drug smuggling Whittington brothers, Don and Bill, of Fort Lauderdale, FL, who in their heyday in the early 1980s had been historic figures in the rise of the trade, commanding fleets of fishing trawlers, sailboats, power boats, and jets.

The Whittington Brothers were among the handful of major smugglers in the late 1970s and early 1980s, when tons of marijuana, and the oceans of cash it created, flowed freely through the streets and canals of Fort Lauderdale.

When *their* prized Learjet was seized—after their indictment for smuggling and tax evasion—it went to the man then on his way to becoming the biggest drug smuggler in American history, Barry Seal. Nor was this by accident. Here we were on familiar ground. Seal was the subject of our book *Barry and the Boys: the CIA, the Mob, and America's Secret History.*

Until his assassination in 1986 at the reported behest of then-Vice President George H. W. Bush, Barry Seal was a close associate of Iran-Contra figures like Frank Moss and Dietrich Reinhardt, who, as we have seen, are still "active," in the middle of all kinds of intrigue at the Charlotte County Airport.

The Learjet confiscated in Orlando didn't *get to* Hilliard by accident either. The man who owned it, Gary Levitz, 61, was killed in 1999 when his modified P-51 Mustang crashed during the National Championship Air Races in Reno, Nevada. Levitz, grandson of Levitz Furniture Corp. founder Richard Levitz, was an avid pilot and member of the Confederate Air Force, an organization of pilots whose members fly vintage war planes... and sometimes other things as well.

"Gary was a pretty amazing man," one of his managers told reporters. "He was a larger-than-life character. He would run the company day to day, and he flew warplanes and was a big-game hunter."

Gary Levitz was also a big-time drug smuggler. Back in the early '80s he was convicted of money laundering with the same Whittington brothers who sold his Lear to Hilliard.

Court documents said Levitz deposited large sums of money into bank accounts in Nogales, Mexico, and "helped disguise William Whittington's narcotics profits by investing into legitimate business ventures."

What we were seeing were clues left behind by a vast but hidden and still-unnamed global network.

The recently-deceased Gary Levitz also had ties in Venice, Florida, with a man whose name we'd heard whispered about.

"Ben Bradley's a DEA informant at the Venice Airport who got arrested for beating his wife," one aviation source in Venice told us bluntly, when we first asked around about Bradley.

"He set people up in Ft. Lauderdale and was given some of their toys. Gary Levitz got in the drug trade. He rolled on the Whittingtons and so did Bradley. His life was threatened, he went to Polk County, and ended up mooring his boat in Venice."

Small world. Barry Seal got a Lear jet after a small-time informant "snitched out" the Whittington brothers, making one available. Wally Hilliard's Learjet came from a guy who got busted with the Whittingtons twenty years ago and died in a crash, making one available. We were looking at institutionally-deep corruption—what sociologists call "elite deviance"—on a scale so massive that the only rational response is a boogie board, some suntan oil, and an extra large pitcher of margaritas.

Maybe that's where the FBI's been all along on 9/11. And maybe that's why FBI agents drink so much. It's hard to do your job with a straight face when you know the fix is in.

As early as a week after September 11 the FBI was pointedly stating that they had known about terrorists rotating through flight schools like Rudi Dekkers in Venice, Florida.

"The FBI Knew Terrorists Were Using Flight Schools," said a *Washington Post* headline one week after the attack.

"Federal authorities have been aware for years that suspected terrorists with ties to Osama bin Laden were receiving flight training at schools in the United States," the article stated.

What the FBI left unanswered was why they had done nothing to shut it down. But if what we were witnessing was some kind of CIA-protected drug trafficking operation, then the FBI's failure to take action against terrorists which the Bureau has acknowledged knowing were flight training in the U.S. can be explained by the Bureau's historical reluctance to meddle on another Federal Agency's turf.

"Early on I gleaned that these guys had Government protection," said a former Huffman executive. "We heard that 16 of the 19 terrorists had been on Interpol's Most Wanted list. They were let into this country for a specific purpose. It was a business deal."

The new information added to long-standing suspicions of drug trafficking voiced by local aviation observers in Venice. One told us he had learned that Dekkers and Hilliard's operation had what he termed a "green light" from the DEA at the Venice Airport.

"They were told to stay away from that (Dekkers) operation."

"*Who* was told?" we asked.

"The Sarasota County Drug Interdiction people," came the response. "They were told that they had a green light to operate and that they were to stay away from them, that they were some type of… alluded to the fact that they may have some type of government protection. And the local Venice Police Department were also warned to leave them alone."

Government protection of Rudi Dekkers would explain his sweetheart coverage in the major media. The notion of a Federal "hands-off" policy towards the Venice operation would also explain another suspicious circumstance provoking speculation: how Rudi Dekkers, whose various businesses were all utter and abject failures, managed to live in a $2.5 million mansion in a private gated community. The rumor was that Dekkers had other sources of income.

Which part of the government was he being "protected" by? Who employed his services? As we've seen, the FBI was only one of several federal agencies that had pursued an interest in Dekkers. While still in Naples, Dekkers stirred the interest of the DEA as well.

The question of the extent of Wally Hilliard's charter company's involvement in trafficking needs to be asked by someone with the authority to compel answers.

"I used to ask myself: Why is Wally doing business with all these foreigners?" said jet mechanic Dave Montgomery, Hilliard's former chief aviation mechanic. "There was Diego Levine, Alfonso Bowe, Mark Shubin, Pervez Khan... It didn't make sense."

Alfonso Bowe, we will learn, is a black South African, and also a former high-ranking Jamaican military officer. He runs Hilliard's FBO in Nassau in the Bahamas. Mark Shubin is Russian, and once flew for the Israeli air force. And Pervez Khan is Pakistani, and is one of only two people in the entire world with the State Department's permission to run regular flights to Havana.

Hilliard's business associates are the very definition of a "motley crew," and we'd barely scratched the surface. An air of mystery surrounded the activities of Wallace J. Hilliard as well as unanswered questions about the terrorist conspiracy's activities in Florida.

Wally Hilliard is not a peripheral character in the story of the terrorist conspiracy in Florida. He denied it, but at least one eyewitness says he knew Mohamed Atta.

During one of his periodic visits to Venice, Amanda Keller said she stood beside Hilliard, looking out the window at Huffman Aviation. Hilliard only came around, she told us as an aside, "to meet the newer jets, it seemed."

"What's a pretty girl like you doing with a guy like Mohamed?" Hilliard asked her.

We would all, I'm sure, love to know what he meant by that.

"I know more about Wally Hilliard than I ever want to know, said a former Huffman Aviation executive. "Why do you think the U.S. military didn't close the passes into Pakistan during the Tora Bora bombing? This all goes far deeper than you think."

Like many others, this executive demanded anonymity.

He explained, "I've got a family."

CHAPTER TWENTY

WALLY WORLD

Although in his many media appearances Rudi Dekkers portrayed himself as both president and owner of Huffman Aviation, this claim, like so many other of Dekkers pronouncements, was untrue.

"We all knew that the money he (Dekkers) flaunted was not even *his* money," stated Tom Hammersley. "What we heard was that he (Dekkers) had somebody in Naples backing him financially, that he was just a 'front' man for the man who had the money."

Dekkers never actually owned the flight school, we discovered. It was a ruse, a paper agreement which was never executed, or meant to be. Wally Hilliard owned Huffman Aviation. He was the sole owner, and had been all along.

We discovered this only after Hilliard sued Dekkers, his erstwhile partner. Hilliard was in the midst, in fact, of suing a number of his employees and business partners.

He sued Stuart Burchill, his accountant, and he sued business partner Mark Shubin. If it came to it, his defense was going to be that he had been victimized by unscrupulous employees.

A *lot* of unscrupulous employees.

Court documents filed at the Sarasota Courthouse in Hilliard's suit against Rudi revealed that Dekkers never completed the terms of the Huffman sale with Hilliard. Rudi "neglected" to pay for his shares of stock in the resulting corporation, said Hilliard's filing.

In the suit, Hilliard accused Dekkers of failing to pay for 1,000 shares of Huffman Aviation stock called for in their partnership agreement, as well as failing to repay loans he'd made to Dekkers since 1999.

Hilliard's lawsuit said that, as a matter of contract law, he had been Huffman Aviation's true owner… at *exactly the same time* a Hilliard-owned Lear jet was involved in narcotics smuggling.

This is probably just a coincidence.

Still, it was time to take a closer look at 70 year-old financier and multi-millionaire businessman Hilliard, the linchpin to the "goings-on" in Venice when the terrorists came to town.

When we finally met him, Wally Hilliard turned out to be a slim well-preserved 70 year-old man, with thinning reddish hair and still-bright blue eyes, impeccably attired in slacks and a gray golf sweater affixed with the insignia of the Augusta National Country Club.

As Huffman Aviation's secretive owner you're well-known in southwest Florida aviation circles, we began, as the "money man" and deep-pocketed financial backer of Rudi Dekkers. So, just who is Wally Hilliard, the "man who had the money?"

He refused our offer to tell. We'd have to find out for ourselves.

Wally Hilliard is the founder and former president of several Green Bay, WI-based health insurance companies. At the age of 65 he'd retired to Naples, Florida, in 1996. He was described in local newspaper articles as "a Florida businessman who made his career as an insurance executive in Green Bay, Wis."

How did a bland Midwestern "insurance executive" get involved in major intrigue in Florida? Even among those who work with him, few professed to have a clue. He was considered in aviation circles to be something of a mystery.

"I was Wally's jet manager. My office was next to his. I could over-hear everything he said. I still don't know who he is." John Villada stated flatly.

Hilliard's business partners professed to be mystified, as well. "Nobody knows for sure who Wally works for," said Mark Shubin, himself a bit of a mystery, as well as a partner of Wally's several aviation ventures.

Wally was colorful as well. Not many business execs can boast a 21 year-old secretary who gets arrested for trafficking heroin while she's working for them. Wally (and Rudi) can.

Summer Jeffries worked in Hilliard and Dekkers' Naples office.

"Summer was street smart but had a coke problem," said Villada. "She was busted for 10 bags of heroin."

Summer's bust revealed the level of surveillance Hilliard's operations were receiving... before 9/11.

"She told me that when they brought her in for interrogation," Villada said, "that they showed her *dozens* of surveillance photos of her, with Wally and Rudi. And she said there was even one of *me* getting in a Lear Jet with Wally. When I asked the FBI later why they had so many pictures of me, they said 'Just be careful, because you've got your name on a list.'

"Summer was busted for *trafficking*. Not possession. How does a 20 year-old girl get involved trafficking heroin?"

The question hung in the air.

Rudi Dekkers didn't impress locals as a budding James Bond. But Wally was a different story. Some in aviation at the Venice Airport thought it conceivable that Wally might be—of all things—a spy.

"You think of these guys looking like James Bond, or, you know, wearing flowered shirts and carrying Walther PPK's," said Coy Jacob. "It seemed like he (Rudi) wasn't quite as astute as I would have thought someone in the intelligence community would be."

"Wally certainly could be, though... I mean, Wally was unassuming, a nice guy, had a cell phone ringing all the time, and had an affinity for Lear Jets."

Wally may have been a man with a busy cell phone and an affinity for Lear jets, but he wasn't a *businessman* anymore. His aviation businesses weren't designed to make money, we heard over and over.

When we learned of the staggering sums Hilliard has invested in aviation after supposedly *retiring* to Florida, we were stunned.

"Wally's lost $40 million in the last 3 years, which is easy to do if you are spending $14 million on jets in one year as he did," explained jet manager Villada.

How does a retired insurance executive from Green Bay, WI "lose" $40 million? Whose money was Hilliard throwing around?

"I managed all of his jets. And I said to him, 'You have people flying all over the world and you don't know where they are, and where they are going. This is crazy.' Wally's planes went all over the free world, flying wildly," Villada said.

"How could you have a fleet of jets and not even know what they're doing?' But the pilots' attitude was always: 'I'm not telling you where I've been and I'm not telling you where I'm going.'"

Whatever Hilliard was doing cost lots of money…

"The man quickly bought—in very short order—a fleet of 12 to 15 jets. He spent between $30 and $40 million on planes and he still has 20 very expensive airplanes left, including Lear 35s, and Gulfstreams."

Flight manager Danielle Clarke in Naples told us Hilliard liked to portray himself as a "pious man."

"Wally came in quite a bit, seemed very compassionate, made a lot of references to God," she said. "You'd be talking about business and all of a sudden he'd mention the good Lord, and it got to be a bit much."

As a man of God, Hilliard's taste in secretaries was fairly un-Godly.

"Summer was 5-7 with long blond hair. She wore exceedingly short skirts and very low cut tops. You were struggling to find a bit of cloth on the woman," said Danielle tartly.

Another odd note was that Hilliard also hobnobbed with characters you might not expect a Midwestern insurance executive to come across.

Aviation mechanic Dave Montgomery, known as "Jet Dave" at the Naples Airport, told of witnessing a secretive meeting between Wally and Miami Dolphins owner Wayne Huizenga, for example, who choppered in on a large helicopter with the Dolphins logo emblazoned on the side.

Hilliard got into the helicopter, and the two men held a meeting that lasted almost an hour, before Hilliard exited and the helicopter took off.

Almost 40 years ago Wayne Huizenga was a founder of Waste Management, we learned, which grew to become the nation's largest trash hauler. As anyone who's ever watched *The Sopranos* can tell you, garbage is a big, big business.

Hilliard flirted with disaster in ways more staid executives avoided. He was recently subpoenaed by a Federal Court in Denver, for example, in a case in which he bought a plane from a man with connections to a Colombian drug cartel.

We wondered: How does a Midwestern insurance executive get connected to a guy fronting planes for drug kingpins from Colombia? Had he sold Group Health to the Medellin Cartel? Maybe Green Bay Wisconsin had a sister city somewhere in Colombia.

"Why Wally went to Colorado (to testify)," said the source, "was because years ago Wally bought a King Air B-200 from the Colombian mafia."

According to Stuart Burchill, Hilliard's former accountant, "Donald Pritchard was taking deposits on planes and then not producing the planes. He called Wally and told him he had a plane in South America and said he was going to ship it up. He (Pritchard) would advertise a plane for sale, do a contract, wire a deposit, then he'd start stalling and would never deliver the planes."

Why would a retired insurance executive be dealing with an international thief?

"Everybody knows a general in South America who they can get really good deals from on planes," replied Burchill. "You can get a jet in Mexico for a million less than its invoice. Pay $1.5 mill instead of $3 mill, and people do it, it's greed. I just don't get it. He (Hilliard) had some mysterious understanding about the deal that I didn't see. I saw him throwing money away."

Why was Wally "throwing money away?" Did he suffer from premature senility? Had he fallen prey to people who took advantage of old men?

If he was such a sucker, how did he get so *rich?*

Not too many suckers are friends with the President of the United States. Hilliard was friends with Bill Clinton. He kept a picture taken of himself with Clinton prominently displayed in his $3 million Naples, FL home.

"Wally knew Clinton well," confirmed a former employee. "Clinton called Wally a couple of times when I was there."

Hilliard had been in business with an international cast. We recalled the doubts expressed by jet mechanic Dave Montgomery. "Why is Wally doing business with all these foreigners? There's Diego Levine, Alfonso Bowe—a black South African who runs Wally's FBO in Nassau, Bahamas… Wally went to South Africa with him to *see the vine-yards*… And Pervez Khan, Pakistani, and Mark Shubin, who's Russian, and used to fly for the Israeli Air Force…"

Mark Shubin was Hilliard's business partner in a number of airplanes, including a $35 million Gulfstream.

Shubin lived in Miami. We had heard a number of different stories about him, each more lurid than the next.

"Mark Shubin is a KGB agent married to an American woman," said one usually reliable aviation source.

"Mark Shubin is ex-Jamaican military in his 50s and ex-KGB Colonel," said another. "His family was in the trade for the pilot who got shot down over Russia in a U-2. Shubin's an ex-CIA pilot who also flew U-2's over Russia. He's also flown for the Israeli military. He's also connected with the Russian mob."

A third source said, "Mark Shubin *used* to fly for the KGB. He used to fly the President of Russia, Putin. And he still has one of Wally's Falcon 10 jets."

If only one-tenth of this was true, it was quite a curriculum vitae.

We were anxious to meet Mr. Shubin. He sounded like a swash-bucklingly-interesting character.

If Wally Hilliard, the man who owned Huffman Aviation, was in business with a KGB agent—even a *former* KGB agent—it would be pretty big news. We figured news that big would have already been on CNN. On the off chance it hadn't, we traveled to Fort Lauderdale to meet the man himself.

In his office in a hangar at the Ft. Lauderdale Executive Airport, Mark Shubin came across as a pleasant and highly intelligent man in his later fifties, who carried, or so it seemed to us, an aura of authority. The first thing we noted when we arrived was that the offices of his company, Sky Bus, Inc., were located in the same hangar as the Whittington Brother's company, World Jet.

Somehow it seemed prudent not to mention it. At least, not right off the bat. We told him what we'd heard about him. He smiled a little in bemusement as we spoke. Then he nodded, and said, "You know more about me than the FBI."

The true story was that Shubin's father was indeed a KGB Colonel imprisoned after being caught by his own government spying for the United States. He and his family, including young Mark, had been "traded out" of Russia in the spy exchange involving Francis Gary Powers, the pilot of a U-2 shot down over Russia in a famous incident in 1960.

After settling in America, the KGB Colonel's son grew up to become a CIA pilot flying U-2's over Russia, where his native Russian language skills proved useful.

We were already well into spy lore, and we'd barely sat down.

"Wally was manipulated by somebody with a lot of power," said Mark Shubin. "He was blackmailed. Rudi was the one person who knew what was going on."

Shubin had quite a bit of business with Wally Hilliard, we learned. He had a company, Sky Bus, Inc., whose planes were shared in common with Hilliard's Plane 1 Leasing. Three of Skybus's four planes moved from Plane 1 Leasing to Sky Bus between March and August 2000. Plane 1 Leasing remained an "owner of sorts."

Two of the planes that flowed from Hilliard's Plane 1 Leasing, tail numbers N11UN and N111UN, were listed as being owned by both Plane 1 Leasing and Sky Bus.

We thought the "UN" designation on the tail number might be a clue. We were right. We discovered Shubin had established a company called "International Diplomatic Courier Services," on August 28, 2001.

We asked an aviation business owner about the planes with "UN" numbers. Coy Jacob said the last letters in an "N" number are picked by the individual plane owner. So Shubin and Hilliard's two planes either flew for the UN or were trying to look like they did.

Then we recognized the name of another business partner of Shubin's, a man who gained a bit of fame during the Savings and Loan Scandal of a decade ago. Mark Shubin was in business with the notorious Ken Good.

Kenneth Good was a big part of the Silverado Savings and Loan collapse. He was in business with Neil Bush. In fact, Ken Good had been so clearly a Bush family retainer that it strained credulity to think that Shubin—and Wally Hilliard—now were not similarly connected.

In 1983 Neil Bush, President George H. W. Bush's son, and our current president's brother, became partners in an oil venture with Ken Good and William Walters, a Denver developer.

Two years later Bush joined the board of Silverado, a Denver S&L to which Walters and Good already owed more than $100 million that was never to see the light of day again.

Neil Bush received a $100,000 "gift" from Good, as well as other major financial assistance. Yet he was pressing Silverado's management—without mentioning these favors—to let Good off the hook on his debts.

There was no conflict of interest. It was all just a coincidence.

By the late summer of 1988, examiners made ready to seize the company. But then they got a phone call from the White House, according to *Time* magazine. The election was too close; Silverado's collapse would inevitably have spotlighted the Republican candidate's son, whose conduct had certainly been unethical and possibly illegal. So the bank board's seizure of Silverado was delayed.

When Silverado finally collapsed, it cost U.S. taxpayers over $1 billion. But it hadn't been anybody's fault…

The *Houston Post's* Peter Brewton, who broke the CIA-Mob connection to the Savings and Loan Scandal, said Neil Bush's Silverado partners "all had connections to individuals or S&L's in Texas that did business with organized crime figures or CIA operatives. Good is one Silverado borrower who got a large loan at a Texas S&L connected to (Herman) Beebe, allegedly connected to the underworld."

Herman Beebe was an intimate, as they say, of New Orleans "Mafia Kingfish," Carlos Marcello. So Ken Good hung with both the Bushes and the Mob.

Ken Good cost Americans over $132 million, just from loans from Silverado.

He was destitute, said Bush. Yet the very next year, the supposedly destitute Good donated $100,000 to the Republican Party.

Shubin's former partner Kenneth Good was an example of a certain type of rich person who is bankrupt for purposes of paying their bills, yet remains a fat cat when it comes time to buy political influence.

Sociologists call them "elite deviants." They think of themselves as Masters of the Universe.

When Neil Bush was called before Congress to defend himself against charges he'd failed to disclose potential conflicts of interest as a director of Silverado, he conceded he was a go-between with Silverado and his partner Kenneth Good.

But although the disclosure wasn't reflected in documents provided to Silverado directors, Neil Bush insisted he had told Silverado officials that he was involved in an Argentina oil venture with Good.

When a government attorney asked him whether he should have corrected the document, Bush said, "Well, yeah, I would have, if I were a real technical, nit-picky guy."

How strange to find ourselves, while profiling Atta's American associates, right back in the realm of spectacular and unsolved crime. Mohamed Atta's American connections were with people who were crooks. But a certain *kind* of crook…

The well-connected kind.

Shubin and Good's partnership seemed to share a lot in common with Hilliard, Dekkers and Richard Boehlke's. Good's airline, Express One International, supplied both aircraft and crews to Sky Bus, the way Boehlke had for Dekkers and Hilliard. And Shubin's Fort Lauderdale based carrier was soon-to-be-bankrupt, a fate which Atta's Florida associates seem to face with an awful regularity. Good's Express One—drat the luck—will itself soon be bankrupt, and in bankruptcy proceedings the company's leading lessor will be revealed to be Finova Capital, a Canadian company "linked" to the CIA, and which also financed Iran-Contra-era proprietary airlines like Richard Secord's Southern Air Transport.

Mark Shubin was every bit as fascinating a character as we'd been told. Shubin told us much we didn't know about Wally Hilliard's international "associates."

"Wally owns an FBO in Nassau called Executive Jet Support with a guy named Alfonso Bowe," stated Shubin, "whose sister is married to the Prime Minister of the Bahamas. He (Bowe) also runs a flight school he started with Pervez Kahn."

Alfonso Bowe we'd heard about. P.J. Kahn, we knew, had crashed one of Wally's Lear jets in September of 2002, with eight doctors on board. All eight needed treatment. Other than that, he was a mystery, a Pakistani national who had somehow ingratiated himself with southern Florida's movers and shakers.

"Hilliard signed a contract with P.J. Kahn, who bought the old Air Florida Certificate," said an aviation observer. "P.J. Kahn moved in with Mr. Hilliard's backing. He's an Arab operator with a license to fly (an airline). Kahn's got a contract with the U.S. Treasury Foreign Assets Control to fly directly to Havana. He has special permission as an authorized carrier to fly direct to Havana."

We were puzzled. Foreign nationals aren't allowed to own U.S. air carriers. Also, U.S. air carriers aren't supposed to be flying to Havana. Puzzlement turned to incredulity when we heard from several people that P.J. Kahn had disappeared.

"I heard he has to flee the country for some reason," shrugged an aviation insider in Naples, who would say no more.

Another of Hilliard's executives in Naples was Chuck Hathaway, the VP of Ambassador Charter. We discovered a police report in Naples about a stolen Lear jet Hathaway had supposedly flown in from Canada in 1999. Eventually no charges were filed. Still, it was interesting enough. So we asked around about it in Naples.

"Chuck Hathaway flies for Continental Aviation," said John Villada. "The Lear in Canada that Hathaway was suspected of stealing—Kevin Frater talked this Canadian guy into buying the Lear. Kevin Frater is involved in this."

Frater, we were informed, had also disappeared recently, after a partner was arrested with 400 pounds of heroin. He, too, had been in business with Mark Shubin, in a $25 million company they jointly owned.

Heroin seemed to be a *leitmotif* running through many of Wally Hilliard's business connections. But these weren't *dese-dem-and-dose* kind of guys.

We'd already heard that the pilot on Hilliard's seized Lear jet doubled as chief pilot on Venezuela's Air Force One. Now we discovered that the co-pilot, conspicuously unnamed in court documents, had an interesting second career as well.

He's a DEA agent.

"Mike Brassington was co-pilot with Diego Levine on the heroin runs on the Lear Jet," an insider in Naples said. "He is DEA, assigned to Guyana."

Several people told us that Hilliard's former accountant, Stuart Burchill, had intimate knowledge of what was going on. So we set out to find him, after hearing several versions of what was obviously an incredible story. According to some, Wally Hilliard's operation was penetrated by the KGB.

"Stuart ran all of Wally's businesses," Danielle Clarke began. "Wally said he wasn't happy with Rudi. Rudi said he would have his own accountant to do the books. Enter Stuart. Stuart was very efficient.

"Then one day we heard Stuart was going to Russia, he'd found someone on the Internet," said Danielle. "So Stuart went to Russia. And I'll never forget the day he came back with Anna, his new bride. She was about 6'3" and looked like Bridget Nielson, Sly Stallone's ex-wife.

"She was just like a Barbie doll, and I thought, 'Why does somebody that looks like this have to advertise on the Internet for a friend?' She had a 6 year-old daughter and when they were together they looked like big Barbie and little Barbie. She was a very spectacular looking woman.

"And Stuart is rather slight, you know," recalled Danielle with a smirk. "He was for a while at quite some risk of domestic violence."

Mark Shubin got Stuart involved with Anna, said John Villada. He compressed the story this way:

"A really tall blond woman got deported. Anna's parents were KGB. Stuart brought a Russian girl back from the KGB, married her, and brought her here.

"Stuart was warned that if anything ever happened to Anna, he was dead. Then Wally started wondering how Stuart knew so much all of a sudden. And that's when it came out that Stuart's new girlfriend was involved with the KGB."

"Stuart went from a little rinky-dink apartment to a brand new million dollar home, with all new furniture, maids, the whole bit. And that's when Wally started getting suspicious and went through the roof.

Hilliard expressed his disappointment by having employee Burchill charged with embezzlement. "Rudi and Stuart embezzled $500,000 from Wally," said another former Hilliard employee. "Then Stuart took the rap. Nobody knows why."

"Stuart took the rap for Rudi in the embezzlement case," confirmed a source. "Wally turned him in. And then Wally sued him. *But...* he kept Stuart working for him. And I said to him, 'How can you sue Stuart and still have him working for you at the same time?'"

Hilliard's response had been non-committal. At least he was consistent.

After a brief search, we found Stuart Burchill, still in Naples, and still working occasionally for Hilliard.

"I am still friendly with my ex-wife today," Stuart told us. "Anna *is* haughty and egotistical. Her uncle was a big businessman in aviation over in Russia—in the Russian mob."

"I met her on the internet at Russianbride.com. Anna's father's name is Boris Georgeva. He's a former Russian Olympic gold medalist in the shotput."

When we questioned Wally Hilliard about Stuart Burchill, a guy he had busted for the embezzlement of $500,000, we asked if his displeasure with Burchill owed anything to his Russian bride's curious connections.

"I don't know anything about a Russian bride," Hilliard replied blandly. "I don't know anything about her connections. All I know is that he started writing checks a week after he came to work for me, and never stopped, and so that is why he got charged with embezzlement. If he doesn't do a couple of years, I'll be disappointed."

"I'm not mad at him," Hilliard explained. "I'd just be disappointed."

Someone still working for Hilliard explained the Burchill imbroglio this way: "Wally's accountant, Stuart, discovered that money for Wally's flight schools was really being used for something else."

All of this might be of nothing more than anecdotal or even prurient interest, but for the fact that there were so many important and unanswered questions about the man who financed Rudi Dekkers' terror flight school.

One of Hilliard's ventures, for example, is called Oryx, LLC. An "Oryx" is a kind of African gazelle, we learned. And a British mining company in Africa named Oryx was accused by the BBC of having links to Al Qaeda and trading blood diamonds.

We asked Hilliard to tell us how he had come to name a company Oryx. He declined. "There is a company called Oryx," said Hilliard. "If I thought it was germane to anything I would tell you, but I don't see it is germane to anything."

We persisted. "It is a strange name, I just wanted to know why you named the company Oryx?"

"I didn't," replied Hilliard. "There's no relationship. My relationship with them is small, there are other people involved and therefore I'm not going to talk about a company that is owned by others."

Whoever Oryx is, and whatever it was incorporated to do, Wallace J. Hilliard most assuredly owns the company, according to filings with the Florida Dept. of Corporations and FAA.

We always get intrigued when we discover we've been lied to.

When people lie, it's always for a reason. Did diamonds fit into Wally's South African dealings? Was that where the name Oryx comes from?

When we finally got the chance to ask Hilliard about Mark Shubin, his reply was, "Another name I wish I never heard of."

"How do you meet these guys; especially since you look like you should be playing golf?" we asked.

Hilliard used an aphorism to describe his version of the series of seemingly-inexplicable business decisions that ultimately had horrifyingly tragic results. "I have done some very stupid things with airplanes, and it has cost me lots of money," he said, pausing before delivering the punch line:

"Brilliance has its limitations, but stupidity has none."

It sounded like a line scripted by one of Bob Hope's writers, but he kept coming back to it to answer our "specific" questions. Hilliard actually used it so frequently that it got to the point where he just alluded to it in shorthand:

"The difference between brilliance and stupidity," he'd say tersely. It developed a rhythm; Hilliard began to sound like somebody practicing pleading the Fifth: "I refuse to answer that question, Senator."

The difference between genius and stupidity.

Sadly for Hilliard, however, we don't think "stupidity"—should it ever come to it—is a valid legal defense. And even if it were, the slim and sharp-eyed man lounging elegantly across from us in a gray golf sweater affixed with the insignia of the Augusta National Country Club would have a difficult time convincing a jury that he was in any way mentally challenged or impaired. Why?

The thought came unbidden: Very few "stupid" people ever own that many Lear jets.

Or get near that much heroin.

CHAPTER TWENTY-ONE

LIVING WITH MOHAMED

Revelations about "shadowy financier" Wally Hilliard had been coming fast and furious. They were frankly more than we'd bargained for. While interviewing Wally's partner Mark Shubin we'd realized we were overmatched, never a happy conclusion.

We'd never met anyone who'd alledgedly worked for both the CIA and the KGB. How do you ask somebody about something like that? We didn't know where to start.

And we still couldn't figure out Wally Hilliard, a retired-to-Florida insurance executive now living like a Midwestern James Bond. Maybe not as much razzle-dazzle, but owning twenty jets was impressive.

We had no idea what made Wally so... *different.* A lot of people retire to Florida. But most retired men settle for hobbies like woodworking. Boating. Golf. Shuffleboard. We'd never heard of anyone retiring to Florida to pursue espionage and drug trafficking. Worrying that your organization's been penetrated by a foreign intelligence service cuts down on hammock time.

So we turned our attention back to Mohamed Atta's activities in Venice, to see if his behavior offered any clues to the riddle of Wally Hilliard's motivation. Since they knew each other, we thought maybe we'd find a common thread. We re-visited our interview with Amanda Keller.

We have to admit we weren't immune to the tabloid aspects of the story of her living with a terrorist ringleader. We'd wondered what terrorists like to do for fun, during the odd hour when not planning mass murders. If America had a free press anymore, we figure we would already have seen headlines like "Terrorist's Stripper Girlfriend Bares All—The Mohamed no one knew."

But of course we haven't. It's a puzzlement. Had good taste suddenly become fashionable on the networks?

Maybe we missed it.

"When they first mentioned Venice on the news," Amanda Keller told us, "I went oh my god, what if I knew one of them? Then they mentioned the name Mohamed, and I was like, oh my god."

We sympathized. If the FBI called and told us we were buddies with a major terrorist, we'd be like, "Oh my god, too."

"Then the FBI started calling. They asked me what I knew, I told them, and they told me not to talk to anybody, to keep my mouth shut."

We asked her, "When you first saw his picture on TV afterwards, how did you know that that was the guy you'd been living with?"

"It was that look on his face. That was the look he kept on his face most of the time," she replied. "Very moody, somber, but he had a little goatee, very close-shaven, when I knew him. So he looked a little different too."

Amanda's sister Tammy met Atta when he drove up to her mother's house in Lady Lake. Looking to her sister for confirmation, she told us, "It was in March that you brought him up to Lady Lake, remember?"

"I waited and waited for them to get here, and then finally took my lunch break, and that's when they showed up," explained Tammy.

"He got pissed off and told me I was a rude bitch for not waiting for him. He smelled of patchouli oil."

We'd heard this patchouli oil story from several people. Amanda confirmed it. "He had a very intimidating look about him. He smelled like patchouli oil, wore a foreign cologne every day," she said. "And it stunk."

Almost by accident we learned from Amanda that two other of the nineteen terrorists—the less publicized ones—also lived in Venice. "Majed Moqed" moved in to the Sandpiper, she recalled. Also "Ahmed

Alghamdi" (another Alghamdi). "I recognized his picture," she said. "He used to come to the beach, and hit on my friend Tania."

Atta's two months with an American girlfriend went as badly as you'd expect. And his American girlfriend, as American girlfriends do, let him know about her disappointment in him… *a lot.*

"After I lived with him, I noticed he was an asshole," Amanda stated flatly. "He called me an infidel all the time. But I was working non-stop at Tampico Bay (a nursing home in Venice) and Papa John's because I needed to buy a car."

What she meant was she wasn't yet ready to lower the boom on Mohamed. But it was coming…

She ticked off a litany of his irritating qualities. "Mohamed was really anal," she explained. "Very anal about the way he hung his clothes. He ironed everything, and got mad at me because I didn't iron. So he bought an ironing board and an iron. He would sit there and press his pants. He had to have perfect creases in his pants. He had a particular way he hung everything. He was very anal retentive."

"Even his bathroom routine was exactly the same every day," she continued. "Exactly. He would go in shave his goatee, trim his hair, wash his face, brush his teeth, go the bathroom then take a shower."

"I remember lying in bed listening to the different noises he made and they were always exactly the same… exactly. Every single day, same order, the same time."

She made him sound like a dripping water faucet. The litany continued…

"He didn't like animals. Charlie (Grapentine, the apt. mgr.) had a great big dog, a puppy, and he would paw on my door, come to our door and I would let it in. And I would give him lunch meat, and that pissed Mohamed off to no end. He said, 'You let that dirty beast in here?'"

"So I said, 'Well, I let your ass in here. What's the difference?'"

"Then there were always dirty dishes in the sink," she continued. "He said 'Aren't you going to do the dishes?' I said 'You made the mess, you clean it up.' He said, 'That's your role.' I said 'No, you're in America, and it's my name on the lease. This is my house.'"

A moment of truth was approaching. Mohamed Atta's last girlfriend on Earth, (that we know about), was getting ready to do him wrong.

"See, I had talked him into using his money to get the apartment, but it was in my name," she said. "Basically, I was just using him."

It was, ironically, Amanda's new job at Fantasies & Lingerie that led to the split. We'll let her tell it:

"As soon as I started making good money there, I kicked him (Atta) out," she said. "I was pulling like three grand a week. You wouldn't believe how many doctors, lawyers, judges, came in there. All high profile people. To spend money there, you had to have money. They sucked me in."

"I started working there, and Mohamed called me a whore, cause I was stripping. He started cussing at me. Either Harley or Page drove me to work. And Mohamed would start arguing with him, (the driver) and Page once said to him, 'I wear 6-inch stilettos, and I'll kick you right in your head.'"

"Page had a crush on me," Amanda explained, "they were all lesbians that worked there, and she was the one that picked up my dead cats."

We heard another anecdote casting Mohamed Atta in a less than manly light. "We went to a club called In Extremis one night in Sarasota," Amanda explained. "They have a fight night on Wednesday night with a wet T-shirt contest afterwards, which I had talked my friend Tania into joining."

While waiting around for the T-shirt competition, someone in the ring pointed to Atta. "Some guy called him up to fight, they were in the same weight category, and Mohamed wouldn't do it."

This was not considered good form at "fight night."

"The dude totally punk-ed him out," Amanda said disgustedly.

"Right in the middle of the club with 1,400 people in it, the dude punk-ed him out. It was awful. My trainer was in there, and all these people that I knew and I just sort of walked off to the side because I didn't want to be seen with him."

We heard more about the social set in Venice.

"Angelina knew Mohamed too, through Olivia, who knew the big Dutch guy that lived in the apartment at the Sentinel," she said. "Angelina was a nanny, and Olivia was working at Publix, then Denny's. She designed lingerie on the side, that was her passion."

"Me and Angelina were looking for new jobs; I was sick of working at the nursing home. I didn't like the way they treated the patients.

We looked in the paper. Saw an ad: 'Lingerie models wanted.' I said, 'Cool.'"

By way of explanation, she says, "My hair was hot pink at the time."

Life at Fantasies & Lingerie provided Amanda an education into the colorful strains of "elite deviance" which flourish in southwest Florida. Amanda told of Nick, a bald former N.Y. City cop who worked security, and protected them. She said all the girls had stage names: Alexis, Harley, Faith...

"Joy was my stage name," she explained. "Richard (the owner) named me Joy. They made me keep my hair hot pink, down to my ass. He owns Extremis boat racing. Extreme boat racing. Owns the boat racing franchise."

"For a half-hour session I made $600, that was just my money. In the dungeon it was $1000 a session."

There was even a whiff of blackmail wafting over the scandalous proceedings.

"There was one politician in Florida who came in there, Lexi told me about it. He liked his penis to be downgraded, got off on us telling him how small it is and stuff. That's how Richard made his money," Amanda alleged.

"They have cameras and monitors set up in those rooms, and they blackmail people. When I left, Richard threatened to blackmail *me*. He was pissed, 'cause a lot of customers would ask for me, and I was embarrassed about having worked there and he knew it, and he threatened to give pictures of me to people that knew me."

Blackmailing politicians in Florida appeared to be a growth industry. Presumably the FBI is on top of the situation.

Although they've released nothing to the public which pays for all their long lunches, the FBI must know that Atta frequented places like Fantasies & Lingerie. In fact, it was the last place Amanda Keller ever saw him, when he stumbled in late one night after they had broken up, shouting her name.

"I was in a session one day and Mohamed and a bunch of his cronies, drunk and stoned out of their minds, came in screaming his head off. 'Where's Amanda! I want to see Amanda!'"

"And none of the people I worked with knew my real name, because it was all supposed to be confidential. And he was throwing a fit.

They had to get security to throw him out. Security stuck around and walked me out to my car at 5 a.m.," she said.

"I was in a session, and Bobbie wouldn't let me come out, cause they were drunk and hopped up on whatever, and she wouldn't let me come out. She chased them out as quickly as possible. But I had to pay a fine for that cause they thought it was my fault. And that pissed me off even more."

"And that was the last time I saw him."

Did he have any good points?

"He was somewhat decent at some point. He had a gold necklace with a figure on it, and I asked him what it was. He told me it was Palestine he wore around his neck. He called it the home country. He told me his father was a pilot, he wanted to be like his father, he'd gone to private school in Lebanon, he spoke highly of his mom, cause she was obedient," Amanda explained.

Here's a newsflash we don't know what to do with: Atta listened to the Beastie boys, non-stop.

"One time I got mad cause he broke one of my knick-knacks, so I snapped his CD's in half," said Amanda. "I broke all of his CD's, cause they drove me crazy, he played the 'Beastie Boys' nonstop."

In the aftermath of the argument, Atta told her why he was such a big Beastie Boys fan.

"He told me about this girl he'd dated in France, that had his son. He didn't tell anyone else about that, for some reason he felt he could spill his guts to me. His son was like nine, he said. He said his son was the reason he liked the Beastie Boys so much, cause they were his son's favorite band."

Did Mohamed Atta have a nine-year-old son in France? Or was this just part of Atta's "cover story?" We didn't, and still don't, know.

But consider: we can imagine a spy making up a nine-year-old son as part of a cover story for "civilians." But we have a harder time envisioning that spook going to the trouble of inventing for his phantom son a favorite band, which then becomes his own.

Amanda confirmed that the story we'd heard from Stephanie Frederickson about beatings, and her throwing his clothes out was true.

"Mohamed hit me, threw stuff at me, hard. Left bruises. We had three very nasty arguments. The first was over the way he talked to me, the second over religion, and the third one... that one came after

I had slept with Garret. After the last one, I threw his shit over the railing onto the parking lot below. He was gone at the time.

"We argued a *lot* over how I dressed when I went to work or to go out to a club," she said. "I was thin, I wore little bitty clothes, And I was gonna wear what I wanted to wear."

Amanda described the arc of the relationship as not having a favorable trajectory. But it had had it's moments.

"He did have some good points. When I first met him, he knew exactly what to say to me, 'cause I guess he could see. He talked in French all the time, saying little sweet things… But then he turned into a wicked monster. After that he was an asshole, always downgrading me.

"After I met Garret, I guess I did flaunt Garret in his face," she admitted. "I used to have Garret spend the night with me, and I'd make Mohamed sleep on the couch, for the last week before I kicked him out."

They fought over Garret, not surprisingly.

"And Mohamed said, 'You are a typical American bitch, fickle and an infidel.' He also called me infantile. 'You American women are all alike, all you want is money.'"

"And I said, 'What the hell else do you have to offer?'"

Things were going more than slightly downhill.

Amanda called her sister Tammy for advice. "I told my sister he had called me an infidel, and she said you must mean 'infidelity,' and I said, no, that's not it."

We asked Amanda: What was he like in bed? We didn't have to, but we did. And when we did, Amanda's sister Tammy giggled and went into convulsions, and then held up her pinky finger and wiggled it in the universal symbol for the under-endowed.

"His dick was like, almost invisible, it made my skin crawl," said Amanda. Her sister interrupted excitedly. "What did you tell me about him?" she asked.

Amanda remembered: "God gave me hands for a reason, so I could do it better myself… Seriously, sex with Mohamed was terrible. He wasn't passionate. The most passionate thing he did was when he molested my foot while I was sleeping."

This was "sticky wicket" territory. We scolded ourself for asking such a shameless question. Then we motioned to Amanda to—please, by all means—go on…

"I was sleeping, and I had already met Garret," she began, "and I sleep on my stomach, and I can't stand my feet to be covered, and I woke up from a nap one day because my leg was shaking, and I'm all, what the hell?

"And I looked down, and he was standing at the foot of my bed with my left foot in his hand, and rubbing it against himself. And I kicked him as hard as I could—just reared my leg back and just clocked him right in his stuff. I just got him. Right there. And I said 'What the hell are you doing?'"

If Atta had a ready answer, Amanda didn't tell us what it was. But for a guy with a foot fetish, he prayed a lot, Amanda said. He prayed in the morning, and later in the afternoon, and then after he got back from flying. One of their three big fights had been (ostensibly) about religion...

"He would make fun of how we believe in God. He said, 'What do you people do for your god? You don't do anything for him.' And I just looked at him.

"I pray sometimes, too. I was sitting at the table reading my Bible and he came in and snatched it out of my hands, and tore it in half. And he broke the crosses I had on my walls. He was mad cause I had interrupted his prayer session... he had two candles around a little gold something, had his head down and was praying.

"I lived with him almost two months. He was gone for two weeks in the middle, to New Orleans, he said. When he got back, he was more moody than before.

"I don't remember him saying anything about Mardi Gras when he got back, though. I figure if they would have gone to Mardi Gras they'd have come back with beads. But he didn't."

This would have been the early April time frame, when Atta is reputed to have gone to Europe, and met in the south of Spain with fellow conspirators.

Amanda had noticed discrepancies in Atta's "flight student" cover story. Mohamed wanted his commercial license really bad, she said. But that never made any sense to her.

"It doesn't make any sense because he was allowed to fly students at that airport... He was allowed to fly new students. He flew to Tampa with Timothy. But Timothy was flying and Mohamed was in the co-pilot's seat, telling Timothy what to do, just like an instructor."

"Timothy," we later discovered, is Timothy Hupfeld, a German friend of Atta's from Hamburg, about whom we have heard nothing from the major media. Timothy had a sister, Sabrina, who was close to Atta as well.

All of Atta's friends already had pilot licenses from other countries, she said.

"This is what I don't understand," she continued. "He (Mohamed) said he was a student, yet he was allowed to fly other students, he was allowed to go off on his own, and he had the privileges of an instructor, which is why Mohamed didn't fly the plane when I went up (to Tampa) with him, he just sat there and told (Timothy) what to do."

This is crucial information. It clearly indicates that the government and media have not come anywhere close to clean about the status of Mohamed Atta in the United States.

And then Amanda started to tell us about the drugs. Atta's one-time girlfriend had a ringside seat to the debauchery.

"In Key West, they were doing drugs, but not in front of me," she explained. "They would go into the locked-down room where no one slept, saying they needed to look at their manuals, and when they came out you can tell their jaws were locked, and they started chewing gum like there was no tomorrow. They would go brush their teeth, wash their faces.

"They didn't do drugs in front of me until after I had met everyone at the apartment," she said. "The Sentinel Apartments. After we got back from Key West, Mohamed introduced me to everyone in the apartment, the first time I went over there."

On the FBI's Suspects List, 400 E. Base Ave., in Venice, the address of the Sentinel Apartments, is given as the address for a number of the terrorists, but not Atta.

"I met Angelina and Olivia and a big Dutch guy who was like almost seven feet tall. Peter, Stephan, Timothy, and Juergen were there too. And a guy with dark hair who looked kind of like Mohamed but had real long hair, moody, said he was from France."

"Frank said he was from France, he and Mohamed acted like they knew each other for a long time," she said. "I drove Frank to Tampa.

He was dressed in a pilot's uniform, looked like a pilot, said he had a job interview there. He was one of the top flight instructors (at Huffman)."

This would be Francois Nicolai, a French flight instructor, who we heard was today flying for a living in Saudi Arabia.

"They were always drinking. Beer or wine, or liquor. Always. Once I met everyone there (at the Sentinel condominium) they felt comfortable with me and they pulled out the coke."

The first time we heard this we'd been flabbergasted. We made her repeat it: "You saw Mohamed Atta do coke?"

She nodded. "The first time I saw him use it, he borrowed a dollar from me to roll up as a straw, and then asked me if I wanted to do a line laid out on a glass table in the living room they used to cut it on. I said no. To me it was like something you'd see in a movie. It was the first time I'd ever even seen cocaine.

"These guys had money flowing out their ass," she said. "They never seemed to run out of money. And they had massive supplies of cocaine. Whenever they'd run out, they'd go over to the flight school.

"I followed them one day with Sabrina (Timothy's sister, from Hamburg) to see where they were going, and saw them go into Florida Flight Training."

That's the Florida Flight Training Center, owned by Arne Kruithof, which also maintained a condo at the Sentinel, right across the hall from that used by Atta and his crew, which belonged to Rudi Dekkers.

Amanda described a typical night out with Atta when nothing much seemed to happen at all.

"Area 51 club was another place we went, sink or swim night," she said. "Mohamed didn't like the music, which was all rap. And Juergen had to take Sabrina home, cause she was epileptic, and there were strobe lights, and it was causing her to have a seizure."

"Me and Olivia stayed, and also Timothy (Hupfeld), the outgoing one of the bunch, a real nice guy, younger than the others. We met more pilots, from Africa, Germany, and Arabs."

"Marwan was in the reggae room drinking with a bunch of women at the bar, there were a lot of women around him, and he was just flaunting money."

It's one thing to hear Atta described as living it up with wine, women and song. But Marwan flaunting money at the bar pretty much puts the lie to the *Islamic fundamentalist* tag.

In conversation with Amanda we were amazed at the number of associates of Atta's whose names didn't sound Arab.

"Him and Wolfgang drove around in the red convertible a lot," she said. "Their favorite place to eat was Hooters in Sarasota. They got kicked out of Hooters for grabbing their boobs.

"He spoke German with Wolfgang, who was in his thirties. Wolfgang was with Mohamed when he came by the nursing home to see me one time. They told me he was here. When I saw him I said, 'What are you doing here?' He said 'I wanted to make sure you were at work.'"

Not a very trusting soul, apparently.

More puzzling was learning of Atta's deep ties with a number of Germans. "Mohamed called certain people—Arabic people—'my brother.' And I was wondering how he had so many family members. Like gang members do, 'this is my brother,'" she said.

"But not *all* Arabs. So it wasn't like anyone Muslim was his brother. He called Wolfgang and Juergen 'my brother,' too. He and Wolfgang were very tight, they went everywhere together. When he came into the picture they were together all the time.

"Him and Juergen acted like they had known each other forever. He told me he went back and forth to Germany, but lived in France.

"Juergen was a pervert, straight out," she said. "Every woman that walked by, he had something to say to them, commenting on their butt or whatever. He would go up to a woman, say I'm from Germany, and I want to touch an American woman's butt. He was a lush, mid-30s."

Who was this "Wolfgang?" Who was this "Juergen?"

Why have they not stepped forward to explain themselves? Even as these questions rolled around in our head, Amanda plunged forward with her narrative, to the all-time low moment in her romance with Mohamed Atta.

"I made him cry one time," she said, with some satisfaction. "So he obviously thought more of me than I did of him. He asked me how come I wouldn't sleep with him anymore, and I said, you don't want to know. And he was like, 'Yes I do,' and I said, 'Leave it alone, you don't want to know.'

"And he kept picking and picking at it, and so I finally looked at him and said, "because my pinky is bigger than your penis.""

Well into the last year of his life, Atta may well have been reaching out for a little human comfort. That he so clearly picked the wrong girl is small compensation. But small compensation is better than none.

For Amanda Keller, summing up her brief brush with a terrorist—with a terrorist *ringleader*—will always be difficult. It would be hard to remember the good times, even if there'd been any.

"There were moments he'd be laughing and joking, then the next minute angry and violent, in 2.5 seconds. Then, as soon as you'd blink your eye, he'd change," she said.

"Although he did like pork chops."

CHAPTER TWENTY-TWO

THEY'RE TRYING TO KILL THE "MAGIC DUTCH BOYS"

Half-way through our investigation into the people and organization operating at the Venice Airport, our efforts took on a certain urgency, after it became apparent that somebody was trying to kill the "Magic Dutch Boys"

Rudi Dekkers and Arne Kruithof, the targets of our investigation; had also been targeted in ways less benign.

Less than five months apart, Kruithof and Dekkers were involved in separate air accidents. Kruithof in a Cessna on his way (supposedly) to Cancun and Dekkers in his helicopter on his way to a showdown meeting with his now-estranged partner Wally Hilliard. Aviation observers said the crashes could have—or *should* have—killed both men.

Neither man had any history of air crashes. It was enough to remind some—certainly the conspiracy-minded—of the suspicious deaths of Kennedy assassination witnesses, who no longer had any comment on what they'd seen, because they were no longer with us.

"Paging Miss Dorothy Kilgallen."

So even though we'd made some headway in understanding what was going on, and in the process unearthed evidence of a large and on-going 9/11 cover-up in Florida, it might not be enough to meet our unstated goal: aiding a successful effort to compel sworn testimony from people assisting the terrorist conspiracy while they were in this country.

Because if there was a 9/11 clean-up crew at work in Florida, its activities could instantly make all our efforts unavailing.

We were playing Beat the Clock with the Grim Reaper.

Dekkers' brush with death happened with such inauspicious timing that eyebrows were raised all over Florida.

On Friday morning, January 24, 2003, Rudi and his helicopter "splashed down" at the mouth of a river spilling into the Gulf. He had been en route to a showdown over Huffman Aviation with his erstwhile partner Wally Hilliard, with whom he had been publicly feuding.

Just a few short months earlier it had been fellow Magic Dutch Boy Arne Kruithof's turn. Kruithof was one of three men who barely survived the crash of their Twin Beech D-18, which plummeted from 100 feet in the air to a runway at the Venice Airport. The men were able to drag themselves out of the mangled fuselage and dash to safety moments before the plane's 300 gallons of fuel exploded in a fireball.

It made for a great picture in the next-day's *Venice Gondolier.*

When the tumultuous Dekkers crashed his helicopter into the Caloosahatchee River, his latest misadventure made the news everywhere from Sarasota to South Africa. The coverage revealed an abiding and continuing public curiosity about him, even in the face of the official blackout.

What was most revealing about Dekkers' crash was that before he took off for what was to be a showdown with Hilliard, he had been seriously worried about having an in-flight "mishap."

Although the flight from the Naples-Fort Myers area to Venice takes barely half an hour, Dekkers prevailed on another helicopter pilot headed in the same direction, Tony Douangdara, to fly alongside him in an effort, as he explained it, unconvincingly, "to stave off boredom."

Either Dekkers was psychic, or he was afraid someone might want him dead. Something clearly was going very wrong for Rudi Dekkers even before his chopper began experiencing difficulties.

The first sign of trouble-to-come came when one of the helicopters began pulling away. When his more powerful helicopter surged ahead, pilot Tony Douangdara told the *Venice Gondolier,* Dekkers seemed remarkably upset.

"He was calling me on he radio saying, 'Slow down, slow down!'" said Douangdara. "Then, just a couple of minutes later, I heard him say, 'I'm going down!'"

Douangdara seemed to be suggesting he'd been recruited to be nearby if something went wrong. He circled back to see what had happened.

"'Oh, shit! I'm going down,'" Douangdara heard Dekkers cry out over the radio. "I thought it was a joke at first," he told the *Sarasota Herald-Tribune.* "But when I couldn't hear the motor or any rotor noise, I knew he was in trouble. He was in bad shape and in no condition to swim. He was just hanging onto (his craft's) skid to stay afloat."

"The helicopter he (Dekkers) was in flipped over and crashed into the Caloosahatchee River near downtown Fort Myers at 7:25 a.m.," reported the January 25, 2003 *Miami Herald.*

"Dekkers climbed on part of his helicopter that had not submerged. He then grabbed the landing runners on Douangdara's helicopter and was pulled from the river."

Once ashore, Dekkers hopped into a nearby swimming pool to warm up, said news accounts. "After Douangdara took Dekkers to a nearby home (actually someone's back yard in a quick drop) he went into the pool to wash off the fuel that was stinging his skin."

Startled at the sight of a fully-dressed Magic Dutch Boy floating in his pool, the homeowner called 911. Strangely, by the time officers arrived, Dekkers had left. "The sopping wet Dekkers braved the 30-degree weather, wandering down the streets in search of help," said the Sarasota paper.

Odd. He'd been trying to flag people down to take him to the hospital, he said later. But he had a hard time getting people to believe his story. Because if Dekkers was seeking medical attention, he didn't tell the people who owned the oil-slicked pool. He was clearly in a hurry: taking a dip in a pool, then disappearing. Was he worried about compensating the homeowner for the cost of having jet fuel sopped from their swimming pool? He went wandering down the street, soaking wet...

"Dekkers received another lucky turn: Rescue crews, on their way to the crash scene, spied him and rushed him to Lee Memorial Hospital in Fort Myers," said the *Tribune*. "Dekkers was treated and released about 11:30 a.m. By early afternoon (he) was apparently feeling well enough to hold business meetings at Huffman Aviation."

Rudi Dekkers' unexplained helicopter crash came while he was on his way to a Venice meeting to sign papers relinquishing control of terror flight school Huffman Aviation to Wally Hilliard.

The two simultaneous events—the crash, and being forced out of business by his partner—weren't linked by law enforcement. But the strange timing added another bizarre twist to the saga of the 46 year-old Dutch national, who had already achieved international notoriety.

When we checked both men's FAA records for previous crashes, they hadn't shown any. But the search proved fruitful anyway: records obtained from the Naples Airport Authority reveal that Rudi Dekkers has received numerous citations for negligence, non-payment of bills, leaving a helicopter running with no one at the controls, numerous noise complaints, and a lot of suspicious low flying well-below safe limits.

But no previous plane crashes.

Dekkers was in the middle of a fairly rough patch. In the space of little more than a week he learned he would be arrested on felony fraud by the state attorney's office, crashed his helicopter into the Caloosahatchee River, and signed over the flight school that gave him his 15 minutes of fame.

Told he was about to be arrested for fraud, Dekkers told the *Venice Gondolier*, "Wow, I'm surprised."

After overcoming his incredulity, however, he called the charge "political," heaping some thinly-veiled scorn on the man prosecuting him, State's Attorney Jonathon Greene, for not knowing that everything had been taken care of already.

"We're drawing the paperwork as we speak that resolves the deal," Dekkers told reporters defiantly. "We have a deal, we know about it. Everybody knows about it except the State Attorney."

He said, "We don't have problems anymore."

Wally Hilliard, present at the contract signing the afternoon of Rudi's crash, was agreeable to dismissing the suit, confirmed Jim Beach, director of operations for Triple Diamond Jet Center, the new owners of Huffman Aviation.

Not so fast, said State's Attorney Jonathon Greene.

"Wally Hilliard called me and asked for a waiver of prosecution," he told us. "But I told him that nothing has changed on our end. We're going forward with the charges."

The charges would keep Dekkers in the U.S. for a year, preserving the hope that investigators will have the opportunity to question him.

We asked about Rudi's "rap sheet." We'd wanted to know since our first day in Venice, when we were told his police file had been confiscated by the FBI. State's Atty. Greene indicated Dekkers' prior record included a number of *blemishes;* like owing $3 million in the Netherlands, for example, the result of the same criminal activity he'd just been charged with again—pledging assets he didn't own to secure loans he didn't plan to repay.

A Dutch court had adjudged him guilty of acting "in a manifestly improper fashion," according to documents we had translated. They said his "manifest failure to properly manage the company was an important cause of bankruptcy" of an Ede, Netherlands-based company Dekkers had stripped of its assets before fleeing to the U.S.

Rudi Dekkers was a *repeat* offender. Not just a fraudster, but a *professional* fraudster. Many people with his history are assumed to be working with organized crime.

When he completed the sale of Huffman, Dekkers expected his problems to go away, he'd indicated. His legal woes would end when Hilliard dropped his lawsuit, an action he believed would trigger the dismissal of the criminal fraud charge, which concerned a $200,000 loan from a crony of Hilliard's in Wisconsin "secured" with a mortgage on property in the name of a company which didn't own, the property being used as security.

This must be what people mean when they say, "Nice work if you can get it."

Yet despite settling his lawsuit with now-former partner Hilliard, his woes appeared to be just beginning. Now someone in the government was saying "wait a minute." In the two years since the 9/11 disaster, it was the first time officials had taken action that wasn't designed to pass over "inconvenient details" of the 9/11 attack.

The second Magic Dutch Boy, Arne Kruithof, kept a much lower profile. So it was somewhat surprising to discover that his plane crash was even more life-threatening than Dekkers'. Arne and two others barely survived the crash of their private plane on Wednesday, June 26, 2002, when it nose-dived to earth after a troubled take-off from the Venice Airport.

From over a hundred feet in the air the plane plunged onto the runway of the Venice Airport. And subsequent events left aviation observers wondering if Kruithof's near brush with death was an accident… or something more sinister.

Onboard, along with co-pilot Kruithof, were the pilot, Glenn Goodman, and a passenger, John Mills. The men told investigators they were on their way for a pleasure trip to Cancun.

They were "shaken up, but essentially without injuries," according to a Venice Police spokesman, who also said, "They were really lucky to walk away from this."

Coming just months after Rudi Dekkers' helicopter crash, Kruithof's plunge had observers wondering out loud if the crash was just an accident. Local observers were skeptical. While "mechanical failure" was believed to be responsible, there were suspicions the plane had been sabotaged.

Citing a commonly used method of provoking plane crashes, one wag at the Airport asked, "Did they check the fuel tanks for rubber balloons?"

And that was *before* the plane's wreckage was towed out of the Airport and destroyed in an unseemly and possibly criminal haste, before investigators had even determined the cause of the crash.

If someone *were* attempting to ensure Kruithof's ultimate silence in front of Congressional investigators, a plane crash, historically, would be the way to go.

Did someone want the Magic Dutch Boys dead?

Glenn Goodman's plane was uninsured when it went down, supposedly on the way to Cancun ferrying parts for another plane that had broken down there. But one of the men, John Mills, was wearing his mechanic's coveralls in the cockpit of a plane flying to Mexico in sweltering late June. It was like flying to Hawaii wearing a three-piece suit, someone told us.

Then, too, going to Cancun to spend a weekend in July is like taking a three-day vacation in February in Green Bay, Wisconsin.

We could hear in our head the slow drawl of our friend the Southern lawman, who sometimes spoke so slow he made two words out of one. When he said, "It's un-tidy," you could drive a truck between "un" and "tidee."

There were suspicious irregularities in the official investigation into Kruithof's plane crash that observers at the airport said had never before happened. Without any finding on the cause of the crash… before investigators were even able to get a *look* at the downed plane, the wreckage was gone.

Things like that weren't supposed to happen.

"Even though the FAA hadn't yet determined the cause for the crash," said one shocked observer, "the plane was almost immediately dragged off to be compacted."

He looked stunned. "That's not just irregular. It's *highly* irregular. We're all kind of wondering just what the hell's going on."

Though both Dekkers and Kruithof got a free ride from the national press, they didn't get one from their aviation peers; in the community of aviation professionals in southwest Florida, there was a cloud of suspicion hanging over them already, even before their near-disasters.

One concern we heard voiced was that the two schools had catered almost exclusively to international students. Dekkers told reporters he'd trained more than 800 foreign students during just the past two years. And Venice residents said the city's other flight school, Florida Flight Training, had numerous international students as well.

Speculation about Kruithof centered on his relationship with Rudi Dekkers, and also to another partner, Pascal Schreier.

A German national living in Munich, Schreier and Kruithof had a co-venture, called Aviation Aspirations. According to its literature the company provided financial assistance and a "Mentor Programme."

About their "mentoring programme," the company's literature said, "The help is both financial and practical. We now provide one-to-one practical assistance from experienced Professional Pilots (our Mentors) whom we have established throughout the world."

"Mentor" sounded a lot like "handler" to us. Were we being too cynical? French newspaper *Le Monde* had reported that Osama Bin

Laden's brother Yeslam sent student pilots to Venice for training. Nothing more about this mechanism has surfaced. Was Aviation Aspirations the vehicle that had been used to insert Yeslam bin Laden's pilots into the Venice flight schools?

Schreier's job was recruiting flight students from his Munich base. Had he recruited in Hamburg? We didn't know. We did know that the company's motto was "Better training because we care."

Who was Pascal Schreier, and why did *he* care?

"Pascal Schreier has an inferiority complex," Venice Airport insider Max Burge told us. "He's 6'2" blond, good-looking, German, and you could see it in him. Rudi and Arne, too."

We didn't get to meet him, but we learned a few interesting tidbits to share. "Pascal Schreier is married to a lady who took over the 135 School at Port Charlotte," said one aviation source.

We checked it out. It was true. Small world.

Pascal's wife, Sandra K. Hamouda, who was half-French and half-Tunisian, now owned the flight school in Punta Gorda once known as Professional Aviation, the one which went bankrupt in February 2001, while Mohamed Atta and all those Tunisians were there.

Now it appeared that they'd kept the school in the family.

Later we learned that the new owners of Huffman Aviation were from the largest flight school in the Netherlands, which used to train up in Lakeland, Florida. It was near Rotterdam, the city from which Arne Kruithof hailed.

Pascal Schreier was also apparently involved with Wally and Rudi's failed aviation ventures. The true name of their flop airline, which flew as Florida Air, was Sunrise Airlines. And Pascal Schreier owned a company called Florida Sunrise with an address at the Venice Airport. It was too close for coincidence

Kruithof's plane crash also threw a spotlight on the pilot of the downed plane, Glenn Goodman, the pilot at the controls of the downed Beech D-18. Goodman and Kruithof were partners in Arne's flight school at the Venice Airport, just like Rudi and Wally were in theirs.

Goodman received praise for controlling the crash, and keeping the plane from flipping end over end down the runway. Some credited his skillful flying for the three men still being alive.

Who is Glenn Goodman? Goodman, we learned, is the scion of the Budweiser distributor family in nearby Tampa. His family also owns the Sarasota Yacht Club, which attests to a certain level of attainment. Glenn, however, lived on the floor of a cabin out at Eagle's Point Landing, we were told.

We asked someone who knew him to describe him. Was Goodman eccentric? "Glenn Goodman has a gold mine in the Caribbean, and owns a sailboat he sometimes lives on at Marathon Key," said the source. "He looks like Howard Hughes with a ponytail."

We took that for a *yes*.

Kruithof and Goodman formed "Florida Flight Maintenance," in July of 2000, just as Mohamed Atta and Marwan began training at the Venice Airport. Goodman also owned a DC-3 that sat at the Venice Airport for two years before being donated to an air museum in July, 2000, called the "Florida Military Aviation Museum."

This was a major red flag. Donating planes and then getting them back from air museums is a ruse which has been used to provide planes over the years to a rich and colorful crop of elite deviants with intelligence connections.

A Military flight museum was the same venue used by the CIA in the past to *liberate* military planes and helicopters in various sordid paramilitary schemes. It was being used right next door in Charlotte County, we remembered, to "re-assign" 23 helicopters to new billets.

Also troubling was the fact that as Goodman's company was closed involuntarily by the State of Florida on September 21, 2001.

Was it's closure 9/11-related?

Known as N90079, Inc., the company was named for the "N-Number" of the business's sole asset, the aging DC-3. Because the company never filed an annual report, much about it remains a mystery.

When we ran the plane's registration, or "N" number, we discovered that the plane's colorful history has included long stints in exotic locales. It spent quite a bit of time, for example, back in the '80s, in Manuel Noriega's Panama.

The DC-3 could be traced back to an infamous South Florida Customs airplane "bone yard," where "planes with checkered pasts" sit in a fenced storage yard, like the sister ship to the famous C-123 shot down over Nicaragua in 1986 with Eugene Hasenfus aboard.

Probably just a coincidence.

We heard a funny "only in Florida" anecdote about another proud local owner of a DC-3, a man reputed to be in the "import-export business" and apparently as colorful as Goodman's impersonation of Howard Hughes with a pony tail. "Any time I need cash," said this aviator, "I go out in the back yard and dig up a Mason jar."

The most interesting thing we heard about Glenn Goodman was that the DEA—surprisingly active at the tiny Venice Airport—had asked a local Confidential Informant of theirs to follow him around.

Maybe the aborted Cancun trip had something to do with it. Even more incredible was that the DEA informant being asked to keep an eye on a guy walking around looking like Howard Hughes with a ponytail was involved in other events in our story as well, and had his own colorful history…

"He set up people in Ft. Lauderdale and was given some of their toys," said an airport insider. "He rolled on the Whittingtons."

The Whittingtons? *Those* Whittingtons?

We were momentarily speechless. We thought… wow. Who knew? Small world.

When we finally interviewed Wally Hilliard, it came after we'd dropped into his offices unannounced. It got us an audience.

We began by asking him to explain the numbers of Arab students "marching across the tarmac at his flight schools."

"I'm sorry, what you are saying is grossly untrue," Hilliard stated, angrily denying reports about the number of suspected terrorists who had flocked to his two Dekkers'-run flight schools.

"I believe that there were two Arab students, not 22, only two," Hilliard told us, dismissive and emphatic. "There were two, period. Two total."

If we were speaking of Dekkers, we'd say he was lying. But Mr. Hilliard, as an elder, deserves a touch more respect, we figure.

Hilliard wasn't *lying*. He was just mistaken.

In point of fact, the revelation of an additional four terror suspects (in Chap. 14) had brought just the already-*known* total of 9/11 cadre terrorists enrolled at flight schools owned by Dutch nationals Rudi Dekkers and Arne Kruithof, to eight.

Rudi Dekkers' toll alone was five. And counting.

What made Dekkers more than a run-of-the-mill con man and quick-fading historical footnote is something which remains unacknowledged, except obliquely, by U.S. officials.

When the Hamburg cadre made their fateful leap across the Atlantic, it was Rudi Dekkers assigning them bunks on the Left Side of the Big Pond. Dekkers sat at the critical nexus where the terrorist conspiracy met the United States of America.

If Dekkers had been lying while claiming to be an innocent business owner victimized by wily terrorists—an action we've documented him taking with an awe-inspiring regularity—the conclusion is unavoidable that Mohamed Atta didn't "just happen" to stumble onto Venice, Florida.

And if Atta didn't "stumble" on Venice, then *we* have stumbled... onto the fabled Global Network, and flatly contradicted the FBI's scenario that the terrorists received no outside help while they were in the U.S... a position they have held tenaciously during the years since the disaster. Even though it's wrong, the position has allowed the Bureau to discourage speculation about the anomalies visible in the terrorists' workplace. In their *milieu*.

The FBI probably figures—and rightly—that when you're playing for time, every little bit helps.

Within spitting distance of communities of "retired" CIA agents, large numbers of Middle Eastern men were enrolled as students at flight schools operated by people reeking with shady and clandestine connections.

In the indifferently-motivated September 11th investigations so far, the one really burning question hasn't even come *up...*

"What's been going on in Florida?"

When Rudi Dekkers turned himself in to be arrested on the fraud charge, local observers said they were disappointed that there hadn't been a "perp walk." It would have been, all in all, small satisfaction.

But then, small satisfaction is better than none.

CHAPTER TWENTY-THREE

ANATOMY OF A COVER-UP

By this point in our investigation we had proved to our satisfaction that it was not mere happenstance that led Mohamed Atta and his Hamburg cadre to Huffman Aviation in Venice. Things were not what they seemed in Florida. And the FBI's full attention seemed to have been engaged—not in investigating what had happened—but in suppressing evidence and even intimidating the witnesses who had seen and heard things that fly in the face of the "official story," everyone from Mohamed Atta's American girlfriend to the Sarasota Fire Captain who witnessed four Arab men attempt to get close to President George W. Bush on the morning of September 11 have been subjected to sometimes ham-handed efforts to keep them silent.

There is a demonstrable, provable, and *massive* federally-supervised cover-up in place in Florida. But the real question, of course, is: *What* are they covering up? What's the *reason* for it?

Late in our investigation, we found a piece of it.

On at least three occasions during the last six weeks of his life, terrorist ringleader Mohamed Atta left the jazzier precincts of Miami to travel across the state to the retirement community of Venice.

The FBI has said nothing about this. The FBI says Atta didn't live there anymore. The FBI says Atta was nine months gone.

The FBI is lying.

Who was Atta meeting with in Venice? We realized that this is one thing the FBI might be eager to hide. Because this discovery would lead inexorably to identifying the organization, or global network, that so clearly smoothed the progress of Atta's Hamburg cadre through America.

And then... then we would know just who in the United States was doing business with Osama bin Laden's thugs—on *this* end, the *U.S. end*—while they were here.

That this knowledge "might could" prove highly explosive was driven home to us with a vengeance when, by lucky accident, we stumbled onto a piece of what the FBI is covering up in Florida, evidence which indicates that—whatever the reason for the attack on America on September 11, 2001—*the enemy is still inside the gates.*

During the month before the 9/11 attack, Mohamed Atta was seen meeting in Venice with "flight school owner" and international con man Rudi Dekkers, who has sworn in testimony before Congress that he never saw Atta again after he "left" his flight school nearly nine months earlier, in December, 2000.

This awful truth should have come from our taxpayer-funded federal investigative agency, the FBI, charged with the responsibility of solving the mass murder of 3,000 people on American soil. The conclusion is unmistakable: *Somebody is "protecting" Rudi Dekkers.*

Sadly, it appears the FBI's investigation was slanted—or jimmied—in the same way U.S. intelligence estimates were twisted in the run up to the war in Iraq, in order to present the American people the idea that it was the next logical step in America's War on Terror.

For what it's worth, we feel that America's War on Terror is wholly-justified. Lying to the American people in matters pertaining to the deaths of 3,000 people, on the other hand, is not.

We found numerous credible eyewitnesses to Atta's presence in Venice in the final days of the terrorist conspiracy: a rent-a-car agent who took a call from Atta from there... a deli clerk who served him a sub... the owners of a restaurant just a half block from Atta and Marwan's rental home... a cab driver who had him as a fare...

Their eyewitness testimony is clear proof of a massive government 9/11 coverup in Florida.

Becky Cover works in the deli of Publix supermarket, a mile from the Venice Airport. She says Mohamed Atta was in Venice just one week before the attack.

"On September 11, I was on the phone with my mother-in-law the time the buildings got hit," she told us. "They showed pictures of three different guys—Atta was one of them—on TV. And immediately I recognized the faces and I told my husband, 'My God, those are the three guys! They were just in the store a week ago! The week before, they were in the store. They got subs.'"

The FBI never spoke with her.

Tom and Rene Adorna also saw Mohamed Atta in Venice—along with Marwan Al-Shehhi and a third, unidentified man—just a few weeks before the attack. For reasons which will soon become clear, they have vivid memories of his visit to their eatery a month before the attack. So when reporters showed up the day after September 11, Rene Adorna says she immediately knew why they were there...

"Right after the incident happened, we had newspapers come down, and right away I knew what it was about, because I remembered the table. Tommy knew, Jeff knew, and we said right away, and they showed us one picture and we knew immediately."

Why did she vividly remember Mohamed Atta and Marwan Al-Shehhi? Because they caused a scene in her restaurant, she told us. "They were loud, making comments, one was pounding his hand on the table, saying: 'We're talking $200,000! We have to answer to the family!'"

"There were three of them," Rene recounted. "And they all looked of the Egyptian persuasion, dark skin, dark hair, lots of jewelry, *lots* of jewelry. They were dressed in Florida type shirts—the silk, you know, with the pattern, that kind of thing—and I could have sworn there was a cross, the one guy had a big cross, the big gaudy gold cross thing, I thought, but you know, I'm not sure now, but I know he had the big watch on."

Gold jewelry, expensive watches, and silk shirts. Not exactly a description of Islamic fundamentalists.

"I thought they were Mafia," said Rene.

This comment may not be too far afield, either. What they were arguing about—the disposition of a "loose" pile of nearly a quarter million dollars—not the proper interpretation of the Koran.

She confirmed what numerous other women whom we met who knew Atta had said about him. Atta wouldn't talk to her, Rene said. "He barely spoke a word to me, but when I'd come over I'd feel like, jeez, what's his problem, because he had that really mean, *mean* look on his face all the time, like he was *very* unhappy."

Marwan, as always, served as buffer and go-between. "Then there was the other guy, the heavier-set guy, he did all the talking, with me, anyway. He was very outgoing, very pleasant actually."

It was Marwan loudly arguing with Atta, we learned to our surprise. "The big guy... actually he, the big guy, was yelling at the other guy (Atta). I tried to stay away from the table pretty much, and then went and told the owner and the manager, 'you better watch his table, they're getting a little out of hand.'"

Her husband Tom came out front to see what the trouble was about. "He (Marwan) was a pretty big guy," he said. "And he was doing most of the talking. He kept saying stuff to them, about money, we kept hearing about money. The other guy (Atta), I guess, was the main guy, but he wasn't saying a word, he just sat there with a look on his face and he didn't say anything."

Their restaurant, the Pelican Alley, is a block from the rented home which Atta and Marwan supposedly vacated the prior December. Both Tom and Rene Adorna remain surprised that the FBI hadn't bothered to interview them. When we told them they were in good company, they sounded slightly mollified. "Two newspapers came by," said Tom. "That was it. And they (the terrorists) were living right down the street, right down the block. But they (the FBI) never came over here to see us."

"I did think it was strange," added Rene. She shrugged. "We thought like they might want some information. But maybe they had everything that they needed."

Brad Warrick, owner of Warrick's Rental Car in Pompano Beach, also knows that Atta was in Venice in the weeks before the attack because he says they used his rental car to drive there. Warrick said he called the FBI on Wednesday afternoon, the day after the attack, after he recognized a picture of Atta on television.

"They rented two cars over three different contracts, a total of about five weeks," Warrick told us. "They picked up that car at about closing time, and that one was going to be for two weeks, he told me it was going to be for two weeks. And he told me he had to go over to the west coast of Florida and he wanted to know if that would be a problem.

"While he was gone during those two weeks he called me from Venice, I saw it on the caller ID," stated Warrick. "I thought oh, wonderful. I've got a car broke down over on the west coast of Florida. He had called because the service engine soon light was on."

During his questioning by the FBI, Warrick said he learned details of the attack which the Bureau has chosen not to tell the American people. "The FBI told me that Marwan almost missed the building. Marwan was flying one hundred miles per hour faster than Atta, they said. And that's why he flew into the building deeper and that's why that building came down first, because there was so much fuel deeper into the building."

"Their explanation was Atta was very cool, calm, collected, just zeroed right in on it, just bingo. And Marwan on the other hand, ten years younger, was just scared to death and he flew erratic, and at the last minute nearly missed the building."

This illustrates how little we have been told about what really happened.

Brad Warrick's description of Mohamed Atta makes him sound like a perfect spy. "He had Allstate Insurance," said Warrick. "The address on his insurance card matched his drivers license. He was a perfect customer.

"Mohamed dressed to the nines," said Warrick. "Nice, nice pants and shirt. Nice clothes, business like. He carried a briefcase and he had all the credentials he needed... credit card, drivers license, and proof of insurance and he had that, everything matched."

When they returned their last rental car days before the attack, Atta and Marwan exhibited behavior at his rental agency when they showed up to return the car, Warrick said, that seems flatly inconsistent with two men on their way to meet their fate.

"If they were on a suicide mission, and knew they were going to be gone in a couple of days, why did they go to the trouble to return their rental car to us two days before? Why didn't they just leave the car at the airport? Why would they care?"

But not only did Atta and Marwan politely return the car, they engaged in a contest to see who would pay for the rental. "On the last contract, we already had a signed credit card slip for Mohamed,"

Warrick explained. "But Marwan said no, don't put it on his credit card. 'Here, put it on mine.'

"Well in order to take it on somebody else's credit card for the contract, you have to *be* on the contract. So that means he had to give us his drivers license, and he had to sign everything. We had to tear up the contract and write out a new one," stated Warrick.

"He (Marwan) gave us his drivers license, got on the contract. We tore up Mohamed's credit card slip, and charged it on Marwan."

Warrick paused, looking pained, then said, slowly, "Why go to all this trouble? What difference does this make if you are going to be dead in a couple of days?"

It was a question he has contemplated often since.

We learned that Mohamed Atta was meeting with terror flight school owner Rudi Dekkers in Venice in the month before he crashed American Airlines Flight 11 into the North Tower of the World Trade Center through a lucky cab ride in Venice taken by a friend and associate who had come down to spend a few weeks assisting the investigation.

Lois Battuello, a researcher whose considerable assistance can be seen throughout the pages of this book, was spending an extended fortnight in Venice, when one day she needed to take a cab across town.

And that's how she met "Bob the cabbie." Her cabdriver, who she got to know over the course of a week, was a retired Navy man named Bob Simpson, who had seen duty during the '80s off the coast of Libya, among other places. Simpson comes from a law enforcement background: his father was Chief of Police in a mid-sized town in California, his brother is a cop, and an uncle works for the DEA. He appears neither mentally disordered nor suicidal. These factors will be important in evaluating his report of what he saw.

"Bob asked me why I was in town," Lois explained, telling how their conversation began. "And I said, 'To probe around a bit into September 11.' I said, 'I was helping someone who was writing a book.'"

Bob said, "Atta was here, he was right in this cab, and so was the other guy, Marwan, and right here is where I would pick them up." He indicated a convenience store, then across the street, the apartment building where he was dropping her off to come and meet us. We live there. It was the building we have lived in for over a year in Venice. Atta had been a frequent visitor to *our* apartment building in downtown Venice, Burgundy Square.

"I had the FBI come over and question me about them," the cabbie continued. "They (the FBI) had videotape of me with them (Atta and Marwan) taken at Orlando Executive Airport; they said they went through the film on security cameras at the Airport and saw my cab number. That's how the FBI knew to contact me and they let me know that I was just an innocent cab driver even before they asked me questions.

"That apartment where you're staying, their best friend used to live upstairs on the second floor," stated Simpson. "I saw Atta and Al-Shehhi there. Most of the time, I'd be called by their friend, who owned the convenience market across the street, or they would call saying pick them up there at the market."

The owner of the convenience store was "their best friend here," he said. "They were always hanging out together at the store." He knew this, he said, because he would stop in his cab and give Atta and Al-Shehhi a lift to Huffman, during the time they were students at the flight school.

Atta's friend, the man who owned the market across the street, a KwikChek, disappeared immediately after the attack, we learned, and has not been seen since.

According to Venice Yellow Cab employees interviewed by the FBI three days after the attack, Atta took numerous cab rides in August 2001 to and from Huffman Aviation as well as other locations in Venice.

Yellow Cab driver Bob Simpson, who was the only cabbie on the day shift in Venice, stated that on two of these occasions Atta was accompanied by Rudi Dekkers. "They knew each other well, really well. They were friends. They were going to a nightclub in Sarasota, talking and very sociable with each other. He and Atta were friends, you could tell."

Could Simpson be mistaken in his identification? Not likely; he knew Rudi Dekkers well, he said, from numerous trips to Huffman Aviation to pick up arriving flight students.

"He (Dekkers) would walk them out to the cab, and give me the address to take them to," states Simpson. "Then a lot of times, with a new flight student, Rudi would take them over to Sharkey's for lunch, and I'd get the call to pick them up. Dekkers also regularly used our cabs to do things like go to lunch, because he usually flew in by heli-copter and didn't have a car at the Venice Airport."

Simpson said he first took Atta and Dekkers from Huffman Aviation to James' Place, a restaurant in downtown Venice. Then on a second occasion he picked the two up at the Pompano Road residence of former Huffman employee Charlie Voss, and took them to a Sarasota nightclub Atta is known to have frequented. It was Voss, we recalled, whose home was made available to Atta and Marwan when they arrived in Venice.

The Yellow Cab office manager in Sarasota confirmed that the trips were recorded in the firm's cab logs, and said the FBI had also expressed a keen interest in cab rides Atta had taken with the company's other driver, who worked nights.

Atta's presence in Venice during final preparations for the attack directly contradicts the FBI's official chronology of his movements in the month before Sept. 11, and totally contradicts numerous statements made by Dekkers to the news media.

In sworn testimony in front of the House Judiciary Committee in March 2002, Dekkers insisted his relationship with the terrorist ringleader had been distant, and ended the previous December, nine months before the attack.

Dekkers told the hearing about complaints from his staff that Atta and Al-Shehhi had behavioral problems, that they were not following instructions, and that they also had bad attitudes. "On December 24th, 2000, Atta and Al-Shehhi rented a Warrior (N555HA) from Huffman Aviation for a flight," the Dutch national stated, telling of his last encounter with Atta.

"Atta and Al-Shehhi returned to Huffman Aviation to make final payments on their outstanding bills. Because they were not taking any more flying lessons, they were asked to leave the facility due to their bad attitudes and not being liked by staff and clients alike. Huffman never heard about or from them again until September 11th, 2001."

Speaking with reporters, he had been more colloquial. "They did not socialize with anyone," Dekkers said three days after the attack. "They did not go to the bar with us. That Atta guy was an asshole."

On Friday, Sept. 14, three days after the Sept. 11 attack, cab driver Simpson was contacted by the FBI, who questioned him closely about an associate of Atta's, a Middle Eastern man who owned the convenience store across the street from the apartment building where Simpson said he picked him up. Simpson elaborated:

"I heard a voice say, 'This is Special Agent Joe Anderson from the FBI calling,'" remembers Simpson. "My heart sort of skipped a beat. Then he said, 'Don't worry, you haven't done anything wrong,' and asked if I'd seen pictures of the terrorists, and if I had, wanted to know if I recognized any."

"I said, 'Yes, I recognized Mohamed Atta,'" Simpson continued. "'I'm the day driver for Yellow Cab in Venice, and he was in my cab a bunch of times in August, 2001. The night driver had him even more than I did.'"

So the FBI clearly knew—much earlier than we—that Atta was in Venice just before the attack.

"They were especially interested in a rich Saudi guy that I'd been sent to pick up at the Orlando Executive Airport. They said they already knew that he'd ridden in my cab because they'd gotten my cab number from a surveillance camera there."

The FBI agents asked specific and direct questions focused on several trips to the Orlando Executive Airport beginning in December 2000, said Simpson.

Simpson told the FBI he had been asked to drive to Orlando by a convenience store owner in Venice, a Middle Eastern man who was an associate of Atta's, and who left town shortly after the attack.

"I took the store owner, and when he got to Orlando Executive Airport, we waited together for a flight to come in. Then out comes this really wealthy Saudi businessman, dressed in Armani and shades, as well as his wife, who was wearing traditional Arab clothing."

"The store owner knew him really well. They hugged, and I am sure he was bringing the store owner a lot of money, because you could tell that he *had* a lot of money. The first thing they wanted to do was go to a good restaurant, so there we were, steak, lobster, everything. The guy had a *lot* of money. I just know this meeting had to do with this wealthy Saudi businessman bringing him money."

After dinner they proceeded back to the Venice apartment of the convenience store owner, the one where Simpson said he picked up Atta several times. "I took them back to Venice, and to the apartment, where I had to carry in luggage. I guess this wealthy Saudi businessman stayed there at the apartment too, at least that's where I left him."

Six weeks later, Simpson said, he drove the wealthy Saudi's wife back to the Orlando Airport, once again leaving from the convenience store owner's Venice apartment. When he arrived to pick up the fare, he was asked to help carry a chest down to the cab.

The chest was so heavy, he said, it took two people to carry. The man who helped him carry it down the stairs to the cab, says Simpson, was Zacharias Moussaoui, the so-called 20th hijacker. "He was a big bald guy, and he helped me with the chest."

Simpson's identification of Moussaoui in Venice added confirmation to the story we'd heard about the second "Magic Dutch Boy," Arne Kruithof, being grilled for two days at the Sarasota FL. courthouse about his connections to Moussaoui by a Justice Dept. Asst. Attorney General and top-level officials from the FBI, there taking depositions from potential witnesses in Moussaoui's upcoming trial. So Moussaoui was in Venice too. The FBI has said nothing about it.

Also of major significance was Simpson's statement that on several occasions he drove Mohamed Atta and Marwan Al-Shehhi from Venice to the Orlando Executive Airport, a considerable distance, on one-way trips. This places the two men at the same scene where Huffman Aviation's true owner, Wally Hilliard, lost a Lear jet after it was discovered to have 43 pounds of heroin onboard. Hilliard also owns a flight school and commuter airline in Orlando as well.

Was Mohamed Atta flying out of Orlando Executive Airport for Wally Hilliard? Dekkers' partner in their failed airline venture, Richard Boehlke, told a reporter that Dekkers' proposed using flight students to ride along as co-pilots as a way to save money.

"The thought that terrorists might have been allowed access to secure airport facilities is chilling," said Boehlke.

As we've seen, in the official chronology of this period—January to April, 2001—FBI investigators state they are not sure where Atta and Al-Shehhi were, suggesting they may have traveled back to Germany, since Atta reportedly received a visitor's visa in Hamburg and reentered the United States during this time.

Once again we have heard eyewitness testimony which indicates the FBI is lying. So is Rudi Dekkers. If Dekkers is lying about his relationship with Mohamed Atta, this concerns material evidence in the deaths of 3,000 people. Why hasn't he been arrested? Why have federal authorities as yet done nothing about it? Why is he still walking the streets a free man?

When we called a man we know who used to work at something like the CIA, to ask him what could have been in that chest that was so heavy, his reply was swift and immediate, and seemed to put everything going on in Florida in its proper perspective...

"Gold," he said firmly. "There was gold in that chest."

Who deals in heroin? Who deals in gold?

Islamic fundmentalists?

Or Islamic *spooks*.

CHAPTER TWENTY-FOUR

"GUNRUNNERS, DRUG SMUGGLERS & SUITCASE SALESMEN"

If the FBI was "covering" for Rudi Dekkers, it wouldn't be out of love for the chubby flight school owner, universally loathed. No; they would, instead, be shielding the involvement of the entity, or organization, for whom Dekkers toiled. If the entity being shielded was, say, another Federal Agency, the FBI might have a lot of incentive to cover-up.

The task of identifying the organization being shielded by the FBI's incompetent and indifferently-motivated 9/11 investigation was made easier by events which played out right in front of us in Venice, which clearly demonstrate the scope and reach of the organization involved, and which seem to point a finger towards, in all likelihood, the CIA.

Surprised? We weren't either.

There is even historical precedent for the FBI covering up for the CIA. During the investigation into the Kennedy assassination, the Bureau flatly refused to investigate a CIA covert operation just outside of New Orleans, a training camp for Cuban exiles where CIA agent and all-around freak David Ferrie rubbed elbows with Lee Harvey Oswald at a camp which provided personnel and logistics support for the assassination conspirators.

The camp was studiously ignored by the FBI's New Orleans office, which again covered up for the "renegade" camp a dozen years later in testimony in front of Congressional committees looking into the assassination.

But it will take more than historical precedent to level accusations against the CIA of involvement in Wally Hilliard and Rudi Dekkers' misbegotten Arab training operation. There needs to be hard evidence. And hard evidence is a difficult thing to find in professional intelligence operations. A parking permit from a CIA parking lot in Langley was not going to be discovered on the dashboard of one of Rudi Dekkers' many expensive cars. There wasn't going to be any sort of obvious paper trail. At best there might be some bread crumbs pointing *towards* what used to be a paper trail.

We recalled a recent conversation we'd had with a man who had been the personal pilot for famed CIA pilot and operative Barry Seal for several years before Seal was assassinated in 1986.

Phil Marshall flew Barry Seal's Lear jet for two years. Yet when we asked him what Barry Seal did for a living, Marshall said he'd been kept in the dark about the nature of his boss's business. Still, he said, after a certain amount of time watching Seal move in and out of countries and capitals all over the Western hemisphere, he concluded that his job had something to do with selling guns and drugs. It also involved a moderate amount of heavy lifting: carrying suitcases bulging with money and drugs up and down the steps of the plane.

"I decided that Barry must have been a gunrunner, a drug smuggler, or a suitcase salesman," laughed Marshall.

It was an apt, if wry, description of the world of the covert operative, and we have seen quite a bit of just that kind of behavior in the world inhabited by Mohamed Atta, Rudi Dekkers, and Wallace J. Hilliard.

Then something happened involving Hilliard and Dekkers, not in Venice or Naples, but up in Lynchburg, Virginia, at the Lynchburg Regional Airport, which revealed the two men's connections to American intelligence.

We got a letter from a reporter in Lynchburg, Virginia, telling us that a recent government move out at the Lynchburg Airport had a strange Venice, Florida twist to it that had left aviation observers in Virginia scratching their heads.

"Hello sir," the letter began. "My name is Chris Flores and I'm the business reporter at the *Lynchburg News & Advance,* a 40,000 daily in Lynchburg, VA."

Flores was writing, he said, because an unknown company called Britannia Aviation had just been awarded a five-year contract to run a large regional maintenance facility at the Lynchburg Virginia Regional Airport, over Virginia Aviation, a much better-qualified local firm, in suspicious circumstances that hinted at the involvement of a very influential, if invisible and mysterious, "presence," with the ability to directly affect government decision-making in Lynchburg.

"Virginia Aviation was really pissed that they lost the bid to a little company in Florida for this large facility," explained the reporter. "Right away, Virginia Aviation's VP Jim Lampmann started questioning this company's credentials, to the point where I'd be setting the paper up for liability if I printed it. It seemed like the talk of a monopolist who doesn't want more competition. However, he did point out that Britannia did not have an FAA license to work on planes; (yet) Britannia plans to set up a large operation here to work on regional carriers for Delta and US Air (Express).

"Lampmann said, 'I would hope the city would do due diligence before they turn over a major facility.' And he was right. They *didn't* have the FAA license. Paul Marten, the Brit who is VP of the company, said he didn't have the license because they were just working out of a small hangar on planes for Huffman Aviation under Huffman's license," Flores wrote us...

"Which goes back to your boy Dekkers."

Someone behind the scenes had been pulling strings in Virginia to win a government contract for a company housed in a hangar at Huffman Aviation in Venice. Nobody in Virginia could figure out why.

And that's when the CIA's links to Rudi Dekkers and Wally Hilliard finally began to come into focus. At a Lynchburg City Council hearing on the dispute, we learned there had been vocal objections from local aviation observers baffled at why a company with no qualifications was being awarded a contract over a much better-qualified local Lynchburg aviation company for a large regional maintenance facility designed for major carriers.

"It was as if someone with a learner's permit from the DMV got picked to drive Richard Petty's car at Daytona," explained one Lynchburg aviation executive. "It made absolutely no business sense that anyone could see."

Ah, we thought. Maybe we can help here. We had begun to feel comfortable in the mysterious but increasingly familiar realm of things which make "absolutely no business sense."

When Britannia was chosen for the contract in Lynchburg, local Lynchburg news reports on the controversy questioned why the tiny unknown firm from Venice was being shoe-horned in at the Lynchburg Airport. "Some commission members were concerned that they hadn't seen details of Britannia's bid until this past Wednesday, and that the company's un-audited finances weren't given to commissioners until some had asked for it," the *Lynchburg News and Advance* reported.

The city's response was not to worry about it, as if it were only a question of collecting the rent. "As a result of the questions raised concerning financial fitness," said Airport Manager Mark Courtney, "we put a clause in requiring Britannia to put down the first six months of rent."

Folks in Lynchburg were hardly reassured, and aviation executives began voicing their concerns to reporters at the local paper. They pointed out that Britannia's financial statements, released only after prodding by the local aviation community, showed the "company" to be worth less than $750, with virtually no assets, employees, or corporate history. In fact, it had only recently incorporated.

If ever there was a transparent dummy *front* company Britannia Aviation was it. It didn't even possess the necessary FAA license to perform the aircraft maintenance services for which it had just been contracted. Yet it had been chosen over a respected and successful local Lynchburg company which boasted a multi-million dollar balance sheet and more than 40 employees.

No one knew anything about Britannia Aviation, other than that it had been housed at Huffman Aviation. Still, the airport manager, who had recently moved over from the FAA, greased the way for the company, and the City Fathers of Lynchburg agreed. Out at the Lynchburg Airport, everyone wanted to know what gave Britannia its "stroke" with government officials.

What was it about Huffman Aviation that prompted government officials to so consistently strew rose petals in its path? Recall that Wally Hilliard and Rudi Dekkers' hasty purchase of Huffman without prior government approval had exposed them to serious business losses if they didn't receive quick government approval for a lease at the airport. What made them so certain that the City Council of Venice would rubber stamp their deal?

What was it about these guys that made government officials go out of their way to smooth their progress at every step?

The U.S. Government loves Rudi Dekkers... The man who trained both pilots who hit the World Trade Center was getting a cool million in government cash. The government was *giving away* money to Dutch national Dekkers...

"Rudi was going to get an SBA loan when he was indicted," Venice Airport observer Max Burge told us. "He had a letter of approval for an $800,000 loan."

In light of such massive malfeasance, we thought business reporter Chris Flores struck the right tone of ironic understatement.

"There was some sentiment that there might be something suspicious about Britannia Aviation," he wrote us. "There was a clear feeling that nobody knew who these guys were, or where they were coming from."

What began as a purely local spat has clear national security implications.

The connection between Hilliard, Dekkers, and the CIA was inadvertently revealed during a raucous Lynchburg City Council meeting over citizen complaints about the City awarding a $5 million contract to a company worth less than a typical business lunch. A Lynchburg city official used a little humor to try to wave aside objections that Britannia was insolvent.

"At least they have more on their balance sheet than Enron," joked Lynchburg City Councilman Robert Garber.

The Britannia executive in attendance, Paul Marten, who is British, rose to angrily protest that it was untrue his company was worth less than $750...

Britannia's assets, he felt sure, amounted to *more* than that. How much more was a question he left unanswered.

To illustrate the company's solidity and reassure those in attendance, Marten boasted that his company had already and for some time been successfully providing aviation maintenance services at

Huffman's hangar at the Venice Airport, for a Caribbean carrier called Caribe Air.

"Marten has said in the past that he works on planes in a hangar in Venice for Huffman Aviation," reported the *Lynchburg News-Advance*. "Marten also said Britannia does a similar service to what it wants to do in Lynchburg at the Venice Airport with Caribbean airlines, including Caribe Air."

And that's how we learned that under Rudi Dekkers' FAA license Paul Marten's little dummy front company worked for a notorious CIA proprietary air carrier.

"You might want to look at the history of Caribe Air," said reporter Flores drolly. "I think one of the original co-owners was some huge drug runner for the Medellin Cartel."

Even by the standards of a CIA proprietary, Caribe Air has had a particularly checkered past, including such "blemishes" as having its aircraft seized at the infamous Mena, Arkansas airport in 1990, after being accused by government prosecutors of using as many as 20 planes to ship drugs worth—get this—*billions* of dollars into the country.

Caribe Air also made headlines during the Iran-Contra scandal after one of their planes, a C130 military cargo plane, was shot down over Angola with the loss of everyone aboard.

Unfortunately for Caribe Air, the "everyone on board" included a US Congressman's nephew. In the resulting publicity it was let slip that the plane, laden with a cargo of whiskey and cigarettes, had been on a mission for the Angolan government.

Observers at the time had noted this fact with some surprise, since the CIA had been for years covertly supporting the Angolan government's opposition, Jonas Savimbi's UNITA rebels. The death of the Congressman's nephew revealed the Agency to once again be playing both ends against the middle... at least when it came to planeloads of swag.

Although the Congressman with a dead nephew was unamused, the matter was quickly dropped.

Today Caribe Air is controlled by an offshore bank located on the Caribbean island of Dominica, Banc Caribe, a private bank which is being investigated by authorities pursuing Enron's secret offshore partnerships, some of which have the name "Caribe" in their title.

This is probably just coincidence.

When details of the Lynchburg controversy reached Venice, local aviation executives professed amazement. "No one here had ever heard of Britannia Aviation before," Coy Jacob told us. "And this is a very small airport."

Someone had decided there was too much heat on the Venice Airport for a covert operation housed at Huffman Aviation to remain there, observers speculated. So they moved it to Lynchburg.

Intrigued, Venice aviation business owner Coy Jacob called a DEA source he knew at the airport and asked what he knew about Britannia Aviation.

"This guy got all excited as soon as I asked," Jacob told us later. "He immediately wanted to know why I was so interested in Britannia. Finally he reluctantly told me that Britannia had a 'green light' from the DEA at the Venice Airport, whatever that means."

"He said the local Venice Police Department (which mounted round-the-clock patrols at the Airport since Sept. 11) had been warned to leave them alone."

Rudi Dekkers was in trouble with the DEA (Drug Enforcement Administration) while still located at the Naples Airport in the mid-1990s. But things had changed.

There were some sinister currents swirling around the aviation scene in Southwest Florida. But the notion of a Federal "hands-off" policy towards the operation at Huffman helped explain what it means to have a "green light from the DEA." It certainly sounded like an impressive credential. So one day we wandered in to see Paul Martens—unannounced of course, as he would never have spoken to us otherwise—at his office in a Huffman Aviation hangar at the Venice Airport.

Martens refused to comment on the reports of covert influences having been responsible for winning the Lynchburg contract. He was just an honest British businessman, he protested. He had ties to Lynchburg Virginia. He met his wife there, while she was a student at Jerry Falwell's Liberty University, he said. Her father had been a pastor for the Reverend Falwell.

Was there an evangelical Christian connection to our story? We had earlier noted that many of the flight trainers who trained the Arab terrorists moonlighted by flying missionary flights out of the Venice and Sarasota Airports for Christian missionary services like televangelist Pat Robertson's Operation Blessing.

"Islamic fundamentalist" Osama bin laden reportedly cloaked his covert activities under the cover of religious charities. Were our own government intelligence agencies using the same ruse?

"Jerry Falwell got bailed out in the early '90s by a local Lynchburg businessman with interesting associations," one Lynchburg observer told us. "Since then Falwell runs a missionary service called World Help, which flies all over the world."

Pat Robertson, we recalled, made the news after 9/11 when he invited Jerry Falwell onto his 700 Club to point a manicured finger at segments of American society both men felt were responsible for 9/11. Falwell surmised out loud that the horrors of 9/11 indicated God had lifted His "veil of protection" from the United States because of various transgressions, including attempts to "secularize" the nation by pagans, abortionists, feminists, homosexuals, and the American Civil Liberties Union.

"The pagans and the abortionists and the feminists and the gays and the lesbians who are actively trying to make that an alternative lifestyle," decreed Falwell. "The ACLU, People for the American Way— all of them who have tried to secularize America, I point the finger in their face and say, 'You helped make this happen.'"

"Well, I totally concur," responded Pat Robertson, who went Falwell one better by adding that "rampant Internet pornography" was also to blame for God's anger.

"If we don't repent, then more events might happen in the future," Falwell chimed in.

Venerable CBS news anchor Walter Cronkite expressed his disgust at the duo to TV Guide. "It makes you wonder if Falwell and Robertson are worshipping the same God as the people who bombed the Trade Center and the Pentagon."

Meanwhile, the consternation in Lynchburg did not diminish in the months after Britannia moved in. Instead, suspicions grew even greater, Lynchburg aviation observers told us, because of the "secretive nature" of the operations going on at the facility.

"No one knows anything about this group," Virginia Aviation's Jim Lampmann said.

"They took over a sizeable maintenance facility and all they're doing is working on a few old, broken-down Jetstreams. But they keep their hangar doors down and closed. They stay strictly to themselves and keep their shades pulled down. Their activity consists of one plane coming in and one plane going out every few weeks or so."

We knew what he was getting at: the "no business sense" thing. He said, "There's no way they can be making any money in an operation like that." Christian-linked or not, a transparent dummy front company had a *green light* from the DEA. So it was natural to wonder whether Robertson and Falwell were part of some as-yet unrevealed U.S. covert operation.

Our suspicions grew when we discovered one reason Britannia was able to move so smoothly from Venice to Lynchburg. Huffman Aviation's shadowy financier, Wally Hilliard, loaned Jerry Falwell a million bucks which the televangelist has shown no indication of repaying.

Only a cynic would suggest Falwell may have spread some of the money around town. But then, a million bucks *does* buy a lot of "looking the other way."

Falwell certainly needed the money. He was being foreclosed on—in a supreme irony—by a creditor who chose to place business before sentiment when Falwell couldn't repay his debts: Stephens, Inc., the Arkansas financial institution run by Jackson Stephens, who has been so influential, as we've seen, in Venice. In 1991 Stevens, Inc., foreclosed on the North Campus of Jerry's pride and joy, Liberty University.

That Jackson Stephens was also a generous patron of that minion of Satan, Bill Clinton, didn't stop Falwell from taking his money.

Business is business.

Financier Wallace J. Hilliard, 70, managed to avoid being caught in the glare of publicity surrounding his partner Dekkers. But that changed when Britannia Aviation became embroiled in controversy in Falwell's Lynchburg, VA.

The revelation of Hilliard's ties with Falwell shed light on things.

The Lord works in mysterious ways; but this was clearly no coincidence. Was Hilliard a representative of a large and powerful but largely invisible "Company"?

Had he been tasked with the covert flight training operation in Florida.

So, what did we really know about Wally Hilliard? The answer was not enough. A successful entrepreneur from Green Bay, WI., Hilliard supposedly retired to Naples, FL in the mid-'90s, only to go on a buying spree of aviation assets in southwest Florida that ran into the tens of millions of dollars with a partner, Rudi Dekkers, who had been the subject of a recent multi-agency Federal investigation and whose reputation as a deadbeat was so bad that no one would sell him aviation fuel at the Naples, FL. Airport… for *cash*.

As we learned more about Hilliard, a picture of the shadowy financier began to slowly fall into place. We discovered, for example, that the health insurance company he founded had a highly unusual corporate motto:

"Hate Sin, Fight Communism, and Back the Pack!"

While this may cover a lot of bases, motivation-wise, with insurance salesmen, it is way too odd for a regular health insurance company.

We learned more odd facts about Hilliard from Stuart Burchill, his former accountant. We virtually staked out Burchill's house in Naples after hearing several aviation executives close to Hilliard's operations in Naples state emphatically that Burchill didn't just know where all the bodies were buried, he also knew where they were sent to be cut up *before* they were buried.

Metaphorically speaking, of course.

Burchill told us that at one time Hilliard had assigned him the task of dunning deadbeat Falwell, the founder of Liberty University and Pastor of the Thomas Road Baptist Church, to repay the money Falwell owed his boss.

"The Falwell note was an outstanding receivable I was assigned to collect," Burchill explained.

This was almost too rich. As always, truth is stranger than fiction. But it got even better. In the course of trying to get Falwell to address the unpaid debt, Burchill said, he learned details of the Reverend's accounting practices upon which the Almighty Himself would presumably frown.

"I talked to Falwell's accountant, who was very apologetic," said Burchill. "He said there was plenty of money to pay off the loan. Except any time there was money left in the account at the end of the month, Jerry always stripped it out."

At this point we admit to being slightly giddy with glee. If the avuncular Southern Baptist minister had been "stripping out" his church's bank account at the end of the month, his pastoral image might suffer.

Burchill said, "Falwell's accountant told me, 'If I can pay you in chunks off the books so Jerry doesn't see it, I can get it handled.' So we worked out a payment schedule. And after that checks drawn on Liberty University came in for a few months, until Falwell figured out what was going on and put a stop to it."

Hilliard also had other ties to the Evangelical Christian milieu. Ties that—given his involvement with Atta's Hamburg cadre—were frankly disturbing…

In addition to the loan to televangelist Falwell to bail out his failing religious enterprises, he served on the board of an avowedly Christian aeronautics company planning to manufacture a new business jet in Israel.

He was a Director of a company in St. Louis, VisionAire Corp, an aircraft developer attempting to attract funding to manufacture a six-seat business jet in Israel.

Like Hilliard's failed airline, which announced new service between Orlando and Daytona Beach and failed to attract a single customer, VisionAire spent millions developing a business jet…

But they never sold a plane.

The company's CEO and head "VisionAire," Jim Rice, was a former religious fund-raiser who ran the business as something of a religious crusade. When Rice was asked why he founded the company, for example, he credited divine inspiration. "I had been wondering what God wanted me to do next," he said in an interview. "When I pray, it's more listening than asking. The more I listened, the more I felt this is what He wanted me to do."

VisionAire's headquarters at Spirit of St. Louis Airport was described by the *St. Louis Post-Dispatch* as having an "undercurrent of spirituality," with one employee telling the paper she was attracted to working at the company by the "strong Christian faith" of top management.

Faith must have been sorely tested, however, during the brouhaha surrounding a $30 million civil lawsuit filed against the company by two former officers. After they complained to CEO Rice that he had misled investors about the company's prospects for FAA certification, they alleged, all—forgive the expression—*hell* broke loose.

The two had been having an illicit affair. In retaliation for their allegations, the company "caused video recordings to be made of plaintiffs' private activities," and then "unreasonably publicized private and personal details of plaintiffs' lives."

Ouch! That must have hurt. How Christian is that?

VisionAire Corp. officials eventually won dismissal of the suit, but it was a Pyrrhic Victory, since they never won FAA approval for their plane. As the company's finances worsened, some "enraptured" employees ended up working for free, or even subsidizing their employer by using their personal credit cards to pay for company expenses.

One former employee told a reporter, "A lot of us felt the company let us down. Not intentionally, but we felt bitter and kind of stupid for listening to Jim Rice in the first place."

CEO Rice was confronted by one investor who angrily told him, "My investment isn't worth anything now!"

Yet another company connected to the people connected to Mohamed Atta suffering the cruel indignity of forced bankruptcy.

In a bid to keep the company and plane alive, Rice solicited Israeli involvement. A July 3, 2001 press release from Israel Aircraft Industries (IAI) describes Israeli plans to help the manufacturer attract funding to manufacture the six-seat business jet in Israel.

Wally Hilliard's political connections continued to surprise us… He has ties extending well into the upper reaches of American political circles. These ties hold the answers to questions about how sophisticated operators like Hilliard and Dekkers could have been hoodwinked and taken in by foreign student pilots who demonstrated none of "the right stuff."

At the same time his Venice flight school was training dozens of terrorists to fly he was involved with Truman Arnold, a multi-millionaire Texas oil-man who played a prominent role in the Whitewater Scandal.

Arnold, chief fund-raiser for the Democratic Party in 1995 when the scandal broke, was investigated for a variety of dubious money-raising schemes ranging from renting out the White House's Lincoln Bedroom to selling tickets on Air Force One. And he was fingered for procuring cash (read hush money) for convicted Clinton friend Web Hubbell.

Arnold, who played golf with Clinton regularly, coordinated payments to Webster Hubbell from businesses controlled by old friends of the President's, as well as campaign donors that included the Lippo Group, in business with (who else?) Jackson Stephens, and organizers of a multibillion-dollar development in China that had received the endorsement of the Clinton administration.

Truman Arnold's name surfaced in connection with our investigation into the Venice flight schools in a curious aircraft transaction we unearthed while probing into Hilliard's tangled business affairs.

Arnold, it appears, "loaned" Hilliard—for a dollar—a Beechcraft King Air 200 worth over $2 million. It wasn't until almost a year after the airplane sale that Hilliard got around to arranging financing to pay for the plane.

Truman Arnold engaged in his act of munificence in December 2000. So Wally Hilliard had a benefactor at the heart of the American political process, again raising the question of whether the appearance of Mohamed Atta and his terrorist buddies in Venice was—as the official story has it—a matter of mere happenstance.

Truman Arnold's lawyer during the Whitewater Investigation was Democratic power-broker Richard Ben-Veniste, who is currently serving on the official 9/11 probe. So if Ben-Veniste's client Truman Arnold's business dealings with terror flight school owner Wally Hilliard come under scrutiny, the slick Washington lawyer will find himself playing two different angles in a major American scandal for the second time!

Richard Ben-Veniste has been a player in major American scandals, in roles that are often not clearly-defined, going all the way back to Watergate. Now serving on his third major national investigative panel (Watergate, Whitewater, and 9/11), he may be about to face the same criticism all over again.

Ben-Veniste already served as Majority Counsel to the Congressional Whitewater probe investigating Truman Arnold. He went on to defend Arnold before Ken Starr's Whitewater grand jury, an action for which he was roundly criticized.

Observers tarred the Democratic super lawyer, claiming Ben-Veniste, while serving as Democratic counsel to the Whitewater Committee, blocked inquiries about Webster Hubbell's hiring by the Lippo Group, and then turned around and defended a man, Truman Arnold, whom he had just been investigating.

"Truman Arnold's name never came up during the Whitewater investigation," Ben-Veniste wrote, addressing his critics, "because of the entirely collateral nature of the inquiry about Hubbell and Lippo… And given Arnold's total lack of involvement in any aspect of the matters before the Whitewater Committee, no honest argument can be made that my representation of Arnold transgresses professional guidelines."

But Ben-Veniste's turning up at the "scene of the crime," is by no means the oddest thing about Truman Arnold and Wallace Hilliard's aviation transaction.... That distinction would have to go to the aircraft bill of sale which conveyed the plane from Arnold to Hilliard.

Dated December 10, 2000, it was not submitted to the FAA until over a year later, January 31, 2002. While the purpose of this arrangement is unclear, one reason, aviation sources indicated, might be that had the plane come under law enforcement scrutiny during this interregnum, the person coming under suspicion would have been—not Wally Hilliard, the man using the plane—but Truman Arnold, still the owner of record.

Considering that the December 10, 2000 transfer date for the twin-engine King Air came right after Hilliard had lost his bid to retain possession of his Lear jet confiscated by the DEA, this is no small benefit. Because after the "blemish" of having a plane he owned found with 43 pounds of heroin, Mr. Hilliard's name, understandably, was "mud" for a while with federal authorities.

Nonetheless, Hilliard continued putting together a company, Florida Air Holdings, which again was bravely planning to offer commuter air service in Florida. After briefly flying in the Spring of 2001, when it was touted by Florida political luminary Katherine Harris, Hilliard was no doubt eager to lose some more money.

We could hear it in our head, like a mantra. "When things don't make business sense, sometimes it's because they *do* make sense… just in some other way."

Hilliard's latest ill-starred aviation enterprise also offered commuter service under the name Discover Air. After not one ticket was sold on its inaugural route, it went—almost immediately—out of business.

Notwithstanding this uniquely dismal record, for reasons unknown, Florida political luminary Gov. Jeb Bush stepped forward to tour the facilities and praise its completely un-praiseworthy management.

One of the first decisions of the current U.S. Administration was, strangely enough, a change in drug policy. After President Bush's swearing-in in January 2000, the State Department announced the change of policy, instructing the U.S. Ambassador to Columbia,

Anne Hamilton to "stop its opium eradication activities in favor of eliminating coca."

When he found out, Republican Dan Burton was livid, and brought the matter before his House Government Reform Committee. "In 2000 we saw initial success with the heroin strategy," Burton stated in the hearing. "Our allies and the Colombian National Police eradicated 9,200 hectares of opium poppy plants in Colombia's high Andes Mountains. This put a serious dent into the supply of heroin coming into the United States.

"It was then that the State Department chose to stop opium eradication," fumed Burton, "to, as Ambassador Patterson put it, 'take advantage of a historic opportunity to eradicate coca.'

"Eradication of opium with the new Black Hawks that we gave them last year was stopped—stopped while the coca eradication in the south took a priority," Burton said during the hearings.

"And the only problem is Colombia's cocaine is now increasingly headed in another direction: to Europe. And the opium poppy used to make more deadly Colombian heroin is almost exclusively headed to the United States of American and our East Coast."

The Truman Arnold Company today tops the Arkansas Business list of that state's largest private companies. It unseated—you can't make this stuff up—Jackson Stephens Inc., of Little Rock, long unchallenged as the state's largest private company.

No doubt all of this is mere coincidence, without the slightest relevance to an understanding of what happened in America on September 11th, 2001.

Because, according to the FBI, which should know, the 19 hijackers had no help from any outside organization while in this country. They were a *Lone Cadre*.

Wally Hilliard and Rudi Dekkers' purchase of Huffman Aviation in 1999 set in motion a chain of events that led directly to people hanging out of 100th story office windows in New York and asking themselves whether it would be less painful to jump.

Like the Arab terrorist bombers of the early '90s, some of whom also attended U.S. flight schools, Atta's terrorist cadre clustered around a handful of flight schools, leading to speculation that the hijackers may not have enjoyed completely unfettered access to any flight school in America they pleased. They appear to have been siphoned into only a few. It is not clear to us that if Hilliard and Dekkers had not teamed up in their unholy alliance that the terrorists would have just gone to another school.

Do the political connections of the owner of the flight school Mohamed Atta called home, provide a rationale for questioning the official story told by the U.S. Government about the terrorists being in this country on their own and receiving no outside help?

Hell yes.

CHAPTER TWENTY-FIVE

THE EUROPEAN CONNECTION

So Mohamed Atta's American hosts—Rudi Dekkers and Wally Hilliard—are not who they pretend to be.

But the same could be said of Atta as well. As we've seen, he exhibited behavior which is totally inconsistent with that of an "Islamic fundamentalist," however broadly defined. But his behavior *was* consistent with that of a member of his society's—Arab society's—privileged elite, who also happened to be a spy.

The people he consorted with in Florida, his Florida associates, were not exclusively—perhaps even predominantly—Arab.

From information gleaned first in interviews with Amanda Keller, Atta's one-time American girlfriend, and corroborated by independent sources in Venice and Naples, we confirmed that at least *seven* of Mohamed Atta's close associates in Florida during the year leading up to the 9/11 attack were European: German, Swiss and French.

Today we know at least something—but by no means enough—about the identities of each. Their names haven't surfaced in any press accounts about Atta's stay in the U.S., nor has their existence been mentioned or alluded to in official statements.

We know they were all pilots.

According to Amanda, all of them already had pilot licenses from other countries when they arrived in the U.S. Traveling with Atta, or meeting him around the state, Atta's European friends appeared to share relationships with him of long-standing. Their meetings were serious business; when they returned, said Amanda, Atta *and* his German associates "always came back glum."

Only one of the seven still resides in the U.S.; five live in Germany or Switzerland. The seventh has a criminal record in his native Germany, and today lives in Saudi Arabia.

Cabdriver Bob Simpson referred to Rudi and Mohamed as "partners in crime." He thought the two men shared both social and business connections. He said they were very close socially. As we've seen on one pickup during the summer of 2001, Simpson drove them to Sarasota to a bar on Main Street.

Amanda had made frequent references to a close friend of Atta's named "Wolfgang," a friend so close Atta called him "my brother."

"He called certain people, Arabic people, 'my brother,'" Amanda said. "And I was wondering how he had so many family members. Like gang members do, you know, 'this is my brother.' But not *all* Arabs. So it wasn't like anyone who was Muslim was his brother."

"He called Wolfgang and Juergen 'my brother,'" she said. "He and Wolfgang were very tight, they went everywhere together. When he came into the picture they were together all the time."

Keller said Atta always spoke German with Wolfgang, which contradicts the testimony of Rudi Dekkers to a Congressional Committee that when he addressed Atta in German, Atta merely looked at him strangely.

Wolfgang's story, according to people we spoke with who knew him, includes a life studded with things like sailing around the world on a 47-foot yacht, on a trip where he met his wife Sujita, a native of Bombay. But when we went looking for Wolfgang, we found him through records of his scrapes with authorities in Florida. In airport records in Naples he was referenced in Aero Jet/Ambassador correspondence. A letter was sent by a former employee soliciting to offer private flight instruction without authority and in violation of FAA rules.

Wolfgang Bohringer is a pilot in his thirties. In Spring 2002, he became a naturalized U.S. citizen. He was one of the first of the "German element" to arrive in Florida, in 1996, when he opened a flight school in Naples. Prior to arriving in Naples he was associated with an organization called "The Flying Club of Munich," in Augsburg, Germany.

Like Rudi and Wally, Wolfgang was notorious in aviation circles for bad behavior. "Wolfgang showed up from Munich in the mid-1990s and immediately began operating a flight school illegally," stated Marcus Huber, a flight instructor in Naples. "He's half Swiss, half German."

Also like Rudi and Wally, Wolfgang seemed to have a "hall pass" from federal authorities. This embittered other foreign flight trainers not similarly well-connected. "When Wolfgang applied for an E-2 Visa, he made up a fake company, a cleaning service," Huber told us. "Sometimes it makes me mad that a criminal gets preference."

Welcome to TerrorLand.

Wolfgang was instrumental in bringing another of Atta's German associates to Florida, a pilot named "Stephan," who has done jail time in Germany, was on parole when he came to the U.S., and thus not supposed to be flying. But "being connected means never having to say you're sorry," and while regular German flight students struggle to obtain the necessary visas, Wolfgang and Stephan had inside connections which smoothed their progress. Stephan purchased Wolfgang's flight training business.

Two other German associates of Mohamed Atta's in Florida were brothers, Peter and Stephan. "Stephan did eight months of jail time," Huber told us.

"He was convicted Oct 1, 1997 and released from parole in Nov. 2000. Wolfgang signed off on Stephan's books, and so Stephan also got in on a fraudulent business investor's visa."

Yet Stephan was running a Florida flight school, although there are more than a few laws that say he shouldn't have been. Presumably the FAA was "looking the other way."

Stephan today reportedly flies in Saudi Arabia for a Swiss carrier, Farnair.

Atta also was often seen with Rudi's head flight instructor, Francois Nicolai. "He's another guy with no papers," an aviation source told us, "but at least he's an excellent pilot. He's French, and Swiss."

From what she saw, Amanda said that all of Atta's friends, with the exception of Marwan Al-Shehhi, were either German and Dutch, including Dutchmen Rudi Dekkers and Arne Kruithof, and another man from the Netherlands named "Paul." There was also Arne Kruithof's "agent" from Munich, as well as his business partner in Aviation

Aspirations, Pascal Schreier. Pascal was close to Bohringer, Atta's closest friend among the German nationals.

Pascal Schreier is married to a woman named Sandra Hamouda, French Tunisian, who as we have seen bought the bankrupt flight school in Punta Gorda where Atta hung out early in 2001. She is an executive with a Florida flight school called Pelican Flight Training Center, a fact we might have overlooked except for a curious *coincidence*...

When the *New York Times* did a two year anniversary story on 9/11 called "Hard Times Are Plaguing Flight Schools in Florida" (Sept. 14, 2003) focusing on the fact that pilot-training schools in Florida have been struggling since 9/11, the two schools profiled in their story are Magic Dutch Boy Arne Kruithof's... and Pelican Flight Training Center, where Pascal Schreirer's wife works.

There are over 220 flight schools in Florida. That the *New York Times* profiled these two "well-connected schools" is no doubt just a freak coincidence.

Another "old friend" of Atta's was a German named "Juergen," who was not the smoothest of operators. "Juergen was a pervert, straight out," Amanda had said "He was a lush, mid-30s. Every woman that walked by, he had something to say to them, commenting on their butt or whatever. He would go up to a woman, say, 'I'm from Germany, and I want to touch an American woman's butt.'"

We *may* have found "Juergen," working as a realtor in nearby Sarasota. Amanda recognized him from the picture in a YAHOO swinger's profile. Kurgus Juergen is the owner of Europe One, a company whose Florida incorporation papers lists the phone number of The Continental Café in Sarasota, a fictitious business name of Casablanca Rose Inc., whose two directors are Abeltif Mamdouh and Mustafa Ettaki.

Although he did tell us, unprompted, that he knew many people in the FBI, Juergen denied knowing Atta. And because we don't have a second source for the identification, we have to leave open the possibility that Amanda's photo confirmation was in error.

But not everyone has business partners named Abeltif and Mustafa.

The fact that Atta was being subsidized by U.S. taxpayers while he was in Hamburg hasn't been played up anywhere that we know about. But it's true...

For at least four of Atta's seven years living in Hamburg he was part of a "joint venture" between the U.S. and German Governments, an elite international "exchange" program run by a little-known private organization which has close ties to powerful American political figures like David Rockefeller and former Secretary of State Henry Kissinger.

This fact has escaped notice as well.

Before becoming a terrorist ringleader, Atta enjoyed the patronage of a government initiative known as the "Congress-Bundestag Program," overseen by the U.S. State Department and the German Ministry of Economic Cooperation and Development, the German equivalent of the U.S. Agency for International Development.

The jointly-funded U.S.-German government effort picked up the tab for Atta on sojourns in Cairo, Istanbul, and Aleppo in Syria during the years 1994 and 1995, as well as employing him as a "tutor" and "seminar participant" during 1996 and 1997.

Atta's financial relationship with the U.S.-German government program probably extends back to his initial move from Egypt to Germany in 1992.

The news that Mohamed Atta had been on the payroll of the elite international program only surfaced in a whisper, just as quietly as news that Venice flight schools had trained a third terrorist pilot. It was in a brief seven-line report by German newspaper *Frankfurter Allgemeine Zeitung* on Oct. 18, 2001, under the headline "ATTA WAS TUTOR FOR SCHOLARSHIP HOLDERS."

The story quoted spokesmen for "Carl Duisberg Gesellschaft," described as a "German international further education organization," as having admitted paying Hamburg cadre principal Atta as a "scholarship holder" and "tutor," between 1995 and 1997.

When we found it, what seemed to make this story especially curious is that the German paper concealed the truly shocking implication of their story: that Mohamed Atta had been on the payroll of a joint U.S.-German government program. They did this through the simple expedient of neglecting to mention in the article that the "Carl Duisberg Gesellschaft" was a private entity administering the "exchange" initiative of the two governments.

Maybe they forgot.

The U.S. end of the program, we discovered, is run out of an address at United Nations Plaza in New York, by the U.S. arm, called

CDS International. The letters stand for Carl Duisberg Society, also the name of its German counterpart in Cologne, the Carl Duisberg Gesellschaft. They are named for the German chemist and industrialist who headed the Bayer Corporation during the 1920s.

The list of elite power brokers backing CDS International ranges from the aforementioned Kissinger and Rockefeller to former President Bill Clinton, and other Democratic heavyweights like former First Lady Hillary Clinton, and Clinton adviser Ira Magaziner.

Kissinger showed his support by addressing over 100 international business leaders at an anniversary dinner organized and celebrating CDS International held at the River Club of New York June 2, 1987, where he congratulated CDS International on its 20 years of service in keeping close business ties, not only between Germany and the United States, but more recently through career development programs for participants from "other countries" as well.

Five years later, Mohamed Atta became a participant from one of these "other" countries.

Then-President Bill Clinton also found a lot to like about CDS International. During his visit to Germany to commemorate the Berlin Airlift, he noted that the United States "will be working hard to expand our support" for the "Congress-Bundestag" exchange which "has already given more than 10,000 German and American students the chance to visit each other's countries."

Were he to give the same speech today, he would no doubt amend the wording to read "visit and vaporize."

CDS International, states the organization's literature, provides opportunities for young German engineers. Mohamed Atta wasn't, strictly speaking, a "young German engineer"; but apparently Kissinger's praise for "career development programs for participants from other countries as well" had been taken to heart.

"These young German engineers earn real world experience and are given assignments to contribute from the start," a program spokesman enthused in a newspaper interview.

The organization is today understandably shy about mentioning that their most famous recent graduate's "real world experience" included murdering almost 3,000 people in New York City in slightly less than two hours.

A financial relationship between the terrorist ringleader and the U.S. and German Governments has not previously even been *hinted* at in

America's major media. The conspiracy-minded might conclude that this may owe something to the program's raft of politically-powerful boosters, giving it "big juice."

We prefer to think of it as an oversight.

Having "big juice" may also explain omissions in the story about Mohamed Atta's time in Germany in the March 7, 2003 *Chicago Tribune.*

Under the headline "9/11 haunts hijacker's sponsors; German couple talks of living with pilot Atta," the article described the 1992 meeting in Cairo between Atta and a German couple running an "international student exchange program."

Atta was recruited in Cairo by this mysterious German couple, dubbed the "hijacker's sponsors." It was this meeting, said the *Tribune,* which led Atta to move to Hamburg.

But although *Tribune* correspondent Stevenson Swanson cites this German couple for "having played such an important role in Atta's move to Germany," he never gives their *names,* nor that of the organization they worked for.

We thought good journalism was all about... you know. Who. What. When. Where. Why.

The *Chicago Tribune* got unaccountably stuck on "Who."

During a visit to the Egyptian capital in fall 1991, the *Tribune* reported, the German couple stayed with friends who knew Atta's father, a Cairo lawyer, and his father's friends had then introduced the German couple to Atta.

"Atta, who had recently graduated with a degree in architectural engineering from the University of Cairo, told the couple he wanted to study architecture in Germany, but he had no particular idea where he should go," the paper reported.

Though the article neglects to mention it, the reason Atta found himself with "no particular idea where he should go" was that although he'd studied engineering at prestigious Cairo University, he hadn't done well enough to gain admission to its graduate school.

The paper quotes the German wife telling investigators, "In this first conversation, we suggested he continue his studies in Hamburg and offered him a place to live at our house."

Atta, she states, accepted their offer right away.

This magnanimous gesture by the German couple to an undistin-guished young man they have just met may be normal behavior for this couple. Perhaps their gesture was just the very milk of human kindness.

Then again, perhaps it is something else. Why did this German couple leap at the opportunity to help a young man not considered promising enough to gain entrance to graduate school in Cairo? Of-fering him a place to live at their own home? The *Tribune* doesn't say. It also fails to identify either the couple or the "international" program they ran.

The story is 1,200 words in length. So it's not as if they didn't report the names for space reasons. "Jane and John Doe from Help-A-Student International" would have sufficed. Just an extra ten words and they would have had it. You know: Who What When Where and Why.

Either the *Tribune* just forgot the "Who." Or something more sin-ister occurred.

After studying German in Cairo, Atta arrived in Germany on July 24, 1992, according to investigator's records, and then lived rent-free for at least the next six months in the couple's home in a quiet, middle-class neighborhood.

Since just three years later Atta was on the payroll of the "Congress-Bundestag Program" it is reasonable to conclude—no thanks to the *Chicago Tribune*—that this was the "exchange program" responsible for bringing him to Germany in the first place.

CDS International's elite sponsors are apparently influential enough to have kept their organization's name out of the newspapers. Or, at any rate, out of the *Chicago Tribune*.

Here's something else we found curious about reports of Atta's time in Hamburg.... When he returned home for a three-month visit to Cairo in 1995, it was just as the Egyptian government was beginning to crack down viciously on Islamic fundamentalists.

Yet, strangely, Atta chose this exact time to grow a beard, tradition-ally a sign of a devout Muslim. It is assumed that Atta did this as a defiant political gesture to register his disgust at the secular elite that ruled his homeland.

At least, that's the way they tell the story... Atta's two German trav-eling "companions" report that Atta said he would not be cowed by his home country's "fat cats," who he believed were criminalizing religious traditionalists while bowing shamefully to the West in foreign and economic policies.

At least that's what they *say* he said.

A more plausible explanation might be that growing a beard and assuming an "Islamic fundamentalist" pose was the act of a man "singing for his supper," by going undercover on behalf of people who were paying his room and board in Hamburg.

CHAPTER TWENTY-SIX

"THINK. IT AIN'T ILLEGAL YET."

A ctions have consequences. At least they're supposed to. But the people, forces, and institutions in the U.S. before 9/11 that were dealing with, and doing business with Mohamed Atta and Osama bin Laden's terrorist thugs have yet to be named and identi-fied, let alone face justice.

Why was training narco-terrorists to fly a growth industry in South-west Florida a few short years ago?

Even the FBI admitted knowing about it.

"The FBI Knew Terrorists Were Using Flight Schools," read a *Wash-ington Post* headline one week after the attack

What the FBI left unanswered—both in the *Post* article and since— is why they did nothing to shut it down.

Maybe it was business. Maybe it was too lucrative to shut down.

One former Huffman aviation executive said, "Early on I gleaned that these guys had Government protection. They were let into this country for a specific purpose. It was a business deal."

Purchased in haste for top dollar and with no due diligence just a year before Arab terrorists began arriving, Hilliard and Dekkers' flight schools, Huffman Aviation in Venice, and Ambassador Avia-tion in Naples, made "no business sense."

So they must have made sense some other way… Was there an of-ficially-sanctioned drug trafficking operation run out of Venice, Flor-ida concurrent with Mohamed Atta's presence ?

There has been a big taboo surrounding some of the most obvious questions. 9/11 has been treated as if it were an event that occurred in a vacuum, instead of in time, in a specific set of circumstances known only to the participants in the negotiation then said to be transpiring.

9/11 happened in a world in which Osama bin Laden controlled one commodity on this planet, a strategic one: opium.

He was the King of Heroin.

With the capture of Kandahar in October 1994 the Taliban gained command of the southern gate of the vast smuggling empire built during the Soviet war with assistance from the Pakistani ISI and the CIA. Later that same year Afghanistan scooted past Burma to become the world's leading producer, and the narcotics industry in Afghanistan continued to grow enormously, serving the interests of the new masters of Kabul and their "fundamentalist" friends.

They were the world's only Islamic drug cartel.

If it's the end of the week, and George W. Bush announces its Friday, there are lots of people who'll still say he's lying. Yet some of these same people naïvely or disingenuously believe at face value Mullah Omar's pronouncement on July 27, 2000 "banning" the growing of opium in Afghanistan .

Mullah Omar was lying.

Satellite surveillance carried out for the United Nations revealed that the surface area devoted to growing opium poppies in Afghanistan had just grown by half, in one year.

After the Soviet war, poppy growing in Afghanistan began to take on the characteristics of modern agro-business, according to Professor Alfred McCoy's *The Politics of Heroin*.

Opium production in Mullah Omar's home district doubled after the Taliban take-over, said Amnesty International in a Nov '96 report.

What Mohamed Atta was really up to while he was in the U.S. can be seen in court documents and testimony concerning the transactions being engaged in by other bin Laden terrorists at the same time, doing business in the U.S. in a murky netherworld where government and organized crime intersect.

In a New Jersey Stinger missile case, for example, Arab terrorists got caught trying to buy Stinger missiles from the Mob.

The deal they got caught doing was typical, according to government prosecutors...

It involved oil and heroin for guns and training.

Osama the Heroin King would definitely have been trading heroin into the U.S., the world's richest market. Wouldn't he? There always seems plenty of heroin on U.S. "heroin store" shelves, which are probably re-stocked quicker than any convenience store. So *somebody* in the U.S., just logically, was doing business with him.

America's heroin supply has to enter the U.S. *someplace.* Traffickers look for someplace congenial, someplace cozy. Someplace where they could do *business...*

Someplace like Florida.

We've heard nothing about this from the FBI. It is a big taboo. Yet the pilot of Wally Hilliard's "Heroin Express" told investigators he'd flown the exact same flight 30 times in the previous nine months, a weekly "milk run" down and back to Venezuela.

Hilliard's operation wasn't legitimate. They got paid after each flight in *cash.*

Getting paid in cash by a Latin male for a once-a-week round-trip charter jet to Venezuela, in the unanimous opinion of law enforcement and aviation observers in Southwest Florida, is not a fact that will look very good at trial.

"It's just blatant," said one aviation executive. "They obviously weren't even bothering to hide what they were doing."

So the outlines of case for a Continuing Criminal Conspiracy are visible to any prosecutor. Any *courageous* prosecutor, that is.

Learning that Mohamed Atta was a coke-head had put the permanent kibosh on notions of Atta as any sort of recognizable "Islamic fundamentalist." Even if Al Qaeda's training manual urged them to blend in, that would mean having an occasional beer. Snorting cocaine was not part of Mohamed Atta's *cover...*

It was part of his *life,* or, if you prefer, his *life-style.*

Drug smugglers live that kind of life-style. Maybe spies do too. Do spies trade in drugs?

Watching the Venice Airport for a year and a half felt like seeing the movie *Casablanca* playing over and over. Apparently the DEA felt the same way we did. "The DEA rolls videotape from an apartment across from the Venice Airport," a business owner there informed us.

Hell will freeze over before *those* DEA tapes ever become public.

When Bill Clinton was elected President in 1992, his campaign stressed at every opportunity the message: "It's the economy, stupid!"

When all of the nationalistic and "fundamentalist" jingoism is stripped out, we think the 9/11 attack will ultimately prove to be about what most wars are about: Money.

Maybe the secret history of 9/11 is: "It's the drugs." A falling out between two business partners. A double-cross. A deal gone wrong. Wally Hilliard's own pilots talked freely about the nature of the endeavor going on around them.

"I flew Wally's Turbo-Commander to Venezuela and then got detained in Haiti on the way back, because both U.S. Customs and the DEA wanted to inspect the aircraft," said one pilot who flew for Hilliard. "When I asked them what was up, they said the plane you are flying is known to be smuggling drugs in and out of the country."

"Another time, one of our planes was being serviced in Jamaica, and they called and said, 'You need to pay us $10,000 to get the log books back,'" recalled the pilot and aviation executive. "'There's a fee involved.' When I asked, 'Why,' they said, 'Because the plane was supposed to fly a drug run and something had gone wrong and it hadn't kept its commitment.'"

U.S. officials spoke of the drug connection to 9/11 only in the immediate aftermath of the attack. "Frankly, we can't differentiate between terrorism and organized crime and drug dealing," Assistant Attorney General Michael Chertoff told a Senate Banking Committee hearing about the terrorists' money trail.

Osama bin Laden controlled the heroin trade in Afghanistan.

And Afghanistan controlled the heroin trade worldwide, producing as much as the rest of the world combined. His organization was said by officials to derive much of its funding from heroin and opium.

Even today, two years after being deposed, the Taliban are said to be deeply involved in a trade which last year generated sums said to be at least equal to the amount being spent on reconstruction aid for the country.

Today we think back to a comment made to us by a Special Forces Commander who was working out of McDill AFB in Tampa, and who'd just returned from Afghanistan. He offered an off-the-cuff but candid assessment of the reasons for the hostility between the U.S. and the "Evil Ones" that led to the heinous September 11 attack.

"The Taliban were launching an effort to take over the worldwide heroin trade," stated this grizzled veteran of recent rescue missions behind enemy lines matter-of-factly. "They were going to use that as a basis to move into cocaine distribution as well. They were planning on supplanting the Cali Cartel."

We Wondered: Whose nose might have gotten bent out of joint over *that?*

Nothing better illustrated how pathetically-little we know about the circumstances surrounding the 9/11 attack than the fact that Rudi Dekkers and Wallace J. Hilliard, whose Florida flight schools were "marching Arabs across the tarmac," are not who they pretend to be. We have seen through each man's "cover."

Who could have guessed that the man who owned the school where Mohamed Atta hung out was at the same time pursuing a diplomatic opening to Fidel Castro's Cuba?

"While Wally was supposedly flying Missionary flights to Havana, he was passing out Rolex watches instead," explained John Villada, Hilliard's former jet manager. "And somebody turned him in to the State Department for flying illegal charters to Cuba, and the State Department seized his account."

We heard the same story from four separate sources, each of whom added colorful detail. Those weren't just any ol' Rolexes Wally was handing out in Havana, either…

They were Presidential Rolexes.

"Did you know that Wally Hilliard went illegally over to Cuba providing money and Presidential Rolex watches?" asked an indignant aviation exec in Naples. "He said he was going over there to do a missionary job for his church, but nobody knew what he was doing."

Hilliard knew people in Naples politically well-connected with Fidel Castro. "They got Wally involved in Cuba," confirmed another source. "Rob has a DC-3 at the Immoklakee Airport. They're the one's who got Wally involved and Cuba. They got busted for running illegal charters to Cuba."

Odd behavior for a *retired Midwestern insurance executive.* "Somebody turned him in to the State Department for flying illegal charters to Cuba," stated one source. "How he got caught was one of his pilots turned in an expense report, and Wally's accountant, Stuart Burchill, actually wrote on the expense report: Expenses for Cuba."

Then this source, a man involved in aviation in Naples for several decades, spent a long moment looking down at his feet. When he lifted his eyes he asked, "Can you *believe* this shit?"

Our sentiments exactly.

The evidence added up. Testimony from one eyewitnesses corroborated that of others. For example, from one source we'd learned, just in passing, that Wally and Rudi had formed a fictitious company to keep Rudi in the U.S. back in the mid-90s, and that Wally also had an aircraft maintenance facility in Nassau in the Bahamas, run by a South African man named Alfonso Bowe.

"Nobody knows for sure who Wally works for," the source had said. "He owns an FBO in Nassau called Executive Jet Support with a guy named Alfonso Bowe, whose sister is married to the Prime Minister of the Bahamas. He (Bowe) also runs a flight school he started with Pervez Kahn."

We filed this away. We didn't need to go to the Bahamas to find the story. It was all around us in Venice. Then months later someone told us something Bowe said about Rudi Dekkers.

"When Alfonso Bowe heard that the terrorists had trained at Rudi Dekkers' flight school, he said, 'It figures that out of all the flight schools in the nation the terrorists would go to Rudi.'"

Nothing could be more clear. Wally Hilliard was not who he pretended to be.

"I think common sense should prevail," said Coy Jacob. "And I think if you are a thinking person and you have common sense I think that you examine the person making the statement and see if there is any reason for falsehoods."

"It all looks pretty suspicious to me."

It appears increasingly likely that one of History's Greatest Crimes—
the September 11 terrorist attack—is being followed by one of History's Greatest Cover-Ups. We don't even have the satisfaction of having brought to justice the killers of our 3,000 dead. Although President Bush is careful to avoid mentioning his name these days, Osama bin Laden is still on the minds of Americans, whose thinking is Biblically-simple.

They want his head.

As I write these words it's been almost 800 days since hundreds of millions watched 3,000 of our number perish in gruesome and terrible ways. Late on the day of the attack, NBC anchor Brian Williams opined, "There will be many people asking tonight just what it is we are getting for all those tens of billions of dollars being spent on intelligence."

Almost 800 days later, the question still seems valid. And now we have others as well.

The brutal reality of American life at the beginning of the 21st century seems to be the same as that faced by the citizens of Rome 2,000 years ago, as they looked with despair at the swaggering and corrupt Praetorian Guard which had made a mockery of their once proud Republic, and asked out loud the question which echoes down to us across the centuries:

"Who will guard the *guards?*"

CHAPTER TWENTY-SEVEN

LATE BREAKING NEWS: THE RUSSIAN MOB AND 9/11

Four years after the 9/11 attack, events in two out of the way corners of the world added to our ability to identify and put "uniforms" on the "players" involved in the terror plot that resulted in the loss of almost 3,000 innocent civilians.

The search for the truth eventually led us halfway around the world in either direction; to places which have not before now been associated with the events of that terrible day, and to events involving Russian Mobsters in the Ukraine, and a German CIA asset with Russian Mob connections on a tiny island in the middle of the Pacific.

Rather than being the "lone cadre" portrayed by the FBI, receiving no outside help while in the U.S., Mohamed Atta and his terrorist buddies were, in fact, outstandingly well-connected, to state intelligence agencies like the CIA, and to the shadowy world of international organized crime.

The biggest lie told about the September 11th attack was the first one, which stated "19 hijackers moved through Europe and America unnoticed."

The first occurred on a runway in the Ukraine in the dead of winter, about as far from Florida, where we had based out 9/11 investigation, as you can get.

What happened there, and what it revealed, will widen the scope of the story of the terrorist hijackings, and introduce elements not yet widely considered pertinent. The terrorist hijackers had connections that go far beyond what the U.S. Government has been willing to admit; with a motley crew of weapons merchants, narcotics traffickers, diamond smugglers, Russian-Israeli mafia tycoons, and Islamic terrorists, all shivering as one under a slate gray Ukrainian winter sky.

Here's how it went down, based on government documents and interviews with one of the crew members onboard at the time, who asked for anonymity.

Snow was falling and visibility was poor underneath the low-hanging gray clouds at Zhuliany Airport outside Kiev, the capital of the Ukraine. Overhead a plane, a Challenger 600 luxury ten passenger executive jet (N-number N187AP) began to maneuver in preparation for landing. It was the morning of January 4 2005.

Inside the Challenger jet sat Russian oligarch Vitaly Gaiduk, his wife and daughter, and a handful of employees of an air charter company, including several pilots and an aviation mechanic; all were comfortably seated on six ivory-leather swivel chairs, clustered around a dark cherry hardwood table, upon which sat an unread Russian newspaper.

The family amused themselves looking up at twin 14-inch TV monitors, mounted on the forward and aft cabin bulkheads. They were oblivious to the mounting tension in the cockpit of the plane, hidden behind a cockpit door. And the rising tension in the cockpit had nothing to do with the lowering weather.

Sitting in the co-pilot's seat was Mark Shubin, a much-traveled former CIA pilot of U-2 and SR-71 high-altitude reconnaissance planes over Russia and other Cold War hotspots. Instead of piloting the plane, Shubin had been cajoled into letting an inexperienced American pilot and journeyman adventurer named Travis Paul have the controls, while he sat in the co-pilot's seat. Shubin had allowed Paul to take over the controls to demonstrate that he was ready to be more than a co-pilot on one of the small fleet of private jets Shubin provided for his employer.

Now Shubin began to regret the decision. He was studying Travis Paul through narrowed eyes. As they prepared to land Paul had done something suspicious...

Rather than of clasping his seat belt across his lap, he had instead strapped himself into the more-bulky shoulder harness. This was highly unusual for a routine landing; they were usually only worn during emergencies and for crash landings.

And it added to the unease Shubin felt that something was amiss, which he had so far kept to himself.

Even before take-off in Geneva, Travis Paul and William Kerry spent an hour on the phone talking with Rabaev in Kiev. Later Shubin realized that their attitude had changed after the phone conversation.

Shubin was the chief pilot and head honcho of a charter aviation company with a contract to fly for a Ukrainian conglomerate, one of the Ukraine's biggest concerns, called the Industrial Union of Donbas, and based in Kiev and the industrial city of Donetsk.

It was owned by his passenger Vitaly Haiduk and his two partners, Serge Taruta, and Oleg Makartchan. The trio was among the wealthiest men in the country, and belonged to the new class known as "the oligarchs," people who had grown rich buying up state-owned enterprises on the cheap after the fall of Communism.

All three men were supporters in the upcoming election of the man who would soon become the new president, but only after being poisoned and disfigured, reportedly by KGB agents backing the other candidate and current President of the Ukraine, who was, and is, a close associate of Vladimir Putin.

The Challenger landing in Kiev carried one of the key players in the struggle. Gaiduk was a West-leaning Ukrainian Minister of Energy who had made enemies because of his pro-Western positions and the hostility towards Russia he'd shown on a controversial energy issues, including the recent showdown between Ukrainian and Russian officials over whether to hand over Ukraine's gas transport system under a concession agreement with Russia.

What happened next was apparently the culmination of weeks of intrigue by a man claiming to have been a 767 pilot in Uzbekistan who Shubin had recently hired named Felix Igor Rabaev.

The conflict between the men was not over personalities, but over conflicting hidden agendas, and their struggle highlights the often-murderous nature of the geo-political intrigue swirling then, ad now, between Russia and the West in the modern version of what in former times was called the "Great Game."

Then Russia and Great Britain were contending over the Russian's desire to expand and gain warm water ports for their fleet. Today the intrigue is about Central Asia's vast oil reserves. It's a game played by oilmen, politicians, and petroleum geologists, supported by a motley cast of soldiers of fortune, raffish adventurers, weapons merchants, narcotics traffickers, Russian-Israeli mafia tycoons, and terrorists.

It was an epic struggle, a Trojan War with no Helen, just lots of black oily goop.

And at that moment in January of 2005, tensions had been running especially high, as the world watched to see what else might happen while awaiting the inauguration of Western-backed President Viktor Yushchenko, a man who had been scarred by poisoning during the election campaign.

One big prize was control of the Ukraine, which would be a crucial terminus for moving the vast oil reserves of Central Asia to Europe.

It was a deadly serious game. In Uzbekistan, one of the battlegrounds, and a former Republic of the USSR known collectively as the "Stans," and which will shortly figure in our story, losers in such struggles were even sometimes boiled alive. Since Idi Amin had been forced to leave Uganda for the safety of Muslim motherland Saudi Arabia, among the nations of the Earth only Uzbekistan still indulged in the custom of boiling alive political dissidents.

And because Gaiduk had aligned himself with the West, someone was now trying to make him think twice about that decision, or, if they were lucky, disable or even eliminate him.

In Florida, Shubin enlisted several pilots: Travis Paul, another pilot who was an ex-colonel in the Russian Air force, Lev Soburnov, a former MIG pilot with an FAA license and years flying jets, and a man Paul recommended, William Kerry, who claimed to be experience pilot on Hawker aircraft.

Also coming aboard the aviation venture was a man who went by several names: he was Felix or Igor or Boris Rabaev, depending on circumstances. He was hired after Shubin was prevailed upon by German Galilov, Operations Manager for a Fort Lauderdale-based charter jet company which flew air cargo flights between an abandoned military base in West Germany and Tashkent, Uzbekistan, and was partly-owned by government officials in Tashkent.

Galilov, who lives in Miami, wanted Shubin to help a relative of his, an immigrant from Tadzikistan living in New York, who reportedly had a pilot's license, but little experience.

Kerry flew one of the charter companies' jets to Kiev to meet Rabaev. Later, when Kerry began ignoring phone calls from Shubin, he knew something was going wrong.

He was right. In his very first flight, Kerry began flying erratically, Shubin learned. He violated military airspace three times, and after landing the airplane was arrested by the FSB, the successor to the KGB.

Kerry would also disappear from the crew's hotel in Geneva before the fateful flight aboard the Challenger to Kiev which was sabotaged by its own pilot.

Shubin later discovered that Felix Rabaev had begun causing problems with Kerry and other members of the flight crew almost immediately after being hired.

Rabaev also grew cozy with a former KGB officer named Alexander Koshevoi.

Just after Christmas, Shubin had flown Gaiduk and his family to Geneva on the Challenger for a few days vacation. Now they were returning to the overheated atmosphere surrounding the disputed Ukrainian Presidential election.

"The way I heard it, Gaiduk felt safe with Shubin, and never wore his seatbelts; his family the same way," said a pilot who had flown in Central Europe with Shubin. "The other side used that information to try to eliminate, or at least send a message to, Gaiduk."

This is an important piece of information necessary to understand what follows, the source stated. Shubin had been Haiduk's personal pilot for long enough for the Ukrainian Minister to be so confident in his abilities that he rarely bothered to strap-in, even during take-offs and landings, but made it his custom to easily wander up and down the plane's aisles.

But this time, instead of piloting the plane, Mark Shubin had been cajoled into letting an inexperienced American pilot and journeyman adventurer named Travis Paul have the controls, while he sat in the co-pilot's seat.

"Shubin told me that things were strange from the start," the observer continued.

"After we took off from Geneva, he said, Paul was warned by the control tower for not maintaining the proper altitude and heading.

They threatened to order us back. They asked who the hell the pilot was. And Travis said, 'Captain Mark Shubin.'"

An aircraft mechanic who had been also been onboard told us, "We were coming in way too fast. I heard Shubin yell, 'You're going too fast! Please slow down!'"

By all accounts, there had been no response from Travis, who was hunched over the controls. "Shubin told me later that he noticed he had been breathing heavily breathing and sweating," said the source. "He began pleading with Paul to let him land the airplane, but I didn't hear any response.

"The runway quickly rose to meet the plane. And then it was too late. The airplane bounced once and then went flying down the runway. Later Shubin told me Travis was breathing heavy and sweating profusely, but wasn't trying to stop airplane, or exit to the taxi way."

We reached Shubin, who at first didn't want to discuss the crash. After mulling it over a few days, he relented, and confirmed the outlines of the story. He would later begin to receive phone threats on his life in an attempt to dissuade him from revealing too much detail of the incident.

The aviation mechanic onboard, Alvin Hegner, stated, "I could hear Shubin screaming at Paul to 'Turn the plane, turn the plane!' But only from the Captain's seat can you turn the plane, and coming up almost immediately on our right was the last taxiway."

"It's true we came in way too fast," Shubin confirmed. "It's also true that after we touched down the plane was running down the runway at full throttle. It was just hurtling. And I could see that Travis Paul wasn't braking. I screamed at him to brake. He said "I am stepping on the brakes! We have no brakes!

"So I slammed on the brakes on my side of the controls. The airplane started to slow down. But we were already approaching the last taxiway to turn off before the end of the runway."

The eyewitness to the crash continued: "Paul started turning to the right. It looked like he'd make it. But it had been a real close call. But a few seconds later as I sat back and began to relax, the plane's engines revved and we turned back into the runway and began accelerating again.

"Shubin grabbed the throttle, and cut the engine, but it was too late. The Challenger rolled off the runway straight across the frozen grass and pitched forward, it landing gear broken.

"We went sliding for couple hundred feet on the snow and into the dirt until airplane finally came to a halt. Behind me I could heard people rolling and bouncing all over the cabin. I ran to the back to check the condition of the passengers. Vitaly and his family were shaken, but okay. One of the members of the crew that was 'dead-heading' with us had a sprained ankle.

"Up front I saw Shubin opening the emergency door. We got out and everything was dark and eerily quiet. In the distance were some twinkling lights, like Christmas tree lights. They began to get closer. And then we could hear the sirens. A minute later there were ambulances, fire trucks and police vehicles everywhere."

Shubin suspected sabotage. Several days later he got confirmation that the crash had been deliberate. Igor "Felix" Rabaev had enlisted several of the plane's motley crew in a plan. No one would suspect a crash-landing on an icy runway in the dead of winter of being an attempt to do the Ukrainian Minister bodily harm.

The next day Ukrainian investigators started the investigation of accident. Our aviation source spent the night with the crew, including Shubin, in their rented house.

"At four in the morning the phone rang in our apartment," he told us. "Shubin answered, and spoke briefly in Russian. I asked him what's happening, and he said, "Somebody just told me they will blow up the house if we go in for an investigation of the crash in the morning. We have to leave Ukraine immediately."

A year later, a non-fatal accident report from the National Transportation & Safety Administration contained none of this intrigue. Instead, it set out a set of facts in dry language:

"On January 4, 2005, at about 1701 coordinated universal time, a Canadair CL-600 airplane, N187AP, received minor damage when it departed the end of runway 26 during the landing roll at the Zhuliany Airport, Kyiv, Ukraine," said the NTSB accident report.

"The airplane was registered to Wells Fargo Bank Northwest, Trustee, Salt Lake, Utah, and operated by Vladimir Kravets, Kiev, Ukraine, under the provisions of Ukraine Civil Aviation Regulations.

"The pilot, copilot, and an unknown number of passengers were not injured. Information provided by the Government of Ukraine, and from a statement provided by the pilot, indicated that the runway was contaminated by ice and snow. The runway braking action was reported as fair.

"Upon touchdown, the crew was unable to deploy the thrust reversers because they were not armed. The captain applied maximum braking but was unable to prevent the airplane from departing the end of the runway. The nose gear then collapsed. The captain provided a calculated landing distance, including surface contamination, which was 4,513 feet. Runway 26 is 5,905 feet long, and 16 feet wide."

"The NTSB report is bullshit," a member of the doomed flight's crew told us. "Rabaev spread money around to keep the true story from coming out, but it wasn't enough to keep everybody's mouth shut. He's a cheap bastard, and that's a fact."

Shubin later told our source that aviation mechanic Hegner had overheard a heated argument in Donetsk between the crew members over bribe money Rabaev had promised them, after Travis Paul and William Kerry showed up to meet Rabaev and receive the money, $25,000 each, including airline tickets back to the US.

Travis said to Rabaev $25.000 it is not enough and if Rabaev didn't bring more money he will go see the big bosses in Kiev and tell them what happened.

Rabaev then promised both men jobs when everything calm down in ISD Avia on a new Challenger 300 jet managed by Jet Aviation and owned by Wells Fargo /Kravets.

Rabaev said that he had been named "chief pilot" by general manager Alexander Koshevoi to ensure their silence.

Koshevoi was KGB. And Igor Rabaev and Alexander Koshevoi were now in business.

So Igor Rabaev had paid Travis Paul and William Kerry $50,000 for the attempt to murder or incapacitate Gaiduk. Rabaev was also involved with the Russian Mob in Tashkent, trafficking heroin from next-door Afghanistan.

It looked more and more like a plot, a high-level power play. So when he returned to the States, Shubin started investigating the man, Igor Rabaev, who he believed had set him up. He learned Rabaev had not just been trafficking heroin; but terrorists to Russia, as well, and for years.

"Rabaev claimed he had been flying for Uzbekistan Airways as Captain of a 767," an aviation executive in Fort Lauderdale told Shubin, waving his hand through the air dismissively. "He was lying."

Shubin found a flight school in New Jersey that had updated Rabaev's license.

"Rabaev came to our flight school to convert his Uzbek license to an FAA license," said a New Jersey flight instructor who had trained Rabaev. "I flew with him several times. His pilot log book and Russian license looked very suspicious. And he could hardly keep airplane on taxiway. I told him he should stop flying. He was that bad."

He always paid cash from a roll of twenties," said the instructor. "I don't understand how he get his license and where was money coming from. He certainly not a pilot. But he *is* a dangerous man...you could feel it."

Rabaev's negatives went beyond merely being a poor pilot. One of Shubin's most experienced Captains, Lev Soburnov, a Russian, who refused to fly with Rabaev a second time, said he also "apparently had a fear of flying."

But he did have a few things of value: a "cousin" in Miami, a number of aliases: "Igor Rabaev; Edgar Rabaev; Felix Rabaev... and, most importantly, connections to international narcotics traffickers.

By chance, Shubin was friends with Diego Levine, the pilot who had been flying Learjets down and back to Venezuela for Wally Hilliard.

And that's why a minor plane crash in the Ukraine tells us some important facts about the 9/11 attack, because this pilot had information which allows us to connect the Ukrainian crash with the biggest piece of the 9/11 puzzle we'd discovered in Venice, Florida, the home of three of the four terrorist pilots:

That during the same month Mohamed Atta arrived to attend his flight school, the *owner* of the flight school had his Lear jet confiscated, on July 25, 2000, on the runway of Orlando Executive Airport, by DEA agents brandishing submachine guns.

They did a search of the plane and discovered 43 pounds of heroin. The flight school owner's Learjet was seized carrying what drug smugglers term "heavy weight," at the same time that Mohamed Atta arrived at his flight school.

Remind us: What is it, again, that they produce in Afghanistan? This was the "smoking gun." And it is the place where any real 9/11 investigation will begin.

The heroin kingpin from Venezuela who was arrested in Orlando, Edgar Valles-Diaz, had paid cash each week for the Learjet's flights. A mysterious Venezuelan, Edgar Valles-Diaz had been chartering Wally Hilliard's Learjet once a week until he got caught with 43 pounds of heroin hidden inside tennis shoes in his luggage.

We wanted to know more about Edgar Valles-Diaz, the mysterious Venezuelan left almost literally holding the bag, filled with 43 lbs. of heroin hidden in his luggage. He had gone to prison in early 2001 for a few years.

We had learned little else about him.

The pilot of the drug flights on Wally Hilliard's Lear jet, Diego Taxar-Levine, told authorities he'd known Valles-Diaz for just nine months, during which he flew him from Venezuela to Fort Lauderdale and then on to New York at least 30 times.

Each of the more than thirty weekly flights began in Venezuela, made a stop-over in Fort Lauderdale, and occasionally Orlando, before terminating at a general aviation airport just outside New York City in Teeterboro, New Jersey.

The Learjet made 39 weekly flights without incident before getting busted.

It was a *milk run.*

Valles-Diaz was no ordinary South American drug dealer, Diego Levine told Shubin.

He reportedly had close ties to Venezuelan President Hugo Chavez, and a serious involvement in geopolitical intrigue in, of all places, Central Asia.

Valles Diaz was making all those trips in Wally Hilliard's Learjet while working for a Russian Mobster, one who will be discovered to have a strange connection to fundamentalist Islamists in Tashkent, Uzbekistan.

During most of the year 2000, Levine told authorities, a Russian Mobster named Felix Igor Borisovich Rabaev, living in the Russian enclave in Brighton Beach in New York City was there to meet Venezuelan drug trafficker Edgar Valles-Diaz on his arrival.

When they landed in New York Valles-Diaz was met by his "boy-friend," Levine stated. "He gets picked up at the airport by an Uzbek named Igor Rabaev, his heroin 'connection' from Central Asia."

The heroin was being delivered each week to *Felix "Igor" Rabaev*, whose feud with former CIA pilot Mark Shubin had caused the plane crash in the Ukraine.

"Igor Rabaev is a name to be conjured with in certain circles," a former U.S. covert operative in Central Asia told us.

Rabaev was a member of one of the three largest Russian Mob families in the U.S., who flitted in and out of Central Asia at will, using the Uzbek capital of Tashkent as a transshipment point for heroin from Afghanistan wending its way to Russia and the West.

"He's from Uzbekistan, and escaped from Russia to Israel by saying he was Jewish, back when it was the only way you could get out. But he's not Jewish. He's Muslim, and he's got close ties with radical Muslim circles in the 'Stans' who serve as a conduit for heroin coming out of Afghanistan."

"Non-Jewish Russian mobsters often fraudulently claimed Jewish ancestry in order to gain easier movement in and out of Israel, where the Russian Mafia has established a large operating base," said the source.

"It was a real scam by Russian organized crime; it was easier for lots of these people to say they were Jewish to get into Israel, and then from Israel to become instant citizens, get Israeli passports, and then into the U.S."

We received confirmation that there were, indeed, Muslim Mobsters from the former USSR posing as Jews in *Red Mafiya*, by Stephen I. Friedman, the definitive book about the Russian Mob in Brighton Beach.

The head of the New York FBI's Russian Mob unit told Friedman that there were three or four major Russian crime families operating in Brighton Beach; the largest consisted primarily of Jewish émigrés from Odessa, followed by a second family from Tashkent, in Uzbekistan, which the FBI had pegged as Muslim, but which people in the community insisted was Jewish.

And Edgar Valles-Diaz had been deeply involved in geopolitical activity more than half a world away, in Tashkent. "Igor Rabaev was in business with Edgar Valles-Diaz," an aviation executive in Fort Lauderdale confirmed.

"You should ask Hilliard's partner about Rabaev. Mark Shubin knows him. Rabaev and Shubin had a run-in just last year, I hear. They were in an accident together."

Russian Mobster Igor Borisovich "Felix" Rabaev—the heroin trafficker waiting at the receiving end for the arrival of a weekly drug flight coming in from Venezuela during the year 2000 on a Lear jet owned by terror flight school impresario Wallace J. Hilliard—masterminded, just four years later, the crash of the Challenger in the Ukraine with former CIA pilot Mark Shubin aboard.

Small world.

We went to the DEA to ask about Rabaev. We had already profiled Shubin for this book because of his association with Wally Hilliard, the supposed Florida "retiree" who owned the flight school Mohamed Atta called home.

Rabaev was from Tashkent, a key transshipment location for Afghan heroin as it wends its way to Russia and the West.

Was there a connection between Mohamed Atta and Felix Rabaev?

As per usual, *mum's the word* at the DEA.

And what of terror flight school owner Wally Hilliard? In addition to being associated with the Russian Mob, Valles Diaz was also a partner of the 75-year old Hilliard in the company "leasing" the Lear jet, American Jet Charters.

Hilliard was a Wisconsin insurance executive who says he "retired" to Florida, but who, instead—within a year of his supposed "retirement"—had assembled a fleet of between twenty to thirty long-range private jets, as well as flight schools like the now-infamous Huffman Aviation.

A lot of people retire to Florida. But most retired men settle for a hobby like woodworking. A boat. A golf game. Shuffleboard. Tennis. Not Hilliard.

Hilliard bought a fleet of 30-40 jets. What was a retiree in Naples doing with a bigger Air Force than Panama?

"I used to ask myself, Why is Wally doing business with all these foreigners?" asked Dave Montgomery, Hilliard's one-time chief mechanic. "There was Diego Levine, Alfonso Bowe, Mark Shubin, Pervez Khan.... It didn't make sense."

We'd never heard of anybody retiring to pursue a second career in espionage, international organized crime, or drug trafficking. At a minimum, worrying your organization has been penetrated by a foreign intelligence service must wreak havoc on your backswing.

How did a retired-to-Florida insurance executive named Wallace J. Hilliard from Green Bay Wisconsin become such a central figure in the story of terrorist hijackers?

Who'd ever heard of a Midwestern James Bond?

There are questions that need to be asked, by authorities with the legal ability to compel answers.

Mark Shubin and Wally Hilliard had been in business together.

Shubin's company, Sky Bus Inc., shared ownership of four planes with Hilliard's Plane 1 Leasing, including two with highly unusual "tail" numbers: N11UN and N111UN. And in August of 2001, Shubin incorporated a company in Florida called "International Diplomatic Courier Services."

Was the "UN" designation on the tail number a clue?

Both companies, Sky Bus Inc. and International Diplomatic Courier Services, had been launched with CIA money, our pilot informant told us.

Shubin was later active as a pilot for some of the infamous "rendering" flights in Europe and Central Asia, we learned, after discovering a note written by one of the ubiquitous "plane spotters" who made it their business to observe the movements of suspected CIA planes.

"N777SA has just dropped in at 0150 Local!" wrote an English plane spotter in Birmingham. "Another due today is VP-BKZ. Nuff said."

The laconic "nuff said" drew our attention. We had already identified N77SA as a jet registered to Shubin. The comment seemed to indicate it was connected in some way with the second plane mentioned, VP-BKZ, which we soon learned was registered in Mclean, VA.

There's a rather large enterprise headquartered near there. It's called the CIA. Then, in early 2004, Shubin and the CIA parted ways, a source told us. Shubin went looking for clients in the Ukraine. We heard he even flew Vladimir Putin around for a while.

But Shubin had flown Presidents and Ministers all over the world. Why back to Russia? One rumor we heard indicated he may have been sent back by the CIA to protect Vitaly Gaiduk, who later would become the Ukraine's Secretary of Defense.

This is the hidden sub-text to 9/11. Terror flight school owner Wallace J. Hilliard lost his heroin Learjet after he was adjudged to be anything but an innocent charter flight operator in early 2001. He was forced by the DEA and the Orlando U.S. Attorney's office to relinquish the plane.

However, even after that, a blemish which would seem to scare away any politician espousing "Republican family values," both Governor Jeb Bush and Florida Secretary of State Katherine Harris provided celebrity endorsements to his bogus front "airline," which on a least one route never sold a single ticket.

All of this is just a small, but significant, part of America's secret history.

And it's why you haven't heard anything about any of this before now.

CHAPTER TWENTY-EIGHT

THE RUSSIAN MOB AND 9/11: PART TWO

There was a second big revelation after the publication of *Welcome to TERRORLAND* that warrants inclusion in the trade paperback edition.

In interviews with Atta's former American girlfriend, Amanda Keller, we had learned that a half-dozen of Mohamed Atta's closest associates in Florida during the year leading up to the 9/11 attack were not Arab, but German, Swiss, and Austrian.

And the name of the German closest to Atta, with whom Atta was "inseparable" once he arrived on the scene, said Keller, was Wolfgang Bohringer. He was one of the handful of people the terrorist ring-leader called "my brother."

Traveling with Atta, or meeting him around the state, at least some of Atta's German friends appeared to share a relationship with him of long-standing, according to eyewitnesses, dating back to his days in Hamburg. The names of these individuals, all pilots, surfaced in no press accounts after the 9/11 attack, nor has their existence been mentioned or alluded to in official statements. There existence was revealed exclusively in this book.

The meetings, in places like Key West and Miami, were apparently very serious business; when they returned, said someone who was there, Atta and his German associates "always came back glum."

As readers of the *MadCowMorningNews* (www.madcowprod.com) know, there was a concerted campaign to discredit Keller's testimony. Then, right in the middle of this disinformation effort, came news that he had recently resurfaced on a tiny island in the South Pacific, in the Republic of Kiribati.

"An FBI terror alert has been issued in the South Pacific for Wolfgang Bohringer, a German pilot identified as a "close associate" of Mohamed Atta," the Associated Press reported.

"U.S. authorities have uncovered a plot to set up a flight training school in Kiribati and suspect the man behind it may have had links to September 11 mastermind Mohamed Atta," reported the Associated Press.

While none of the stories which followed deigned to mention that we had broken the story, or that the first identification of Wolfgang Bohringer had come three years ago in the opening chapter to *Welcome to TERRORLAND*, it was a sweet victory nonetheless.

Wolfgang Bohringer readily admitted knowing Mohamed Atta, island residents told us, stating that another German pilot in Naples, Rex Gasteiger, was to blame for linking him to 9/11.

Bohringer said he and Atta mixed frequently together, said island resident Chuck Corbett. "He (Bohringer) explained the connection by saying that he owned a flight school beside the airfield where the 9/11 hijackers trained."

The woman traveling with Bohringer said that "He seemed to running from something."

"So she told him what she'd read about him on the internet (on our website) about the 9/11 thing," she told Corbett. "Bohringer alleviated her concerns with simple explanations about an unhappy business partnership with the guy who bought his flight school," the resident wrote us.

"But, it was clear he hated Jews. He told some very bad jokes about ovens, Jews, bread, and blacks."

The news completely vindicated our reporting.

Here's what happened: The story in the South Pacific begins after Bohringer showed on a yacht up a year ago at tiny Fanning Island, tucked away in a far corner of the South Pacific. Several local residents, including Chuck Fanning, grew suspicious after

Bohringer announced his intention to open a flight school to teach pilots to fly DC-3's, a vintage aircraft much-favored for its ability to fly into dirt airstrips by pilots carrying contraband cargo like weapons and drugs.

Fanning Island, almost a thousand miles south of Hawaii is one of the most remote places on Earth, an island with no electricity and barely a hundred inhabitants.

We learned of Bohringer's presence there after being contacted by several alarmed local residents who said they'd read about Bohringer on our website. Bohringer, island residents told us, arrived on a 42-foot yacht, complete with a chest filled with several million dollars in brand new bills, several automatic weapons, and passports from a half-dozen nations.

Moreover, he told island residents stories about working for a major international financier and swindler wanted on two continents who has close ties to both political figures in the U.S. as well as the Russian Mob.

On his yacht, the "Argos," Bohringer was carrying a chest filled with "stacks of brand new hundred dollar bills, more money that I have ever seen in my life," wrote one local resident.

"Then there was the cash. Lots of it," Chuck Corbett told New Zealand TV. "I would offer to go shopping for him. He would always give me a $100 bill. Once it was seven $100 bills and they were always crisp and neat."

For Corbett, who spent months with Bohringer, things did not add up. "One particular night he laid out seven passports on the table," Corbett said. "I recall one from Ireland, from the Bahamas, one from Grenada, India, the US, Germany and one or two others.

Mohamed Atta and Wolfgang Bohringer were obviously no slouches in the passport department. Bohringer claimed to be an arms dealer, and acknowledged his involvement with Eastern European Mobsters.

Soon several residents quietly reported surprisingly-deep suspicions to local authorities. "To me Wolfgang is carrying dirty money, lots of it," wrote one.

"If he can gets a flight school going it does not take a stretch of the imagination to see he would sell it to some else who sells it to someone else and Honolulu gets vaporized. He seems to know the money tree and could be working to set things up for others to do so and so has been funded to do so."

Then Wolfgang Bohringer fled tiny Fanning Island in the South Pacific aboard his yacht, after we wrote a story in the *MadCowMorningNews* (headlined "Close Associate of Mohamed Atta Surfaces in South Pacific") revealing his presence there, as well as his suspicious intention to open a flight school to train pilots to fly *only* DC-3s, a 70-year old aviation workhorse frequently used in weapons and drug smuggling.

"The FBI is on the trail of a man with alleged links to one of the 9/11 masterminds after he tried to set up a pilot training school on a remote island bordering US territory, despite the island having no airport or telephones," reported Barbara Dreaver of New Zealand network TVNZ.

"The isolated Kiribati islands are grappling with being catapulted into the world of terrorism. The man causing the alarm is Wolfgang Bohringer, who sailed into Kiribati's Fanning Island a year ago."

Amanda Keller had told us she called Bohringer "The Iceman," because of his resemblance to a character in the movie "Top Gun," the rival to Tom Cruise played by Val Kilmer. They forwarded some pictures they had taken of him. The resemblance is uncanny.

Keller also said Wolfgang won a lottery to get his green card. The locals on Fanning Island reported that Bohringer told them that story too.

Clearly Amanda Keller had known Wolfgang Bohringer. Time after time, Keller's testimony has proven correct. Here's what she said about him: "Him (Atta) and Wolfgang drove around in the red convertible a lot," she said. "Their favorite place to eat was Hooters in Sarasota. They got kicked out of Hooters for grabbing their boobs."

"He spoke German with Wolfgang, who was in his thirties. Wolfgang was with Mohamed when he came by the nursing home to see me one time. Mohamed called certain people—Arabic people—'my brother.' And I was wondering how he had so many family members. Like gang members do, 'this is my brother,'" she said.

"But not all Arabs. So it wasn't like just anyone Muslim was his brother. He called Wolfgang and Juergen 'my brother,' too. He and Wolfgang were very tight, they went everywhere together. When he came into the picture they were together all the time."

Moreover, Amanda Keller was not the only eyewitness quoted mentioning Atta's German associates. Atta's landlord for a brief week told reporters about a wild 3-day weekend Amanda and Atta spent in Key West, along with another girl named Linda.

"The two girls were introduced to two men from Germany that they said were Mohamed's friends," Tony LaConca told the *Charlotte Sun-Herald*.

When we first learned that all of Atta's associates in Florida had not been Arab, we were understandably eager to learn more about the terrorist ringleaders' two German friends. *Sun-Herald* reporter Elaine Allen-Emrich had apparently felt the same way...

"The FBI in Tampa would neither confirm nor deny that any agents were interviewing people in the North Port area," she reported. "Asked for more information about Atta's wild weekend, an FBI spokesperson identified only as "Pam" said, "We recommend that you check in with CNN for current information. Any press statements can be found on televised stations like CNN."

We went looking for ourselves. The results are in this book. We didn't feel like "checking in with CNN."

Like Rudi Dekkers, Wolfgang was notorious in aviation circles for bad behavior. We found records of his scrapes in the files of airport authorities in Florida, including a letter sent by a former employee soliciting to offer private flight instruction at his Wolf Aero, Bohringer's flight school, without authority and in violation of FAA rules was in the airport records in Naples.

Bohringer had opened a flight school in Naples, Florida in 1996, illegal for a foreigner. But he hadn't gotten in any trouble with the FAA.

"Wolfgang showed up from Munich in the mid-1990s and immediately began operating a flight school illegally," stated Naples flight instructor Marcus Huber, a flight instructor in Naples. "He's half Swiss, half German."

"When Wolfgang applied for an E-2 Visa, he made up a fake company, a cleaning service," Huber told us. "Sometimes it makes me mad that a criminal gets preference."

The new details island residents offered led us to probe more deeply into his background. And what we discovered indicates that he may belong to the elusive "global network" which British Prime Minister Tony Blair said had assisted the terrorist hijackers.

During the same period Wolfgang Bohringer was hanging out with Mohamed Atta, we learned, he had been the personal pilot for a major Eastern European Mafia figure named Victor Kozeny, known both as the "Pirate of Prague."

Kozeny, we were shocked to discover, had at some point in the mid-90s controlled one-third of the entire Czechoslovakian economy. "Kozeny bought factories and 'rides' on pipelines, meaning they crossed land he owned and paid big for the privilege."

With his ill-gotten gains, Kozeny tried to buy off top officials in the former Soviet Republic of Azerbaijan to gain control of that country's state-owned oil company. One man already convicted in the scheme, Hans Bodmer, belonged to a network of Russian oligarchs, one of whom, Pyotr Aven, has been accused by a Russian corruption task force of being engaged in drug trafficking.

Kozeny's partners in the Azeri scheme included a managing director of Hank Greenberg's American Insurance Group (AIG). Greenberg was forced to step down amid the Eliot Spitzer probe, a scandal, it is rumored, which involved a major Bush family and associates' international money-laundering operation that has spanned more than a generation and has been used to illegally fund US elections since the Nixon era.

AIG was founded from Asia Life/CV Starr, a Shanghai-based international import/export and insurance firm founded in 1919 by Cornelius V. Starr, an Office of Strategic Services (OSS) operative in Southeast Asia during World War II. Clinton antagonist Kenneth Starr is his nephew.

Today Kozeny owns a private island in the Bahamas, travels on an Irish passport, and is fighting extradition to the U.S. on charges of massive financial fraud and allegedly paying multi-million dollar bribes to government officials in the Republic of Azerbaijan in an effort to take-over the State Oil Company of Azerbaijan.

He stands accused on two continents of defrauding thousands of people around the world, including, interestingly enough, the chairman of the Northern Ireland peace talks, Senator George Mitchell, Kozeny sought refuge in the Bahamas.

Wolfgang Bohringer moved to Atlanta to began a position as corporate pilot in February 1, 2001, according to his online bio, for a software company called HBOC. No doubt it is just a coincidence, or dashed bad luck, but Bohringer's new employer was involved in a major accounting scandal which cost shareholders $9 billion of lost value in a single day.

"HBOC was found to be a mob bust-out," a financial analyst emailed us.

At least four of Viktor Kozeny's partners, we discovered, are in some way connected with American intelligence, like John Sununu, the former chief of staff for the first President George Bush, who took a position in a private Cyprus-based company used to funnel as much as a half-billion dollars from investors in Czechoslovakia into the hands of Kozeny and his cronies.

Kozeny's other cronies with intelligence connections include former Senate Majority Leader George Mitchell, who used Kozeny's private Lear jet during his shuttle diplomacy to bring an end to the conflict in Northern Ireland; Michael Dingman, former chief of major defense contractor Allied Signal; and Hank Greenberg, of AIG, one of whose top executives was also indicted for helping facilitate the massive theft.

Greenberg—in a move that would make a bad situation incalculably worse—is said to be currently contemplating a takeover bid for the *New York Times*.

So Mohamed Atta's German buddy Wolfgang Bohringer clearly had worked for a global network. Did it assist Atta and the terrorist hijackers? Was there a connection between the larger organization, or network, behind gangster financier Victor Kozeny, and that of the terrorists in Florida plotting to kill Americans on the 11th of September in 2001?

In the wake of the September 11 disaster, U.S. officials repeatedly promised explanations. But it was left to British Prime Minister Tony Blair to sketch out the CliffNotes version of the case against Osama bin Laden. He said, "Al Qaeda is a terrorist organization with ties to a global network."

Almost five years after Tony Blair first told the world that a "global network" provided assistance to the terrorist hijackers while they were in the U.S., what is happening on a tiny island in the South Pacific may point towards the international organization in question.

"You have a network of people who obtain certain information and… sell it to whomever would be the highest bidder," explained Sibel Edmonds, former FBI translator, who was muzzled by U.S. Attorney General John Ashcroft, who went to the Supreme Court to ensure her silence about… something.

"There are certain points where you have your drug-related activities combined with money laundering and information laundering, converging with your terrorist activities… Post-9/11 intelligence 'failures' include the willful quashing by the Government of investigations tracing these criminal networks."

So here's the real scoop: A close associate of Mohamed Atta's in Florida was flying, at the same time he was "hangin" with Mohamed," for a Russian Mob-connected "oligarch" reported to control (after the demise of Communism) fully one-third of the entire economy of the nation of Czechoslovakia.

In some places, this might be called "news."

APPENDIX

At this guard shack at the Colony Beach Resort on Longboat Key in Sarasota, where President George W. Bush was staying the night before the 9/11 attack, four Arab men in a white van attempted to gain entrance using a ruse identical to that used just two days earlier to assassinate the Taliban's chief foe, Shah Massoud.

A long history in the Venice Gulf Coast area: Corporate fundraising vehicle used by George W. Bush in his Texas Governor's campaign, inexplicably incorporated in Sarasota, FL.

Glen Sapp ✦

From: Bob Hart [bob@avionix.com]
Sent: Friday, September 14, 2001 10:35 AM
To: sapp@ccso.org
Subject: FW: Shaikh Ibn al-Uthaymeen

Forwarded per Jim Kantor/Eastern Avionics/Punta Gorda/FL
-----Original Message-----
From: YasMine Muslima [mailto:yasmuslima@hotmail.com]
Sent: Thursday, January 11, 2001 12:00 PM
To: ahmed_alalfi@hotmail.com; aaislam@hotmail.com; daliahashad@hotmail.com; gidamy@hotmail.com; meid74@hotmail.com; nora_abd_el_hamid@hotmail.com; odkiko@hotmail.com; weamthabet@hotmail.com; niletrac@starnet.com.eg; darwish@vt.edu; dodiiii@yahoo.com; athabet@kemetint.com; amconegy@egyptonline.com; aoazizi@positron.qc.ca; bindlmk@emirates.net.ae; bfrank@dataradio.com; cltr@celsiustech.se; garaya@intouch.com; gtadros@igs.net; ghakl@iprimus.ca; hala@dns.ncs.com.kw; sswilson@pathcom.com; lee@virtualprototypes.ca; jroireau@cima.qc.ca; joseph@virtualprototypes.ca; hassan.ki@pg.com; klahjioui@positron.qc.ca; kpo@lhmobil.dk; loumi_h@usa.net; marceld@emirates.net.ae; elrefaie@yahoo.com; zoneta@starnet.com.eg; mstawfik@intouch.com; minabil@alexnet.com.eg; figla2000@yahoo.com; rob@avionix.com; rudi_r@usa.net; SKabbas@dataradio.com; TMorin@dataradio.com; aboualy@eg.ibm.com; wahby@qs.ie-eg.com; wnassar@menanet.net; zekry@positron.qc.ca
Subject: Fwd: Shaikh Ibn al-Uthaymeen

>Assalaamu alaikum
>
>We are saddened to learn and inform the ummah of the death of one of its
>greatest scholars just moments ago after salat al-Magrib (Saudi Arabia
>Time), he is Imaam Muhammad bin Saleh al-Uthaymeen may the peak of heaven
>be his resort.
>They will perform prayer on him Thursday 1/11/01 after Asr in Makkah, in
>shaa' Allaah.
>
>Inna lillahi wa inna ilaihi raaji'oon, allahumma ujurni fee museebati wa
>akhlif li khairan minha
>
>(To Allah we belong and to Him we will return, Oh Allah take me out of my
>plight and bring after it something better)
>
>
>_____
>To unsubscribe, write to A5-unsubscribe@listbot.com
>

Get Your Private, Free E-mail from MSN Hotmail at http://www.hotmail.com.

Mohamed Atta's e-mails: Local law enforcement in the Venice area came up with evidence contradicting the FBI's "official story," like these emails from Atta, written while he lived in the area months after the FBI says he left.

Al-Sunnah - http://www.al-sunnah.com

As Salamu Alaikum Wa Rahmatu Allah ☻

Eid: Etiquette and rulings ☙

Praise be to Allaah, Lord of the Worlds, and peace and blessings be upon

>our Prophet Muhammad and upon all his family and companions.

"Eid" is an Arabic word referring to something habitual, that returns and is repeated. Eids or festivals are symbols to be found in every nation, including those that are based on revealed scriptures and those that are idolatrous, as well as others, because celebrating festivals is something that is an instinctive part of human nature. All people like to have special occasions to celebrate, where they can come together and express their joy and happiness.

Glen Sapp

From:	Bob Hart [bob@avionix.com]
Sent:	Friday, September 14, 2001 10:34 AM
To:	sapp@ccso.org
Subject:	FW: >> ÍÇä æÞÊ ÇáäÞÇÞÇøÚØÚ

Forwarded per Jim Kantor/Eastern Avionics/Punta Gorda/FL
-----Original Message-----
From: YasMine Muslima [mailto:yasmuslima@hotmail.com]
Sent: Thursday, January 04, 2001 4:20 AM
To: ahmed_alalfi@hotmail.com; aaislam@hotmail.com; daliahashad@hotmail.com; gidamy@hotmail.com; meid74@hotmail.com; nora_abd_el_hamid@hotmail.com; odkiko@hotmail.com; weamthabet@hotmail.com; niletrac@starnet.com.eg; darwish@vt.edu; dodiiii@yahoo.com; athabet@kemetint.com; amconegy@egyptonline.com; aoazizi@positron.qc.ca; bindlmk@emirates.net.ae; bfrank@dataradio.com; cltr@celsiustech.se; garaya@intouch.com; gtadros@igs.net; ghakl@iprimus.ca; hala@dns.ncs.com.kw; sswilson@pathcom.com; lee@virtualprototypes.ca; jroireau@cima.qc.ca; joseph@virtualprototypes.ca; hassan.ki@pg.com; klahjioui@positron.qc.ca; kpo@lhmobil.dk; loumi_h@usa.net; marceld@emirates.net.ae; elrefaie@yahoo.com; zoneta@starnet.com.eg; mstawfik@intouch.com; minabil@alexnet.com.eg; figla2000@yahoo.com; rob@avionix.com; rudi_r@usa.net; SKabbas@dataradio.com; TMorin@dataradio.com; aboualy@eg.ibm.com; wahby@qs.ie-eg.com; wnassar@menanet.net; zekry@positron.qc.ca; arasheed62@hotmail.comparadisehasaprice@hotmail.comwsberrie@emirates.net.ae
Subject: Fwd: >> ÍÇä æÞÊ ÇáäÞÇÞÇøÚØÚ

Es-salamu Alykum we RahmatulLahi we Barakatoh,☻

This a forwarded email to something I felt was important!✎

Please do tell me if you don't want to recieve any of these e-mails!

and do accept my apology if I bothered you☙*!*

Your sis, Yasmine☻

Friends in strange places: Several of the names on Atta's email list appear to have been employees of U.S. Defense contractors.

Condemning the violation of Muslim Women rights

Anti-Islamic Pracitces @ AUC

Niqab is an Islamic Dress

Stop Attacking our Beliefs

- condemn the violation of the rights of Muslim girls to choose their dress code.

- I demand the decision-makers in the American University in Cairo (AUC) to withdraw their threats of dismissing the Muslim female student who chose to wear the Niqab. I demand them to stop exerting pressures on the Muslim girl to take off the Niqab or to be expelled from the University.

- I demand them to adhere to their claimed "Non- Discrimination Policy" printed on every American University catalogue: " Students of any race, color, religion, sex or ethnic origin have all the'rights and privileges generally accorded to student at the university. Students are not subject to discrimination on the basis of race, color, religion, sex, or ethnic origin in the administration of the university's academic policies, admission policies, scholarship and loan programs, and athletic and other school-administered programs. "

- I remind the decision-makers at the AUC, that the American University in Cairo tolerated Zionists, Homosexuals, micro skirts books insulting Islam as well as Prophet Muhammad (peace and prayers be upon him and the rest of the Prophets), all of which are not tolerated by the Egyptian society. I demand and hope that the decision-makers at the AUC administration tdlerate the dress code of a Muslim female student as well.

Read, Act & Promote :

The American University in Cairo (AUC) has expelled a Muslim emale student because she wore the niqab (a full veil that covers that fac -) .

We ask all brothers and sisters to support the sisters' right to wear her Islamic dress and attend her school so please participate in this mission which aim to show the violation of human rights and freedom made by AUC to o~r sister in Islam.

What is our Role ?

All we have to do is to protest against AUC ,undergoes the American law, which prohibits, the abuse of human rights and freedom.

Brother/Sister just spend 1 or 2 minutes to object on this human rights violations and may Allah reward you for your time !

Please send your objections to the AUC authorities :

facultyv@aucegypt.edu jgerhart@aucegypt.edu

N RTH PORT POLICE DEPARTM T
COM LAINT/FIELD INTERVIEW RE ORT   Juvenile ☐   Confidential ☐

| Offense | Threat / Harrassment. | Agency Report Number | 0 1 0 2 1 7 7 8 |
| Location | 8323 Agress Ave. | | 0 2 2 5 0 1 2 2 5 2 G 07 |

COMPLAINANT — Anonymous ☐ Self-Initiated ☐ No Contact ☐ Name (Last, First, Middle or Business): **Keller Amandra M** — Race W — Sex F — Date of Birth or Age 9-29-81

Address (Street, Apt. Number): **8323 Agress Ave** — City **North Port** — State **FL** — Zip **34287** — Phone **941/626-3005**

SUBJECT — Name (Last, First, Middle): **Owens Robert**   Residence Phone **NO PHONE**

Last Known Address (Street, Apt. Number): **414 Brannda Blv. Apt. B** — City **Warm Mineral Springs FL** — Zip **34257**

Race **W** — Sex **M** — Date of Birth or Age **09 17 78**

Details:

Complainant advised that the above Subject keeps
Calling her on the Cell Phone and Calling her Names.
I advised the Complainant that she needed to call her Cell
Phone Company to see if they can get a print out of all
in Coming Calls.
I explained to Keller that we needed a print out of all the
Calls before we could Charge anyone.
A Wanks/warrants Check Revealed a warrant for the
Complainant for worthless Checks.
Keller was Arrested and transported to the Venice Jail.

[stamp: NPPD Entered FEB 26 2001 J. AYRES]

Officer **N. Coward** I.D.# **064** Signature
Supervisor's I.D.# **094** Signature

Page 1 of 1

After a wild three-day weekend in Key West with Mohamed Atta, Amanda Keller returned to an enraged now-former boyfriend. After she was briefly jailed in the aftermath of the melee which followed, Atta wrote a check to bail her out.

Then and now: Amanda Keller's mug shot from her brief incarceration. Today, the mother of three small children, her wild younger days appear behind her.

"Party hearty." Amanda and Garret (top three photos) the young man for whom she "left" Atta.

The "Magic Dutch Boys." Rudi Dekkers(top) and Arne Kruithof, the two Dutch nationals whose flight schools trained three of the four terrorist pilots to fly.

Dekkers arrested

Attorney: ' Charge is totally unfounded'

By Tommy McIntyre
Staff Writer

Former Huffman Aviation owner Rudi Dekkers has been arrested on a warrant charging him with fraud involving a security interest.

Collier County Sheriff's Office deputies made the arrest last show that the charge is totally unfounded," McGill said. "Even the victim has signed a waiver of prosecution because he understands it is a civil matter."

McGill said he has talked to assistant state attorney Jonathan Greene and

Dekkers

International con man Rudi Dekkers was charged with criminal fraud in a case observers speculated might be a "holding' charge to keep him in the country.

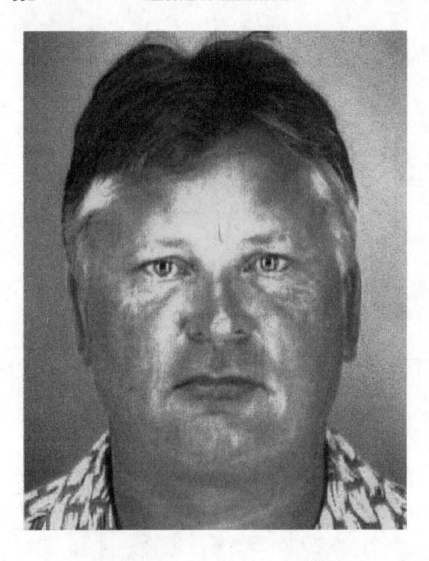

Facing the music: Rudi Dekkers' mug shot. Local reporters bemoaned the fact that there hadn't been a "perp walk."

RECORDED IN OFFICIAL RECORDS
INSTRUMENT # 2001173813 2 PGS
2001 DEC 03 09:19 AM
KAREN E. RUSHING
CLERK OF CIRCUIT COURT
SARASOTA COUNTY, FLORIDA
LKROHN Receipt#110700

IN THE CIRCUIT COURT IN AND FOR ESCAMBIA COUNTY, FLORIDA
CIRCUIT COURT AND
COUNTY COURT
ESCAMBIA COUNTY, FL

FH1100 MANUFACTURING CORP.,
a Florida corporation,

    Plaintiff,

2001 NOV 16 P 3:50

vs.

FILED AND RECORDED
CASE NUMBER: 2001 CA 1932
DIVISION: "A"

DEKKERS AVIATION GROUP, INC.,
a Florida corporation, HUFFMAN
AVIATION, INC., a Florida corporation,
and RUDI DEKKERS, an individual,

    Defendants.

_____/

FINAL JUDGMENT

THIS ACTION was heard after entry of Default against the Defendants and

IT IS ADJUDGED that Plaintiff, FH1100 MANUFACTURING CORP., a Florida

corporation (Florida Department of State Document Number P99000103427, Federal Employer

Identification Number 59-3367403, address: 6080 Industrial Boulevard, Century, Florida 32535),

recover from Defendants, DEKKERS AVIATION GROUP, INC., a Florida corporation (Florida

Department of State Document Number P00000028289, Federal Employer Identification unknown,

address: 240 Aviation Drive North, Naples, Florida 34104), HUFFMAN AVIATION, INC., a

Florida corporation (Florida Department of State Document Number J80391, Federal Employer

Identification Number 59-2822407, address: 400 East Airport Avenue, Venice, Florida 34285), and

RUDI DEKKERS, an individual (Social Security Number unknown, address: 178 Topanga Drive,

Bonita Springs, Florida 34134), the sum of $48,473.31 on principal, $ 4,958.00 for

attorney's fees with cost in the sum of $ 130,50 making a subtotal of

$ 53,561.81 that shall bear interest at the rate of 11% a year and in addition the

Plaintiff shall recover prejudgment interest of $ 2,921.68, for which let execution issue.

Unable to pay the rent on time at his flight school in Venice for six months in a row before the 9/11 attack, Dekkers was somehow flush enough afterward to pay this $50,000 judgment one month after the attack. Observers wonder where he got the money.

Parcel ID Number 0430-16-1015

Warranty Deed

This Indenture, Made this 12th day of August , 2002 AD , Between
RUDI H.G. DEKKERS, a married man

of the County of Collier , State of Florida , grantor, and
D.H.J.M. YPKEMEULE and M.T. YPKEMEULE WERNINK, husband and wife

whose address is Larixlaan 8, 6711 NL EDE, Netherlands

of the City of 6711 NL EDE , Country of Netherlands , grantees.

Witnesseth that the GRANTOR, for and in consideration of the sum of
-------------------------TEN DOLLARS ($10)---------------------- DOLLARS,
and other good and valuable consideration to GRANTOR in hand paid by GRANTEES, the receipt whereof is hereby acknowledged, has granted, bargained and sold to the said GRANTEES and GRANTEES' heirs, successors and assigns forever, the following described land, situate, lying and being in the County of Sarasota State of Florida to wit

Unit 124, Building 1, THE SENTINEL, a Condominium according to the
Declaration of Condominium recorded in Official Records Book 999,
Page 674, and all amendments thereto, and as per plat thereof
recorded in Condominium Book 6, Page 36, and amendments thereto, of
the Public Records of Sarasota County, Florida, together with an
undivided interest in the common elements appurtenant thereto.

Subject to all valid restrictions, reservations, and easements of
record, if any, zoning, applicable governmental regulations, and
taxes and assessments for the year 2002, and subsequent years.

Grantor warrants and covenants that the above-described property does
not constitute the homestead of the Grantor, nor is it contiguous
thereto.

This transfer approved by The Sentinel Condominium Association,Inc.,
and document attached hereto.

and the grantor does hereby fully warrant the title to said land, and will defend the same against lawful claims of all persons whomsoever
In Witness Whereof, the grantor has hereunto set his hand and seal the day and year first above written.
Signed, sealed and delivered in our presence:

_____ _____(Seal)
Printed Name: BOB D. MARTIN   RUDI H.G. DEKKERS
Witness   PO Address 178 Topanga Drive, Bonita Springs, FL 34134

_____
Printed Name: Donna L. Russano
Witness

STATE OF Florida
COUNTY OF Sarasota
The foregoing instrument was acknowledged before me this 12th day of August , 2002 by
RUDI H.G. DEKKERS, a married man

he is personally known to me or he has produced his Florida driver's license as identification

_____
Printed Name: Donna L. Russano
Notary Public
My Commission Expires

02-0317   Laser Generated by © Display Systems Inc 2000 (863) 763-5555 Form FLWD 1

Transferring assets out of the country, Dekkers made a bid to avoid his U.S. creditors.

CRAIG & MURRAY, LLP
ATTORNEYS AT LAW
1250 TAMIAMI TRAIL NORTH
SUITE 201
NAPLES, FLORIDA 34102
TELEPHONE (941) 434-5454

TELEFAX (941) 484-8425

ROGER R. CRAIG*
PAUL A. MURRAY, P.A.*

*ADMITTED IN MICHIGAN & FLORIDA

January 26, 1998

Via Facsimile: 643-4084

Theodore Soliday, Director
Naples Airport Authority
160 Aviation Drive
Naples, FL 34104

RE: Refusal to sell fuel to Aero Jet Service Center, Inc.

Dear Mr. Soliday:

This office represents the interests of Aero Jet Service Center, Inc. (hereinafter "Aero-Jet"), as it concerns the Naples Airport Authority' refusal to sell aviation fuel to Aero-Jet. My client has informed me that he has tried, unsuccessfully to purchase aviation fuel from the Naples Airport Authority on several occasions, for cash. Mr Rudi Dekkers, President of Aero-Jet has been refused the sale of fuel personally, and in addition, Naples Airport Authority has refused to fuel Aero-Jet planes which had previously been leased to separate entities. This could be viewed by a court of law as a pattern of willful discrimination.

DEMAND IS HEREBY MADE for the immediate cessation of your imprudent refusal to sell Aero-Jet, aviation fuel. This action has already had severe ramifications on my client's ability to operate his business. In fact, he is on the brink of financial ruin and your actions are in great measure, if not totally responsible. I have instructed my client to attempt to purchase fuel, on a cash basis, tomorrow, January 27, 1998. If you again discriminate and refuse any such sale, legal action may instituted immediately seeking an injunction and monetary damages.

PLEASE GOVERN YOURSELF ACCORDINGLY.

Very truly yours,
Paul A. Murray, P.A.

Paul A. Murray

PAM:sh
cc: original via US Mail
Rudi Dekkers

"No gas…not even for cash" Dekkers' reputation as a deadbeat was so bad they wouldn't even sell him gas for cash.

CITY OF NAPLES AIRPORT AUTHORITY

160 AVIATION DRIVE NORTH   NAPLES, FLORIDA 34104

31 January 1997

Mr. Rudi H. G. Dekkers, President
Aerojet Service Center, Inc.
200 Aviation Drive North, Suite 6
Naples, FL 34104

Dear Mr. Dekkers:

Today, between 2:45 and 2:50 p.m., I observed your helicopter operation on the ramp. It appears to me that you left your helicopter unattended while you went into your office. I know there was a gentlemen sitting in the helicopter. His hands were completely free of the cyclic control for that helicopter in a significantly gusty wind condition. I would like to know if that man is a helicopter pilot. If so, I will re-think the situation. If he wasn't, I'd like you to explain that operation to me and tell me why I should not submit what I observed to the FAA for their consideration and handling.

Further, as you departed that day, you did not follow the procedures, in accordance with the helicopter arrival and departure routes, as published in the attached document. We are sincere about our desire to be responsive to our neighbors and reduce the amount of noise impact of our airport on our community. It is important that our tenants be aware of the airport's rules and regulations and make every effort to comply.

Rudy, you're asking for us to work with you and to help you expand your operations on this airport. I must tell you that it is very difficult if we can not get you to play by the rules. I'd appreciate your response prior to February 7th, or I will submit this letter and my testimony to the Federal Aviation Administration.

Sincerely,

Theodore D. Soliday

Theodore D. Soliday
Executive Director

Protected by the FAA. Numerous serious violations, which would have grounded anyone else, were ignored by the FAA. The question is *why…*

BERKEL
ADVOCATEN

IN THE CIRCUIT COURT OF THE TWENTIETH JUDICIAL CIRCUIT IN AND FOR
<u>COLLIER COUNTY, FLORIDA</u>   CIVIL ACTION

W. J. BEKS, in his capacity as Trustee
in the bankruptcy of Dekkers Onroerende
Goederen Ede B.V., LLC,

       Plaintiff,

vs.   CASE NO. 02-454-CA

RUDI HENDRIKUS GERRIT DEKKERS

       Defendant.
_____/

OR: 2974 PG: 2944

<u>AFFIDAVIT OF LAST KNOWN ADDRESS OF</u>
<u>JUDGMENT DEBTOR AND JUDGMENT CREDITOR</u>

COUNTRY OF THE NETHERLANDS)

CITY/PROVINCE OF VEENENDAAL)

    BEFORE ME, the undersigned officer, duly authorized to administer oaths and

take acknowledgments, personally appeared Affiant, **<u>Mr. W.J. Beks</u>**, who, being first

duly sworn, deposes and says:

    1.   That he is the Trustee in Bankruptcy of Dekkers Onroerende Goederen

Ede B.V., a private limited liability company.

    2.   That on December 2, 1993, a judgment was executed in District Court No.

533, Arnhem, The Netherlands, Case No. 92/201, in favor of Mr. W.J. Beks in his

capacity as Trustee in Bankruptcy against Defendants, R. DEKKERS HOLDING B.V.

and RUDI HENDRIKUS GERRIT DEKKERS, in which judgment Mr. Dekkers was

ordered to pay to the Trustee the sum of NLG 100 (one hundred Dutch guilders),

increased by statutory interest on that amount as from January 24, 1991, to the date of

payment in full and also to pay to the Trustee the bankruptcy deficit of Dekkers

A wanted man. As a result of criminal activates in his native Holland, including skipping out on hundreds of thousands of dollars worth of judgments, Dekkers is unable to return there.

FILE NOW: FILING FEE AFTER MAY 1 IS $225.00

PROFIT CORPORATION ANNUAL REPORT 1996

FLORIDA DEPARTMENT OF STATE
Sandra B Mortham
Secretary of State
DIVISION OF CORPORATIONS

FILED
Apr 23 1996 8:00 am
Secretary of State

DOCUMENT # P93000086498 (1)

1. Corporation Name
INTERNATIONAL COMPUTER PRODUCTS U.S.A., INC.

Principal Place of Business
710 HARBOUR DR
STE 2B
NAPLES FL 33940
US

Mailing Address
710 ARBOUR DR
STE 2B
NAPLES FL 33940
US

3. Date Incorporated or Qualified 12/13/1983
3a. Date of Last Report 06/28/1995

4. FEI Number 65-0452879 — Applied For / Not Applicable

5. Certificate of Status Desired ☐ $8.75 Additional Fee Required

6. Election Campaign Financing Trust Fund Contribution ☐ $5.00 May Be Added to Fees

8. This corporation has liability for intangible tax under s 199.032. Florida Statutes. ☒ Yes ☐ No

2. Principal Place of Business
21 | 225 Airport Rd S
22 | Suite, Apt. #, etc. —
23 | City & State NAPLES, FL
24 | Zip 33942 | 25 Country USA

2a. Mailing Address
26 | 225 Airport Rd S
27 | Suite, Apt. #, etc.
28 | City & State NAPLES, FL
29 | Zip 33942 | 30 Country USA

9. Name and Address of Current Registered Agent
DEKKERS, RUDI D
180 TOPANGA DR
BONITA SPRINGS FL 33923

10. Name and Address of New Registered Agent
B1 Name
B2 Street Address (P.O. Box Number is Not Acceptable)
B3
B4 City ___ FL B5 Zip Code

11. Pursuant to the provisions of Sections 607.0502 and 607.1508, Florida Statutes, the above-named corporation submits this statement for the purpose of changing its registered office or registered agent, or both, in the State of Florida. Such change was authorized by the corporation's board of directors. I hereby accept the appointment as registered agent. I am familiar with, and accept the obligations of, Section 607.0505, Florida Statutes.

SIGNATURE:
Signature typed or printed name of registered agent and title if applicable. (NOTE: Registered Agent signature required when reinstating) DATE

12. OFFICERS AND DIRECTORS		13. ADDITIONS/CHANGES TO OFFICERS AND DIRECTORS IN 12	
TITLE D	☐ DELETE	1.1 TITLE	☐ Change ☐ Addition
NAME DEKKERS, RUDI H		1.2 NAME	
STREET ADDRESS 180 TOPANGA DR		1.3 STREET ADDRESS	
CITY-ST-ZIP BONITA SPRINGS FL		1.4 CITY-ST-ZIP	
TITLE	☐ DELETE	2.1 TITLE	☐ Change ☐ Addition
NAME		2.2 NAME	
STREET ADDRESS		2.3 STREET ADDRESS	
CITY-ST-ZIP		2.4 CITY-ST-ZIP	
TITLE	☐ DELETE	3.1 TITLE	☐ Change ☐ Addition
NAME		3.2 NAME	
STREET ADDRESS		3.3 STREET ADDRESS	
CITY-ST-ZIP		3.4 CITY-ST-ZIP	
TITLE	☐ DELETE	4.1 TITLE	☐ Change ☐ Addition
NAME		4.2 NAME	
STREET ADDRESS		4.3 STREET ADDRESS	
CITY-ST-ZIP		4.4 CITY-ST-ZIP	
TITLE	☐ DELETE	5.1 TITLE	☐ Change ☐ Addition
NAME		5.2 NAME	
STREET ADDRESS		5.3 STREET ADDRESS	
CITY-ST-ZIP		5.4 CITY-ST-ZIP	
TITLE	☐ DELETE	6.1 TITLE	☐ Change ☐ Addition
NAME		6.2 NAME	
STREET ADDRESS		6.3 STREET ADDRESS	
CITY-ST-ZIP		6.4 CITY-ST-ZIP	

14. I do hereby certify that the information supplied with this filing is voluntarily furnished and does not qualify for the exemption stated in Section 119.07(3)(k), Florida Statutes. I further certify that the information indicated on this annual report or supplemental annual report is true and accurate and that my signature shall have the same legal effect as if made under oath; that I am an officer or director of the corporation or the receiver or trustee empowered to execute this report as required by Chapter 607, Florida Statutes; and that my name appears in Block 12 or Block 13 if changed, or on an attachment with an address.

SIGNATURE: ___ SIGNATURE AND TYPED OR PRINTED NAME OF SIGNING OFFICER OR DIRECTOR ___ Date ___ Daytime Phone #

High tech smuggling. Using dummy "front" companies, Dekkers was caught, but never charged with, smuggling high technology components out of the U.S. by a multi-agency investigation in the mid-90s.

FILE NOW: FILING FEE AFTER MAY 1 IS $225.00

PROFIT
CORPORATION
ANNUAL REPORT
1996

FLORIDA DEPARTMENT OF STATE
Sandra B. Mortham
Secretary of State
DIVISION OF CORPORATIONS

FILED
Apr 19 1996 8:00 am
Secretary of State

DOCUMENT # **P95000067994 (0)**
1. Corporation Name
MEMORY & STORAGE INTERNATIONAL, INC.

Principal Place of Business
**240 AVIATION DRIVE
NAPLES FL 33942**

Mailing Address
**240 AVIATION DRIVE
NAPLES FL 33942**

3. Date Incorporated or Qualified
09/01/1995

3a. Date of Last Report

4. FEI Number
65-0610551

Applied For / Not Applicable

5. Certificate of Status Desired ☐ — **$8.75** Additional Fee Required

6. Election Campaign Financing Trust Fund Contribution ☐ — **$5.00** May Be Added to Fees

8. This corporation has liability for intangible tax under s 199.032, Florida Statutes. ☒ Yes ☐ No

9. Name and Address of Current Registered Agent

**DEKKERS, RUDI H
240 AVIATION DRIVE
NAPLES FL 33942**

10. Name and Address of New Registered Agent

81 Name
82 Street Address (P.O. Box Number is Not Acceptable)
83
84 City   FL   85 Zip Code

11. *(legal text regarding registered agent acceptance)*

SIGNATURE

12.	OFFICERS AND DIRECTORS		13.	ADDITIONS/CHANGES TO OFFICERS AND DIRECTORS IN 12	
TITLE	D	☐ DELETE	1. TITLE	☐ Change	☐ Addition
NAME	DEKKERS, RUDI H		1.2 NAME		
STREET ADDRESS	240 AVIATION DR.		1.3 STREET ADDRESS		
CITY, ST, ZIP	NAPLES FL 33942		1.4 CITY, ST, ZIP		
TITLE	D	☐ DELETE	2. TITLE	☐ Change	☐ Addition
NAME	BODDI, CHRISTIAN H		2.2 NAME		
STREET ADDRESS	240 AVIATION DR.		2.3 STREET ADDRESS		
CITY, ST, ZIP	NAPLES FL 33942		2.4 CITY, ST, ZIP		
TITLE	D	☐ DELETE	3. TITLE	☐ Change	☐ Addition
NAME	CLARK, JOHN		3.2 NAME		
STREET ADDRESS	240 AVIATION DR.		3.3 STREET ADDRESS		
CITY, ST, ZIP	NAPLES FL 33942		3.4 CITY, ST, ZIP		
TITLE		☐ DELETE	4. TITLE	☐ Change	☐ Addition
NAME			4.2 NAME		
STREET ADDRESS			4.3 STREET ADDRESS		
CITY, ST, ZIP			4.4 CITY, ST, ZIP		
TITLE		☐ DELETE	5. TITLE	☐ Change	☐ Addition
NAME			5.2 NAME		
STREET ADDRESS			5.3 STREET ADDRESS		
CITY, ST, ZIP			5.4 CITY, ST, ZIP		
TITLE		☐ DELETE	6. TITLE	☐ Change	☐ Addition
NAME			6.2 NAME		
STREET ADDRESS			6.3 STREET ADDRESS		
CITY, ST, ZIP			6.4 CITY, ST, ZIP		

14. I do hereby certify that the information supplied with this filing is true and accurate... *(certification legal text)*

SIGNATURE: *(signature)*   CHRISTIAN BODDI   Vice president   4/15/96   941 6430707

WELCOME TO TERRORLAND

The famous visa application, used by Dekkers six months after the attack to claim vindication, was filled out by an 18-year-old girl just then being sexually harassed by her middle-aged boss.

CHARGE OF DISCRIMINATION	ENTER CHARGE NUMBER

This form is protected by the Privacy Act, 1974; see Privacy Act Statement on reverse before completing this form.

☐ FEPA
☐ EEOC

FLORIDA HUMAN RIGHTS COMMISSION and EEOC
(State or local Agency, if any)

NAME (indicate Mr., Ms., or Mrs.) **Nicole Antini**
HOME TELEPHONE NO. (include Area Code) **941 426-2298**

STREET ADDRESS **6693 Kenwood Drive** CITY, STATE AND ZIP CODE **North Port, FL 34287** COUNTY **Sarasota**

NAMED IS THE EMPLOYER, LABOR ORGANIZATION, EMPLOYMENT AGENCY, APPRENTICESHIP COMMITTEE, STATE OR LOCAL GOVERNMENT AGENCY WHO DISCRIMINATED AGAINST ME *(If more than one, list below.)*

NAME **Huffman Aviation** NO. OF EMPLOYEES/MEMBERS **over 30** TELEPHONE NUMBER (include Area Code) **485-6474 or 484-64**

STREET ADDRESS **400 E. Airport Ave., Venice Florida** CITY, STATE AND ZIP CODE **34285**

NAME

STREET ADDRESS CITY, STATE AND ZIP CODE

TELEPHONE NUMBER (include Area Code)

CAUSE OF DISCRIMINATION BASED ON (Check appropriate box(es))
☐ RACE ☐ COLOR ☒ SEX ☐ RELIGION ☐ NATIONAL ORIGIN
☐ AGE ☐ RETALIATION ☐ OTHER (specify)

DATE MOST RECENT OR CONTINUING DISCRIMINATION TOOK PLACE (Month, day, year) **12/12/00 (est.)**

THE PARTICULARS ARE (If additional space is needed, attach extra sheet(s))

Personal Harm: I was forced to quit my job because of sexual harassment.

Reason for Adverse Action: I complained and told him to leave me alone but the harassment continued.

Discrimination Statement:

I believe I have been discriminated against on the basis of __my sex, female__, in violation of Title VII, 42 USC §2000e et seq, and the FCRA.

☒ I want this charge filed with both the EEOC and the State or local agency, if any. I will advise the agencies if I change my address or telephone number and I will cooperate fully with them in the processing of my charge in accordance with their procedures.

NOTARY

I swear or affirm that I have read the above charge and that it is true to the best of my knowledge, information and belief.

I declare under penalty of perjury that the foregoing is true and correct.

SIGNATURE OF COMPLAINANT

Date **1/18/01** Charging Party (Signature)

SUBSCRIBED AND SWORN TO BEFORE ME THIS DATE (Day, month, and year) **1/18/01**

Amy Lynn Sargent
MY COMMISSION # CC763549 EXPIRES
July 6, 2004

EEOC FORM 5 PREVIOUS EDITIONS OF THIS FORM ARE OBSOLETE AND MUST NOT BE USED CHARGING PARTY COPY

"Can I buy you?" When Dekkers reneged on the settlement terms of the sexual harassment suit with his 18-year-old former employee, details of the previously-sealed suit became public record.

Coffee Room 8.15 April 7-00

Everybody has to vote because I can't.
So I have to push everybody to vote
because I can't.

He came at me like he was going to hug
me against the counter. He says why do
you have to look so good. I said what
are you doing? I want something. Well, I
don't want to know about that. I
push on his chest, he says; I want
some sweetener. Turn around you
have something on your skirt. Can I
bite into you. No that's sick. I know.
I just can't help it. Look at you. Your
                                    you're a hot girl.
face, hair, your ass. you're good, I'm
leaving. Oh, did you get the E-mail from
Paul Cowen? Not yet. Oh oh OK. he's sending
more students.

My office: 8:55 11-7-00

You know you can see through that blouse rubs finger on my arm. That's why there's a shirt on underneath. (Blue & white flower mesh shirt w/ light blue shirt under it). Well you shouldn't have that shirt on under it. Oh, yes I should. Can I buy you. Buy me what? You know. Can I just buy you? ~~So~~ No, what the hell are you talking about? It should be like the olden days when I could buy you. No, I don't think so! I'm going to undress! No, ~~scribbled out~~ you're not. OK, I'm just tucking my shirt in my pants. Wouldn't that be funny if someone walked in now as I'm putting my shirt away. They'd think I was fucking you. That's grosse! XO.

My Office 4:15 PM 11-7-00
Would you sleep with me?
What? Sleep! I'm tired, you tired?
Iff your tired go to bed.

Did you see that girl Russian girl
I had in here. Yea, did you hire her

No she's Russian citizen I can't, but I
told her I had, a job for her. What,
the pilot shop?
No, I told her she could give me
a blow job. You did not say that?
No, I couldn't say that it'd
probably scare the hell out of me

No, she wouldn't do that but you
probably will someday. Ha. I just
sit straight faced. You better
not because if you did you'd be very
very sorry!

Nikku do you have all your ducks
sitting in a row? As he's going
through everything in my office
Drawers.

"Retired insurance executive' Wally Hilliard, who purchased a fleet of 30-40 planes after retiring to Florida, including several Lear jets like this one.

STATE OF FLORIDA:

COUNTY OF ORANGE: CASE NO. 00-3098

AFFIDAVIT

1.   I am a Special Agent (SA) with the United States Drug Enforcement Administration (DEA). I have been so employed since February 1997. Prior to my appointment as a SA I was a Task Force Agent (TFA) with DEA from October 1990 to 1997. I was a Deputy Sheriff with the Seminole County Sheriff's Office from 1982 to 1997. My duties include investigation of violations of federal criminal drug laws and the collection of evidence related to such investigations.

2.   The information and evidence in this affidavit was gathered through my personal investigation and observations and the observations of other law enforcement agents.

3   Between July 16, and July 25, 2000, a cooperating source (CS) had a series of telephone conversations at my direction. As a result of those conversations, the CS told me that an aircraft would be able to meet him at the Orlando Executive Airport (OEA) with approximately five kilograms of heroin. The CS was to pay $40,000 from a prior heroin debt during the delivery of the 5 kilograms of heroin.

4.   On July 25, 2000, I accompanied the CS to the OEA. At approximately 7:10 p.m., an aircraft approached OEA. The aircraft landed and proceeded to the Executive Air Center (EAC). The CS identified EDGAR JAVIER VALLES and NEYRA RIVAS as they were leaving the aircraft as individuals who had delivered heroin to him in similar fashion on three separate prior occasions. Both individuals had luggage in their possession. They

DEA affidavit on the biggest seizure of heroin in central Florida history, found on Hilliard's Lear jet.

were detained as they approached the building at the EAC.

5.   The luggage in possession of these individuals was searched at my direction. In the luggage were located certain items of foot apparel which were similar to those previously associated with the CS and which each contained approximately one quarter to one half kilogram of heroin. I directed that one of the items be opened. Inside the item was a quantity of a white substance which appeared to be heroin and which field tested positive for heroin. The luggage which was taken off the aircraft contained approximately five kilograms of heroin.

6.   The aircraft in which these individuals had traveled to Orlando is a white Lear Jet Model 35 with identification number N351WB on its tail assembly. The air crew, consisting of a pilot, copilot and flight attendant, and one other passenger were interviewed at the scene. These individuals stated that the Lear jet is a charter aircraft which had picked up the passengers in Caracas, Venezuela earlier on July 25, 2000. The jet was then flown to Ft. Lauderdale, Florida, and then to Orlando.

7.   After RIVAS and VALLES-DIAZ were taken into custody, agents and uniformed officers approached the Lear Jet. As agents approached the aircraft DIEGO LEVINE-TEXAR , the pilot of the aircraft, frantically attempted to make a telephone call using a cellular telephone. LEVINE-TEXAR ignored agents and police officers who repeatedly ordered him to drop the telephone. Agents had to physically remove the telephone from LEVINE-TEXAR's hands. Agents then secured the remaining individuals on the aircraft. Based on my experience I know that narcotics traffickers and their associates maintain frequent contact with each other while transporting narcotics and currency. I believe that LEVINE-TEXAR attempted to contact other accomplices as to the presence of agents and other law enforcement officials.

8.   DEA SA Rob Patterson interviewed LEVINE-TEXAR, who stated that he

has known VALLES-DIAZ for approximately 9 months. He has flown VALLES-DIAZ to New York and Fort Lauderdale from Venezuela approximately 30 times during that time. LEVINE-TEXAR said that he and his company were paid a total of $600,000 for those trips and that he was going to be paid $80,000 for the current trip after arriving in Orlando.

9.   DEA SA Steve Collins interviewed VALLES-DIAZ. VALLES-DIAZ told agents that he has known LEVINE-TEXAR for approximately 15 years. VALLES-DIAZ told agents that LEVINE-TEXAR has flown him to New York numerous times. VALLES-DIAZ told agents that LEVINE-TEXAR was introduced to VALLES-DIAZ' sources for heroin supply in Venezuela. According to VALLES-DIAZ, he told LEVINE-TEXAR that they were involved in the meat business.

10.   On July 25, 2000 DEA TFA Burlin Webster interviewed NEYRA RIVAS. She told TFA Webster that she had accompanied VALLES-DIAZ from Venezuela to the United States to assist in the distribution of heroin.

11.   On July 25, 2000 a search warrant was obtained for the aircraft. A search of the aircraft and its contents revealed approximately 8 additional kilograms of heroin hidden in several pairs of shoes and sandals stored in three separate suitcases.

12.   LEVINE-TEXAR told U.S. Customs SA Tony Howell that he was introduced by VALLES-DIAZ to Ramon Cacho. LEVINE-TEXAR said that Cacho was VALLES-DIAZ' business associate from Puerto Rico. LEVINE-TEXAR said that VALLES-DIAZ and Cacho hired him to fly routes from Caracas, Venezuela, to Puerto Ayacucho, Provo, Turk Caico, Ft. Lauderdale, and New Jersey and return.

2001 UNIFORM BUSINESS REPORT (UBR)

DOCUMENT # **L00000008230**

1. Entity Name
AMERICAN JET CHARTERS, LLC

FILED

Apr 16, 2001 08:00 AM
Secretary of State

Principal Place of Business	Mailing Address	
100 AVIATION DRIVE SOUTH, SUITE 202	100 AVIATION DRIVE SOUTH, SUITE 202	
NAPLES FL	NAPLES FL	
34104	34104	

2. Principal Place of Business	3. Mailing Address	
1651 NW. 51ST. PLACE HANGAR 32	1651 NW. 51ST. PLACE HANGAR 32	
Suite, Apt. #, etc.	Suite, Apt. #, etc.	
SUITE 111	SUITE 111	
City & State	City & State	
FT.LAUDERDALE FL	FT.LAUDERDALE FL	
Zip Country	Zip Country	
33309	33309	

DO NOT WRITE IN THIS SPACE

4. FEI Number	Applied For
59-3659396	Not Applicable

5. Certificate of Status Desired ☐ $5.00 Additional Fee Required

6. Name and Address of Current Registered Agent

MCARDLE   MICHAEL   W
850 PARKSHORE DRIVE

NAPLES   FL
34103   US

7. Name and Address of New Registered Agent

Name

Street Address (P.O. Box Number is Not Acceptable)

City   **FL** Zip Code

8. The above named entity submits this statement for the purpose of changing its registered office or registered agent, or both, in the State of Florida.

SIGNATURE _____ 04/16/2001

Signature, typed or printed name of registered agent and title if applicable. (NOTE: Registered Agent signature required when reinstating) DATE

FILE NOW!!! FEE IS $50.00
Make Check Payable to Department of State

9. MANAGING MEMBERS/MEMBERS

				10.	ADDITIONS/CHANGES	
TITLE	MGR		☐ Delete	TITLE	MGR	☒ Change ☐ Addition
NAME	BURCHILL G. STUART			NAME	HILLIARD WALLACE J	
STREET ADDRESS	100 AVIATION DRIVE SOUTH, SUITE 202			STREET ADDRESS	100 AVIATION DRIVE SOUTH, SUITE 202	
CITY-ST-ZIP	NAPLES	FL 34104		CITY-ST-ZIP	NAPLES FL 34104	
TITLE	MGR		☐ Delete	TITLE	MGR	☒ Change ☐ Addition
NAME	LEVINE DIEGO			NAME	LEVINE DIEGO C	
STREET ADDRESS	100 AVIATION DRIVE SOUTH, SUITE 202			STREET ADDRESS	1631 NW. 51ST. PLACE HANGAR 32 SUITE111	
CITY-ST-ZIP	NAPLES	FL 34104		CITY-ST-ZIP	FT.LAUDERDALE FL 33309	
TITLE			☐ Delete	TITLE		☐ Change ☐ Addition
NAME				NAME		
STREET ADDRESS				STREET ADDRESS		
CITY-ST-ZIP				CITY-ST-ZIP		
TITLE			☐ Delete	TITLE		☐ Change ☐ Addition
NAME				NAME		
STREET ADDRESS				STREET ADDRESS		
CITY-ST-ZIP				CITY-ST-ZIP		
TITLE			☐ Delete	TITLE		☐ Change ☐ Addition
NAME				NAME		
STREET ADDRESS				STREET ADDRESS		
CITY-ST-ZIP				CITY-ST-ZIP		
TITLE			☐ Delete	TITLE		☐ Change ☐ Addition
NAME				NAME		
STREET ADDRESS				STREET ADDRESS		
CITY-ST-ZIP				CITY-ST-ZIP		

11. I hereby certify that the information supplied with this filing does not qualify for the exemption stated in Section 119.07(3)(i), Florida Statutes. I further certify that the information indicated on this report is true and accurate and that my signature shall have the same legal effect as if made under oath; that I am a managing member or manager of the limited liability company or the receiver or trustee empowered to execute this report as required by Chapter 608, Florida Statutes.

SIGNATURE: ___DIEGO LEVINE___   MGR   04/16/2001

SIGNATURE AND TYPED OR PRINTED NAME OF SIGNING MANAGING MEMBER, MANAGER, OR AUTHORIZED REPRESENTATIVE   Date   Daytime Phone #

Hilliard's partners in American Jet Charters included the pilot, suspected by the DEA of being involved but never charged, as well as a Venezuelan currently incarcerated.

UNITED STATES OF AMERICA
DEPARTMENT OF TRANSPORTATION

AIRCRAFT BILL OF SALE

FOR AND IN CONSIDERATION OF $ 1 ∞ε THE
UNDERSIGNED OWNER(S) OF THE FULL LEGAL
AND BENEFICIAL TITLE OF THE AIRCRAFT DES-
CRIBED AS FOLLOWS:

UNITED STATES
REGISTRATION NUMBER N 351WB
AIRCRAFT MANUFACTURER & MODEL
Learjet 35A
AIRCRAFT SERIAL No.
355

DOES THIS 10ᵗʰ DAY OF Nov., 1999,
HEREBY SELL, GRANT, TRANSFER AND
DELIVER ALL RIGHTS, TITLE, AND INTERESTS
IN AND TO SUCH AIRCRAFT UNTO:

Do Not Write In This Block
FOR FAA USE ONLY

NAME AND ADDRESS
(IF INDIVIDUAL(S), GIVE LAST NAME, FIRST NAME, AND MIDDLE INITIAL.)

PLANE I LEASING CO., INC.

240 Aviation Dr. N.
Naples, FL 34104

PURCHASER

DEALER CERTIFICATE NUMBER
AND TO ITS EXECUTORS, ADMINISTRATORS, AND ASSIGNS TO HAVE AND TO HOLD
SINGULARLY THE SAID AIRCRAFT FOREVER, AND WARRANTS THE TITLE THEREOF.

IN TESTIMONY WHEREOF WE HAVE SET OUR HAND AND SEAL THIS 10ᵗʰ DAY OF Nov, 1999.

NAME(S) OF SELLER   SIGNATURE(S)   TITLE
(TYPED OR PRINTED)   (IN INK) (IF EXECUTED   (TYPED OR PRINTED)
                    FOR CO-OWNERSHIP, ALL MUST
                         SIGN.)

World Jet, Inc.   President

SELLER

Hilliard's Lear jet was supplied to him by the same source that years earlier
supplied a Lear to the man called the "biggest drug smuggler in American
history": Barry Seal.

U.S. DEPARTMENT OF JUSTICE
DRUG ENFORCEMENT ADMINISTRATION

Asset Id:	00-DEA-382152
Case Number:	GB-98-0021
Property:	LearJet 35A, Style #355
Serial Number:	#SOFSDO-17
Asset Value:	$2,700,000.00
Seizure Date:	07/25/00
Seizure Place:	Orlando, FL
Owner Name:	Plane I Leasing Co. Inc.
Seized From:	Levine Taxar, Diego Chevet
Judicial District:	Middle District of Florida

Plane I Leasing Co. Inc.
ATTN: Wallace J. Hilliard
240 Aviation Drive N.
Naples, FL 34104

NOTICE MAILING DATE: August 30, 2000

NOTICE OF SEIZURE

The above-described property was seized by Special Agents of the Drug Enforcement Administration (DEA) for forfeiture pursuant to Title 21, United States Code (U.S.C.), Section 881, because the property was used or acquired as a result of a violation of the Controlled Substances Act (Title 21, U.S.C., Sections 801 et seq.). The seizure date and place, as well as other pertinent information regarding the property are listed above.

Pursuant to Title 18, U.S.C., Section 983 and Title 19, U.S.C., Sections 1602-1619, procedures to administratively forfeit this property are underway. You may petition the DEA for return of the property or your interest in the property (remission or mitigation), and/or you may contest the seizure and forfeiture of the property in Federal court. You should review the following procedures very carefully.

INCIDENT REPORT --12/21/99   S/O G.PALLETTE

STOLEN AIRCRAFT - LEAR 443RK

   AT 2230 12/20 I RECEIVED A CELL CALL FROM FLL POLICE STATING WE MAY HAVE A STOLEN LEAR HERE AT APF. I ASKED FOR THE TAIL # AND I TOLD THEM THAT THE AIRCRAFT ARRIVED AT APPROX 2150 JUST A LITTLE BEFORE MY SHIFT WAS TO BEGIN.
   AT 0030 I RECEIVED A CALL FROM THE NPD AND THEY WERE AT THE GAT AND THEY WANTED TO SEE THE JET. THE OFFICERS EATON AND TROAC ASKED IF I KNEW WHO CAME IN ON THE AIRCRAFT AND I CALLED SHANNON BECAUSE HE KNEW THE GENTLEMAN AND HE IS A REGULAR CUSTOMER OF OURS. SHANNON GAVE ALL THE PERTINENT INFORMATION TO THE POLICE . WHEN THE AIRCRAFT ARRIVED SHANNON RECOGNIZED IT AS NEW .WHEN THE OWNER MR HATHAWAY CAME INTO THE GAT HE ADVISED THE STAFF NOT TO MOVE THE AIRCRAFT BECAUSE HE WOULD BE LEAVING AROUND 1000.
   THE NPD STAYED UNTIL 0230 /THEY TAPED THE DOOR AND THE AIRCRAFT IS NOT TO BE RELEASED FROM APF UNTIL FURTHER NOTICE FROM THE POLICE. EVIDENTLY THE AIRCRAFTS PRIOR OWNER IN IN CANADA AND THE PROPER PAPERWORK HAS NOT BEEN COMPLETED. THERE HAS ALSO BEEN A STOLEN AIRCRAFT REPORT DONE ACCORDING TO NPD.
   OFFICER EATON SAID HE WILL ADVISE US IF THERE IS ANY FURTHER INFORMATION ASAP.

S/O G.PALLETE 12-21-99

Aviation crime. Notice of seizure of Hilliard's Lear (top). Another Lear jet flown to Naples by Hilliard's chief pilot was suspected of having been stolen in Canada.

In business with the CIA? Hilliard owns jets worth tens of millions with a Miami man, Mark Shubin, who was a CIA U-2 pilot over Russia.

`0 0 0 0 0 0 0 2 1 4`

UNITED STATES OF AMERICA DEPARTMENT OF TRANSPORTATION
FEDERAL AVIATION ADMINISTRATION-MIKE MONRONEY AERONAUTICAL CENTER
AIRCRAFT REGISTRATION APPLICATION

26-1

CERT. ISSUE DATE

UNITED STATES
REGISTRATION NUMBER **N 911UN**

AIRCRAFT MANUFACTURER & MODEL
Dassault Falcon DA-10

YY MAR 2 9 2002

AIRCRAFT SERIAL No.
122

FOR FAA USE ONLY

TYPE OF REGISTRATION (Check one box)

☐ 1. Individual ☐ 2. Partnership ☒ 3. Corporation ☐ 4. Co-owner ☐ 5. Gov't. ☐ 6. Non-Citizen Corporation

NAME OF APPLICANT (Person(s) shown on evidence of ownership. If individual, give last name, first name, and middle initial.)

Sky Bus, Inc.

TELEPHONE NUMBER: (   )

ADDRESS (Permanent mailing address for first applicant listed.)

Number and street: **1020 NW 62nd Street**

Rural Route: P.O. Box:

CITY	STATE	ZIP CODE
Fort Lauderdale	**Florida**	**33309**

☐ CHECK HERE IF YOU ARE ONLY REPORTING A CHANGE OF ADDRESS
ATTENTION! Read the following statement before signing this application.
This portion MUST be completed.

A false or dishonest answer to any question in this application may be grounds for punishment by fine and / or imprisonment (U.S. Code, Title 18, Sec. 1001).

CERTIFICATION

I/WE CERTIFY:

(1) That the above aircraft is owned by the undersigned applicant, who is a citizen (including corporations) of the United States.

(For voting trust, give name of trustee: _____), or:

CHECK ONE AS APPROPRIATE:

a. ☐ A resident alien, with alien registration (Form 1-151 or Form 1-551) No. _____

b. ☐ A non-citizen corporation organized and doing business under the laws of (state) _____ and said aircraft is based and primarily used in the United States. Records or flight hours are available for inspection at _____

(2) That the aircraft is not registered under the laws of any foreign country; and

(3) That legal evidence of ownership is attached or has been filed with the Federal Aviation Administration.

NOTE: If executed for co-ownership all applicants must sign. Use reverse side if necessary.

TYPE OR PRINT NAME BELOW SIGNATURE

SIGNATURE	TITLE	DATE
Mark Shubin	President	3-26-02
SIGNATURE	TITLE	DATE

UN planes? The registration numbers of several of Hilliard and Shubin's planes end in UN, an unusual designation informed aviation observers have never seen before.

```
                    UNITED STATES OF AMERICA                          FORM APPROVED
U.S. DEPARTMENT OF TRANSPORTATION FEDERAL AVIATION ADMINISTRATION     OMB NO. 2120-0042
                    AIRCRAFT BILL OF SALE          00174  9 1
                                                                     28-1
FOR AND IN CONSIDERATION OF $        THE
UNDERSIGNED OWNER(S) OF THE FULL LEGAL                                M 3 7 0 9 7
AND BENEFICIAL TITLE OF THE AIRCRAFT DES-
CRIBED AS FOLLOWS:
                                                                     CONVEYANCE
UNITED STATES        N11UN                                           RECORDED
REGISTRATION NUMBER
AIRCRAFT MANUFACTURER & MODEL
GULFSTREAM G1-59                                                     Do not write in this block
AIRCRAFT SERIAL No.                                                  FOR FAA USE ONLY
SN 102
                                                                     FEDERAL AVIATION
        DOES THIS        DAY OF        19                            ADMINISTRATION
        HEREBY SELL, GRANT, TRANSFER AND
        DELIVER ALL RIGHTS, TITLE, AND INTERESTS
        IN AND TO SUCH AIRCRAFT UNTO:

NAME AND ADDRESS
(IF INDIVIDUAL(S), GIVE LAST NAME, FIRST NAME, AND MIDDLE INITIAL.)

Plane 1 Leasing Co. Inc.
240 Aviation Drive N.
Naples, FL 34104-3512
and
Sky Bus, INC.
1020 NW 62nd Street #9
Fort Lauderdale, FL 33309


DEALER CERTIFICATE NUMBER

AND TO                                EXECUTORS, ADMINISTRATORS, AND ASSIGNS TO HAVE AND TO HOLD
SINGULARLY THE SAID AIRCRAFT FOREVER, AND WARRANTS THE TITLE THEREOF.

IN TESTIMONY WHEREOF      HAVE SET      HAND AND SEAL THIS           DAY OF        19

NAME (S) OF SELLER         SIGNATURE (S)                    TITLE
(TYPED OR PRINTED)     (IN INK) (IF EXECUTED           (TYPED OR PRINTED)
                       FOR CO-OWNERSHIP; ALL MUST
                       SIGN)
Wallace J Hilliard
Plane I Leasing Co      W J Hilliard           Pres.



ACKNOWLEDGMENT (NOT REQUIRED FOR PURPOSES OF FAA RECORDING: HOWEVER, MAY BE REQUIRED
BY LOCAL LAW FOR VALIDITY OF THE INSTRUMENT.)

ORIGINAL: TO FAA

AC Form 8050-2 (9/92) (NSN 0052-00-629-0003) Supersedes Previous Edition
```

"It's in the pouch." The UN designation for this $30 million plane owned by Shubin and Hilliard may have something to do with another of Shubin's companies: "International Diplomatic Courier Services, Inc."

PLEASE READ ALL INSTRUCTIONS BEFORE COMPLETING THIS FORM.

APPLICATION FOR Reinstatement

FLORIDA DEPARTMENT OF STATE

DOCUMENT # **P98000095974**

1. Corporation Name

AMBASSADOR AVIATION, INC.

FILED

99 NOV 24 PM 4: 28

SECRETARY OF STATE
TALLAHASSEE FLORIDA

Principal Place of Business	Mailing Address
240 AVIATION DRIVE NAPLES FL 34104	240 AVIATION DRIVE NAPLES FL 34104

REINSTATEMENT 1999

If above addresses are incorrect in any way, line through incorrect information and enter correction below.

2 New Principal Office Address, if Applicable	3 New Mailing Office Address, if Applicable	4. Date Incorporated or Qualified To Do Business in Florida 11/13/1998
Suite, Apt. #. etc.	Suite, Apt. #, etc.	5. FEI Number Applied For / Not Applicable
City & State	City & State	6.
Zip Country	Zip Country	CERTIFICATE OF STATUS DESIRED ☐

7. Names and Street Addresses of Each Officer and/or Director (Florida nonprofit corporations must list at least 3 directors)

Title(s) 1	Name of Officers and/or Directors 2	Street Address of Each Officer and/or Director 3	City / State / Zip 4
D	HILLIARD, WALLACE J	240 AVIATION DRIVE	NAPLES FL 34104
D	DEKKERS, RUDI	240 AVIATION DRIVE	NAPLES FL 34104
		300003071413----0	
		-12/15/99--01076--007	
		♦♦♦♦750.00 ♦♦♦♦750.00	

8. Name and Address of Current Registered Agent	9. Name and Address of New Registered Agent
WHITE, JOHN P 5121 CASTELLO DRIVE SUITE 2 NAPLES FL 34103	Name *Summer Jeffries* Street Address (P.O. Box Number is Not Acceptable) *240 Prismons Pk Pl.* Suite, Apt. #, Etc. City *Naples* State *FL* Zip Code *34104*

10. I, being appointed the registered agent of the above named corporation, am familiar with and accept the obligations of Section 607.0505, F.S.

Signature of Registered Agent _____   Date *1/23/99*

REGISTERED AGENT MUST SIGN

11. I certify that I am an officer or director or the receiver or trustees empowered to execute this application as provided for in chapter 607 or 617, F.S. I further certify that when filing this reinstatement application, the reason for dissolution has been eliminated, the corporate name satisfies the requirements of section 607.0401 or 617.0401, F.S., that all fees owed by the corporation have been paid and the names of individuals listed on this form do not qualify for an exemption under section 119.07(3)(i), F.S. The information indicated on this application is true and accurate, and my signature shall have the same legal effect as if made under oath.

SIGNATURE: _____   Date *11/23/99*

SIGNATURE AND TYPED OR PRINTED NAME OF SIGNING OFFICER OR DIRECTOR   Daytime Phone #

Rudi Dekkers, President

This Hilliard-Dekkers flight school was training suspected terrorists who fled just before 9/11. The "new business agent" on this form, secretary Summer Jeffries, was later caught with heroin.

AMS may go public, but not now

■ Health-care reform makes a decision difficult

By Julie Bell May 26,94
Press-Gazette

American Medical Security and its joint venture partner, United Wisconsin Services, have talked about taking AMS public, and the option remains under consideration, United Wisconsin's chief executive officer said Wednesday.

But Thomas Hefty said health-care reform has created such volatility in the market that it's difficult to determine whether now is a good time for any move.

"We've had discussions on it," Hefty said in an interview after United Wisconsin Service's annual shareholders meeting at American Medical Security in Howard. "We continue to evaluate all of our joint ventures."

United Wisconsin is the holding company for all the for-profit entities of its parent company, Blue Cross & Blue Shield United of Wisconsin, including AMS.

AMS has outperformed all of United Wisconsin's holdings, last year generating $463.2 million in premium revenue — a 555 percent jump over the $70.7 million it generated in 1989.

The company marketed products in 27 states last year, up from 10 in its first full year of operation.

In this year's first quarter, United Wisconsin premium revenue attributable to AMS increased 68 percent to $78.2 million from $46.5 million in 1993. Overall, United Wisconsin Services earned $7.8 million in the year's first quarter on $169.2 million in revenue.

The two companies split AMS earnings down the middle. Under the joint venture agreement, United Wisconsin has an option to buy out AMS in 1996. But if the management of both companies agreed, they could take the company public before that.

Or either company could buy the other one out.

"It's a mixture of getting a common course among the partners and then assessing the prospects of health-care reform and the impact on the market," Hefty said. "If you could predict what Bill and Hillary are going to do, it would be easier to make plans."

United Wisconsin is leery, however, after aborting a planned stock issue last year that was unrelated to AMS.

About 40 people attended the shareholders meeting in an AMS meeting room off the cafeteria. In a board of directors meeting afterward, United Wisconsin declared a quarterly dividend on its common stock of 12 cents a share. The dividend is payable June 22 to shareholders of record on June 8.

The dividends paid to United Wisconsin's parent company, Blue Cross & Blue Shield United of Wisconsin — which owns about 81 percent of United Wisconsin's outstanding stock — will be returned to UWS in the form of a capital contribution.

In other business, shareholders elected Jane Taylor Coleman to the United Wisconsin board for a three-year term. She has been executive director of the Madison Community Foundation since 1986.

Falwell visits: From left, Wally Hilliard, the Rev. Jerry Falwell and Ron Weyers talk before the United Wisconsin Services meeting. Weyers and Hilliard started American Medical Security, which has a joint venture with United Wisconsin.

Special to the Press-Gazette

Hilliard
New firm's president

"The Company he keeps." Hilliard and Jerry Falwell, to whom he "loaned" $1 million in the mid-90s.

<u>**Request To Conduct
Operations As
"Florida Air"**</u>

Pursuant to 14 C.F.R. Part 215, Sunrise Airlines, Inc. ("Sunrise") respectfully requests that the Department of Transportation approve and register the trade name of "Florida Air" as a Sunrise trade name.

1.   The trade name of "Florida Air" will be used for marketing purposes in conjunction with flights to be operated by Sunrise.

2.   As the Department is aware, Harbor Air, Inc. used the trade name "Florida Air" earlier this year in conjunction with service that Harbor Air was providing in Florida. Harbor Air ceased providing those services in Florida in late April (at which time its right to use the name "Florida Air" ceased as well), and, as Sunrise understands it, Harbor Air has since ceased all services and surrendered its Operating Certificate to the Federal Aviation Administration.

3.   Sunrise will provide, under separate cover, three (3) executed originals of DOT Form 4523 (Montreal Agreement or Agreement 18800) using the trade name as required by 14 C.F.R. § 215.4(b).

For these reasons, Sunrise Airlines, Inc. respectfully requests that the Department of Transportation approve and register the trade name of "Florida Air."

Boxes within boxes. Hilliard and Dekkers' brief-lived commuter airline, Florida Air, wasn't really Florida Air, but Sunrise Air, of Nevada, which wasn't really Sunrise Air, but Express Air of Utah, which was really Express Air of Page, Arizona.

Order 2003-2-14

Served: February 26, 2003

**UNITED STATES OF AMERICA
DEPARTMENT OF TRANSPORTATION
OFFICE OF THE SECRETARY
WASHINGTON, D.C.**

Issued by the Department of Transportation
on the 21st day of February, 2003

Notice of	
SUNRISE AIRLINES, INC. **d/b/a FLAIR AIRLINES**	**Docket OST-2001-8695**
of intent to resume operations under 14 CFR 204.7	

**ORDER DISMISSING APPLICATION
AND REVOKING COMMUTER AIR CARRIER AUTHORITY**

By Order 91-12-45, issued December 30, 1991, the Department found Sunrise Airlines, Inc.
(Sunrise) fit to engage in scheduled passenger air transportation operations as a commuter air
carrier. It operated under its commuter authority until November 3, 2000, when it ceased those
operations and filed for protection under Chapter 11 of the United States Bankruptcy Code. As a
result of the cessation of its commuter operations, under section 204.7 of our rules (14 CFR 204.7),
the carrier's commuter authority was automatically suspended. On January 16, 2001, Sunrise filed
a notice under section 204.7 requesting approval to resume commuter operations.

By Order 2002-2-5, issued February 8, 2002, we tentatively found Sunrise fit to resume commuter
services on a limited basis. Shortly thereafter, the Department received new information that had
compliance-related implications for the company's fitness. At that time, we requested further
information from Sunrise. Several months later, Sunrise responded and, at the same time, advised
us that it had undergone changes in other fitness-related areas since the issuance of Order 2002-2-5.
Sunrise advised us that it would file updated information relative to these changes in the above
docket. When such information was not received, on July 10, 2002, we issued Order 2002-7-18
vacating our earlier tentative fitness finding. Although Sunrise subsequently filed updated fitness
information, in December 2002, we were informally advised that the carrier had again undergone
material changes in areas affecting its fitness. On February 14, 2003, Sunrise filed a motion
requesting that its application be withdrawn.

We will grant the carrier's request and dismiss the notice to resume operations filed in Docket OST-
2001-8695. At the same time, we will also revoke Sunrise's dormant commuter air carrier
authority. In this regard, section 204.7 of our rules provides that, if a carrier ceases conducting the
commuter operations for which it was found fit, it has one year from the date of cessation to resume
those operations or its commuter authority can be revoked for dormancy. Sunrise ceased operations
on November 3, 2000; thus, its one-year dormancy period expired on November 3, 2001. The
carrier's notice to resume operations had the effect of staying the revocation date for its commuter
authority. Given the carrier's withdrawal here of its notice to resume operations, there is no basis

Unfit to fly. The Department of Transportation regularly found Hilliard's various
airline ventures to be dubious propositions.

FLORIDA AIR HOLDINGS, INC.
ACQUISITION OF
DISCOVER AIR, INC.

On May 9, 2002, Florida Air Holdings, Inc. ("Florida Air") entered into a series of agreements by which it acquired Discover Air, Inc. ("Discover Air"). Discover Air is an air carrier providing public charter and on-demand charter flights in accordance with Part 298 of the Department's regulations and Part 135 of the Federal Aviation Regulations. Discover Air will continue to operate as a charter carrier and Sunrise Airlines, Inc. ("Sunrise") will, after being found fit to continue service, operate as a separate scheduled airline, each owned by Florida Air. The following is a description of the transaction, the reconstituted Florida Air board of directors and the management of Florida Air:

Transaction

In an agreement entered into as of May 9, 2002, Florida Air agreed to purchase all of the shares in Discover Air from its two shareholders, James R. Williams and Ruth M. Williams. In exchange for the Discover Air shares, the Discover Air shareholders received 40% of the issued and outstanding shares of Florida Air as well as $750,000 paid pursuant to a Promissory Note. In addition, Florida Air and Discover Air entered into a Stockholders Agreement by which, among other things, the previously existing shareholders of Florida Air (the so-called "Hilliard Group") are authorized to nominate four Florida Air directors, the Discover Air shareholders (the so-called "Discover Air Group") are authorized to nominate four Florida Air directors and these eight directors will jointly nominate a ninth director. Copies of these agreements will be provided to the Department under separate cover.

Stripping assets. The assets of an Orlando flight school were concealed inside Discover Air and transferred to Hilliard just before the flight school went bankrupt, taking with it the life savings of several hundred students.

Friends in high places. Hilliard "bought" a plane from Truman Arnold, former chief Clinton fundraiser, but didn't arrange financing to pay for it until over a year later

Boehlke dream crumbles amid Capital debacle

Upscale retirement condominiums are in receivership

> **"Always make sure that you get it in cash. I learned that the hard way."**
>
> — *Richard Boehlke, about his finances*

The Company he keeps, pt II. Hilliard and Dekkers partner in Florida Air was Richard Boehlke, a participant in the spectacular $350 million "Mob-led" bust-out of union pension funds in Portland, Oregon, from what were called "mostly Mob-led unions."

Packets of heroin bearing the name of Osama bin Laden.

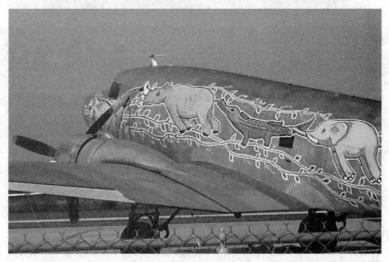

Wally Hilliard served as a director of a company planning on building this new jet in Israel, with the help of the IDF (top). At the Charlotte County Airport sits this seized DC-3, which belonged to Iran-Contra operative Frank Moss (bottom).

While the revelations turned up by our investigaton for *Welcome To TerrorLand* were censored in the major media in America, they were not verboten in the largest daily circulation newspaper in the world, Germany's *Der Bild*, which ran a two-page spread about the revelations about Mohamed Atta we learned from his American girlfriend.

CIA U2 pilot Mark Shubin (front left) in group shot; Shubin "owned" at least four planes with terror flight school owner Wally Hilliard that were part of the CIA's air fleet, including the plane with the curious 'N' number pictured here.

International intrigue: Boris "Felix" Rabaev is a Russian Mob link to 9/11; he met Wally Hilliard's Lear jet in New York, the terminus of each of the 30 weekly drug flights. Shubin believes he is also responsible for the crash in the Ukraine of this plane, with the West-leaning Minister of Energy for the Ukraine onboard.

The FBI in 2006 issued a terror alert in the Suth Pacific for Wolfgang Bohringer, identified by Amanda Keller as a "close associate" of Mohamed Atta's in Florida. Surf enthusiast Chuck Corbett blew the whistle when Bohringer sailed into tiny Fanning Island.

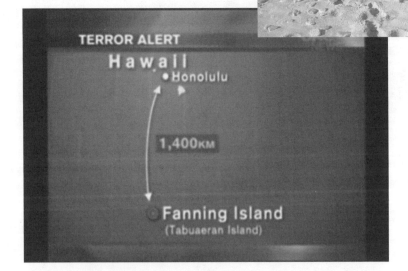

Wolfgang and Anna after completing the long upload to Foreign Investment, Xmas 2006

Two pictures taken on Fanning Island of Wolfgang Bohringer, who looks remarkably like Amanda Keller's description of him as a dead ringer for the character "Ice Man" in the movie *Top Gun* played by Val Kilmer.

Index

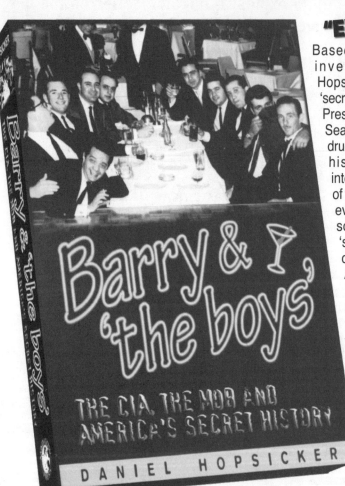